The Stalin school *of* falsification

The Stalin school *of* falsification

BY LEON TROTSKY

Pathfinder

New York London Montreal Sydney

Translated by John G. Wright
Annotated by Max Shachtman

ISBN 978-0-87348-881-5
Library of Congress Catalog Card Number 99-74733
Manufactured in Canada

First edition, 1937
Second edition, 1962
Third edition, 1972
Fourth edition, 2004
Tenth printing, 2026

COVER DESIGN: Eva Braiman

COVER PHOTOGRAPHS: Two versions of the same 1920 photo of V.I. Lenin, at left. The crudely doctored version below eliminates Leon Trotsky and another person. (David King Collection)

PATHFINDER
pathfinderpress.com
Email: pathfinder@pathfinderpress.com

Contents

An illustration of the Stalinist doctoring of history similar to that on the cover. Top picture shows Lenin speaking while Trotsky and Kamenev wait their turn. Lower picture, taken within a few seconds of upper one, has been retouched to eliminate Trotsky and Kamenev.

Publisher's note to the fourth edition

This new edition of *The Stalin School of Falsification* is being brought out just as it was originally published in 1937 under Trotsky's supervision, with new typography and a new cover. We have added to this edition Trotsky's 1932 article "On the suppressed testament of Lenin." It is included as an appendix following the Explanatory notes.

Steve Clark
APRIL 2004

Foreword to the American edition

The Moscow Trials, which so shocked the world, signify the death agony of Stalinism. A political régime constrained to use such methods is doomed. Depending upon external and internal circumstances, this agony may endure for a longer or shorter period of time. But no power in the world can any longer save Stalin and his system. The Soviet régime will either rid itself of the bureaucratic shell or be sucked into the abyss.

This volume does not deal with the Moscow trials, to which my new book, *The Crimes of Stalin,* is wholly devoted. The Moscow juridical amalgams did not, however, fall from the sky, but were the inexorable products of the past, first of all, that is, of the "Stalin school of falsification." The present volume will, I believe, prove of assistance to everyone who seeks to understand the ideological and political genesis of the Moscow trials. Without possessing the knowledge of its genesis, it is in general impossible to understand anything in this world, including a frame-up.

To enter now into a theoretical controversy with the Stalinists would be a complete anachronism. These people—and I have in mind of course the leaders and not the duped and befuddled followers—have completely and decisively broken with Marxism and are veering convulsively from one empirical formula to another, accommodating themselves to the needs of the Soviet ruling caste. But it remains an incontestable historical fact that the preparation of the bloody judicial frame-ups had its inception in the "minor" historical distortions and "innocent" falsification of citations. The bureaucracy found it indispensably necessary to adapt Bolshevism to its own needs. This could not be done otherwise than by corroding the soul of Bolshevism. To the revolutionary essence of Bolshevism the bureaucracy gave the name of "Trotskyism." Thus it created the spindle on which to wind in the future its falsifications in all the spheres of theory and practice.

In the political sphere, the initiative in this work—it is impermissible to slur over this in silence—was assumed by the deceased Zinoviev, the herald of the struggle against Trotskyism from 1923 to 1925. But already at the end of 1925, Zinoviev became frightened by the consequences of his own initiative and came over to the ranks of the Opposition. What happened thereafter is only too well known. In the *economic* sphere, the theoretical weapons against Trotskyism were forged by Bukharin: "the underestimation of the peasantry," "super-industrialization," etc. The fate of Bukharin is no less well known: the official champion of pure Leninism was soon proclaimed a "bourgeois liberal," was later pardoned and is now in jail awaiting trial.

The most prominent place in the struggle against "Trotskyism" was accorded to *historical questions*. These involved both the history of the development of Russia as a whole, as well as the history of the Bolshevik party and the October Revolution, in particular. The deceased M.N. Pokrovsky must unquestionably be acknowledged as the most authoritative Soviet historian. For a number of years, he waged, with a vehemence peculiar to him, a struggle against my general views on the history of Russia and especially my conception of the October Revolution. Everything written by the other "communist" critics on this theme was merely a parroting of the ideas of Pokrovsky. While taking due cognizance of the erudition, conscientiousness and talent of the deceased scholar, it is impermissible not to state that Pokrovsky failed to master the method of Marxism, and instead of providing an analysis of the continued inter-action of all the elements in the historical process, he provided for each occasion mechanistic constructions *ad hoc,* without bothering about their dialectic inter-connection. A few years ago such an appraisal sounded like blasphemy. Pokrovsky was the supreme authority of Soviet science. The reign of his school was absolute. His textbooks or the textbooks of his disciples circulated in millions of copies. Shortly before his death, he was idolized as the lawgiver in the domain of scientific thought. But already in 1935, steps were taken suddenly and all the more drastically to review his heritage. In the course of a few months, Pokrovsky was completely cashiered, crushed and discredited. He probably escaped the prisoners' dock only by his timely demise. It would naturally be absurd to expect that Pokrovsky's school has been liquidated in the interests of Marxism. No, Pokrovsky is accused of lacking patriotism, of irreverence toward Russia's past, of lacking national pride!

In what did Stalin's own theoretical work express itself? In nothing. All he did was to exploit his fellow-traveler theorists, in the interests of the new ruling caste. He will enter into the annals of the history of "thought" only as the organizer of the greatest school of falsification. But for this very reason Stalin, more truly and completely than anybody else, expresses the ideological physiognomy of the new ruling stratum. Each theoretical formula of anti-Trotskyism (whether it involved Zinoviev, Bukharin or Pokrovsky) became at the very next stage an intolerable burden to the new masters of the situation. Official "theory" is today transformed into a blank sheet of paper on which the unfortunate theoreticians reverently trace the contours of the Stalinist boot. Retreating with seven league strides from its Bolshevik past, the bureaucracy at first devoured at each successive stage its own theoreticians. Nowadays that is no longer adequate. The bureaucracy cannot be reconciled with anything but the destruction of the entire old generation of Bolsheviks. Such is the consummation of the Soviet Thermidor!

❖

This volume contains no little material for the political characterization of the four most prominent men in the last two Moscow trials: Zinoviev-Kamenev, on the one hand; Radek-Piatakov on the other. The previous aberrations in politics and theory of both these couples act to facilitate in the extreme the understanding of their conduct in court, just as, on the other hand, the judicial trials cast a livid light on the preceding zigzags of these unfortunate victims of the G.P.U.

Zinoviev and Kamenev were the initiators of the struggle against me in 1923. Piatakov and Radek—the former by three-quarters, the latter by half—stood in the camp of the Opposition. In 1926, Zinoviev and Kamenev joined the Opposition; at the same time, Radek and Piatakov became stauncher in their oppositional credo. In November 1927, Zinoviev and Kamenev turned to the path of capitulation. They were followed first by Piatakov, and then by Radek.

The spectre of Trotskyism was first pushed forward by the "triumvirate" (Zinoviev, Kamenev and Stalin) in 1924. In 1926, Zinoviev, at a meeting of the Opposition center, told how the "triumvirate" had decided to revive artificially the old, pre-revolutionary, long-forgotten differences between Lenin and myself in order, by using the spectre of Trotskyism as a cover, to wage a struggle against Trotsky. This story of Zinoviev is corroborated by the letters of Radek (December 25, 1927) and Piatakov (January 2, 1928) which the reader will find in this volume. Both these letters were written in the days when Zinoviev and Kamenev, to justify their capitulation, were once again pushing forward the spectre of Trotskyism which they themselves had already exposed, while Radek and Piatakov were still seeking to maintain their old positions. But in the course of the very next year, Piatakov and after him Radek, too, found themselves compelled to resort to the official legend of Trotskyism, so as to prepare and justify their own capitulation. In these instances of ideological demoralization was reflected the growing social pressure of the bureaucracy.

The old accusations ("permanent revolution," "underestimation of the peasantry," etc.) proved altogether inadequate for the purpose of crushing the Opposition and, later, of rooting it out physically. There ensued an epoch of criminal amalgams, at first petty and partial, and later ever more monstrous. The series of recantations of Zinoviev-Kamenev, growing in geometric progression, brought them in August, 1936 to the prisoners' dock, charged with the assassination of Kirov, *i.e.*, a crime with which they certainly had less connection than Stalin himself. In the days of the trial of Zinoviev and Kamenev, Radek and Piatakov rushed into print with exceptionally revolting articles in which, pretending a belief in the indictment, they demanded death for the accused. But soon thereafter, both of them found themselves in the prisoners' dock and were compelled to make confessions infinitely surpassing in monstrosity the fictitious crimes of Zinoviev-Kamenev. Conclusion? To play tricks with history is impermissible, especially in an epoch of great shocks and convulsions.

But how can one believe—naïve people will say—that Stalin was capable of such a frightful frame-up, that he was able to find for this frame-up a staff of executives, including the accused themselves, and did not, at the same time, meet with any resistance either on the part of his closest associates or in the judicial apparatus? Only those can be astonished by it who were asleep during the preceding evolution of the U.S.S.R. The process of handpicking and training the apparatus in the spirit of the Stalin school of falsification has already endured for fourteen years. Even though in fragmentary form, this book contains numerous authentic documents which serve to characterize the different stages of the subjugation of the party, the corruption of the apparatus and the poisoning of the conscience of the ruling stratum, in the name of a "monolithism" that is false through and through. The innumerable theoretical forgeries and historical frame-ups, referred to in these pages, represent in essence nothing but a series of designs and sketches for those hellish frescoes with which Stalin has shocked the conscience of the entire world. Control Commissions, as far back as 1924, got used to demanding false confessions from former Oppositionists. Emulating Zinoviev, Kamenev, Radek and Piatakov, many thousands of capitulators got used to issuing false statements. The papers carried articles dealing with these statements, which neither the authors nor the informed readers believed in for an instant. In each new edition of Lenin's *Collected Works,* the notes were subjected to a drastic revision: the minuses were replaced by pluses, the pluses by minuses. In encyclopaedias and other reference books, the biographies were made over anew every year or so and events were delineated in a new manner—for the sake of exalting some while demoting others. Thousands of writers, historians and economists in the U.S.S.R. write by command what they do not believe. Professors in universities and school teachers are compelled to change written textbooks in a hurry in order to accommodate themselves to the successive stage of the official lie. The spirit of the Inquisition thoroughly impregnating the atmosphere of the country feeds, as we have already said, from profound social sources. To justify their privileges the ruling caste perverts the theory which has as its aim the elimination of all privileges. The lie serves, therefore, as the fundamental ideological cement of the bureaucracy. The more irreconcilable becomes the contradiction between the bureaucracy and the people, all the ruder becomes the lie, all the more brazenly is it converted into criminal falsification and judicial frame-up. Whoever has not understood this inner dialectic of the Stalinist régime will likewise fail to understand the Moscow trials.

The death agony of Stalinism signifies the death agony of the Comintern. This international organization is now the main internal obstacle in the path of the emancipation of the working class. The selection of people without honor and without conscience has reached the same appalling proportions in the Comintern as in the state apparatus of the U.S.S.R. The "leaders" by special appointment change their "convictions" upon instructions by telegraph. They organize campaigns of vilification against Zinoviev who used to be their infallible authority, against Bukharin whom they used to acclaim as their leader, against Radek whom only yesterday they reverently cited in the struggle against Trotskyism. The functionaries of the Comintern represent in all relations—theoretical, political and moral—a type which is the polar opposite of the revolutionist. They hang on to Stalin, who in turn needs them for the maintenance of his tyranny in the U.S.S.R. The Moscow trials reveal to the very bottom the inner rottenness of the Comintern. After an initial period of bewilderment and vacillation, its swift disintegration is inevitable. It may take place much sooner than the collapse of the Stalinist system in the Soviet Union. The Second International has contrived in a number of countries to establish intimate connections with the Comintern in the period of its complete degeneration. The collapse of the Comintern must inevitably deal a cruel blow to the social democracy. But this does not mean that the world proletariat will be left without leadership. At the cost of terrible defeats and sacrifices, the main responsibility for which falls upon the Soviet bureaucracy, the proletarian vanguard will find its historic road. Ever more confidently will it rally its ranks under the banner of the Fourth International, which is already rising today on the shoulders of its predecessors.

Leon Trotsky
MARCH 3, 1937

Foreword to the Russian edition

There is hardly a gentle knight left among the world's imperialist politicians or among their "democratic" errand boys who has not expressed his indignation at the cynical attitude of the Bolsheviks toward the precepts of morality. British Tories who, without blinking an eyelash, put the "Zinoviev letter" in circulation, Russian liberals who sought to strangle the revolution by resorting to the most contemptible slander against the Bolsheviks, the ruling classes of France—with their Panama scandal, their Dreyfus affair, their Oustric affair, and their leading newspaper, *Le Temps*[1]—all these gentlemen feel themselves called upon to indict the immorality of the Bolsheviks, contrasting it with lofty exemplars of loyalty and rectitude.

In point of fact, the lie in politics, as in daily life, serves as a function of the class structure of society. The oppressors erect the lie into a system of befuddling the masses in order to maintain their rule. On the part of the oppressed the lie is a defensive weapon of weakness. Revolution explodes the social lie. Revolution speaks the truth. Revolution begins by giving things and social relationships their real names.

In the eyes of the practitioners of the imperialist lie, the revolutionary Marxists appear as a party of "demagogues." Yet Marx, who devoted his entire life to the study of profound social processes and who made a microscopic analysis of the cell of the social organism, abhorred demagogy as a medical scientist abhors the sideshow incantation of a medicine-man. Lenin, with his profound revolutionary realism, exemplifies a political type which is the polar opposite of the demagogue. Indeed, what is demagogy? It is a deliberate play with sham values in politics, the dissemination of false promises and the solace of non-existent blessings. Is not the church then one of the fundamental institutions of demagogy—the church which, in exchange for a wax candle, offers eternal beatitude, all extras included? Meanwhile, the church, as Lloyd George has correctly and aptly said, is the central power plant, feeding all the parties of law and order. But even the purely political programs of capitalistic parties are permeated through and through with the spirit of deliberate deception. Whatever destroys their traditional lie is looked upon as demagogy by the champions of law and order. Revolution, which is the most ruthless exposure of the contradictions of society and all of its falsity, seems to the upholders of the existing order the very spawn of demagogy. Thus, in the conscious attitude of the minority which builds its welfare on the suppression and the spiritual enslavement of the majority, all relationships are stood on their heads.

But revolution itself is neither a single nor a harmonious process. Revolution is full of contradictions. It unfolds only by taking one step back after taking two steps forward. Revolution in its own turn sweeps into power a new ruling stratum which strives to secure its privileged position and is apt to view itself, not as the temporary historical vehicle of revolution, but rather as its completion and its crowning work. The epochs of ideological reaction which, more than once in history, have run parallel with economic successes, engender the need for revising revolutionary ideas and methods; and create their own conventional lie. Such is the content underlying the falsification of history against which this book is directed.

Powerless to conduct policies in the spirit of the party's traditions, the epigones have busied themselves with altering the traditions to fit the requirements of their own policies. The so-called struggle against "Trotskyism" grew out of the bureaucratic reaction against the October Revolution and out of the urge for national tranquillity. That the past was falsified and altered is not at all due to personal intrigue, nor is it an outgrowth of clique squabbles, as commonly depicted by the banal bourgeois historiographers. It is due to the workings of a profound political process, with social roots of its own. Members of the American bourgeoisie, many of whom are the descendants of British convicts, having acquired the requisite number of millions, feel the urge to equip themselves with a respectable genealogy, drawn preferably from the kings of Scotland. The Soviet bureaucracy, likewise, after raising itself above the revolutionary class, could not help experiencing the need, in proportion as it intrenched its independent positions, for such an ideology as would justify its exceptional position and insure it against dissatisfaction from below. It is for this reason that such colossal sweep has been attained by the alteration, perversion and outright counterfeiting of the revolutionary past, still so recent. However, the contradictions of the economic process and of the world situation do not allow the bureaucracy to rest peacefully on the laurels of national socialism. The convulsions of the official policy obstruct the erection of a new theory as well as of a new tradition. With every major historical zigzag, they are compelled to revamp history all over again. Thus far we have had three large-scale alterations.

The first was effected in the course of 1923–1926 by the so-called "Old Guard," the immutable, unwavering and inflexible disciples of Lenin. Let us recall the staff of the basic kernel of the Old Guard: Zinoviev, Kamenev, Stalin, Rykov, Tomsky, Bukharin, Kuibyshev. The history of the party was altered to suit the requirements of that period, principally by Zinoviev.

In 1926, a new opposition appeared on the scene: Zinoviev, Kamenev, Krupskaya, Sokolnikov. Once again history was reviewed, this time by the Stalin-Bukharin bloc, with the "review" so calculated as to maintain the principal course of annihilating "Trotskyism," while demoting retroactively one section of the "Old Guard" headed by Zinoviev and Kamenev, and at the same time exalting another section headed by Stalin and Bukharin. During that period, Bukharin functioned as the theoretician. Yaroslavsky made his début as historian. But for the time being he remained the historian of the bloc between the Centrists and the Rights. Bukharin still remained the "best theoretician" after Lenin. Rykov was still maintained as an old and reliable Bolshevik.

In 1929, after the Stalinists broke with the Rights, theory and history underwent reconstruction for the third time. Stalin steps to the fore as a theoretician. Yaroslavsky becomes a specialist in the sphere of reviewing and correcting history. The theorem is within limits that are strictly confined. It must be proved that there existed no such thing in the past as the "Old Guard." But Stalin did exist. In addition to Stalin there existed a number of mere opportunists and strikebreakers, who for some unknown reason directed the Central Committee of the Bolshevik party.

Every new variant of the past served not only to supplement but also to destroy the preceding variant. As a result, the official history of the party and of the revolution represents, at the present time, a scroll on which various scribes have written as the spirit moved them—each scribe very much unconcerned with what another had written or, in part, one and the same scribe very little concerned with his writings of yesterday.

To decipher the successively accumulated falsifications

of party history is to undertake an instructive labor *sui generis* (of its own kind). The task we set ourselves is more modest. We propose to restore the most fundamental facts and documents which underlie the attempt to counterpose Trotskyism to Leninism. Let us not forget that in all of its variations and permutations, the epigone ideology has always sought to maintain itself on this fundamental antithesis: Trotskyism *versus* Leninism.

❖

The main document in the present volume is my so-called "Letter to the *Istpart*" [Bureau of Party History]. It was written in 1927 in reply to an *Istpart* questionnaire. It circulated from hand to hand in the U.S.S.R. in hundreds of copies, either re-typed or copied by hand. Single copies, often inexact, filtered abroad. Translations of them appeared in several languages. After the author's expulsion from the U.S.S.R., a fuller text of the "Letter" was published in German, French, English, Spanish, Chinese and other languages, but until now it has not appeared in the original—that is, in the Russian language.

Contained in this volume are three speeches by the author, delivered before the highest bodies of the C.P.S.U. They relate to the same question of the distortion of the past for the purpose of justifying new political tendencies. These speeches are also printed for the first time in the Russian language. The necessary explanations are given in the text of this book.

Two chapters: "A Contribution to a Political Biography of Stalin" and "Stalin and the Red Army" have already appeared in the *Bulletin of the Russian Opposition*. The latter chapter ("Stalin and the Red Army") was written by N. Markin, to whom I herewith express my gratitude.

The book includes, in addition, two documents of great

historical significance: the minutes of the so-called "March Conference" of the Bolsheviks in the year 1917, and the recorded minutes of an exceptionally important session of the Petrograd Committee of the party, November 1, 1917, in which Lenin and other members of the Central Committee participated.

The March Conference was attended by Bolshevik delegates who arrived for the All-Russian Congress of the Soviets. The political condition of the upper stratum of the Bolshevik party, especially of Stalin and Co., on the eve of Lenin's arrival in Russia, is characterized with exceptional vividness by the minutes of that Conference. The minutes are vivid but far from flattering. *That is precisely why they are hidden from the party to this very day.* This document is printed here for the first time and is thereby preserved from certain destruction.

The history of the recorded minutes of the November 1 session of the Petrograd Committee is contained in the text of the book. Here again we have before us a document hidden from the party with deliberate malice. The galley proofs bear the notation: "Junk this." By a fortunate accident, the galley proof with the corrections and notations came into our possession. Another precious portion of the history of the October Revolution was thereby saved from being "junked."

Thus the book as a whole comprises a collection of historical documents. But from the recent past, which it encompasses, there run living threads to the present. In that sense the book is not at all a volume for the archives; it is rather a weapon in the political struggle for the theory of Marx, for the policies of Lenin—against the epigones.

Leon Trotsky
KADIKOI
SEPTEMBER 13, 1931

Letter to the Bureau of Party History

Concerning the falsification of the history of the October Revolution, the history of the revolution and the history of the party

Esteemed Comrades:

You have sent me a very detailed printed questionnaire concerning my participation in the October Revolution, and you request an answer. I doubt if I could add much to what is printed in various documents, speeches, articles and books, my own among them. But I permit myself to ask you: What is the sense of questioning me about my participation in the October Revolution when the entire official machine, yours along with the rest, is occupied with concealing, destroying, or at least distorting every trace of that participation?

Hundreds of comrades have asked me again and again why I continue silent in the face of a perfectly outrageous falsification, directed against me, of the history of the October Revolution and the history of our party. I certainly do not intend here to exhaust the theme of these falsifications. That would require several volumes. But in answer to your questionnaire, I will indicate a few dozen examples of this conscious and spiteful distortion of the past, which is now organized on an enormous scale, sustained by the authority of all kinds of public institutions, and even carried into the textbooks.

The war and my arrival in Petrograd (May 1917)

1. I arrived in Petrograd from a Canadian prison at the beginning of May 1917, on the second day after the entry of the Mensheviks and Social Revolutionists into the coalition government.

The organs of the *Istpart,* like many others, are trying at this late date to describe my work during the war as bordering on social-patriotism. In this attempt they "forget" that a collection of my writings during the war (*War and Revolution*) was published in many editions during Lenin's life, was studied in the party schools, and appeared in foreign translation among the publications of the Communist International.

You are trying to deceive the younger generation in regard to my line during the war—to deceive those who do not know that for my revolutionary internationalist struggle during the war, I was condemned in my absence to be imprisoned in Germany as early as the end of 1914. This was for my German book, *The War and the International.* I was deported from France where I worked with the future founders of the Communist party; I was arrested in Spain where I had formed connections with the future Communists; I was deported from Spain to the United States; carried on revolutionary internationalist work in New York; participated with Bolsheviks in the editorship of the newspaper, *Novy Mir,* and there gave a Leninist evaluation of the first stages of the February Revolution. Returning from America to Russia, I was removed from the steamship by the British authorities, spent a month in a concentration camp in Canada along with six or eight hundred German sailors whom I recruited on the side of Liebknecht and Lenin. (Many of them took part afterward in the civil war in Germany and I receive letters from them to this day.)

2. On the subject of an English dispatch as to the causes of my arrest in Canada, Lenin's *Pravda* wrote as follows:

> "Is it possible to believe for a minute in the validity of the dispatch received by the English government stating that Trotsky, the former chairman of the Soviet of Workers' Deputies in St. Petersburg in 1905—a revolutionist devoted for *decades* to the service of the revolution—that this man had any connection with a plan subsidized by the 'German government'? This is clearly a monstrous and unscrupulous slander against a revolutionist!" (*Pravda,* No. 34, April 16, 1917.)

How fresh these words sound now in this epoch of contemptible slanders against the Opposition, differing in no essential from the slanders against the Bolsheviks in 1917!

3. A note on page 482, Volume XIV of the *Collected Works* of Lenin, published in 1921, reads:

> "From the beginning of the imperialist war, [Trotsky] took a clear-cut internationalist position."

Such comments, and still more categorical ones, could be adduced to any number. The writers in our entire party press, both Russian and foreign, have pointed out hundreds of times in reviewing my book, *War and Revolution,* that, considering my work during the war as a whole, one must recognize and understand that my differences with Lenin were of a subordinate character and that my fundamental line was revolutionary and continually brought me nearer to Bolshevism—and this not only in words, but in deeds.

4. You are trying after the event to assemble quotations of certain isolated, sharply polemical remarks of Lenin's against me, among them some that were made during the war. Lenin could never endure any half-statements or unclearness. He was right in dealing double and triple blows when a political thought seemed to him incomplete or equivocal. But a polemical blow struck at a given moment is one thing, the appraisal of a man's political line as a whole is another.

In 1918, in America, a certain F. published a collection of articles[2] by Lenin and me during the war period, among them my articles on the then controversial question of the United States of Europe. How did Lenin react to that? He wrote:

> ". . . the American comrade, F., was wholly right in publishing a big volume containing a series of articles by Trotsky and me and thus giving a handbook of the history of the Russian Revolution." (*Works,* Vol. XVII, p. 96, Russ. ed.)

5. I will not touch upon the conduct of the majority of my present accusers during the war and at the beginning of the February Revolution. Here one could relate many interesting things as to the Skvortsov-Stepanovs, Yaroslavskys, Voroshilovs, Ordjonikidzes and many, many others.[3] I confine myself to a few words concerning comrade Melnichansky who has attempted in the press to bear false witness in regard to my line in May–June 1917.

Everybody in America knew Melnichansky as a Menshevik. In the struggle of the Bolsheviks and revolutionary internationalists against social-patriotism and Centrism, Melnichansky took no part whatsoever. He side-stepped all such questions. He did the same thing in the Canadian camp where he (like many others) landed accidentally along with me and Chudnovsky. In making our plans for future work, Chudnovsky and I took the precaution not to impart them to Melnichansky. But since we had to live side by side in the barracks, Chudnovsky and I decided to put a point-blank question to Melnichansky: With whom was he going to work in Russia, with the Mensheviks or with the Bolsheviks? To Melnichansky's credit it is necessary to state that he answered: "With the Bolsheviks." Only after that did Chudnovsky and I begin to talk with him as with a co-thinker.

Read over what Melnichansky wrote in 1924 and in 1927. Anybody who knew Melnichansky in America could only laugh at it. But why go back to America? You have only to listen to any current speech of Melnichansky in order to recognize the opportunist office-holder to whom Purcellism is much closer than Leninism.

6. On the arrival of our group in Petrograd, comrade Fedorov, then a member of the Bolshevik Central Committee, welcomed us in its name at the Finland Station and in his speech of welcome posed sharply the question of the next stages of the revolution, the dictatorship of the proletariat and the socialist course of development. The reply I gave was in full accord with Lenin's April theses which, for me, flowed unfailingly from the theory of the permanent revolution.[4] As Comrade Fedorov told me subsequently, the fundamental point of his speech had been formulated by him in agreement with Lenin or, more accurately, at Lenin's direction. It goes without saying that Lenin considered this question decisive with regard to the possibility of our collaboration.

7. I did not enter the Bolshevik organization immediately upon my arrival from Canada. Why? Was it because

I had disagreements? You are trying to concoct them now in retrospect. Whoever lived through the year 1917 as a member of the central kernel of the Bolsheviks knows that there was never a hint of any disagreement between Lenin and me from the very first day. On my arrival in Petrograd—or rather at the Finland Station—I learned from the comrades sent to meet me that there existed in Petrograd an organization of revolutionary internationalists (the so-called *"Mezhrayontsi"*[5]) which was postponing the question of fusion with the Bolsheviks; in addition, certain of the leading members of this organization linked their decision on this question with my arrival. Among the personnel of the *"Mezhrayontsi"* organization, which comprised about 4,000 Petrograd workers, were Uritsky, A.A. Joffe, Lunacharsky, Yurenev, Karakhan, Vladimirov, Manuilsky, Pozern, Litkens and others.

Here is the characterization of the *"Mezhrayontsi"* organization given in a note (pp. 488*f*) in Volume XIV of Lenin's *Collected Works:*

> "On the war question the *'Mezhrayontsi'* held an internationalist position and in their tactics were close to the Bolsheviks."

From the earliest days of my arrival, I stated first to comrade Kamenev, afterward to the editorial board of *Pravda,* in the presence of Lenin, Zinoviev and Kamenev, that I was ready to join the Bolshevik organization immediately in view of the absence of any disagreements whatever but that it was necessary to decide the question of the quickest possible way of attracting the *"Mezhrayontsi"* organization into the party. I remember that some one of those present raised the question of how I thought the fusion should be carried out (what member of the *"Mezhrayontsi"* should go into the editorial board of *Pravda,* who into the Central Committee, etc.). I answered that for me that question had no political importance whatsoever in view of the absence of any disagreements.

Among the membership of the *"Mezhrayontsi"* organization there were elements which tried to impede the fusion, advancing this or that condition, etc. (Yurenev and, in part, Manuilsky). Between the Petersburg Committee of the party and the *"Mezhrayontsi"* organization there had piled up, as always in such circumstances, old grudges, lack of confidence, etc. That and that alone caused the delay in our fusion until July.

8. Comrade Raskolnikov has covered no little paper in recent times with attempts to contrast my line in the year 1917 with Lenin's. It is too wearisome a task to adduce such examples, especially since his writing does not differ in the least from all the other falsifications of the same kind.

It might prove more fruitful, therefore, to quote some words which this same Raskolnikov wrote about that period somewhat earlier:

> "The echoes of past disagreements during the prewar period had completely disappeared. No differences existed between the tactical line of Lenin and Trotsky. The fusion, already observable during the war, was completely and definitely achieved from the moment of Leon Davidovich's [Trotsky's] return to Russia. From his first public speech all of us old Leninists felt that he was ours." ("In Kerensky's Jail," *Proletarskaya Revolutsia,* No. 10 [22], 1923, pp. 150*f*.)

Those words were written not in order to prove something or to refute something but just to tell what was. Later on Raskolnikov showed that he also knows how to tell what was not. In republishing his articles issued by the organs of the *Istpart,* Raskolnikov meticulously removed from them what was, in order to replace it with what was not.

Maybe it is not worth while to dwell upon comrade Raskolnikov but this example is rather striking.

In his review of the third volume of my *Collected Works* in *Krasnaya Nov,* No. 7–8, 1924, pp. 395–401, Raskolnikov asks:

> "And what was the position of Trotsky himself in 1917?"

And answers:

> "Comrade Trotsky still considered himself a member of the same general party with the Mensheviks, Tseretelli and Skobelev."

And further:

> "Comrade Trotsky had not yet clarified his attitude towards Bolshevism and Menshevism. At that time comrade Trotsky still occupied a vacillating, indefinite, straddling position."

You might ask how these really impudent assertions can be reconciled with the words of this same Raskolnikov quoted above: "The echoes of past disagreements during the pre-war period had completely disappeared."

If Trotsky had not defined his attitude towards Bolshevism and Menshevism, how did it happen that "all of us old Leninists felt that he was ours"?

But that is not all. In the article of the same Raskolnikov

entitled "July Days," *Proletarskaya Revolutsia,* No. 5 (17), 1923, pp. 71*f*, we read:

> "Leon Davidovich was not formally at that time a member of our party but as a matter of fact he worked continuously within it from the day of his arrival from America. At any rate, immediately after his first speech in the Soviet, we all looked upon him as one of our party leaders."

That seems clear. It seems to be beyond false interpretation. But never fear. Sufficient unto the day is the evil thereof. And how great is the "evil" of our day—an evil systematically organized and reënforced by official command and circular letter.

In order that the conduct of Raskolnikov, characteristic not of him personally but of our entire present system of leadership and education, may appear in its full splendor, I must cite a longer paragraph from his article "In Kerensky's Prison." Here is what he says:

> "Trotsky's attitude to Vladimir Ilyich [Lenin] was one of enormous respect. He esteemed Lenin higher than all contemporaries whom he had met in Russia and abroad. In the tone in which Trotsky spoke of Lenin you felt the devotion of a disciple. At that time Lenin had given thirty years' service to the proletariat, Trotsky twenty."

Then come the lines already quoted above:

> "The echoes of past disagreements of the pre-war period had completely disappeared. . . . All of us old Leninists felt that he was ours."

This testimony of Raskolnikov as to Trotsky's attitude toward Lenin does not, of course, deter Raskolnikov from quoting the "Letter of Trotsky to Chkheidze,"[6] which was extracted from the garbage heap of émigré squabbles for the education of the younger members of the party.

It should be added that Raskolnikov met me often in the line of duty in the summer months of 1917. He frequently drove me to Kronstadt; he turned to me many times for counsel; held long conversations with me in prison, and so forth.

His personal reminiscences represent in this sense a valuable testimonial proof, whereas his later "corrections" are nothing more than the work of a falsifier fulfilling his task under orders.

Before parting with Raskolnikov, let us hear how he portrayed in his reminiscences the reading by the investigator of the testimony of Ermolenko in regard to German gold,[7] etc.:

> "During the reading of his testimony we made, from time to time, ironical comments but when the dispassionate voice of the investigator arrived at the name, so dear to us, of comrade Lenin, Trotsky could not restrain himself. He struck the table with his fist, rose to his full height, and announced with indignation that he refused to listen to this vile and lying testimony. Unable to restrain our wrath in the face of this unconcealed falsification, we all, to the last man, hotly supported comrade Trotsky."

Wrath in the face of "unconcealed falsification" is a perfectly understandable feeling. But leaving aside the trivial falsifications of Raskolnikov himself (also none too well concealed), let me ask: What is the attitude of the present

Raskolnikov, having graduated from the Stalin school, to the latest creations *à la* Ermolenko in regard to the Wrangel officer[8] and the counter-revolutionary conspiracy of the Left Opposition?

From May to October 1917

9. Many of the documents issued by the Bolsheviks in May, June and July 1917 were written by me or with my editorial participation. To this series belong, for instance, the "Declaration of the Bolshevik Fraction of the Soviet Congress as to the Proposed Advance on the Front" (First Congress of the Soviets), the letter to the Central Executive Committee of the Soviets from the Central Committee of the Bolshevik party in the days of the June demonstration, and others. I have chanced upon quite a number of Bolshevik resolutions of this period which I wrote, or participated in writing. In all my speeches at all meetings, as is well known to all the comrades, I identified myself with the Bolsheviks.

10. One of the "Marxian historians" of the new style attempted not long ago to discover disagreements between Lenin and me on the subject of the July days. Everyone tries to contribute his mite, hoping to receive it back a hundredfold. You have to overcome a feeling of disgust even to refute such falsifications. I will not cite personal reminiscences. I limit myself to documents. In my declaration to the Provisional Government, I wrote at that time:

> "1. I share the principled position of Lenin, Zinoviev and Kamenev, and I have developed it in my journal, *Vperyod,* and in general in all my public speeches. . . .
>
> "3. My not participating in the editorship of *Pravda* and not entering the Bolshevik organization are not to be explained by political differences but are due to

conditions in our party history which have now lost all significance." (*Collected Works,* Vol. III, Part I, pp. 165*f*.)

11. In connection with the July days, the Social Revolutionary-Menshevik Praesidium convoked a plenary session of the Central Executive Committee. The Bolshevik fraction of the plenum invited me at that difficult moment to make the report on the question of the new situation and the problems of the party. That was *before* my formal union with the party and notwithstanding the fact that Stalin, for example, was then in Petrograd. The "Marxian historians" of the new style did not yet then exist, and the assembled Bolsheviks unanimously approved the fundamental ideas of my report on the July days and the tasks of the party. There is published testimony on this point, particularly in the memoirs of N.I. Muralov.

12. Lenin, as is well known, did not suffer from benevolent confidence in people when it was a question of ideological line or of political conduct in difficult circumstances, and such benevolence was particularly foreign to him in relation to revolutionists who had stood in a preceding period outside the ranks of the Bolshevik party. It was precisely the July days which broke down the last remnants of the old dividing lines. In his letter to the Central Committee on the slate of Bolshevik candidates for the Constituent Assembly, Vladimir Ilyich wrote:

> "We cannot possibly permit such an immoderate number of candidates from people who have hardly been tested and who have just recently joined the party (such as, U. Larin). . . . We must have special reconsideration and correction of the slate. . . .
>
> "It goes without saying that . . . nobody would oppose such a nomination, for example, as that of L.D.

> Trotsky, for, in the first place, Trotsky immediately upon his arrival, took the position of an internationalist; in the second place, he fought among the *'Mezhrayontsi'* for fusion with the Bolsheviks; and finally, during the onerous July days he proved himself both equal to the task and a devoted adherent of the party of the revolutionary proletariat. Obviously that cannot be said for a majority of the recent members of the party who appear on the slate." (*The First Legal Central Committee of the Bolsheviks in 1917,* Leningrad *Istpart,* pp. 305*f*.)

13. The question of our attitude to the Pre-Parliament[9] was discussed in Lenin's absence. I appeared as the reporter for those Bolsheviks who favored boycotting the Pre-Parliament. The majority of the Bolshevik faction of the Democratic Conference voted, as is well known, against the boycott. Lenin came out decisively in support of the minority. Here is what he wrote to the Central Committee on that score:

> "We must boycott the Pre-Parliament. We must go to the Soviet of Workers', Soldiers' and Peasants' Deputies; we must go to the trade unions—go to the masses in general. We must summon them to struggle. We must give them the correct and clear slogan: Disperse the Bonapartist band of Kerensky together with the bogus Pre-Parliament, with its Tseretelli-Bulyginite Duma. The Mensheviks and Social Revolutionists did not accept our compromise even after the Kornilov events, our proposal of a peaceful transfer of power to the Soviets (in which, at that time, we did not yet have a majority). They sank again into the swamp of dirty and infamous bargains with the Cadets. Down with the Mensheviks and Social Revolutionists! Ruthless struggle against them! Ruthlessly drive them out of all revolutionary

organizations! No negotiations, no conferences with these *friends of the Kishkins,* friends of Kornilov's landlords and capitalists!

"Saturday, September 22.

"Trotsky was for the boycott. Bravo, Comrade Trotsky!

"Boycottism was beaten in the Bolshevik faction attending the Democratic Conference. Long live the boycott!" (*Proletarskaya Revolutsia,* No. 3, 1924.)

The October insurrection

14. As to my participation in the October Revolution—in the notes on p. 482 in Vol. XIV of the *Collected Works* of Lenin, you read:

> "After the majority of the Petrograd Soviet passed into the hands of the Bolsheviks, [Trotsky] was elected its chairman and in that position organized and led the insurrection of October 25."

How much is true here and how much false, let the *Istpart* decide—if not the present one then some future one. Lately, Stalin, at any rate, has categorically denied the truth of this assertion. Thus:

> "I have to say that comrade Trotsky played no particular rôle in the October insurrection and could not do so; that, being chairman of the Petrograd Soviet, he merely fulfilled the will of the corresponding party authority which guided his every step."

And further:

> "Comrade Trotsky played no particular rôle in the party or the October insurrection and could not do so,

> being a man comparatively new to our party in the October period." (J. Stalin: *Trotskyism or Leninism,* pp. 68*f*.)

To be sure, in giving this testimony, Stalin forgot what he himself said on the 6th of November 1918; that is, on the first anniversary of the revolution, when facts and events were still too fresh in the minds of all. Even then, Stalin had already begun that work in relation to me which he has now developed on such a grand scale. But he was then compelled to conduct it far more cautiously and underhandedly than he is doing now. Here is what he wrote then in *Pravda* (No. 241) under the title, "The Rôle of the Most Eminent Party Leaders":

> "All the work of practical organization of the insurrection was conducted under the immediate leadership of the chairman of the Petrograd Soviet, Trotsky. It is possible to declare with certainty that the swift passing of the garrison to the side of the Soviet and the bold execution of the work of the Military Revolutionary Committee, the party owes principally and above all to comrade Trotsky."

These words, written by no means for the purpose of laudatory exaggeration—on the contrary, Stalin's goal was then wholly different: with his article he wanted to "warn" against exaggerating Trotsky's rôle (this is really why the article was written)—these words sound like an absolutely incredible panegyric today, coming from the lips of Stalin. But at that time it was impossible to express oneself otherwise. It was said long ago that a truthful man has this advantage, that even with a bad memory he never contradicts himself, while a disloyal, unscrupulous and dishonest man has always to remember what he said in the past, in order not to shame himself.

15. Stalin, with the help of the Yaroslavskys, is trying to construct a new history of the organization of the October insurrection, basing himself on the fact that the party created a "practical center for the organizational leadership of the insurrection," of which, if you please, Trotsky was not a member. Neither was Lenin a member of that committee. That fact alone demonstrates that the committee had only a subordinate organizational significance. It played no independent rôle whatever. The legend about this committee has been created today for the simple reason that Stalin was a member of it. Here is the membership: Sverdlov, Stalin, Dzerzhinsky, Bubnov, Uritsky.

However unpleasant it is to dig into rubbish, it seems necessary for me, as a fairly close participant in and witness of the events of that time, to testify as follows:

The rôle of Lenin, of course, needs no illumination. Sverdlov I often met and I often turned to him for counsel and for people to help me. Comrade Kamenev, who, as is well known, held then a special position,[10] the incorrectness of which he himself has long ago acknowledged, took, nevertheless, a most active part in the events of the insurrection. The decisive night, from the 25th to the 26th, Kamenev and I spent together in the quarters of the Military Revolutionary Committee, answering questions and giving orders by telephone. But stretch my memory as I will, I cannot answer the question in just what consisted, during those decisive days, the rôle of Stalin. It never once happened that I turned to him for advice or coöperation. He never showed the slightest initiative. He never advanced a single independent proposal. This fact no "Marxian historian" of the new style can alter.

16. (I add this note on November 2, 1927.) Stalin and Yaroslavsky, as I said above, have wasted much effort these

last months in proving that the military revolutionary center created by the Central Committee, consisting of Sverdlov, Stalin, Bubnov, Uritsky and Dzerzhinsky, was, allegedly, the director of the whole course of the insurrection. Stalin has emphasized, in every way he could, the fact that Trotsky was not a member of that center. But alas! through sheer carelessness on the part of Stalin's historians, in *Pravda* of Nov. 2, 1927—that is, after the present letter was written—there appeared an accurate excerpt from the minutes of the Central Committee for the 16th (29th) of October 1917:

> "The Central Committee created a military revolutionary center with the following members: Sverdlov, Stalin, Bubnov, Uritsky and Dzerzhinsky. *This center is to be a constituent part of the Revolutionary Soviet Committee."*

The Revolutionary Soviet Committee is none other than the Military Revolutionary Committee created by the Petrograd Soviet. No other Soviet organ for the leadership of the insurrection existed. Thus, these five comrades, designated by the Central Committee, were required to supplement the staff of that same Military Revolutionary Committee of which Trotsky was chairman. Superfluous, it would seem, for Trotsky to be introduced a second time into the staff of an organization of which he was already chairman! How hard it is, after all, to correct history after the event!

History of the October Revolution

17. At Brest, I wrote a short outline of the October Revolution. This little book went through a large number of editions in various languages. Nobody ever told me that

there is a flagrant omission in my book; namely, that it nowhere points out the chief guide of the insurrection, "the military revolutionary center," of which Stalin and Bubnov were members. If I was so poorly informed of the history of the October insurrection, why did not somebody enlighten me? Why was my book studied with impunity in all the party schools during the early years of the revolution?

But that is not all. Even in the year 1922, the Organization Bureau of the party seemed to think that I understood fairly well the history of the October Revolution. Here is a small but eloquent confirmation of that:

> **"No. 14302**
>
> MOSCOW, MAY 24, 1922.
>
> "To Comrade Trotsky:
>
> "Excerpt from the minutes of the session of the Organization Bureau of the Central Committee for May 22, 1922, No. 21.
>
> "Commission comrade Yakovlev by the first of October to compile, under the editorship of comrade Trotsky, a textbook of the October Revolution.
>
> *"Secretary of the Second*
> *Department of Propaganda*
> (Signature)"

That was in May 1922. Both my book about the October Revolution, as well as my book about the year 1905, having appeared before that time in many editions, must have been well known to the Organization Bureau—which was already at that period headed by Stalin. Nevertheless, the Organization Bureau deemed it necessary to assign me the task of editing the textbook of the history of the October Revolution. How is that? Evidently the eyes of Stalin and the Stalinists were opened to "Trotskyism" only after the eyes of Lenin had closed forever.

Lost documents

18. It was already after the October Revolution that upon the insistence of the Right wing (Kamenev, Rykov, Lunacharsky and others) negotiations were carried on with the Conciliationists regarding a coalition socialist government. As one of the conditions, the Conciliationists demanded the exclusion from the government of Lenin and Trotsky. The Rights were inclined to accept that condition. The question was considered at the session of November 1 (14). This is what the minutes state:

> "Session of the 1st (14th) of November 1917.
>
> "Ultimatum of the majority of the Central Committee to the minority. . . . It is proposed to exclude Lenin and Trotsky. This is a proposal to decapitate our party and we do not accept it."

That very day, that is, on the 1st (14th) of November, Lenin spoke on this issue at the meeting of the Petrograd Committee. The minutes of the Petrograd Committee meetings for 1917 were published on the tenth anniversary of October. Originally the minutes of this session of the 1st (14th) of November 1917, were likewise included in that edition. In the first proof of the table of contents, this session is indicated. But afterwards, under orders from above, the minutes of November 1 (14) were deleted and concealed from the party.[11] It is easy to understand why. On the question of compromise, Lenin spoke to the party as follows:

> "As for a compromise—I cannot even speak about that seriously. Trotsky said long ago that unification

> is impossible. Trotsky understood this and from that time on *there has been no better Bolshevik."*

The speech ends with the slogan: "No compromise! A homogeneous Bolshevik government!"

19. It is worth noting that these same minutes of the session of the Petrograd Committee clearly show what was Lenin's attitude to the question of discipline when discipline was being used to cover a patently opportunistic line. After the report of comrade Fenigstein, Lenin announced:

> "If you want a split, go ahead. If you get the majority, take power in the Central Executive Committee and carry on. *But we'll go to the sailors."*

It was precisely by means of this bold, decisive, irreconcilable way of putting the question that *Lenin saved the party from a split.*

Iron discipline, yes, but on the basis of a revolutionary line. On the fourth of April, Lenin said (at the so-called March Party Conference):[12]

> "Even our Bolsheviks show confidence in the [Provisional] Government. That can be explained only by intoxication incidental to revolution. That is the death of socialism. You, comrades, place confidence in the government. If that's your position, our ways part."

And further:

> "I hear that in Russia there is a trend toward unification. Unification with the defensists[13]—that is betrayal

> of socialism. I think it would be better to stand alone like Liebknecht—one against a hundred and ten."[14]

20. Why did Lenin pose this question so sharply—one against a hundred and ten? Because in the March Conference of 1917, semi-defensist and semi-coalitionist tendencies were very strong.

At that conference, Stalin supported the resolution of the Krasnoyarsk Soviet of Deputies which advocated:

> "Support of the Provisional Government in its activities, only in so far as it follows a course of satisfying the demands of the working class and the revolutionary peasantry in the revolution that is taking place."

More than that, Stalin stood for unification with Tseretelli. Here is the verbatim excerpt from the minutes of the conference:

> "*Order of the day:* Tseretelli's proposal for unification.
>
> "STALIN: We ought to go. It is necessary to define our proposal as to the terms of unification. Unification is possible along the lines of Zimmerwald-Kienthal."[15]

When certain participants of the conference made objections to the effect that such a unification would be heterogeneous, Stalin replied:

> "There is no use running ahead and anticipating disagreements. There is no party life without disagreements. We will live down trivial disagreements within the party."

Disagreements with Tseretelli, Stalin considered "trivial." In his attitude toward the followers of Tseretelli, Stalin was for a broad democracy: "There is no party life without disagreements."

21. Now, comrade directors of the *Istpart* of the Central Committee, permit me to ask you: Why have the minutes of the March 1917 Party Conference never yet seen the light of day? You broadcast questionnaires with innumerable graphs and rubrics. You collect every kind of triviality, often the most insignificant. Why do you keep on hiding the minutes of the March Conference which have tremendous significance for the history of the party? Those minutes reveal the state of mind of the leading elements of the party on the eve of Lenin's return to Russia. In the Secretariat of the Central Committee and in the Praesidium of the Central Control Commission, I have repeatedly asked: Why does the *Istpart* conceal from the party a document of such extraordinary importance? The document is known to you. It is in your possession. You do not publish it for the simple reason that it cruelly reflects upon the political physiognomy of Stalin at the end of March and the beginning of April—that is to say, in that period when Stalin *independently* tried to work out a political line.

22. In his same speech at the Conference of April 4, Lenin said:

> "*Pravda* demands from the *government* that it renounce annexations. . . . Nonsense! Flagrant mockery of. . . ."

The minutes are not edited. There are omissions and unfinished sentences in them. But the general sense and the general trend of the speech are absolutely clear. One of the editors of *Pravda* was Stalin. In *Pravda* Stalin wrote semi-defensist articles and supported the Provisional Government "in so far as." With petty reservations, Stalin welcomed the manifesto of Kerensky and Tseretelli to all the nations—a lying, social-patriotic document which aroused nothing but indignation in Lenin.

That is why, comrades of the *Istpart,* and that is the only reason why, you do not publish the minutes of the Party Conference of March 1917 but hide them from the party.

23. I cited above the speech of Lenin at the session of the Petrograd Committee, November 1 (14). Where are the minutes of that meeting published? Nowhere. Why? Because you have forbidden it. There has just appeared a collection of the minutes of the first legal Petrograd Committee of 1917. The minutes of the session of November 1 (14) were originally included in this collection and were indicated in the table of contents as it was first set up. But afterward, as I said, at the order of the Central *Istpart,* the minutes were deleted from the book with this remarkable explanation, that "obviously" the speech of Lenin was distorted by the secretary in his notes. What does this "obvious" distortion consist in? It consists in this: That Lenin's speech ruthlessly refutes the false assertions of the present historical school of Stalin-Yaroslavsky concerning Trotsky. Everyone who knows Lenin's oratorical style will acknowledge without hesitation the authenticity of his recorded phrases. Behind the words of Lenin about conciliationism, behind his threat—"We will go to the sailors"—you feel the living Lenin of those days. You hide him from the party. Why? Because of his comment on Trotsky. Only that!

You hide the minutes of the March 1917 Conference because they compromise Stalin. You hide the minutes of the session of the Petrograd Committee only because they obstruct your work of falsification against Trotsky.

24. Permit me to touch in passing upon an episode concerning comrade Rykov.

Many comrades were surprised at the publication, in the notes of the Lenin Institute, of an article in which Lenin wrote several unpleasant lines in regard to Rykov. Here is what he wrote:

> "*Rabochaya Gazeta,* an organ of Menshevik Ministerialists, is trying to cast aspersions upon us because the Okhrana[16] in 1911 arrested a Bolshevik conciliator, Rykov, in order to give 'free' activity, 'on the eve of the elections to the Fourth Duma' (*Rabochaya Gazeta* especially emphasizes this) to the Bolsheviks of our party."

Thus, in 1911, Lenin numbered Rykov among the non-party Bolsheviks. How did these lines happen to see the light of day? Ordinarily, in these times, only those harsh comments that bear upon Oppositionists are quoted from the works of Lenin. About the representatives of the present majority, it is permitted to quote only praise (provided there is any). How then did the above lines get into print? Everybody is explaining this fact in exactly the same way: Stalin's historians consider necessary (so soon! so soon!) a complete objectivity—in regard to Rykov.[17]

Concerning Yaroslavsky

25. Nine-tenths of his slanders and falsifications, Yaroslavsky dedicates to the author of these lines. It would be hard to imagine lies more confused and at the same time more spiteful! Do not make the mistake of thinking, however, that Yaroslavsky always wrote in this way. No, he wrote quite differently. It was just as pedestrian, it was in just as bad taste, but to exactly the opposite effect. As late as the spring of 1923, Yaroslavsky devoted an article to the beginnings of the political-literary activity of the author of these lines. The article is a tumultuous panegyric,

unbearable to read. It requires an effort to quote from it. But it can't be helped. In his character of inquisitor, Yaroslavsky takes a voluptuous pleasure in bringing face to face on the witness stand communists guilty of distributing the Testament of Lenin, the letters of Lenin on the national question, and other criminal documents in which Lenin dared to criticize Stalin. Let us bring Yaroslavsky face to face with himself.

> "The brilliant literary-publicistic activity of comrade Trotsky [so Yaroslavsky wrote in 1923] gained him the worldwide renown of 'Prince of Pamphleteers.' The English writer, Bernard Shaw, described him thus. Whoever has followed his activity during the course of a quarter of a century, cannot but be convinced that this talent of the pamphleteer and polemicist developed, grew and blossomed with especial brilliancy during the years of our proletarian revolution. But even at the dawn of his activity, it was observable that we had before us an endowment most profound. All his newspaper articles were saturated with inspiration; they all partook of imagery, color, although they had to be written in the vise of the censorship of Czarist absolutism which mutilated the bold thought and the bold form of everyone who wished to escape from the grip of those jaws and raise himself above the common level. But so great were the ripening underground forces, so strongly was felt the beating of the heart of the awakening people, so sharp were the developing contradictions, that all the censors in the world could not stamp out the creative power of such a shining individual personality as was already in those days the figure of L.D. Trotsky.
>
> "Probably many have seen the quite widely distributed photograph of the youth Trotsky when he was first

sentenced to exile in Siberia—that boisterous head of hair, those characteristic lips and lofty brow. Under that head of hair, under that lofty brow, was boiling even then a turbulent stream of images, thoughts, moods—sometimes diverting comrade Trotsky a little from the broad road of history, compelling him sometimes to choose too long a detour, or, on the other hand, to cut his way fearlessly through where it was impossible to go through. *But in all this questing we had before us a man profoundly dedicated to revolution, a man born to the rôle of tribune,* with a tongue sharply whetted and flexible as steel, slaying his enemies, and a pen scattering in handfuls like artistic pearls the riches of his mind."

And further:

"The articles at our disposal embrace a period of more than two years—from Oct. 15, 1900 to Sept. 12, 1902. The Siberian comrades read with delight these brilliant articles and awaited their appearance with impatience. Only a few knew who was the author, and those knowing Trotsky never guessed in those days that he would be *one of the recognized leaders of the most revolutionary army and of the greatest revolution in the world."*

And finally the conclusion:

"His protest against the pessimism of the demagnetized Russian intelligentsia [Ahem!] comrade Trotsky established later. Not in words, but in deeds he established it, shoulder to shoulder with the revolutionary proletariat of the great proletarian revolution. For this, great powers were needed. The Siberian village did not destroy in him these powers; it only further convinced him of the necessity of radically breaking, to the foundation, that whole social order which made possible the facts described by him." (*Sibirskye Ogni,* Nos. 1–2, Jan.–April 1923.)

Although in some of his recent articles comrade Yaroslavsky has made a turn of 180°, we must grant that in one respect he remains faithfully the same: He is equally unbearable in slander and in praise.

Concerning Olminsky

26. Among the exposers of "Trotskyism," Olminsky, as is known, has occupied a fairly prominent place. He has been especially zealous, I remember, on the subject of my book, *1905,* which appeared originally in the German language. But Olminsky also has had two opinions upon this subject: one in the days of Lenin; another in the days of Stalin.

In October 1921, somebody raised the question of the publication of my book, *1905,* by the *Istpart.* Olminsky wrote me on that subject the following letter:

"Dear Leon Davidovitch:

"The *Istpart* will be delighted, of course, to publish your book in Russian but the question is: To whom shall the translation be entrusted? You can't let the first man you meet translate a book *by Trotsky*! All the beauty and individuality of the style would be lost. Maybe you could squeeze an hour a day from your duties of state importance for this work—also, by the way, of state importance—and dictate the text in Russian to a typist.

"Another question: Why not begin to prepare a complete collection of your writings? We could easily commission someone to take charge of that. It is high time it was done. The new generation, not knowing, as it should, the history of the party, unacquainted with old and recent writings of the leaders, will always be getting off the track. I am returning the book in the hope that it soon comes back to the *Istpart* in a Russian text.

"With best wishes,
"M. Olminsky.
"OCTOBER 17, 1921."

That is how Olminsky wrote at the end of 1921—that is to say, long after the controversies over the Brest-Litovsk peace and over the trade unions, controversies to which Olminsky and Co. are now trying to impart such an exaggerated importance. At the end of 1921, Olminsky considered the publication of *1905* a work of "state importance." Olminsky was the initiator of the publication of my complete works, which he considered necessary for the education of party members. In the autumn of 1921, Olminsky was not a child. He knew the past. My disagreements with Bolshevism were known to him better than to anybody else. He himself had engaged in polemics with me in the old days. All this did not prevent him, in the autumn of 1921, from insisting upon the publication of a complete collection of my works in the interests of educating the party youth. Was Olminsky perhaps a "Trotskyist" in 1921?

A word or two concerning Lunacharsky

27. Lunacharsky also now appears among the "exposers" of the Opposition. Trailing the others, he accuses us of pessimism and lack of faith. This rôle is especially becoming to Lunacharsky.

Trailing the others, Lunacharsky occupies himself not only with contrasting "Trotskyism" and Leninism but also supports in a very slightly disguised form—every kind of insinuation.

Like certain others, Lunacharsky knows how to write on one and the same question, both for and against. In 1923, he issued a little book, *Revolutionary Silhouettes*. There is a chapter in that book dedicated to me. I will not quote this chapter for the oratorical exaggerations of its praise. I will quote merely two passages in which Lunacharsky speaks of my attitude toward Lenin:

> "Trotsky is a prickly person, imperious. Only in his relations with Lenin, after their fusion, Trotsky always showed, and still shows, a tender and touching yieldingness, and with a modesty characteristic of the truly great, recognizes Lenin's superior authority." (p. 25.)

And a few pages earlier:

> "When Lenin lay wounded mortally, as we feared, no one expressed our feeling about him better than Trotsky. In the terrible storm of world events, Trotsky, the other leader of the Russian Revolution, by no means inclined to sentimentalism, said: 'When you think that Lenin might die, it seems as if all of our lives were useless, and you want to stop living'." (*Ibid.,* p. 13.)

What sort of people are these, who know how to write this thing or that depending on who gives them orders—history or the Secretariat!

The Brest-Litovsk and the trade union controversy Martinovism in the limelight

28. What I have demonstrated above, with examples taken from the year 1917, could be carried through all

the years that followed. I do not mean that there were no disagreements between Lenin and me. There were. The disagreements on the question of the Brest-Litovsk peace[18] lasted several weeks and assumed a sharp character for several days.

The attempt to present the differences on the question of the Brest-Litovsk peace as if they derived from my alleged "underestimation of the peasantry" is utterly ridiculous, and at best is an attempt to hang Bukharin's position onto me—a position with which I had nothing in common. Not for a moment did I suppose that in 1917–1918 it was possible to rouse the peasant masses for a revolutionary war. In estimating the moods of the peasant and labor masses after the imperialist war, I was wholly in agreement with Lenin. If I stood, at the time, for postponing as long as possible the moment of capitulation to Hohenzollern, it was not for the purpose of calling forth a revolutionary war but in order to arouse the workers of Germany and Austria-Hungary to as great a revolutionary activity as possible. The decision to announce a state of war as terminated, without signing a forced peace, was dictated by the intention of testing in action whether or not Hohenzollern was still able to wage war against the revolution. This decision was adopted by the majority of our Central Committee and approved by the majority of the fraction of the All-Russian Central Executive Committee of the Soviets. Lenin regarded that decision as the lesser evil since a very considerable section of the party leadership was for the Bukharinist "revolutionary war," ignoring not only the condition of the peasants but also of the labor masses. The signing of the peace treaty with Hohenzollern exhausted entirely my episodic differences with Lenin on that question, and our work proceeded in complete harmony. Bukharin, on the other hand, developed his Brest-Litovsk differences with Lenin into an entire system of "Left Communism," with which I had nothing in common.

Many wiseacres seize every propitious occasion to scintillate on the subject of my slogan: No peace—no war. It obviously appears to them in contradiction with the very nature of things. Yet, between classes, as well as between states, relationships of "no peace—no war" are not at all rare. One need only recall that several months after Brest-Litovsk, when the revolutionary situation in Germany had completely defined itself, we announced that we were breaking the Brest-Litovsk peace without in any way resuming hostilities against Germany. With the countries of the Entente, in the course of the first few years of the revolution, our relationships were those of "no peace—no war." As a matter of fact, the same type of relationship exists between us and England now (with the Tories in power). Throughout the Brest-Litovsk negotiations, the whole question was whether or not, at the beginning of 1918, a revolutionary situation had sufficiently matured in Germany to enable us, without continuing the war (we had no army!), to refrain from signing a peace. Experience showed that such a situation did not exist as yet.

The meaningless "reviews" beginning with 1923 have completely distorted the sense of the Brest-Litovsk controversy. All the fictions concerning my line during the epoch of Brest-Litovsk are discussed in detail and refuted on the basis of the incontrovertible documents in the notes to Volume XVII of my *Collected Works*.

The Brest-Litovsk disagreements, as I have already stated, did not leave the shadow of any bitterness in my personal relations with Lenin. Just a few days after the signing of the peace, I was placed—on the motion of Vladimir Ilyich—at the head of the military work.

29. The conflict on the trade union question was sharper and more protracted. The new theoretician of Stalinism, the Menshevik, Martinov, who came to us on the wave of the N.E.P.,[19] has described the disagreement on the trade union question as a disagreement on the question of the N.E.P. On this subject, Martinov wrote in 1923:

> "L. Trotsky in 1905 argued more logically and consistently than either the Bolsheviks or the Mensheviks. But the flaw in his argument lay in that he was 'too consistent.' *The picture which he drew very accurately anticipated the Bolshevik dictatorship during the first three years of the October Revolution* which, as is well known, arrived in a blind alley, tearing the proletariat away from the peasantry, by reason of which the Bolshevik party was compelled to make a long retreat." (*Krasnaya Nov,* No. 2, 1923, p. 262.)

Before the N.E.P., "Trotskyism" reigned. Bolshevism began only with the New Economic Policy. It is noteworthy that Martinov reasoned in exactly the same way about the revolution of 1905!

According to him, in October, November and December of 1905—that is, in the period of the highest upsurge of the revolution—"Trotskyism" reigned. The real Marxian policy began only after the crushing of the Moscow insurrection—approximately, say, with the elections to the first State Duma. Martinov now contrasts Bolshevism with "Trotskyism" along the self-same line according to which twenty years ago he contrasted Menshevism with "Trotskyism." And these writings are passing for Marxism and are being fed to the young "theoreticians" of the party.

30. In his Testament, Lenin refers to the trade union discussion not in order to represent it as a controversy

called forth by my widely publicized "underestimation of the peasantry." No. Lenin speaks of this discussion as of a controversy over the People's Commissariat of Means and Communication, and he chides me not for "underestimating the peasantry" but for a "disposition to be far too much attracted by the purely administrative side of affairs." I think that these words quite correctly characterize the root of that controversy.

War Communism had exhausted itself. Agriculture and with it everything else had arrived in a blind alley. Industry was disintegrating. The trade unions had become agitational and recruiting organizations which increasingly lost their independence. The crisis of the trade unions was by no means a "crisis of growth"; it was a crisis of the whole system of War Communism. There was no passage out of the blind alley without the introduction of the N.E.P. Proposals sponsored by me to harness the trade union apparatus to the administrative system of economic management (my "disposition to be far too much attracted by the purely administrative side of affairs"), did not point the way out. But neither did the trade union resolution presented by the "Ten" (Lenin, Zinoviev and others) because the trade unions as defenders of the material and cultural interests of the working class and as a school of communism were losing their ground under conditions of an economic impasse.

Under the blows of the Kronstadt uprising,[20] a new economic orientation of the party was effected, which opened up altogether new perspectives for the trade unions as well. But it is significant that at the Tenth Congress, at which the party unanimously approved the initial foundations of the N.E.P., the trade union resolution was not in harmony with these foundations and retained all of its internal contradictions. This became evident within a few months. The trade union resolution which was adopted by the Tenth Congress had to be radically changed without waiting for the Eleventh Congress. The new resolution, drafted by Lenin, which brought the work of the trade unions under the new conditions created by the N.E.P., was unanimously adopted.

To study the trade union discussion without any relation to the question of the turn of our entire economic policy at the time means even now, seven years later, not to understand the meaning of that discussion. This lack of understanding is precisely the source of all efforts to foist the "underestimation of the peasantry" upon me when, indeed, at the time of the trade union discussion, it was I who proposed the slogan: Industry must turn its face to the village!

More consistent falsifiers attempt to represent the matter as if I were opposed to the N.E.P. But irrefutable facts and documents prove that as early as the time of the Ninth Congress I raised time and again the question of the necessity to pass from the food levy to taxes and, within certain limits, to the commodity forms of circulation.

Only the rejection of these proposals, in the face of a continuing decline of economy, compelled me to seek a way out, along the opposite road, i.e., along the road of rigid management and closer inclusion of the trade unions—not as mass organizations but as administrative machinery—into the system of economic management under War Communism. The transition to the N.E.P. not only met with no objections on my part, but, on the contrary, corresponded entirely with all the conclusions I had drawn from my own experience in economic management and administration. Such is the actual content of the so-called trade union discussion.

The volume of my *Collected Works* devoted to this period

has not been published by the State Publishers precisely because that book does not leave a stone unturned in exposing the legend created around the trade union discussion.

31. To believe the present party historians and theoreticians, you might think that the first six years of the revolution were entirely filled with disagreements about Brest-Litovsk and the trade unions. All the rest has disappeared: the preparation of the October insurrection, the insurrection itself, the creation of the government, the creation of the Red Army, the civil war, the four congresses of the Comintern, all the writings on communist propaganda, the work in the sphere of leadership of the foreign communist parties and our own. Of all this work, in which upon all fundamental questions, I was in complete accord with Lenin, there remain, according to the present historians, only two moments: Brest-Litovsk and the trade unions.

32. Stalin and his lackeys have worked hardest over the effort to picture the trade union discussion as my "bitter" struggle against Lenin.

Here is what I said at the height of this discussion at our fraction in the Miners' Congress, January 26, 1921:

> "Comrade Shliapnikov in speaking here—perhaps I express his thought a little crudely—said: 'Don't believe in this disagreement between Trotsky and Lenin. They will unite just the same and the struggle will be waged only against us!' He says: 'Don't believe.' I don't know what this means about believing or not believing. Of course, we will unite. We may dispute in deciding any very important question but the controversy only pushes our thoughts in the direction of 'unification'." (Trotsky, *Concluding Speech,* Second All-Russian Congress of Miners, Jan. 26, 1921.)

Here is another passage from my speech which Lenin quoted in his pamphlet:

> "During the sharpest polemic concerning comrade Tomsky, I always said what is absolutely clear to me, that the leaders in our trade unions can be only people with the greatest experience, with the authority that comrade Tomsky possesses. I said that at the meeting of our fraction during the Fifth Trade Union Congress. I said it again the other day at Zimin's Theatre. An ideological struggle in the party does not imply mutual repulsion. It implies rather influence mutually exerted." (*Collected Works,* Vol. XVIII, Pt. 1, p. 71.)

And here is what Lenin said on this self-same question in his concluding speech at the Tenth Party Congress, summarizing the trade union discussion:

> "The Workers' Opposition said: 'Lenin and Trotsky will unite.' Trotsky taking the floor replied: 'Whoever does not understand that it is necessary to unite is going against the party; of course, we will unite because we are party men.' I supported Trotsky. To be sure, Trotsky and I have differed. When more or less equal groupings arise in the Central Committee, the party decides, and decides in such a way that we unite according to the will and directives of the party. That is the announcement with which Trotsky and I went to the Miners' Congress and have come here, i.e., to the Party Congress." (*Ibid.,* p. 132.)

Is that anything like the spiteful scribbling which is given out these days for a history of the trade union discussion in one political textbook after another?

The thing becomes laughable when Bukharin incautiously proceeds to exploit the trade union discussion as a weapon against "Trotskyism." Here is the way Lenin appraised Bukharin's position in that discussion:

> "Hitherto the 'chief' in the struggle has been Trotsky. But now Bukharin has left him way behind and completely 'eclipsed' him. Bukharin has created a completely new situation in the struggle for he has talked himself into a mistake a hundred times bigger than all the mistakes of Trotsky put together.
>
> "How could Bukharin talk himself into this break with communism? We know all the softness of comrade Bukharin, one of the characteristics for which you love him so, and can't help loving him. We know that he is often jokingly called 'soft wax.' It seems that 'any unprincipled person,' any 'demagogue,' can print on that soft wax anything he wants to. The harsh expression included in the quotation marks was used by comrade Kamenev in the discussion of January 17. And he had a right to use it. But, of course, it would never occur to Kamenev or to anybody else to explain what happened as unprincipled demagogy—to reduce everything to that." (*Ibid.,* p. 35.)

The Third Congress of the Comintern

33. After all, was the trade union question the only question in the life of the party and the Soviet Republic during the years of my collaboration with Lenin? In the same year, 1921, the year of the Tenth Party Congress, occurred the Third World Congress of the Comintern, which played an enormous rôle in the history of the international labor movement. At this Third Congress, a profound struggle unfolded upon the fundamental questions of communist

policies. That struggle was transferred into our Political Bureau. I told something of it briefly at a session of the Political Bureau soon after the Fourteenth Party Congress:

> "There was danger at that time that the policy of the Comintern would follow the line of the March 1921 events[21] in Germany. That is, the attempt to create a revolutionary situation artificially—to 'galvanize' the proletariat, as one of the German comrades expressed it. That mood was the prevailing one in the Congress. Vladimir Ilyich came to the conclusion that, following this course, the International would most certainly go to smash. Before the Congress I wrote my impression of the March events to comrade Radek in a letter of which Vladimir Ilyich knew nothing. Considering the ticklish situation, and not knowing the opinion of Vladimir Ilyich and knowing that Zinoviev, Bukharin and Radek were in general for the German Left, I naturally did not express myself publicly but wrote a letter (in the form of theses) to comrade Radek, asking him to give me his opinion. Radek and I did not agree. Vladimir Ilyich heard about this, sent for me, and characterized the situation in the Comintern as one involving the very greatest dangers. In appraising the situation and its problems, we were in full accord.
>
> "After this conference, Vladimir Ilyich sent for comrade Kamenev in order to assure a majority in the Political Bureau. There were then five members in the Political Bureau. With comrade Kamenev, we were three and consequently a majority, but in our delegation to the Comintern, there were, on one side, comrades Zinoviev, Bukharin and Radek; on the other, Vladimir Ilyich, comrade Kamenev and myself. And, by the way,

> we had formal sittings of these groups. Vladimir Ilyich said at that time: 'Well, we are forming a new faction.' During further negotiations as to the text of the resolutions to be introduced, I served as the representative of the Lenin faction while Radek represented the Zinoviev faction."
>
> ZINOVIEV: "Now the state of affairs is changed."
>
> TROTSKY: "Yes, it has changed. Moreover, comrade Zinoviev rather categorically accused comrade Radek at that time of 'betraying' his faction in those negotiations; that is, of making presumably too great concessions. There was an intense struggle throughout all the parties of the Comintern, and Vladimir Ilyich conferred with me as to what we should do if the Congress voted against us. Should we submit to the Congress whose decisions might be ruinous, or should we not submit?
>
> "The reflection of that conference you can find in the stenographic report of my speech. I said at that time, in agreement with Ilyich, that if you, the Congress, adopt a decision against us, I trust you will leave us a sufficient framework in which to defend our point of view in the future. The meaning of this warning was perfectly clear. I ought to add, however, that the relations then existing within our delegation, thanks to the leadership of Vladimir Ilyich, continued to be perfectly comradely." (*Minutes of the Political Bureau of the C.P.S.U.,* March 18, 1926.)

In agreement with Lenin, I defended our common position in the E.C.C.I., whose session preceded the sessions of the Third World Congress. I was the target of a fierce attack by the so-called "Leftists." Vladimir Ilyich hurried to the session of the E.C.C.I. and this is what he said there:

"... I came here in order to protest against the speech of comrade Bela Kun who took the floor against comrade Trotsky instead of defending him as he ought to have done if he wanted to be a genuine Marxist. . . .

"Comrade Laporte was absolutely wrong and comrade Trotsky, protesting against it, was absolutely right. . . . Comrade Trotsky was a thousand times right when he stressed that point. And here is another Luxemburg comrade who reproached the French party because it did not sabotage the occupation of Luxemburg.[22] There you have it. He thinks that this is a geographical question, just as comrade Bela Kun does. No, this is a political question and comrade Trotsky was entirely right in protesting against it. . . .

"That is why I considered it my duty to support fundamentally all that comrade Trotsky said. . . ."

Throughout all of Lenin's speeches relating to the Third World Congress recurs this sharp emphasis upon his complete solidarity with Trotsky.

The question of educating the party youth

34. In 1922, there was created upon the initiative of comrade Ter-Vaganyan a magazine, *Pod Znamenyem Marxisma* [*Under the Banner of Marxism*]. For the first issue, I contributed an article on the difference in the conditions of education of the two generations of the party—the old and the new—and on the necessity of a special theoretical approach toward the new generation in order to safeguard the theoretical and political heritage in the development of the party. In the following issue of the new magazine, Lenin wrote:

"Concerning the general task of the magazine *Under the Banner of Marxism,* comrade Trotsky in No. 1–2 said

> all that was essential and said it excellently. I should like to dwell upon certain questions defining more closely the content and program of work issued by the editors of the journal in their preliminary announcement to No. 1–2." (*Collected Works,* Supplementary Vol. XX, Pt. 2, p. 492.)

Could our solidarity upon these fundamental questions have been accidental? No, the only accident lies in the fact that the solidarity happened to be so clearly recorded in the press. In the overwhelming majority of cases, our solidarity was sealed only in deeds. Yet it was precisely on the question of attitude to the youth that innumerable legends have been created in recent years.

Attitude toward the peasantry

35. After Bukharin, out of sheer rejection of or disregard for the peasantry, had arrived at his kulak slogan:[23] "Enrich yourselves," he came to the conclusion that he had thereby forever corrected all of his old mistakes. More than that, he thought he could string on the same thread with the peasant question, my disagreement about Brest-Litovsk and my other *partial* disagreements with Vladimir Ilyich. The stupidities and abominations put in circulation by the Bukharin school on this theme are absolutely incalculable. It would take a volume to refute them all specifically. I will mention only the most important points:

(a) I do not touch here upon the old pre-revolutionary disagreements that really existed.[24] I will say only that they have been monstrously distended, distorted and perverted by Stalin's agents and the petty school of Bukharin.

(b) In 1917 there was no disagreement whatever upon this question between Lenin and me.

(c) The "adoption" of the Social Revolutionary land

program was carried out by Vladimir Ilyich in full agreement with me.

(d) I happened to be the first to read Lenin's penciled draft of the decree on the land question. There was not even a hint of disagreement. We were of one mind.

(e) In the food policy the peasant question occupied, obviously, no small place. Vulgarians like Martinov are saying that this policy was "Trotskyist" (c.f., Martinov's article in *Krasnaya Nov,* 1923). No, it was a Bolshevik policy. I took part in its enactment hand in hand with Lenin. There was not a shadow of disagreement.

(f) The policy based on the middle peasantry was adopted with my most active participation. The members of the Political Bureau know that after the death of Sverdlov, the first thought of Vladimir Ilyich was to name comrade Kamenev chairman of the All-Russian Central Executive Committee. The proposal to select instead a "worker-peasant" figure came from me. I nominated comrade Kalinin for the post. It was also on my suggestion that he was called "All-Russian *Starosta*" [village elder]. All this is, of course, a trivial matter upon which it would not be worth while to pause. But at present these trivialities, these symptoms, are murderous evidence against the falsifiers of our past.

(g) Nine-tenths of all our military policy and organization reduced itself to the policy of the relation of the workers to the peasantry. That policy—against petty bourgeois guerrilla and amateur methods (Stalin, Voroshilov and Co.)—I carried out hand in hand with Vladimir Ilyich.

I cite, for example, a whole series of my telegrams from Simbirsk and Ruzaevka (March 1919) stressing the necessity of applying energetic measures in order to improve relations with the middle peasantry. I demanded that an authorized commission be sent to the Volga region for the purpose of checking up on the activities of local authorities and of making a study of the causes of peasant dissatisfaction. My third telegram—by direct wire to Stalin, Kremlin, Moscow (urgent)—reads as follows:

> "The Commission's task should be to strengthen the faith of the Volga peasantry in the Central Soviet Government, to remove the most crying cases of local maladministration and to punish the guilty representatives of the Soviet power; to gather all complaints and materials to be used as *a basis of demonstrative decrees in favor of the middle peasants*. Smilga could be appointed a member on this commission; Kamenev is likewise desirable, or some other authoritative figure." (March 22, 1919, No. 813.)

It was not Stalin who sent me this telegram—one of many—stressing the necessity of decrees to benefit the middle peasants, but it was I who sent it to Stalin. This took place not during the period of the Fourteenth Congress but at the beginning of the year 1919 when Stalin's views on the middle peasants were still unknown to anyone.

Indeed, every page of the old records—without the slightest attempt at selection—rings today like a scathing exposure of the twaddle invented at this late date regarding my "underestimation of the peasantry" or the "underestimation of the middle peasants"!

(h) At the beginning of 1920, basing myself on an analysis of the condition of peasant economy, I introduced in the Political Bureau the proposal of a series of measures similar to the N.E.P. That proposal could not possibly have been dictated by a "disregard" for the peasantry.

(i) The trade union discussion was, as I said, a search for a way out of an economic blind alley. The transition to the N.E.P. was carried out in complete unanimity.

36. All this can be proved on the basis of indisputable documents. Some day it will be. Here I limit myself to two quotations.

In answer to questions asked by peasants as to our relation to the kulaks, the middle and the poor peasants, and as to alleged disagreements between Lenin and Trotsky on the peasant question, I wrote in 1919:

> "No disagreement upon this question in the centers of the Soviet Government have existed or exist. The counter-revolutionists, whose cause is getting more and more hopeless, have nothing left but to deceive the toiling masses as to a pretended conflict supposed to be dividing the Council of People's Commissars within." (*Izvestia,* Feb. 7, 1919.)

Lenin wrote upon this theme, in answer to a question from the peasant Gulov, the following words:

> "In *Izvestia* for February 2, there appeared a letter from Mr. Gulov, a peasant, who asks about the relation of the workers' and peasants' government to the middle peasantry and speaks of rumors to the effect that Lenin and Trotsky are not in harmony; that there are big disagreements between them, and especially upon the subject of the middle peasant.
>
> "Comrade Trotsky has already given his answer in his 'Open Letter to the Middle Peasants' in *Izvestia* for February 7. Comrade Trotsky says in this letter that the rumors of disagreement between him and me are a monstrous and a despicable lie, propagated by the landlords and capitalists and their conscious or unconscious servitors. I, upon my part, fully confirm this statement of comrade Trotsky. There are no

> disagreements between him and me, and in regard to the middle peasants, there are no disagreements not only between Trotsky and me, but in general, in the Communist Party of which we are both members.
>
> "Comrade Trotsky in his letter explained clearly and in detail why the party of the communists and the present workers' and peasants' government elected by the Soviets and members of that party, do not consider the middle peasants their enemies. I subscribe with both hands to what comrade Trotsky said." (*Collected Works,* Vol. XVI, pp. 28*f*. Printed originally in *Pravda,* No. 35, Feb. 15, 1919.)

Here we run into the same fact again. The rumor was first set going by the White Guards. Now it is caught up by the Stalin-Bukharin school, developed and deliberately propagated.

Military work

37. On the subject of my military work which began in the spring of 1918, an attempt has been made, under the guidance of Stalin, to rewrite history. In fact, the attempt has been made to rewrite the entire history of the Civil War for the sole purpose of the struggle against "Trotskyism"—or, to put it more precisely, the struggle against Trotsky.

To rehearse here the story of the creation of the Red Army and the relation of Lenin to that work, would be to write the history of the Civil War. For the time being, the Gusevs are writing it. Later, others will write it. I must limit myself to two or three examples supported by documents.

When Kazan was captured by our troops, I received a telegram of congratulations from Vladimir Ilyich, then rapidly convalescing:

> "I greet with rapture the brilliant victory of the Red Army. Let it serve as a pledge that the union of workers

and revolutionary peasants will shatter the bourgeoisie completely; will break every resistance of the exploiters, and guarantee the victory of world socialism. Long live the workers' revolution!

"SEPT. 10, 1918.
"Lenin."

The intensely elated (for Lenin) tone of the telegram—"I greet with rapture"—testifies to the enormous significance he attributed, and rightly so, to the capture of Kazan. Here occurred the first and essentially decisive trial of strength of the union of workers and revolutionary peasants and of the ability of the party, amid the economic ruin and terrible desolation left by the imperialist war, to create a fighting, revolutionary army. Here the methods of creating the Red Army underwent their trial by fire, and Lenin knew the true value of this trial.

38. At the Eighth Party Congress, a group of military delegates criticized the war policy. The Stalins and Voroshilovs have been talking lately as though I dared not even appear at the Eighth Congress and hear their criticisms. How monstrously far that is from the actual fact! Here is the resolution of the Central Committee on the subject of my departure for the front on the eve of the Eighth Congress:

Excerpt from the minutes of the March 16, 1919, session of the Central Committee, CPR

Present: Comrades Lenin, Zinoviev, Krestinsky, Vladimirsky, Stalin, Schmidt, Smilga, Dzerzhinsky, Lashevich, Bukharin, Sokolnikov, Trotsky, Stassova:

"Points on Agenda

"12. Certain comrades from the front, learning of the Central Committee's resolution for the immediate return of the army comrades to the front, raised the question as to the correctness of this decision which might be interpreted by the organizations at the front as an unwillingness of the Center to hear the voice of the army. Some are even interpreting it as a sort of trick because the departure of comrade Trotsky and the non-admission (recall to the front) of army deputies make it futile even to raise the question of military policy. Comrade Trotsky protests against the interpretation of the resolution of the Central Committee as a 'trick' and calls attention to the extreme seriousness of the situation caused by the retreat from Ufa and still farther west. He insists upon his departure."

"Resolutions passed

"(1) Comrade Trotsky shall depart immediately for the front.

"(2) Comrade Sokolnikov shall announce at a meeting of the comrades from the front that the order for the departure of all of them is annulled, and it is assumed that those should depart immediately who themselves consider their presence at the front necessary.

"(3) The question of military policy shall be placed first on the order of the day of the Congress.

"(4) Comrade Vladimir Mikhailovich Smirnov is granted permission to remain, as requested by him, in Moscow."

There you have a clear example of the party régime of that epoch. All who were *attacking* the Central Committee for its military policy, and especially the leader of the military opposition, V.M. Smirnov, were permitted to remain for the congress, notwithstanding the grave situation at the front. Those who *supported* the official policy were sent to the front before the opening of the congress. Nowadays things are done in exactly the opposite way.

The minutes of the military section of the Eighth Party Congress, where Lenin spoke decisively in defense of the military policy carried out by me at the direction of the Central Committee, have not yet been published. Why? Because they rip to pieces the lies of Stalin, Voroshilov and Gusev concerning the period of the Civil War.

39. Stalin has tried to put in circulation an absurdly exaggerated account of the military disagreement which arose in the Political Bureau in regard to the Eastern front at the beginning of 1919. The essence of the disagreement was this: Should we continue the offensive in Siberia or intrench ourselves in the Urals and throw the maximum of our forces to the south in order to liquidate the threat against Moscow? I was inclined, for a certain period of time, towards the second plan. Many military workers, among them Smilga, Lashevich, I.N. Smirnov, K.I. Gruenstein and many others, were in favor of the first plan. The first plan was adopted and gave admirable results. This disagreement did not involve any principle. It was purely practical. The subsequent test demonstrated that the army of Kolchak was wholly disintegrated. The offensive in Siberia was entirely successful.

40. The military work was harsh work. It was not carried out without pressure, repressions and measures of force. Many prides were hurt—most often through necessity but sometimes by mistake. Much discontent resulted and some of it, of course, was entirely legitimate. When the disagreements arose in regard to the Eastern front, and the Central Committee was to decide the question as to the change of Chief Command, I offered the Central Committee my resignation from the post of People's Commissar for War. On the same day, July 5, 1919, the Central Committee adopted a resolution, of which the principal part follows:

"The Organization Bureau and the Political Bureau of the Central Committee, after considering the statement of comrade Trotsky and discussing it in full, have come to the unanimous conclusion that his resignation cannot be accepted, being entirely out of question.

"The Organization Bureau and the Political Bureau of the Central Committee will do all that they can to make more convenient for comrade Trotsky, and more fruitful for the Republic, that work on the Southern front which comrade Trotsky himself has chosen and which is the most difficult, the most dangerous and the most important at the present moment. In his position as People's Commissar for War and Chairman of the Military Council, comrade Trotsky is also fully empowered to act as a member of the Military Revolutionary Council of the Southern front together with that Commissar of the Southern front (Yegorov) whom he himself proposed and whom the Central Committee has confirmed.

"The Organization Bureau and the Political Bureau of the Central Committee give comrade Trotsky full authority by every means whatsoever, to achieve what he considers a necessary correction of policy on the military question and, if he so desires, to expedite the congress of the party."

The signatures to this resolution were: Lenin, Kamenev, Krestinsky, Kalinin, Serebriakov, Stalin, Stassova.

This resolution speaks for itself. It ended the controversial issue, and we passed on to the next point on the agenda.

A propos of this: At the joint session of the Political Bureau and the Praesidium of the Central Control Commission, Sept. 8, 1927, Stalin entered a statement into the minutes alleging that the Central Committee "forbade" me to touch the Southern front. On that question, too, the above resolution gives a sufficiently exhaustive answer.

41. But was the disagreement about the Eastern front the only disagreement of a strategical nature? Not by any means. There was a disagreement about the strategic plan against Denikin. There was a disagreement about Petrograd—surrender it to Yudenich or defend it? There was a disagreement about the advance on Warsaw[25] and about the possibility of a second campaign after we had retired to Minsk. Disagreements of this kind were born of the practical struggle and were liquidated in struggle.

On the question of the Southern front, the necessary documents are published in my book, *How the Revolution Armed Itself* (Vol. II, Book 1, p. 301).

During the advance of Yudenich upon Petrograd, Lenin at one time thought it was not worthwhile trying to defend the city and that we ought to move the line of defense nearer Moscow. I objected. Comrade Zinoviev supported me and I think also comrade Stalin. On the 17th of October 1919, Lenin communicated with me in Petrograd by direct wire:

> "Comrade Trotsky:
>
> "Last night transmitted in code . . . the decision of the Council of Defense.
>
> "As you see, your plan was adopted. But the withdrawal of the Petrograd workers to the south was, of course, not rejected (I am told that you expounded it to Krassin and Rykov); but to discuss it before the need arises would distract attention from the fight-to-the-finish.
>
> "An attempt to outflank and cut off Petrograd will, of course, bring corresponding changes which you will carry out on the spot.
>
> "Assign someone in each department of the local

executive committee to collect Soviet papers and documents in preparation for an evacuation.

"I enclose a proclamation which I was assigned to draft by the Council of Defense. I did it hastily and it turned out poorly. You had better put my signature under yours.

"Greetings!
"Lenin."

There were many such episodes. They had immense practical importance at the given moment but they never had any principled significance. It was not a struggle over principles but a working out of the best plan for fighting off the enemy at a given moment and a given place.

The Stalins and the Gusevs are trying to rewrite the history of the Civil War. They will not succeed!

42. The most contemptible part of the campaign of the Stalinists against me is their accusation that I had "communists" shot. This accusation was once put in circulation by our enemies, by their "Intelligence Service." That is, the political departments of the White Armies tried to circulate leaflets among our Red Soldiers, accusing the Red Command and Trotsky, in particular, of bloodthirstiness. The agentry of Stalin are now going the same road.

Assume for a minute that this lie is true. Then why were Stalin, Yaroslavsky, Gusev and the other agents of Stalin silent during the entire Civil War? What is implied by these current tardy "revelations" on the lips of the Stalin agentry? It means this:

"Workers, peasants and Red soldiers, the party deceived you when it told you that Trotsky, the Commander of the Army, was fulfilling the will of the party and carrying out its policy. In its innumerable articles about the work of Trotsky, in the resolutions of its party congresses and the congresses of the Soviets, the party deceived you, approving the military work of Trotsky and hiding from you such facts as the execution of communists. Lenin participated in this deceit, decisively supporting the military policy of Trotsky."

That is the real meaning of these tardy "revelations" of Stalin. These "revelations" compromise not Trotsky but the party, its leadership. They undermine the confidence of the masses in all the Bolsheviks. For if, in the past, when Lenin and the main core of his colleagues stood at the head of the party, it was possible to conceal monstrous mistakes and even crimes, what can you expect now, when the personnel of the Central Committee is infinitely less authoritative? If, for example, Yaroslavsky in 1923, when the Civil War was already long past, sang the immoderate praises of Trotsky, his fidelity, his revolutionary devotion to the cause of the working class, then what is the thoughtful young party member going to say today? He is going to ask himself: "Just when was Yaroslavsky lying to me—when he exalted Trotsky above the skies, or now, when he is trying to cover him with mud?"

Such is the real work of Stalin and his agents in their effort to invent a new biography for him after the events. The party mass cannot possibly check upon the greater part of Stalin's "revelations." Instead they become firmly imbued with a loss of confidence in the leadership of the party, past, present and future. We shall have to win this anew—this confidence of the party—against Stalin and Stalinism.

43. As is known, Gusev has devoted special energy to the literary revision of our war history. He has even written a brochure entitled *Our Military Disagreements*. In this brochure, it seems, the poisonous gossip first appeared

about shooting communists (not deserters, not traitors, even though with party cards, but communists).

Gusev's misfortune, like that of many others, is that he has written twice about one and the same fact and question: once in Lenin's time; once in Stalin's.

Here is what Gusev wrote the first time:

> "The arrival of comrade Trotsky [near Kazan] produced a decisive change in the situation. The arrival of Trotsky's train at the wayside station, Sviazhsk, brought a firm will to victory, initiative and momentum for all sides of the work of the army. From the very first day, in that station crowded with the wagon trains of the innumerable regiments, where were the headquarters of the political department and the commissary, as well as among the army troops deployed over a distance of fifteen *versts,* everybody felt that a great turning point had arrived.
>
> "This made itself felt first of all in the sphere of discipline. . . . The stern methods of comrade Trotsky in that epoch of guerrilla warfare, in discipline and provincial egotisms, were especially and above all expedient and necessary. You could do nothing with persuasion. And, moreover, there was no time for it. In the course of those twenty-five days that comrade Trotsky spent in Sviazhsk an enormous work was accomplished. The disorganized and degenerated regiments of the Fifth Army were converted into fighting troops and prepared for the capture of Kazan." (*Proletarskaya Revolutsia,* No. 2 [25], 1924.)

Every member of the party who lived through the experience of the Civil War and has not lost his memory will say, at least to himself, if he is afraid to say it out loud, that you could quote by the score, if not by the hundred, such printed testimonials as this testimonial written by Gusev.

44. I limit myself here to testimonials of the most authoritative character. In his recollections of Lenin, Gorky says:

> "Striking his fist on the table, he [Lenin] exclaimed: 'Show me another man who would be able in a year to organize almost a model army; yes, and win the esteem of the military specialists. We have such a man. We have everything, and you'll see miracles!'" (Maxim Gorky, *Vladimir Lenin,* Leningrad, 1924, p. 23.)

In the same conversation, Lenin said, according to Gorky:

> "Yes, yes, I know. They lie a lot about my relations with him. They lie a great deal, it seems, especially about Trotsky and me." (*Ibid.,* p. 23.)

Yes, they lied a lot about the relations of Lenin and Trotsky. But can you compare the amateurish lying of those days with the properly organized, All-Russian and international lying of today? In those days the liars were the Black Hundreds, the White Guards, in part also the Social Revolutionists and Mensheviks. Now it is the Stalin faction that has seized this weapon.

45. In the Bolshevik fraction of the All-Russian Central Council of Trade Unions, January 12, 1920, Lenin said:

> "If we defeated Denikin and Kolchak, it was because our discipline was higher than that of all the capitalist countries of the world. Comrade Trotsky has introduced the death penalty and we will support him. He has introduced it by means of conscious organization and agitation on the part of communists."

46. I have not at hand the many other speeches of Lenin in defense of the military policy which I carried out in full accord with him. In particular, the minutes of the conference of delegates to the Eighth Congress on Military Affairs remain unpublished. Why are those minutes unpublished? Because Lenin in that conference opposed with all his energy the colleagues of Stalin who are now so industriously falsifying the past.

47. But I have at hand one document which is worth a hundred. I spoke of this document in the Praesidium of the Central Control Commission when Yaroslavsky started a poisonous intrigue against me, under protest from Ordjonikidze. I quoted it at the last joint Plenum, August 1927, when Voroshilov followed in the footsteps of Yaroslavsky.

Lenin gave me, on his own initiative, a blank sheet of paper with the following lines written at the bottom:

> "Comrades, knowing the harsh character of comrade Trotsky's orders, I am so convinced, so absolutely convinced, of the correctness, expedience and necessity for the good of our cause, of orders issued by comrade Trotsky, that I give them my full support.
>
> *"V. Ulianov (Lenin)."*

The purpose of this blank I explained to the Praesidium of the Central Control Commission in the following words:

> "When he [Lenin] handed me that sheet of paper with these lines written at the bottom of a clean page, I was perplexed. He said: "I have been informed that rumors are being started against you that you are shooting communists. I give you this blank and I will give you as many of them as you want, stating that I support your decisions. Above it you can write any

> decision you want to and my signature will be ready.' That was in July 1919. Since much gossip is now abroad about my relations with Vladimir Ilyich, and what is far more important, his attitude toward me, I would suggest that somebody else show me such a blank page with his signature, where Lenin says that he endorses beforehand every decision that I might make. Upon these decisions depended not only the fate of individual communists but often a far greater thing."

Concerning economic questions

48. Martinov maintains, as is well known, that civil war and War Communism are "Trotskyism." This doctrine has now acquired a vast popularity. The creation of industrial armies, the militarization of labor and other measures flowing inevitably, just as did food distribution, from the conditions of that epoch, are portrayed by philistines and vulgarians as manifestations of "Trotskyism." On what side did Lenin stand in these questions?

In the organization section of the Seventh Congress of the Soviets, we were debating the question of bureaucratism in the directing centers. In my speech I pointed out that bossism might choke our industries; that centralism is not an absolute principle; that the necessary coördination between local initiative and the leadership of the center had yet to be found in practise. Lenin in his speech emphasized his full agreement with me on centralism and added:

> "Let me say in conclusion that I agreed entirely with comrade Trotsky when he said that there have been some very wrong attempts made here to present our disputes as a disagreement between workers and peasants and to mix up with this question, the question of

> the dictatorship of the proletariat." (Speech on Dec. 8, 1918, *Collected Works*, Vol. XVI, p. 433.)

"Our disputes"—this means those very prolonged disputes in which Lenin and Trotsky were on one side; Rykov, Tomsky, Larin and others, on the other side. In these disputes, as in so many others, Stalin remained behind the scenes manoeuvring and waiting.

49. At the caucus of the Bolshevik fraction of the All-Russian Central Council of Trade Unions, January 12, 1920, Lenin had the following to say on the subject of "our disputes" with Rykov, Tomsky and others:

> "Who started this disgusting departmental squabble? Not comrade Trotsky. There is none of it in his theses. It was comrades Lomov, Rykov and Larin. Every one of them holds the highest office. They are all members of the Praesidium of the All-Russian Council of National Economy. Among them is the chairman of the Council who has so many titles that if I wanted to list them all I should lose five minutes of my ten minute speech. . . . Rykov and others have got up here and started a disgusting literary squabble. Comrade Trotsky posed the question of new problems and they have started a departmental polemic with the Seventh Congress of the Soviets. Of course, we know that comrades Lomov, Rykov and Larin did not say this directly in their extremely stupid article. As some orator here has said: 'You must not indulge in polemics with the Seventh Congress of the Soviets.' If the Seventh Congress of the Soviets made a mistake, correct that mistake in the meeting, say that it is a mistake, and stop babbling about centralization and decentralization. Comrade Rykov says that it is necessary to talk about

> centralization and decentralization because comrade Trotsky did not notice it. This man assumes that the people sitting here are so backward that they have forgotten the first lines of comrade Trotsky's theses which say: 'Economic administration assumes a general plan,' etc. Do you know how to read Russian, most condescending Rykov, Lomov and Larin? Let's go back to the time when you were sixteen years old and start babbling about centralization and decentralization. Is that the governmental work of the members of the collegium, of the Praesidium of the All-Russian Council of National Economy? This is nonsense and pathetic rubbish—it is a shame and disgrace to waste time on it."

And further:

> "War gave us the ability to carry discipline to a maximum and to centralize tens and hundreds of thousands of people, comrades, who died to save the Soviet Republic. Without that we should have all gone to hell."

I might add that this speech, which is at the disposition of the Lenin Institute, has not been published simply because it is inconvenient for the present "historians." The concealment from the party of a part of our ideological inheritance from Lenin is a necessary element in the departure from the Leninist course. The speech of Lenin quoted above will be brought forward when the time comes to decapitate Rykov.

50. About my work on the railway transport service, Lenin said at the Eighth Congress of the Soviets:

> ". . . You have seen already, by the way, from the theses of comrade Emshanov and comrade Trotsky that

in this sphere [the reëstablishment of our transport] we have to do with a real plan, looking ahead many years. Order No. 1042[26] reckons on five years. In five years we can restore our transport, reduce the number of broken-down locomotives and, if you please, as the most *difficult* I emphasize in the ninth thesis the indication that we might even shorten that period, as has been done.

"When big plans are made based on a many years' calculation, there are often skeptics who say: 'How can we calculate years ahead? God help us to do what we have to do right now.' Comrades, it is necessary to learn how to combine both. You can't work without having a plan that assumes a long period and serious success. That this is necessary is proved by the indubitable improvement of the transport work. I want to call your attention to that place in the ninth thesis where it says that the term for reëstablishment would be four and a half years but that it is already shortened because we are working above normal. The term is already cut down to three and a half years. That is the way we should work in the other branches of our industry." (Speech on Dec. 2, 1920, *Collected Works*, Vol. XVII, pp. 423*f.*)

I remark here that a year after I had issued Order No. 1042, in the order of comrade Dzerzhinsky, "Concerning the Fundamental Principles of Further Work of the People's Commissariat of Means of Communication," for May 27, 1921, we read:

"Owing to the fact that the lowering of the norms set by Orders No. 1042 and 1157, *the first brilliant experiment in planned industrial work*, is temporary, and due

> to the existing fuel crisis . . . measures must be taken to support and restore the equipment and the shops. . . ."

51. In 1924, Zinoviev put in circulation a charge against Trotsky that by issuing the railway "Order No. 1042," Trotsky almost ruined the transportation system. With this for a canvas, Stalin, Yaroslavsky and Rudzutak later embroidered various designs. In its day the legend made the rounds of all the publications of the Comintern. We have already quoted Lenin's and Dzerzhinsky's real opinions concerning Order No. 1042 and its significance for transportation. But there is comment of a more recent origin. In the *Yearbook of the Communist International* issued in 1923, that is, on the eve of the campaign against Trotsky, the article entitled "The Transportation System of the R.S.F.S.R. and Its Reëstablishment" has the following to say:

> "At that time the transportation system was already completely disorganized. Not only was there no talk of reëstablishing it but matters had reached such a stage that in the Council of Labor and Defense, Professor Lomonosov, a member of the Collegium of the People's Commissariat of Means of Communication, made a report to the effect that the transportation system was on the verge of complete and inevitable stoppage. Comrade Trotsky, on taking charge of transportation, advanced two slogans which proved of decisive significance not only for transportation but for the economy of the country as a whole. . . . Order No. 1042 is an historical event. According to that order, the locomotive park should have been restored in five years. Communist propaganda based on that order and communist enthusiasm called forth by it must be regarded

> as the highest level attained by the enthusiastic readiness of the masses for heroic achievements in labor." (*Yearbook of the Communist International*, Petrograd-Moscow, 1923, p. 363.)

You will observe that "Order No. 1042" served different functions at different periods.

52. As to the alleged attempt on my part to shut down the Putilov shops: In comrade Rykov's theses written in October 1927—that is, four years after the question arose—there appears again the legend about my urging the shutting down of the Putilov shops. In this case, as, by the way, in many others, comrade Rykov is acting very incautiously, collecting material against himself.

The fact is that the proposal to shut down the Putilov shops was introduced in the Political Bureau at the beginning of 1923 by *comrade Rykov himself as Chairman of the All-Russian Council of National Economy*. Rykov demonstrated that the Putilov shops will not be needed in the course of the next ten years and that trying to maintain them artificially will have a harmful effect upon other factories. The Political Bureau—and I among others—took the data adduced by comrade Rykov for good coin. I was not the only one who voted for the closing of the Putilov shops upon the proposal of comrade Rykov. So did Stalin for that matter. Comrade Zinoviev was away on leave of absence. He protested against the decision. The question was raised again in the Political Bureau and the decision reversed. Thus the initiative in this affair was wholly in the hands of Rykov as Chairman of the All-Russian Council of National Economy. To what extent must the feeling of impunity have grown, when Rykov dares, after a short four years, to attribute to me his own "sin." However, don't worry. This fact will no doubt crop up again . . . in a new form, when the time comes for Stalin to "review" Rykov. You won't have long to wait.

53. You delude the party with tales about how "Lenin wanted to send Trotsky to the Ukraine as People's Commissar of Food Supplies." On that subject you confuse and twist the facts beyond recognition. I made many such journeys at the direction of the Central Committee. In full agreement with Lenin I went to the Ukraine to improve the organization of the coal industry in the Don Basin. In full agreement with Lenin I worked as Chairman of the Soviet of the Industrial Army in the Ural. It is perfectly true that Lenin insisted that I go to the Ukraine for two weeks—for two weeks!—in order to improve the organization of the food supplies. I got in touch with comrade Rakovsky by telephone. He informed me that all the necessary measures to guarantee food for the workers' centers had been taken without my help. Vladimir Ilyich at first insisted upon my going but afterward abandoned the idea. That was all there was to it. It was a question of a practical fighting problem which Lenin considered the most important for the given moment.

54. Here is what Lenin said at the Eighth All-Russian Congress of the Soviets, December 22, 1920, on the question of my journey to the Don Basin:

> "Coal from the Don Basin which we were receiving at the rate of 25,000,000 *poods* a month has now reached 50,000,000, thanks to the work of the Plenipotentiary Commission which was sent to the Don Basin with comrade Trotsky as chairman and which took the decision that experienced and responsible workers should be assigned there. At present, comrade Piatakov has been sent there to direct the work." (*Collected Works*, Vol. XVII, p. 422.)

55. *A propos* of this: Comrade Piatakov was crowded out of the Don Basin by the underground intrigues of Stalin. Lenin considered this a serious blow to the coal industry, expressed his indignation against it in the Political Bureau and protested publicly against the disorganizing activities of Stalin.

> "That we have had immense success was demonstrated especially, for example, in the Don Basin where such comrades as Piatakov have been working with extraordinary devotion and with extraordinary success in the sphere of the large-scale industries." (Lenin's report at the Ninth Congress of the Soviets, Dec. 23, 1921. *Collected Works*, Vol. XVIII, Pt. 1, p. 408.)
>
> "In the central management of the coal industry stood people not only of undoubted devotion but people of real education and great ability, and I think I make no mistake if I say, talented people, and, therefore, the attention of the Central Committee was directed thither. . . . We, the Central Committee, have after all had a certain amount of experience and we decided unanimously not to remove the managing groups. . . . I made inquiries among the Ukrainian comrades. And comrade Ordjonikidze I asked especially, and also the Central Committee directed him to go there and find out what was happening. Quite evidently there was intrigue there and every other kind of mess which the Bureau of Party History will be unable to unravel in ten years, should they ever undertake the job. But the practical result was that, *contrary to the unanimous orders of the Central Committee, the managing group was replaced by another.*" (Lenin's report at the Eleventh Party Congress, March 27, 1922.)

It is known to all the members of the old Political Bureau—Stalin best of all—that the acrid words of Lenin about intrigue against devoted, educated and talented leaders in the Don Basin referred to the intrigue of Stalin against Piatakov.

56. During the Ninth Congress of the Soviets in December 1921, Lenin wrote some theses concerning the fundamental problems of industrial construction. I remember I answered that the theses were excellent and that there was only one point lacking, that about the specialists. (In a few words I indicated the contents of that point.) The same day I received the following letter from Vladimir Ilyich:

"STRICTLY CONFIDENTIAL.

"Comrade Trotsky:

"I am sitting in a meeting of non-party members with Kalinin. He advises me to make a short speech on that resolution which I introduced (and to which you proposed an amendment, entirely correct, about the specialists).

"Couldn't you undertake a very short report on that resolution on Wednesday—at the Plenum of the congress.

"Your military report is, of course, ready and you will be through with it on Tuesday.

"It is impossible for me to undertake a second speech at the congress. Drop me a note or send a telephonogram. It will be best if you agree, and it can be confirmed by telephone with the vote of the Political Bureau.

"Lenin."

Our solidarity on the fundamental problems of socialist construction was so complete that Vladimir Ilyich considered it possible to authorize me to make a report in his place on those questions. I remember that I persuaded him by telephone to appear himself on this important matter if only his health permitted. In the end that was done.

During the last period of Lenin's life

57. The falsifications and fictions in relation to the last period of Lenin's life are especially numerous. It would behoove Stalin to be extremely cautious about this period when Vladimir Ilyich arrived at certain final conclusions about Stalin.

It is naturally difficult to expound the inner history of the Political Bureau during Vladimir Ilyich's active life. There were no minutes taken and only the decisions were recorded. That is why it is so easy to lift out separate, completely insignificant episodes, distort them and puff them up or, indeed, simply invent "disagreements" where there was not a sign of one. Really shameful in its stupidity is the legend about "the cuckoo" which is supposed to indicate, in retrospect, my "pessimism." The "cuckoo" is the last resort of Stalin and Bukharin when they are driven to the wall by arguments or events. The "cuckoo" is borrowed from my conversation with Vladimir Ilyich in the first period of the N.E.P. The drain of our limited state resources awakened in me a serious alarm both from the point of view of the waste of the already limited resources of the workers' government as well as from the point of view of the possibility of swift accumulations of private capital at this critical period. I talked about that more than once with Vladimir Ilyich. In order to investigate the industrial processes in progress in the country, I organized at that time the so-called Moscow Amalgamated Network. In one of my conversations with Lenin, referring to certain flagrant examples of wastefulness, I used approximately this phrase: "If we administer things that way, the cuckoo will soon be singing our death-knell." Something of that kind. Phrases like that were repeated by every one of us more than once. How many times did Lenin exclaim: "If this keeps on, we're gone for sure." It was a strong statement but by no means a "pessimistic" prognosis.

That is approximately the history of the "cuckoo" with the dividends of which Stalin and Bukharin are trying to pay their debts for the Chinese Revolution, the Anglo-Russian Committee, the economic leadership and the party régime.

To be sure, practical disagreements arose often enough in the Political Bureau and among them disagreements between Vladimir Ilyich and me. The whole question is, what place did these disagreements occupy in the common work? On that theme the Stalin faction, with extreme lack of caution, is putting into circulation spiteful legends which go to pieces at the first touch of real fact, and which will ultimately turn wholly against Stalin.

58. To refute these legends it is necessary to take first of all the period of Lenin's illness—more accurately, the period *between* the two heavy attacks of it—when the doctors permitted Lenin to take part in the work, and when many important questions were decided by correspondence. In this correspondence—that is, in unquestionable documents—it is possible to see what debated questions arose in the Central Committee, who had disagreements with whom, and in part also what was the attitude of Vladimir Ilyich toward individual comrades. I will adduce a few examples.

The monopoly of foreign trade

59. In the Central Committee at the end of 1922, there arose a very fundamental disagreement on the question of the monopoly of foreign trade. I do not want to exaggerate its significance in retrospect, but the political groupings created in the Central Committee around that question were, nevertheless, very characteristic.

On the initiative of comrade Sokolnikov, the Central Committee adopted a decision which meant a serious breach in the monopoly of foreign trade. Vladimir Ilyich was decisively against this resolution. Learning from Krassin that I was not present at the Plenum of the Central Committee and that I had expressed myself against the resolution, Lenin entered into correspondence with me. Those letters are not yet published, any more than the correspondence of Lenin with the Political Bureau on the question of the monopoly of foreign trade. The censorship established over our inheritance from Lenin is ruthless. You publish two or three words written by Lenin on a scrap of paper, if only they may directly or indirectly be used to injure the Opposition. You suppress documents of vast and fundamental significance, if they directly or indirectly involve Stalin.

I quote the letters from Lenin touching that question:

"Comrade Trotsky:

"I am sending you a letter from Krestinsky. Write immediately. Do you agree? I will fight at the Plenum for the monopoly. And you?

"Yours,
"Lenin.

"P.S. Better return it *quick.*"

"To Comrades Frumkin and Stomoniakov,* copy to Trotsky:

"In view of my increasing sickness, I cannot be present at the Plenum. I am conscious how awkwardly,

* Non-members of the Central Committee with whom Lenin entered into a "conspiracy" against the majority of the committee!—L.T.

and even worse than awkwardly, I am behaving in relation to you, but all the same, I cannot possibly speak.

"Today I have received the enclosed letter from comrade Trotsky, with which I agree in all essentials, with the exception perhaps of the last lines about the State Planning Commission. I will write Trotsky of my agreement with him and ask him to take upon himself, in view of my sickness, the defense of my position at the Plenum.

"I think that this defense ought to be divided into three parts. *First,* the defense of the fundamental principle of the monopoly of foreign trade, its full and final confirmation; *second,* delegate to a special commission the detailed consideration of those practical plans for realizing this monopoly which are advanced by Avanesov—at least half of this commission ought to consist of representatives from the Commissariat of Foreign Trade; *third,* the question of the work of the State Planning Commission ought to be considered separately. And by the way, I think that there will be no disagreement between me and Trotsky, if he confines himself to the demand that the work of the State Planning Commission, carried on under the aegis of the development of state industry, should give its opinion about all parts of the activity of the People's Commissariat of Foreign Trade.

"I hope to write again today or tomorrow, and send you my declaration on the essence of the given problem at the Plenum of the Central Committee. At any rate, I think that this question is of such fundamental importance that in case I do not get the agreement of the Plenum, I ought to carry it into the party congress, and before that, announce the existing disagreement in the fraction of our party at the coming congress of the Soviets.

"Lenin.

"Dictated to L.F.
[Fotieva, Lenin's Secretary.]
"DEC. 12, 1922."

"To Comrade Trotsky, copy to Frumkin and Stomoniakov:
"Comrade Trotsky:

"I received your comment on the letter of Krestinsky and the plans of Avanesov. I think that we are in maximum agreement, and I think that the question of the State Planning Commission in the given situation excludes (or postpones) the dispute as to whether the State Planning Commission needs to have administrative rights.

"At any rate, I earnestly ask you to take upon yourself at the coming Plenum, the defense of our common opinion of the unconditional necessity of preserving and reënforcing the monopoly of foreign trade.

"Inasmuch as the preceding Plenum adopted a decision going wholly contrary to the monopoly of foreign trade, and since it is impossible to yield on this question, I think, as I say in my letter to Frumkin and Stomoniakov, that in case of our defeat we must carry the question into the party congress. For that we will need a short exposition of our disagreement before the party fraction of the coming congress of the Soviets. If I can, I will write one, and I should be very glad if you would do the same thing. Vacillation on this question will do us untold injury. The argument against the monopoly amounts to an accusation of inadequacy *against* our apparatus. But our apparatus is inadequate here and everywhere, and to renounce the monopoly because of the inadequacy of the apparatus would be to pour the baby out with the bath.

"Lenin.

"Dictated by telephone to L.F.

"DEC. 13, 1922."

"To Comrade Trotsky:

"I send you a letter received today from Frumkin. I also think that it is absolutely necessary to settle this question once and for all. If there is any fear that this question excites me and might have a bad effect on my health, I think this is wholly wrong because I should be ten thousand times more excited by a delay which would make completely unstable our policy upon one of the fundamental questions. Therefore, I call your attention to the enclosed letter and earnestly ask you to support an immediate consideration of this question. I am convinced that if we are in danger of losing out, it would be far more advantageous to lose out before the party congress, and immediately turn to the fraction of the Soviet congress than to lose out after the congress. Perhaps such a compromise as this would be accepted: Adopt the decision about confirmation of the monopoly now but raise the question nevertheless at the party congress and make that agreement now. No other compromise, in my opinion, would be to our interest in any circumstances.

"Lenin.

"Dictated by telephone to L.F.

"DEC. 15, 1922."

"Comrade Trotsky:

"I think we have arrived at a full agreement. I ask you to announce our solidarity in the Plenum. I am in hope that our decision will go through, for a part of those voting *against* in October have now come over partially or completely to our side.

"If, unexpectedly, our decision does not go through, we will turn to our fraction of the Soviet congress and declare that we are going to carry the question into the party congress.

"Notify me in that case and I will send my declaration. If this question should be removed from the order of the day of the present Plenum (which I do not expect and against which, of course, you must protest with all your strength in our common name), then I think we must turn just the same to the fraction of the Soviet congress and demand the transfer of this question to the party congress. For any more wavering is absolutely impermissible.

"All the materials which I sent you, you can keep until after the Plenum.

"Yours,
"Lenin.
"DEC. 15, 1922."

"Leon Davidovich:

"Professor Forster today permitted Vladimir Ilyich to dictate a letter and he dictated to me the following letter to you:

"'Comrade Trotsky:

"'It seems we captured the position without firing a shot by mere movements of manoeuvre. I propose that we should not stop but continue the attack, and to that effect introduce a resolution to raise the question at the party congress of reënforcing the monopoly of foreign trade and of measures looking to its better enactment. Announce this at the fraction of the Soviet congress. I hope you have no objection and will not fail to make a report at the fraction.

"'N. Lenin.'

"Vladimir Ilyich also asks you to telephone an answer.

"N.K. Ulianova.

"DEC. 21, 1922."

Neither the content nor the tone of these letters needs any comment.

On the question of foreign trade, the Central Committee adopted a new decision annulling the old one. The joking words in Lenin's letter about a victory gained "without firing a shot," refer to that.

It remains to ask: Suppose that among those voting for the resolution disrupting the monopoly of foreign trade had appeared the name of Trotsky, while Stalin, in agreement with Lenin, had fought for the annulment of that resolution, how many books, brochures and "cribs" would have been written in proof of the petty bourgeois and kulak deviation of Trotsky?

The question of the State Planning Commission

60. I related our "wastefulness" to the planlessness of our national economy in general. There were differences in the Political Bureau on the question of planned management and the rôle of the State Planning Commission. Among them, differences between Vladimir Ilyich and me. There were debates about the composition of the planning bureaus.

In his letter to the members of the Political Bureau on

the question of the State Planning Commission, Vladimir Ilyich wrote as follows:

> "As to giving legislative functions to the State Planning Commission:
>
> "Comrade Trotsky advanced this idea, it seems, long ago. I opposed it then because I thought that there would be in that case a fundamental incoherence in our system of legislative institutions, but after attentively reconsidering the matter, I find that there is an essentially healthy thought here: The State Planning Commission stands somewhat apart from our legislative institutions, notwithstanding the fact that as a meeting center of the leaders, experts and representatives of science and technology, it possesses, as a matter of fact, the best possible data for a correct judgment of things. . . . In that respect, I think I should and must come over to comrade Trotsky, but not in respect to giving the chairmanship of the State Planning Commission to any one of our political leaders, or to the Chairman of the Supreme Council of National Economy, and so forth." (Dec. 27, 1922.)

These disagreements about the State Planning Commission were mentioned above in Lenin's letters to me on the question of the monopoly of foreign trade. Lenin there proposed to *postpone* that question, describing it—not quite accurately—as a question of the administrative rights of the State Planning Commission. In insisting on the all-sided reënforcement of the State Planning Commission, the subordination to it of the planning work of all the departments, I did not propose to give the State Planning Commission administrative rights, believing that they ought to be concentrated as before in the hands of the Council of Labor and Defense. But that is not the essential thing now. Both the character and the tone of the above letter show how calmly, and purely as a matter of business, Lenin regarded our previously existing disagreements, proposing to the Political Bureau to resolve those disagreements in the direction of a very close approach to the views which I had defended. How many lies have been told the party on this subject!

Lenin's letters on the national question

61. I will not quote here Lenin's principal letter against Stalin on the national question. It is printed in the stenographic reports of the Plenum of July 1926 and, moreover, it is being passed around in individual copies. They will fail to conceal the letter.* But there are other documents on the same theme, completely unknown to the party. The keepers of the archives and the historians of the Stalin school are taking every measure to prevent those documents from appearing. They will continue to do so. They are quite capable, in fact, of simply destroying them.

For that reason I think it necessary to quote here the most important excerpts from an earlier letter of Lenin and the answer of Stalin on the question of the structure of the U.S.S.R. Lenin's letter, dated Sept. 27, 1922, was addressed to comrade Kamenev, a copy being sent to all the members of the Political Bureau. Here is the beginning of the letter:

> "You probably have already received from Stalin the resolution of his commission on the admission of the independent republics into the R.S.F.S.R.
>
> "If you have not received it, get it from the secretary and please read it immediately. I spoke about it

* To my regret, at the moment of the publication of this book, a copy of the letter is not in my possession. It is of exceptional interest.—L.T.

> yesterday with Sokolnikov, today with Stalin, tomorrow I will see Mdivani (a Georgian communist suspected of advocating 'independence').
>
> "In my opinion the question is supremely important. Stalin is somewhat inclined to hurry. You must think it over well; Zinoviev too. You once intended to take this matter up and did so to some extent.
>
> "Stalin has already agreed to one concession in Section I; instead of saying 'entry' into the R.S.F.S.R. to say: 'formal unification with the R.S.F.S.R. in a union of Soviet Republics of Europe and Asia.' I trust the spirit of this concession is obvious. We acknowledge ourselves on an equal basis with the Ukrainian S.S.R. and the other republics and together with them on the basis of equality we enter into a new union, a new federation—'the Union of Soviet Republics of Europe and Asia'."

There follows a whole series of Lenin's corrections made in the same spirit. In the concluding part of his letter, Lenin says:

> "Stalin agreed to postpone introducing the resolution in the Political Bureau until my arrival. I arrive Monday, October 2. I should like to have a meeting with you and Rykov for a couple of hours—in the morning, say, from one to two and, if necessary, in the evening, say five to seven or six to eight.
>
> "Here is my preliminary project. On the basis of conversations with Mdivani and other comrades, I will fight also for other changes. I urge you to do the same and answer me.
>
> "Yours,
>
> *"Lenin.*
>
> "P.S. Send copies to *all* members of the Political Bureau."

Stalin sent his answer to Lenin to the members of the Political Bureau the same day, Sept. 27, 1922. I quote from his answer two important passages:

> "Lenin's correction to paragraph 2, proposing to create, along with the All-Russian Central Executive Committee of the R.S.F.S.R., a Central Executive Committee of the Federation should not, in my opinion, be adopted. The existence of two Central Executive Committees in Moscow, one of which will obviously represent a 'lower house' and the other an 'upper house' will give us nothing but conflict and debate."

And further:

> "4. On the subject of paragraph 4, in my opinion, comrade Lenin himself 'hurried' a little, demanding a fusion of the Commissariats of Finance, Food Supply, Labor and National Economy with the commissariats of the Federation. There is hardly a doubt that this 'hurriedness' will 'supply fuel to the advocates of independence,' to the detriment of the national liberalism of comrade Lenin.
>
> "5. Comrade Lenin's correction of paragraph 5 is, in my opinion, superfluous.
>
> *"J. Stalin."*

This extraordinarily illuminating correspondence, concealed, like many similar documents from the party, preceded the famous letter of Lenin on the national question. In his remarks upon Stalin's draft, Lenin is exceptionally reserved and mild in his expression. Lenin still hoped, in that period, to adjust the matter without a major conflict. He gently accuses Stalin of "hurrying." Stalin's accusation against Mdivani of "independence," Lenin places in quotation marks, obviously dissociating himself from that accusation. Moreover, Lenin especially emphasizes the fact that he is introducing his corrections on the basis of conversations with Mdivani and other comrades.

Stalin's answer, on the contrary, is marked by rudeness; the concluding phrase of the fourth point is especially worthy of attention:

> "There is hardly a doubt that this 'hurriedness' [Lenin's 'hurriedness'—L.T.] will supply fuel to the advocates of independence, to the detriment of the national liberalism [!] of comrade Lenin."

Thus Lenin had come to the point of being accused of national liberalism!

The further course of the struggle over the national question showed Lenin that he could not straighten things out by means of internal and, so to speak, family methods of influencing Stalin; that it was necessary to appeal to the Congress and to the party. With this purpose, Lenin wrote in several installments his letter on the national question.

62. Vladimir Ilyich attached enormous importance to the "Georgian" question, not only because he feared the consequences of a false national policy in Georgia—a fear which had been wholly confirmed—but also because in that question was revealed to him the falseness of Stalin's whole course on the national question. The exhaustive and fundamental letter of Lenin on the national question is concealed from the party to this day. The pretense that Lenin did not intend his letter to be read to the party is false to the core. Did Lenin intend his remarks in note books or on margins of the books he read to be published? The fact is that you publish everything which directly or

indirectly strikes at the Opposition but you hide the programmatic letter of Lenin giving his fundamental position on the national question.

Here are two quotations from this letter:

> "I think that here the hastiness and administrative impulsiveness of Stalin played a fatal rôle, and also his spitefulness against the notorious 'social nationalism.' Spitefulness in general plays the worst possible rôle in politics." (From Lenin's note of December 30, 1922.)

That is clear enough!

> "It is, of course, necessary to hold Stalin and Dzerzhinsky responsible for all this out-and-out Great Russian nationalistic campaign." (From Lenin's letter of December 31, 1922.)

Vladimir Ilyich sent me this letter at the moment when he felt that he would hardly be able to appear at the Twelfth Congress. Here are the notes which I received from him in the course of the last two days of his participation in political life:

"STRICTLY CONFIDENTIAL. PERSONAL.

"Esteemed Comrade Trotsky:

"I earnestly ask you to undertake the defense of the Georgian affair at the Central Committee of the party. That affair is now under 'prosecution' at the hands of Stalin and Dzerzhinsky and I cannot rely on their impartiality. Indeed, quite the contrary! If you would agree to undertake its defense, I could be at rest. If for some reason you do not agree, send me back all the papers. I will consider that a sign of your disagreement.

"With the very best
comradely greetings,
"Lenin.

"Dictated to M.V.
"(Checked by M. Volodicheva)
"MARCH 5, 1923."

"To Comrade Trotsky:

"To his letter, sent to you by telephone, Vladimir Ilyich asks me to add for your information that comrade Kamenev is going to Georgia on Wednesday, and Vladimir Ilyich asks me to find out whether you do not want to send something there from you.

"M. Volodicheva."

"To Comrades Mdivani, Makharadze and others:
(copy to Comrades Trotsky and Kamenev)
"Esteemed comrades:

"I am with you in this matter with all my heart. I am outraged at the rudeness of Ordjonikidze and the connivance of Stalin and Dzerzhinsky. I am preparing for you notes and a speech.

"With esteem,
"Lenin.
"MARCH 6, 1923."

"To Comrade Kamenev (copy to comrade Trotsky):
"Leon Borisovich:

"Supplementing our telephone conversation, I communicate to you as acting chairman of the Political Bureau the following:

"As I already told you, December 31, 1922, Vladimir Ilyich dictated an article on the national question.

"This question has worried him extremely and he was preparing to speak on it at the party congress. Not long before his last illness he told me that he would publish this article, but later. After that he took sick without giving final directions.

"Vladimir Ilyich considered this article to be a guiding one and extremely important. At his direction it was communicated to comrade Trotsky whom Vladimir Ilyich authorized to defend his point of view upon the given question at the party congress in view of their solidarity upon it.

"The only copy of the article in my possession is preserved at the direction of Vladimir Ilyich in his secret archive.

"I bring the above facts to your attention.

"I could not do it earlier since I returned to work only today after a sickness.

"*L. Fotieva* (Personal secretary of Comrade Lenin)

"MARCH 16, 1923."

After all the slanders with which they have surrounded the question of Lenin's attitude to me, I cannot refrain from calling attention to the signature of his first letter—"with the very best comradely greetings." Whoever knows Lenin's parsimony of words and his manner of conversation and correspondence will realize that Lenin did not sign those words to his letter accidentally. It was not accidental either that Stalin, when he was compelled to read this correspondence at the Plenum of July 1926, substituted for the words "with the very best comradely greetings" the official phrase "with communist greetings." Here again

Stalin was true to himself.

63. The above quoted notes of Vladimir Ilyich on the national question require a brief explanation. Vladimir Ilyich was at the time ill in bed. My own health was poor. Vladimir Ilyich's secretaries, comrades Glyasser and Fotieva, came to me during the last day before the second and final illness of Lenin. When Fotieva brought me the so-called "national" letter of Lenin, I suggested that since Kamenev was leaving that day for Georgia to the party congress, it might be advisable to show him the letter so that he might undertake the necessary measures. Fotieva replied: "I don't know. Vladimir Ilyich didn't instruct me to transmit the letter to comrade Kamenev, but I can ask him." A few minutes later she returned with the following message: "It is entirely out of the question. Vladimir Ilyich says that Kamenev would show the letter to Stalin and Stalin would make a rotten compromise in order then to deceive."

However, almost immediately thereafter, it may have been within half an hour, Fotieva returned from Vladimir Ilyich with another message. According to her, Vladimir Ilyich decided to act immediately and wrote the above quoted note to Mdivani and Makharadze, with instructions to transmit copies to Kamenev and myself.

"How do you explain this change?" I asked Fotieva.

"Evidently," she replied, "Vladimir Ilyich is feeling worse and is in haste to do everything he can."

The question of the Central Control Commission and the Commissariat of the Workers' and Peasants' Inspection

64. Lenin's proposal *to reorganize the Commissariat of Workers' and Peasants' Inspection (Rabkrin)* was met with extreme hostility by Stalin's group. I told of this in very

restrained language in one of my former letters to the members of the Central Committee. I reproduce the passage here:

> "But how did the Political Bureau react to Lenin's project for the reorganization of *Rabkrin*? Comrade Bukharin hesitated to print Lenin's article, while Lenin, on his side, insisted upon its immediate appearance. N.K. Krupskaya told me by telephone about this article and asked me to take steps to get it printed as soon as possible. At the meeting of the Political Bureau, called immediately upon my demand, all those present—comrades Stalin, Molotov, Kuibyshev, Rykov, Kalinin, Bukharin—were not only against comrade Lenin's plan but against the very printing of the article. The members of the Secretariat were particularly harsh and categorical in their opposition. In view of the insistent demand of comrade Lenin that the article should be shown to him in print, comrade Kuibyshev, afterwards the head of *Rabkrin*, proposed at the above-mentioned session of the Political Bureau that one special number of *Pravda* should be printed with Lenin's article and shown to him in order to placate him, while the article itself should be concealed from the party.
>
> "I argued that the radical reform proposed by comrade Lenin was progressive in itself—provided, of course, it were properly carried out—but that even if one held that the contrary was true, it would be absurd and ridiculous to defend the party against the proposals of comrade Lenin. I was answered with arguments, all in the same spirit of formalism: 'We are the Central Committee. We will take the responsibility. We will decide.' I was supported only by comrade Kamenev who appeared at the meeting of the Political Bureau

> almost an hour late.
>
> "The chief argument which induced them to print the article was that an article by Lenin could not be concealed from the party in any case. Later on that article became a special weapon in the hands of those who had not wanted to print it, a weapon which they attempted to use *against me*! Comrade Kuibyshev, then a member of the Secretariat, was placed at the head of the Central Control Commission. Instead of a struggle against Lenin's plan, a policy of 'drawing its teeth' was adopted. Whether the Central Control Commission acquired in this way the character of an independent, impartial institution, defending and confirming party justice and unity against all kinds of administrative excesses—it is hardly necessary to go into that question since the answer is perfectly clear." (Trotsky, Letter to the Members of the CC and the CCC, Oct. 23, 1923.)

The conduct of Stalin upon this question first clearly proved to me that the proposal to reorganize the Central Control Commission and the Central Committee was directed solely and entirely against the bureaucratic power of Stalin, then already excessive, and against his disloyalty. Hence Stalin's stubborn opposition to Lenin's plan.

Lenin's last plans

65. At the Praesidium of the Central Control Commission I reported about my *last conversation with Vladimir Ilyich*, not long before the second attack of his illness. I quote from the report:

> "Lenin summoned me to his room in the Kremlin, spoke of the terrible growth of bureaucratism in our Soviet apparatus and of the necessity of finding a lever

with which to get at that problem. He proposed to create a special commission of the Central Committee and asked me to take active part in the work. I answered him: 'Vladimir Ilyich, it is my conviction that in the present struggle with bureaucratism in the Soviet apparatus, we must not forget that there is taking place, both in the provinces and in the center, a special selection of functionaries and specialists, party and non-party, around certain ruling party personalities and groups—in the provinces, in the districts, in the party locals and in the center—that is, the Central Committee. Attacking a functionary you run into the party leader. The specialist is a member of his retinue. Under present circumstances, I could not undertake this work.'

"Vladimir Ilyich reflected a moment and—here I quote him verbatim—said: 'That is, I propose a struggle with Soviet bureaucratism and you are proposing to include the bureaucratism of the Organization Bureau of the Party?'*

"I laughed at the unexpectedness of this, because no such finished formulation of the idea was in my mind.

"I answered: 'I suppose that's it.'

"Then Vladimir Ilyich said: 'Very well, then, I propose a bloc.'

"I said: 'It is a pleasure to form a bloc with a good man.'

"At the end of our conversation, Vladimir Ilyich said that he would propose the creation by the Central Committee of a commission to fight bureaucratism 'in general,' and through that we would be able to reach the Organization Bureau of the Central Committee. The organizational side he promised to think over 'further'! At that we parted. I then waited two weeks for the bell to summon me but Ilyich's health became

* Stalin as General Secretary was at the head of this Bureau.—L.T.

> continually worse and he was soon confined to bed. After that Vladimir Ilyich sent me his letters on the national question through his secretaries. And so that work was never carried through."

In the essence of the matter that plan of Lenin was wholly directed against Stalin. It flowed from the same train of thought which found its expression in the so-called "Testament of Lenin."

66. Yes, I had disagreements with Lenin. But Stalin's attempt, relying upon these "facts," to distort the general character of our relations goes to pieces completely when confronted with the facts of that period when, as I have said, things were decided, not in conversation and in votes, of which no record remained, but by means of correspondence; that is, in the interval between the first and second illnesses of Lenin. To summarize:

(a) On the national question Vladimir Ilyich was preparing for the Twelfth Party Congress a decisive attack upon Stalin. Of this his secretaries told me in his name and at his direction. The phrase of Lenin that they repeated oftenest of all was: "Vladimir Ilyich is preparing a bomb against Stalin."

(b) In his article about the *Rabkrin*, Lenin says:

> "The People's Commissariat of *Rabkrin* does not enjoy at the present moment a shadow of authority. Everybody knows that a worse organized institution than our Commissariat of *Rabkrin* does not exist, and that in the present circumstances you cannot expect a thing of that Commissariat. . . . As a matter of fact, what is the use of creating another commissariat whose work is carried on any old way, not inspiring the slightest confidence, and whose word enjoys

infinitely small authority? . . .

"I ask any of the present leaders of *Rabkrin*, or any of the people connected with it—can they tell me, in good conscience, what is the practical use of such a Commissariat as *Rabkrin*?" (Lenin, "Better Less, but Better," March 4, 1923.)

Stalin stood at the head of *Rabkrin* throughout the first years of the revolution. Lenin's volley here was directed wholly against him.

(c) In the same article we read:

"(We have bureaucratism not only in the Soviet institutions but also in the party.)"

These words, clear enough in themselves, acquire an especially sharp significance in connection with my last conversation with Vladimir Ilyich, quoted above, where he spoke of our forming a "bloc" against the Organization Bureau of the Central Committee as the fountainhead of bureaucratism. The mild and typically Leninist remark in parenthesis was directed wholly against Stalin.

(d) Of the Testament, it is needless to speak. It is filled with distrust of Stalin, his rudeness and disloyalty. It speaks of the possible misuse of power on his part and the danger, due to this, of a party split. The sole organizational inference indicated in the Testament, from all the characterizations made there is this: "Remove Stalin from the post of General Secretary."

(e) Finally, the last letter which Lenin ever wrote in his life, or rather dictated, was a letter to Stalin breaking off all comradely relations with him. Comrade Kamenev told me of that letter on the same night it was written (March 5–6, 1923). Comrade Zinoviev told about that letter at the joint

Plenum of the Central Committee and the Central Control Commission. The existence of the letter was confirmed in the minutes by the testimony of M.I. Ulianova. ("Documents on the subject of this incident exist"—says a declaration of M. Ulianova at the Praesidium of the Plenum.)

Enumerating the "warnings" which Lenin gave to Stalin, comrade Zinoviev said at the July Plenum, 1926:

> "And the third warning consists of this: That at the beginning of the year 1923, Vladimir Ilyich, in a personal letter to comrade Stalin, broke off all comradely relations with him." (*Minutes*, 4th issue, p. 32.)

M. Ulianova tried to present the matter in such a way that the breaking off of comradely relations announced by Lenin to Stalin in the last letter before his death seemed to be evoked by personal and not political causes. (*Minutes*, 4th issue, p. 104.)

Need we recall that with Lenin personal motives always derived from political, revolutionary, party causes? "Rudeness" and "disloyalty" are also personal qualities. But Lenin warned the party about them not for "personal" but for party reasons. Lenin's letter, breaking off comradely relations with Stalin, had exactly the same character. That last letter was written *after* the letter on the national question and *after* the Testament. Attempts are being made in vain to weaken the moral weight of the last letter of Lenin. The party has a right to know that letter!

That is how the facts stand. That is how Stalin is deceiving the party.

Discussion during the years 1923–1927

67. During Lenin's lifetime and especially at the time of the discussions over the Brest-Litovsk peace and over the

trade unions, which have since been so grossly exaggerated and distorted, the word "Trotskyism" did not exist at all.* The party held that whatever occasional differences there were, they unfolded on the historical foundations of Bolshevism. The extreme opponents of Lenin on the question of Brest-Litovsk were: Bukharin, Yaroslavsky, Kuibyshev, Soltz, Safarov and scores of other old Bolsheviks, who made up the faction of the "Left communists." They would have been legitimately amazed had it occurred to any one at that time to say that their position was "Trotskyism," especially since on all the fundamental issues which separated the Left communists from Lenin, I was on the side of Lenin.

The same must be said about the trade union discussion. The tendency to stress the administrative side grew out of the entire practice of War Communism and affected innumerable old Bolsheviks. If, at the time of the discussion, any one had mentioned such a thing as "Trotskyism" he would simply have been regarded as temporarily insane. The bogey of "Trotskyism" was projected after Lenin had withdrawn entirely from work, precisely at the time of the discussion of 1923. It was then that the "criticism of the theory of the permanent revolution" began for the purpose of stringing together the differences which had arisen on a new stage of historical development. They engaged in a struggle against Trotsky not because he had advanced a

* In this connection, the fact might be mentioned that Stalin insistently proposed on the eve of the Twelfth Congress that I make the political report for the Central Committee. He did so in agreement with Kamenev, who was then the acting chairman of the Political Bureau, and with the energetic support of Kalinin and others. I declined, partly on the ground that there were differences of opinion on industrial questions. "One can hardly say differences," objected Kalinin. "In the majority of cases, your proposals are accepted."—L.T.

special theory of "Trotskyism." On the contrary, the critics artificially built a theory of "Trotskyism" in order to carry on the struggle against Trotsky. Some of the original critics confessed as much later on, when the groupings changed.[27]

The permanent revolution

68. As to the theory of the permanent revolution, I shall devote special consideration to it at some future time.*

Here I limit myself to two references.

In the beginning of 1918, in a brochure devoted to the October Revolution, Bukharin wrote:

> "The downfall of the Czarist régime was prepared by the entire preceding history of the revolution. But this downfall, and *the victory of the proletariat* supported by the poor peasantry, a victory which has at a single blow opened up unlimitable vistas throughout the world, *is not yet the beginning of the organic epoch.* . . . The Russian proletariat is confronted more sharply than ever before with the problem of the *international revolution.* . . . The grand total of relationships which have arisen in Europe leads to this inevitable conclusion. Thus, *the permanent revolution in Russia is passing into the European proletarian revolution.*" (*From the Collapse of Czarism to the Fall of the Bourgeoisie*, p. 78. Our emphasis.)

The brochure ends with the following words:

> "Into the powder magazine of old blood-stained Europe was thrown the torch of the Russian socialist

---

* Since that time the author has published a book entitled, *The Permanent Revolution* (Pioneer Publishers, New York, 1931). The exposition of the theory is therefore omitted here.

> revolution. It has not died. It lives. It is spreading. And it will inevitably merge with the great triumphant uprising of the world proletariat." (*Ibid.*, p. 144.)

How infinitely removed was Bukharin of that time from the theory of socialism in one country!

It is common knowledge that Bukharin was the chief and indeed the sole theoretician of the entire campaign against "Trotskyism," summed up in the struggle against the theory of the permanent revolution. But at an earlier period when the lava of the revolutionary upheaval had not yet cooled, Bukharin, as we see, was unable to provide a characterization for revolution different from the one against which, a few years later, he was to wage a ruthless struggle.

Bukharin's brochure was issued by the official party publishing house, Priboy, under the supervision of the Central Committee. Not only did no one declare that pamphlet heretical but, on the contrary, everyone accepted it as the official and unchallenged expression of the views of the Central Committee of the party. This brochure went through several editions in the course of the next few years. Together with another brochure devoted to the February Revolution it appeared in translations into German, French, English and other languages, under the general title, *From the Collapse of Czarism to the Fall of the Bourgeoisie.*

In 1923, the brochure was published—apparently for the last time—by the Kharkov party publishing house, Proletari. The preface to this edition expressed the conviction that this little book "will prove of great interest" not only to new members of the party, the youth and so forth, but also "to the Bolshevik Old Guard of the underground period of our party."

That Bukharin is not very staunch in his views is sufficiently well known. But it is not a question of Bukharin himself. If we are to believe the legend created for the first time in the autumn of 1924, that there was an impassable abyss between Lenin's understanding of revolution and Trotsky's theory of the permanent revolution, and that the old generation of the party was brought up on the understanding of the irreconcilability of these two theories, then it is incomprehensible why Bukharin, at the beginning of 1918, could preach this theory with impunity, calling it by its name—the theory of the permanent revolution. How did it happen that not a single person—literally nobody in the entire party—took issue with Bukharin? How and why did the official publishing house of the Central Committee publish this brochure? How and why did Lenin happen to keep silent? How and why did the Comintern publish in several foreign languages this brochure of Bukharin in defense of the permanent revolution? How and why did Bukharin's brochure retain its status as a party textbook up to the very death of Lenin? How and why was Bukharin's brochure republished as late as 1923 and warmly recommended both to the party youth and to the Bolshevik Old Guard in Kharkov—the future center of Stalinist zealots?

This brochure of Bukharin's differs from his later writings and from the entire latter-day Stalinist historiography, not only in its characterization of the revolution, but also in its manner of portraying the participants of the revolution. For example, we find the following on page 131 of the Kharkov edition:

> "The focal point of political life became . . . not the pathetic Soviet of the Republic, but the impending Congress of the Russian Revolution. In the center of this

> work of mobilization stood the Petersburg Soviet which demonstratively elected as its chairman, Trotsky, the most brilliant tribune of the proletarian uprising. . . ."

And further, on page 138:

> "On the 25th of October, Trotsky, the brilliant and courageous tribune of the insurrection, the indefatigable and flaming herald of revolution, declared in the name of the Military Revolutionary Committee of the Petersburg Soviet, to the thunderous applause of the assembly, that 'the Provisional Government no longer exists.' And as living proof of this fact, greeted by a stormy ovation, Lenin appeared on the tribunal, liberated from illegality by the new revolution."

In 1923–1924, the party was overwhelmed by the flood of so-called discussion against "Trotskyism." It wrecked a great many things that had been reared by the October Revolution. It flooded newspapers, libraries, reading rooms, and buried under its silt and slime countless documents relating to the greatest epoch in the development of the party and the revolution. Now we are compelled to extract these documents in fragments in order to restore the past.

69. In 1921, one of the many editions of Trotsky's old book entitled, *Summaries and Perspectives of the Revolution*, was published in the English language. Contained in it is the most complete exposition of the theory of permanent revolution.

The English edition is supplied with a preface by the author dated March 12, 1919, Kremlin, and originally written for the Russian edition of the brochure issued in 1919. In the period between that Russian edition and the English edition of 1921 appeared several editions in various languages. In his preface of 1919, the author referred to the differences of opinion on this question which had formerly separated him from Bolshevism. The preface states among other things:

> "Having thus conquered power, the proletariat cannot confine itself to bourgeois democracy. The proletariat is compelled to resort to the tactic of the *permanent revolution*—that is to say, it must destroy the barrier between the minimum and maximum programs of social democracy, introduce increasingly radical social reforms and strive for the direct and forthright support of the European revolution. That position was developed in the present brochure which was originally written in 1904–1906."

"Destroy the barrier between the minimum and maximum programs"—that is precisely the formula for the growing over of the bourgeois democratic revolution into the socialist revolution. Such a process is predicated on the conquest of power by the proletariat which, by the logic of its position, is compelled to "introduce increasingly radical social reforms. . . ."

And who published this brochure? The publisher did not at all deem it necessary to hide his criminal identity. The title page reads: "Published by the Communist International, Moscow, 1921." The last page of the brochure bears the notation in Russian: "Printshop of the Comintern." The chairman of the Comintern was Zinoviev. Bukharin was in full-time employ of the Comintern. The edition could not have passed unnoticed by them, especially since there were several editions. Nor could the edition in the Russian language have passed unnoticed by the Central Committee of the party as a whole—especially since the brochure was expressly published by it—nor by Lenin in particular. At that period the question of interpreting the significance of the October Revolution was very sharply posed in the mind of every member of the party, and especially of its leading cadres.

I am compelled to ask again: How was it that on the most important and most burning question, not only the Central Committee but even the Comintern, could disseminate a brochure devoted wholly to the defense and exposition of the theory of the permanent revolution and, moreover, containing a preface written specially for the new edition, in which the author declared that the course of events had confirmed that theory? Is it your contention that until 1924 the Bolshevik party and the Comintern were headed only by blind or ignorant men, or what is worse, Mensheviks and counterrevolutionists? We demand an answer to this question—one of a hundred, one of a thousand similar questions.

'Discussions' in the post-Lenin period

70. I do not propose to analyze here the discussion of 1923. The controversy opened at that time still continues. The fundamental controversial questions were:

(a) The inter-relations between the city and country (the "scissors,"[28] the disproportions; whether the threat to the *smychka*[29] in the next period lay in industry's lagging behind or in the attempt to leap ahead).

(b) The rôle of planned management of national economy from the point of view of the struggle of socialist and capitalist tendencies.

(c) The party régime.

(d) The problems of international revolutionary strategy (Germany, Bulgaria, Esthonia[30]). Since that time the controversial questions have assumed a much clearer aspect and have been expressed in more adequate form in a number of the documents of the Opposition. However, the main line sketched by the Opposition in 1923 has been wholly confirmed.

The July 1926 declaration signed by comrades Zinoviev and Kamenev states the following:

> "At the present moment there can no longer be any doubt that the main nucleus of the Opposition of the year 1923 had correctly warned us of the danger of sliding away from the proletarian line and of the alarming growth of the apparatus régime. Nevertheless, scores and hundreds of leaders of the Opposition of 1923, among them many old worker-Bolsheviks tempered in the struggle, immune to careerism and servility, remain to this day removed from party work, despite their proven constancy and submission to discipline."

That declaration alone suffices to show how puny on the scales of theory is the weight of the phantom of "Trotskyism," created and fostered to befuddle the party.

The label "Trotskyism" has been applied since 1923, and especially since 1924, to the correct application of Marxism with regard to the new stage in the development of the October Revolution and of our party.

A few conclusions

The above is a very small part of those facts, testimonials and quotations which I might adduce in refutation of the history of the last ten years as falsified by Stalin, Yaroslavsky and Co.

I must add that the falsification is not limited to these ten years but spreads over the whole preceding history of the party, converting it into an uninterrupted struggle of

Bolshevism with "Trotskyism." In that sphere the falsifiers feel especially free, for the events belong to an already comparatively remote past, and they can make an arbitrary selection of documents. The thought of Lenin is counterfeited by means of a one-sided selection of quotations. At present, however, I will not enter into the preceding period of my revolutionary activities (1897 to 1917) since the motive of the present letter is your questionnaire as to my participation in the October Revolution and my meetings and relations with Lenin.

As to the twenty years preceding the October Revolution, I will confine myself to a few lines.

I was of that "minority" (*menshinstvo*) of the Second Congress (1903) from which Menshevism subsequently developed. I remained politically and organizationally associated with this minority only until the autumn of 1904—approximately until the so-called "land campaign" of the *New Iskra*, when my irreconcilable conflict with Menshevism upon the questions of bourgeois liberalism and the perspectives of the revolution defined itself. In 1904, that is, twenty-three years ago, I broke politically and organizationally with Menshevism. I never called myself or considered myself a Menshevik.

At the Plenum of the Executive Committee of the Comintern, on December 9, 1926, in connection with the question of "Trotskyism," I made the following statement:

> "Generally speaking, I do not think that the biographical method can lead us to a decision about questions of principle. It is indubitable that I made mistakes upon many questions, especially during my struggle against Bolshevism. From that, however, it hardly follows that political questions ought to be examined not according to their inner content but on the basis of

> biography. Otherwise, we should have to demand an elaboration of the biographies of *all* the delegates. . . .
>
> "I personally may refer to a certain great precedent. In Germany there lived and fought a man by the name of Franz Mehring, who only after a long and energetic struggle against the social democracy (until late years we all called ourselves social democrats), only after he was fully mature, joined the Social Democratic party. Mehring wrote the history of the German social democracy at first as an enemy, not as a lackey of capitalism, but as intellectually opposed to it—and afterward he rewrote it in that splendid work on the German social democracy as its true friend. On the other hand, Kautsky and Bernstein never struggled openly against Marx and they both stood under the whip of Frederick Engels. Bernstein, moreover, is famous as the literary executor of Engels. Nevertheless, Franz Mehring died and was buried as a Marxist, as a communist, whereas the other two, Kautsky and Bernstein, still live the lives of reformist dogs. The biographical element is, of course, important but of itself it decides nothing."

As I have many times stated, in my disagreements with Bolshevism upon a series of fundamental questions, the error was on my side. In order to give an approximate outline in a few words of the nature and extent of those former disagreements of mine with Bolshevism, I will say this:

During the time when I stood outside the Bolshevik party, during that period when my differences with Bolshevism reached their highest point, the distance separating me from the views of Lenin was never as great as the distance which separates the present positions of Stalin-Bukharin from the very foundations of Marxism and Leninism.

Every new stage in the development of the party and

the revolution, every new book, every new fashionable theory, has called forth a new zigzag and a new blunder on the part of Bukharin. His whole theoretical and political biography is a chain of errors committed within the formal framework of Bolshevism. The mistakes of Bukharin since the death of Lenin far exceed in their scale, and especially in their political consequences, all his earlier mistakes. This scholiast, emptying Marxism of all concrete reality, converting it into a game with ideas, often into mere verbal sophistry, has proved naturally the most suitable "theoretician" for the period of the sliding over of the party leadership from the proletarian to the petty bourgeois rails. Without sophistry this cannot be done. Hence the present "theoretical" rôle of Bukharin.

In all those—very few—questions upon which Stalin has attempted to occupy an independent position, or has merely given, without the immediate direction of Lenin, his own answer upon major issues, he has always and invariably, and so to speak, organically, occupied an opportunist position.

The struggle of Lenin against Menshevism, against *Vperyodism,*[31] and Conciliationism, Stalin denounced from exile as an émigré "tempest in a teapot" (*cf., Zarya Vostoka,* Dec. 23, 1925).

No other political documents as to the form of Stalin's thoughts up to 1917 exist, as far as I know, except for a number of more or less correct but school-boy articles on the national question.

The independent position of Stalin (prior to the arrival of Lenin) at the beginning of the February revolution was opportunist through and through.

The independent position of Stalin in relation to the German revolution of 1923 was wholly saturated with tail-endism and conciliationism.

The independent position of Stalin on the problems of the Chinese revolution is nothing but a cheap edition of Martinov's Menshevism of 1903 to 1905.

The independent position of Stalin on the problems of the British labor movement is a Centrist capitulation to Menshevism.[32]

You can juggle quotations, hide the stenographic reports of your own speeches, forbid the circulation of Lenin's letters and articles, fabricate yards of dishonestly selected quotations. You can suppress, conceal and burn up historic documents. You can extend your censorship even to photographic and moving-picture records of revolutionary events. All these things Stalin is doing. But the results do not and will not justify his expectations. Only a limited mind like Stalin's could imagine that these pitiful machinations will make men forget the gigantic events of modern history.

In the year 1918, Stalin, at the very outset of his campaign against me, found it necessary, as we have already learned, to write the following words:

> "All the work of practical organization of the insurrection was carried out under the direct leadership of the Chairman of the Petrograd Soviet, comrade Trotsky. We can say with certainty that the swift passing of the garrison to the side of the Soviet and the bold execution of the work of the Military Revolutionary Committee the party owes principally and above all to comrade Trotsky." (Stalin, *Pravda*, Nov. 6, 1918.)

With full responsibility for my words, I am now compelled to say that the cruel massacre of the Chinese proletariat and the Chinese Revolution at its three most important turning points, the strengthening of the position of the trade union agents of British imperialism after the General Strike of 1926, and, finally, the general weakening of the position of the Communist International and the Soviet Union, the party owes principally and above all to Stalin.

OCTOBER 21, 1927

Some documents relating to the origin of the legend of 'Trotskyism'

In November 1927, Zinoviev and Kamenev, after spending nearly two years in the Opposition, found it necessary to return to the haven of the Stalinist bureaucracy.[33] For their credentials, they sought once again to present a declaration of their disagreement with "Trotskyism." But the misfortune is that Zinoviev and Kamenev, while they were in the Opposition, had bestirred themselves to expose completely the workings of the machine in the preceding period from 1923 to 1926, when they together with Stalin had manufactured the legend of "Trotskyism" in their conspiratorial laboratory.

On the eve of my exile to Central Asia, I sent a letter to a number of comrades. The text of this letter together with the replies is printed below (with minor omissions).

MOSCOW, NOVEMBER 21, 1927.

Dear Comrades:

Zinoviev and Kamenev and their closest associates—after a considerable interval—are again bringing up the legend of "Trotskyism."

For this reason I should like to establish the following facts:

(1) When the so-called "literary discussion" was first kindled (in 1924), certain comrades closest to our group declared that the publication of *The Lessons of October* was a tactical error because it provided the then majority of the Political Bureau with a pretext for launching a "literary discussion."[34] On my part, I maintained that the "literary discussion" would have been launched in any case, on one pretext or another. The gist of the "literary discussion" consisted in piling up as many facts and quotations as possible against me, culling them from the entire past history of the party, and presenting them—in a distorted perspective and in actual violation of historical truth—to the uninformed party masses. In point of fact, the "literary discussion" had no bearing whatever upon my book, *The Lessons of October.* Any one of my books or speeches might have served as a formal pretext for burying the party underneath an avalanche—a drive against "Trotskyism." That was my reply to those comrades who were inclined to view the publication of *The Lessons of October* as a tactical blunder.

After the formation of our bloc with the Leningrad Group, during one of the conferences, in the presence of several other comrades, I put substantially the following question to Zinoviev:

"Could you please tell me whether the so-called literary discussion against 'Trotskyism' would have taken place, if I had not published *The Lessons of October*?"

Without the slightest hesitation, Zinoviev replied: "Yes, indeed. *The Lessons of October* served only as a pretext. Failing that, a different motive would have been found, and the discussion would have assumed somewhat different forms, nothing more."

(2) In the declaration of July 1926, signed by Zinoviev and Kamenev, the following statement occurs:

"There can no longer be any doubt now that the main nucleus of the 1923 Opposition correctly warned against the dangers of the departure from the proletarian line and against the alarming growth of the apparatus régime. Nevertheless, scores and hundreds of the leaders of the 1923 Opposition, among them many old worker-Bolsheviks, tempered in the struggle and immune to careerism and toadyism, remain to this day removed from party work, despite their proven constancy and submission to discipline."

(3) At the joint Plenum of the Central Committee and the Central Control Commission of July 14 to July 23, 1926, Zinoviev said:

"I have made many mistakes. But I consider two mistakes as my most important ones. My first mistake of 1917 is known to all of you. . . . The second mistake I consider *more dangerous* because the first one was made under Lenin. The mistake of 1917 was corrected by Lenin and made good by us within a few days with the help of Lenin, but *my mistake of 1923* consisted in. . . ."

ORDJONIKIDZE (*interrupting*): "Then why did you dupe the entire party?"

ZINOVIEV: "We say, there can no longer be any doubt now that the main nucleus of the 1923 Opposition, as the development of the present ruling faction has shown, correctly warned against the dangers of the departure from the proletarian line, and against the alarming growth of the apparatus régime. . . . Yes, in the question of suppression by the bureaucratized apparatus, Trotsky proved to be right as against us."

(*Minutes,* 4th Issue, p. 33.)

In this manner, Zinoviev admitted his mistake of 1923 (in waging a struggle against "Trotskyism" and even characterized it as much more dangerous than that of 1917 (when he opposed the October insurrection!).

(4) This admission on the part of Zinoviev aroused considerable astonishment among many second-rank leaders of the Leningrad Opposition who were not initiated into the conspiracy and who honestly believed in the legend of "Trotskyism."

Zinoviev told me repeatedly: "In Leningrad we hammered it into the minds of the comrades more deeply than anywhere else and it is, therefore, most difficult to reëducate them."

I recall quite accurately the words that Lashevich shouted at two members of the Leningrad Group who came to Moscow to clarify themselves on the question of Trotskyism:

"Why do you keep standing the matter on its head! We invented 'Trotskyism' together with you in the struggle against Trotsky. Why won't you understand this? You are only helping Stalin! etc."

Zinoviev in his turn said:

"You must keep the circumstances in mind. You must understand it was a struggle for power. The trick was to string together old disagreements with new issues. For this purpose 'Trotskyism' was invented. . . ."

This conversation made a deep impression upon us, the members of the 1923 Group, even though we had had previous knowledge of the mechanics of the struggle against "Trotskyism."

Now that Zinoviev and Kamenev are again resorting to the same trick, that is to say, stringing together old disagreements with the rather current question of their capitulation, I am asking you to recall whether you participated in any of the above-mentioned conversations and what your own recollections are.

With communist greetings,
L. Trotsky.

Letter from E. Preobrazhensky

I confirm everything brought out in the above document. Only Lashevich said: "We invented Trotskyism ourselves, etc." without using the words "together with you." Because, as I recall it, the two Leningrad comrades were quite honestly perturbed about "Trotskyism" and could hardly have been informed of the entire plan of the struggle against "neo-Trotskyism" from its inception. The meeting took place at Kamenev's [home] somewhere around October 16 [1926], perhaps a few days before or after—I cannot recall exactly.

DEC. 29, 1927.
E.A. Preobrazhensky.

Letter from G. Piatakov

Dear Leon Davidovich:

You ask me to inform you what I am able to recall about the speeches of Lashevich and Zinoviev on the occasion of a discussion with Leningrad comrades on "Trotskyism" which took place at Kamenev's home. I no longer remember all that was said. But since I have always been deeply disturbed by the question of so-called "Trotskyism," and since the attitude of the Opposition of 1925–1926 towards this question was always of enormous political interest to me, I remember quite clearly what Zinoviev and Lashevich said to us. I do not recall the exact words but the sense of what

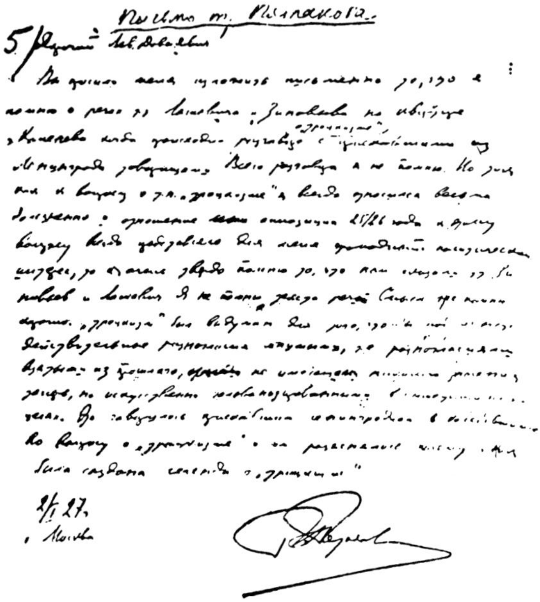

5) Письмо т. Пятакова.
Дорогой Лев Давыдович!

2/I 27.
Москва

Photostat of Piatakov's letter.

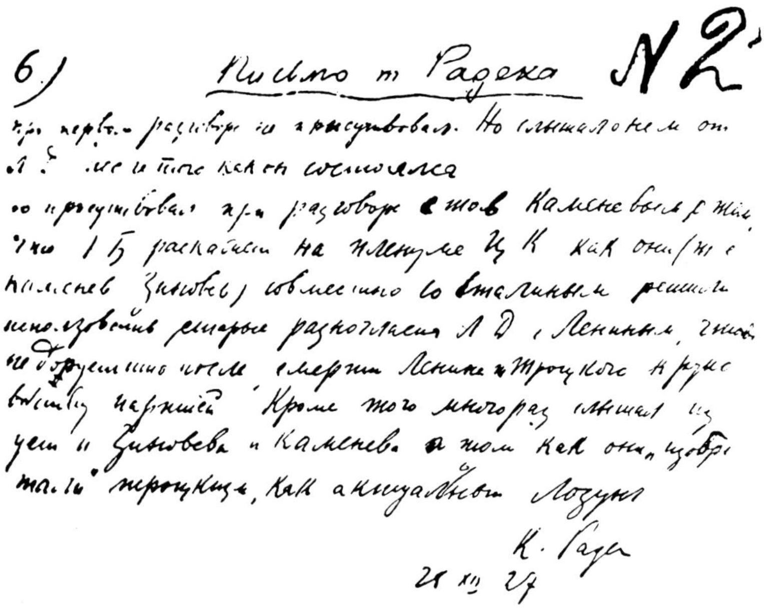

6) Письмо т. Радека N 2

при перв... разговоре не присутствовал. Но слышал потом от
Л. Д. [illegible] и после как он согласился
[illegible] присутствовал при разговоре с тов. Каменевым [illegible]
что [illegible] раскаялись на пленуме ЦК как они (т. е. Каменев Зиновьев) совместно со Сталиным решили использовать старые разногласия Л. Д. с Лениным, чтобы не допустить после смерти Ленина Троцкого к руководству партией. Кроме того многораз слышал из уст и Зиновьева и Каменева о том как они „изобретали" троцкизм, как актуальный лозунг

К. Радек

28 XII 27

Photostat of Radek's letter.

they said I remember well, namely:

"Trotskyism" had been invented in order to replace the real differences of opinion with fictitious differences, that is, to utilize past differences which had no bearing upon the present but which were resurrected artificially for the definite purpose mentioned above. This was told to the comrades from Leningrad who were wavering on the question of "Trotskyism" and to whom it had to be explained how and why the legend of "Trotskyism" had been created.

JAN. 2, 1928.*

Piatakov.

Letter from K. Radek

I was not present during the first conversation but heard of it later from L.D. [Trotsky].

But I was present at the conversation with Kamenev when L.B. [Kamenev] said he would openly declare at the Plenum of the Central Committee how they, that is, Kamenev and Zinoviev, together with Stalin, decided to utilize the old disagreements between L.D. [Trotsky] and Lenin so as to keep comrade Trotsky from the leadership of the party after Lenin's death. Moreover, I have heard repeated from the lips of Zinoviev and Kamenev the tale of how they had "invented" Trotskyism as a topical slogan.

DEC. 25, 1927.

K. Radek.

(Radek here recalls a striking incident that is not mentioned in my letter. During the July Plenum in 1927, Zinoviev and Kamenev were subjected to a particularly heavy barrage of quotations out of their own writings against "Trotskyism."

* The date in the original is mistakenly given as 1927—L.T.

Since Kamenev hoped to get the floor again on the question of the Opposition, he was preparing, as he put it, to take the bull by the horns and declare openly before the Plenum how and why the Trotskyist danger had been invented for the purpose of an organized struggle against Trotsky. But the speakers' list was closed and Kamenev did not get the floor again.—L. Trotsky.)

Letter from C.G. Rakovsky

Dear Leon Davidovich:

I was not present at the conversation to which you refer (I was not in Moscow, having left for Paris after the Plenum). However, on my return in the autumn I heard from you—as well as from Preobrazhensky in Paris—concerning both the conversation with Zinoviev and Lashevich's remarks in particular ("Why do you keep standing the matter on its head?"). Both of them (*i.e.*, Zinoviev and Lashevich) stated themselves that the argument from "Trotskyism" and the "permanent revolution" was dragged in by the hair for the sole purpose of discrediting the 1923 Opposition.

With greetings,
C. Rakovsky.
DEC. 28, 1927.

Letter from V.B. Eltsin

Dear Leon Davidovich:

I have a very clear recollection of the episode relating to the "literary discussion" on *The Lessons of October.* It occurred during one of the conversations in Kamenev's home on the eve of the Declaration of October 16.[35]

To a question put by Leon Davidovich as to whether the discussion against "Trotskyism" would have taken

> place if *The Lessons of October* had not appeared, Zinoviev replied: "Certainly, it would have taken place," for the plan to begin this discussion was already decided upon in advance, and they were only looking for a pretext. None of the supporters of the 1925 Group (the Zinovievists) who were present raised any objections to this. Everyone received this information of Zinoviev's as a generally known fact.
>
> JAN. 2, 1928.
> *V. Eltsin.*

I succeeded in obtaining these written testimonials in Moscow prior to my exile. These testimonials serve only to illustrate what is clear enough to those comrades who are better informed. They cast a rather glaring light upon the repulsive ideological jugglery on the question of "Trotskyism." In the years from 1917 to 1923, there was no mention ever made of Trotskyism. That was the period, apart from other things, of the October insurrection, the Civil War, the construction of the Soviet state and of the Red Army, the elaboration of our party program, the founding of the Communist International, the formation of its cadres, the drafting of its fundamental documents, including the programmatic theses and the manifestoes of the C.I. In 1923, after Lenin's withdrawal from work, serious differences broke out in the main nucleus of the Central Committee. In the course of the next four years, these differences were to develop into two irreconcilable political lines. In 1924, the phantom of Trotskyism was brought into the arena after meticulous preparations behind the scenes. The guiding spirits in the campaign were Zinoviev and Kamenev. They stood at the head of the "Bolshevik Old Guard"—in the terminology of that period. On the opposing side was—"Trotskyism." But the "Old Guard" group suffered a split in 1925. Within a few months, Zinoviev and Kamenev found themselves compelled to admit that the main nucleus of the 1923 Opposition—the so-called "Trotskyists"—proved to be right on the fundamental controversial questions. This admission was the harsh penalty they paid for abuses in the sphere of party theory. But that was not all. Zinoviev and Kamenev soon found themselves enrolled among the "Trotskyists." One could hardly conceive a fate more ruthless in its irony!

The Fifteenth Party Congress brought no change in the political line of the majority. On the contrary, the Congress set its seal of approval upon this line. It condemned the Opposition and banished the latter from the party. So far as Zinoviev and Kamenev were concerned, this provided them with sufficient cause to hide the danger of Thermidor. Instead they sought to resurrect the phantom of Trotskyism. It would not surprise us at all if Zinoviev were to undertake writing a brochure against the Trotskyist danger, while Kamenev begins quoting from his articles and speeches of 1923–1924.

Unprincipled politics carries with it its own punishment. It disintegrates when confronted with facts; it undermines confidence in itself and it ultimately becomes a laughing stock.

Individuals, even such outstanding men as Zinoviev and Kamenev, come and go, but the political line remains.

MOSCOW
JANUARY 3, 1928.

Since the above lines were written, more than two years have elapsed. Piatakov and Radek, the chief witnesses against the falsifiers who had created the legend of Trotskyism, failed to foresee that a few months after signing their eloquent depositions (reproduced here in facsimile) they themselves would take a different road. The paths of ideological backsliding are truly incalculable! The undertow of a revolutionary ebb-tide is so powerful that people flounder in it, and heads and feet become so mixed up in the foam as to be indistinguishable.

Despite its tragi-comic aspects, the fate of the capitulators has a very weighty meaning: The frailty of men serves only to underscore the power of ideas.

It is not the author of this book but rather his adversaries who have built and appraised all party groupings, with their attitude toward "Trotskyism" as a measuring rod. In the struggle against "Trotskyism," Stalin turned "theoretician" and Molotov, leader. Zinoviev and Kamenev marched hand in hand with Stalin, broke with Stalin and returned to Stalin—and each time "Trotskyism" served as the touchstone. The Right wing (Bukharin, Rykov, Tomsky) broke with Stalin, accusing him of "Trotskyism." Stalin, in his wisdom, turned the self-same accusation against the Rights. Piatakov, Radek and other second-draft capitulators were compelled to drink from the self-same fountain.

What does it all mean? First of all, it means that all these individuals and groups possess nothing they can call their own. All of them are repelled by something; they all temporarily gravitate toward something only in order to be repelled again. They call this "something"—"Trotskyism" and they use this pseudonym to settle their accounts with the doctrine of Marx and Lenin.

Revolution is a harsh school. It is unsparing of spines, whether physical or moral. An entire generation has spent itself, becoming drained physically and spiritually. Only a few have survived. The overwhelming majority of the Stalinist tops consists of men drained to the core. The appurtenances of the apparatus invest them with an imposing appearance, serving them as a parade uniform serves a senile general. Historical events will continue to expose and to confirm the hollowness of the Stalinist "Guard" at each new trial. The capitulations on the question of Trotskyism have served thousands and tens of thousands as training in the art of capitulation as such.

The succession of political generations presents a major and a very complex problem which is posed in its own peculiar manner before each class and each party. But all must face it.

Lenin often castigated the so-called "Old Bolsheviks," even remarking on occasion that revolutionists on reaching the age of 50 should be consigned to the Hereafter. This grim jest contains a serious political thought. Each revolutionary generation becomes, after attaining certain limits, an obstacle to the further development of those ideas which it had served. Generally speaking, men are quickly drained by politics and all the more so by revolution. Exceptions are rare. But there are exceptions. Otherwise there would be no such thing as ideological continuity.

Today the theoretical education of the younger generation is our supreme task. This is the meaning of the struggle we are waging against the epigones who despite their seeming strength have already been drained ideologically.

T.
CONSTANTINOPLE,
FEBRUARY 7, 1930.

The lost document

We publish herewith the minutes of the historic session of the Petrograd Committee of the Bolsheviks held November 1 (14),[36] 1917. The conquest of power had already been achieved, at any rate, in the most important centers in the country. Within the party, however, the struggle over the question of power had far from terminated. It had merely passed into a new phase. Prior to October 25, the representatives of the Right wing (Zinoviev, Kamenev, Rykov, Kalinin, Lunacharsky and others) argued that the uprising was premature and could lead only to defeat. After the victorious insurrection, they proceeded to argue that the Bolshevik party would be unable to maintain itself in power unless the Bolsheviks entered into a coalition with the other Socialist parties, *i.e.*, the Social Revolutionists and the Mensheviks. During this new phase, the struggle of the Rights became exceptionally acute, and terminated with the resignation of the representatives of the Right wing from the Council of People's Commissars and from

The first chairman of the Communist International was Gregory Zinoviev, above, a long-time Bolshevik and close associate of Lenin. He was a member of the Political Bureau of the Russian Communist Party and, after the October insurrection, the chairman of the Petrograd Soviet. Although he and Kamenev opposed the 1917 Bolshevik seizure of power, in Lenin's time he continued as a prominent leader of the party and state. Zinoviev and Kamenev were killed by Stalin in the purge of 1936.

the Central Committee of the party. It should be borne in mind that this crisis occurred only a few days after the conquest of power.

How did the present Centrists and, above all, Stalin, conduct themselves on this question? In the nature of things, Stalin was a Centrist even at that time. He occupied a Centrist position whenever he had to take an independent stand or to express his personal opinion. *But this Centrist stood in fear of Lenin.* It is for this reason that there is virtually no political trace of Stalin during the most critical moments of the ideological struggle—from April 4, 1917, up to the time Lenin fell ill.

As these minutes prove, the revolutionary line of the party was defended jointly by Lenin and Trotsky. That is precisely why the minutes we publish were not included in the collection of the minutes of the Petrograd Committee, issued under the title: *The First Legal Petrograd Committee of the Bolsheviks in 1917* (State Publishers, 1927). We must pause to correct ourselves. The minutes of the November 1 session were originally included in the book. They were set in type and the proofs were carefully read. As evidence of this, we present a facsimile reproduction of a section of these proof-sheets. But the minutes of this historical session were in flagrant and virtually intolerable contradiction with the falsification of the history of October, executed under the unenlightened but zealous supervision of Yaroslavsky. What was there left to do? Leningrad phoned Moscow; the Central *Istpart* phoned the Secretariat of the Central Committee, and the latter issued its instructions: That the minutes be expunged from the book, in such a manner as would leave no traces behind. The table of contents was hastily reset and the pages renumbered. Nevertheless, a tell-tale trace remains in the body of the book itself. The session of October 29 concludes by setting Wednesday (November 1) as the date for the next session. Meanwhile, according to the book the "next" session takes place on Thursday, November 2. But a much more important trace is preserved outside the pages of the book itself, in the form of the above-mentioned proof sheets, corrected and annotated in her own handwriting, by P.F. Kudelli, the editor of the volume.

As the official reason for hiding the most important minutes of the Petrograd Committee for the year 1917, Kudelli jotted down the following note on the proofs: "The speech of V.I. Lenin was recorded by the secretary of that session of the Petersburg Committee with considerable omissions and numerous abbreviations of various words and sentences. In places, the record of Lenin's speech cannot be deciphered. To avoid presenting the speech in garbled form, it will, therefore, not be printed."

It is quite true that the record of the minutes is imperfect, containing many omissions and obscure passages. But this is equally true of all the minutes of the Petrograd Committee for the year 1917. The record of the November 1 session is, if anything, superior to several others. It is generally known that Lenin's speeches were always difficult to record even in shorthand, because of the peculiarities of his delivery. He spoke very rapidly, using extremely complex sentences, making sudden and abrupt interpolations, etc. Nevertheless, the full import of Lenin's speech of November 1 (14) is perfectly clear. Lunacharsky's speech and the two speeches of Trotsky are quite adequately recorded. The reason for the excision of these minutes is wholly different. Nor is it difficult to find. The reason is denoted on the margins of the proof sheets by a heavy line accompanied with an enormous question mark. These notations are placed next to the following words in the text:

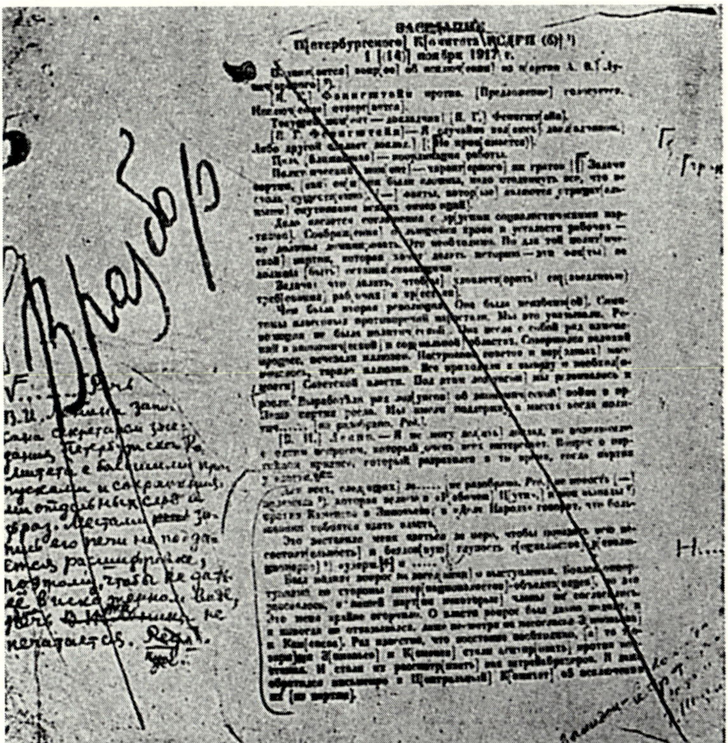

ЗАСЕДАНИЕ
П[етербургского] К[омитета] РСДРП (б)
1 (14) ноября 1917 г.

The handwriting on the margin is that of P.F. Kudelli, the editor of the volume of minutes.

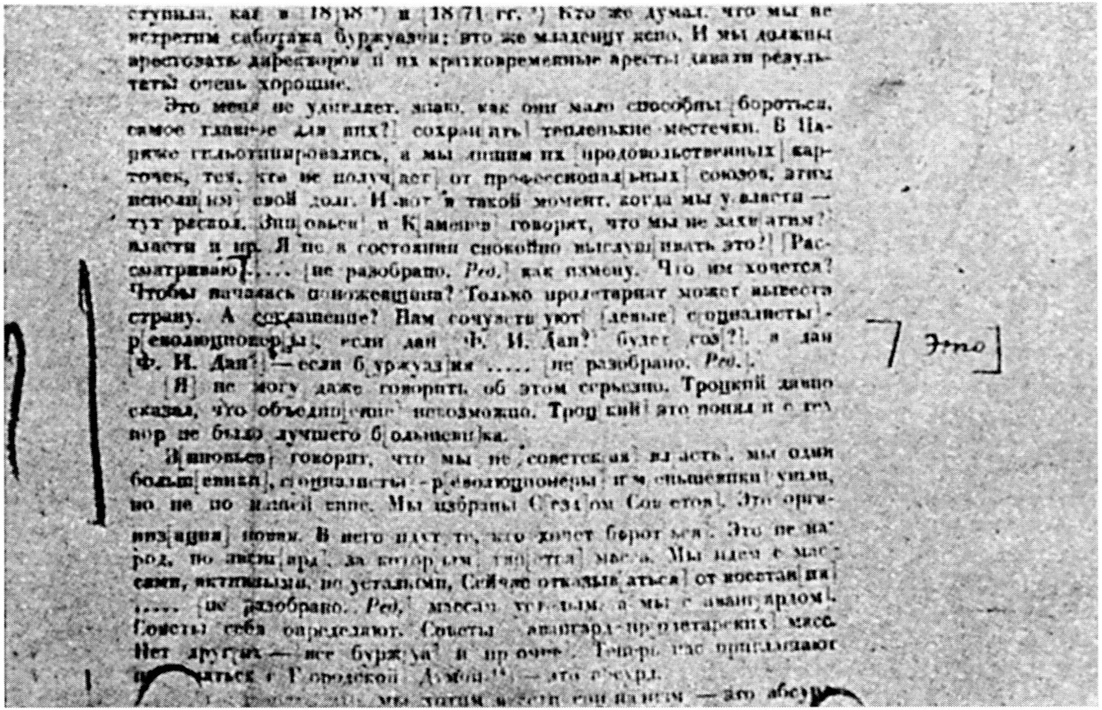

ступила, как в [18]48 ¹) и [18]71 гг. ²) Кто же думал, что мы не встретим саботажа буржуазии; это же младенцу ясно. И мы должны арестовать директоров и их кратковременные аресты давали результаты очень хорошие.

Это меня не удивляет, знаю, как они мало способны [бороться, самое главное для них?] сохран[ять] тепленькие местечки. В Париже гильотинировались, а мы лишим их [продовольственных] карточек, тех, кто не получ[ает] от профессиона[льных] союзов, этим исполн[им] свой долг. И вот в такой момент, когда мы у власти — тут раскол. Зин[овьев] и К[аменев] говорит, что мы не захв[атим] власти и пр. Я не в состоянии спокойно выслуш[ивать это?] [Рассматриваю] . . . . . [не разобрано. *Ред.*] как измену. Что им хочется? Чтобы началась поножовщина? Только пролетариат может вывести страну. А соглашение? Нам сочувств[уют] [левые] с[оциалисты]-р[еволюционе]ры, если дан [Ф. И. Дан?] будет соз[?], а дан [Ф. И. Дан?] — если б[уржуаз]ия . . . . . [не разобрано. *Ред.*].

[Я] не могу даже говорить об этом серьезно. Троцкий давно сказал, что объедин[ение] невозможно. Тро[ц]кий это понял и с тех пор не было лучшего б[ольшеви]ка.

З[иновьев] говорит, что мы не [советская] в[ласть], мы одни больш[евики], с[оциалисты]-р[еволюционеры] и м[еньшевики] ушли, но не по нашей вине. Мы избраны С[ъезд]ом Сов[етов]. Это организ[ация] новая. В него идут те, кто хочет борот[ься]. Это не народ, но авангард, за которым [идут] массы. Мы идем с массами, активными, не усталыми. Сейчас отказыв[аться] от восстан[ия] . . . . . [не разобрано. *Ред.*] массам усталым, а мы с авангардом. Советы себя определяют. Советы [авангард пролетарских] масс. Нет других — все буржуа и прочие. Теперь нас приглашают [соединяться] с Городской Думой ³) — это абсурд.

Photostat of galleys of the “First Legal Petrograd Committee of the Bolsheviks in 1917” (State Publishers, 1927) as originally set up.

> *"As for conciliation* [with the Mensheviks and the Social Revolutionists] *I cannot even speak about that seriously. Trotsky long ago said that unification is impossible. Trotsky understood this and from that time on there has been no better Bolshevik."*

It was *this* passage that completely overwhelmed the Secretariat of the Central Committee and resulted in a reconstruction of the entire book which is unpleasant enough in itself—for even in its present ravaged form it constitutes a deadly document against the falsifiers. Enough to mention that the viewpoint of the Central Committee as presented to the locals was referred to as "the viewpoint of Lenin and Trotsky" (cf., p. 345). Not even a man as assiduous as Yaroslavsky can attend to every detail.

I might remark in passing that it would be highly instructive to reconstruct the independent ideological creative work of this incompetent compiler and spiteful falsifier during the year 1917. We shall recall only a single fact that is little known or conveniently forgotten. After the February Revolution, Yaroslavsky issued in Yakutsk jointly with the Mensheviks a review, *Sotsial-Demokrat,* a model of infinite political sordidness, straddling between Menshevism and the most provincial form of liberalism. Yaroslavsky at that time was at the head of the Yakutsk Chamber of Arbitration, whose function it was to safeguard the splendors of the democratic revolution against clashes between workers and capitalists. This spirit permeated all the articles in the above review, of which Yaroslavsky was the editor. Among his collaborators who, too, did not violate the spirit of the publication were Ordjonikidze and Petrovsky, the present Chairman of the All-Ukrainian Central Executive Committee. In a leading article which might seem incredible had it not appeared in print, Petrovsky literally shed tears to express his emotions over the fact that a government official had donated 50 roubles to charity. Petrovsky expressed his firm conviction that the revolution would attain its full fruition the moment when the ruling classes began to follow the example of the noble titular or, perhaps, aulic councillor. These staunch "Marxists" and inflexible "revolutionists" are now editing Lenin and are seeking to edit all history. On a proof sheet of the November 1 session they write with assurance: "Junk that." (See the facsimile reproduction.) Exactly! "Junk" the history of the October Revolution! "Junk"—Lenin! The history of Russia for a third of a century must be reset—with Yaroslavsky as the author, proofreader and make-up man of the new Stalinist history.

But, sad to say, Yaroslavsky "failed" on this occasion too. He failed to "junk" the minutes. After all, it takes living men to break up the galleys.

The proof sheets with all the notations fell instead immediately into the hands of the Opposition. It is not the only document of this kind!

As to the editing of the text printed by us here, we were guided solely by the same methods as were used by the editors of the above-mentioned collection of the minutes of the Petrograd Committee. Wherever the meaning of the sentences leaves no room for doubt, we have corrected the grammar or the syntax to assist the reader. Half-formed or unintelligible phrases have been deleted. The general trend of the entire session and of the tendencies and groupings represented there can be gleaned quite incontestably from the record which, despite all its defects, bears internal evidence of its authenticity. In publishing the present document, we rescue for the annals of history a living and rather important page of the October Revolution.

SESSION OF THE PETERSBURG COMMITTEE OF THE SOCIAL DEMOCRATIC LABOR PARTY OF RUSSIA (BOLSHEVIK), NOVEMBER 1 (14), 1917

Under discussion—the question of expelling A.V. Lunacharsky* from the party.

J.G. Fenigstein-Daletsky speaks against.

The motion is put to a vote.

Motion to expel defeated.

The current situation—reporter, J.G. Fenigstein.

J.G. FENIGSTEIN: I have been chosen reporter by chance. Perhaps someone else will make the report?

[The proposal (for another reporter) rejected.]

Our goal—the impending coördination of work [with the Mensheviks and S.R.'s]. What is involved here is a coalition with other socialist parties. Such considerations as "blood being spilled" or the workers being weary—should not predominate. For a political party that wants to make history—these facts cannot constitute obstacles. The task is: What to do in order to satisfy the just demands of workers and peasants? What was [the nature of] the second revolution? It was inevitable. Class contradictions were

---

* Lunacharsky came out in favor of a coalition with the Mensheviks and the Social Revolutionists. He resigned from the Government, giving as his reason the (alleged) destruction of the Cathedral of St. Basil the Blessed in Moscow. The proposal to expel Lunacharsky was introduced on the initiative of Lenin.

growing. We have pointed this out. The revolution was not [only] political. It brought with it a series of changes in economic and social spheres. A great process was being consummated. Illusions were being dissipated. The mood of the Soviets and of the popular masses was changing; they were losing the [conciliationist] illusions. All were coming to the conclusion that the Soviet state was necessary. Under this slogan we have developed and grown. We have elaborated a number of slogans relating to the economic struggle, etc. Our party has grown. We have had the support of the masses.

LENIN: I cannot make a report but I shall give some information upon a question which is of great interest to all. That is, the question of the crisis in the party, which broke out [openly] at a time when the party was already in power.

The polemic waged by *Rabochi Put,*[37] and my speeches against Kamenev and Zinoviev are no news to all those who have been following the life of the party. Formerly, *Delo Naroda*[38] used to say that the Bolsheviks would be afraid to take power. This compelled me to take up my pen in order to show the bankruptcy and the infinite stupidity of the Social Revolutionists. I wrote *Will the Bolsheviks Retain Power?*[39] The question of the armed insurrection was raised at the October 1 session of the Central Committee. I had fears of opportunism from the side of the Internationalist-Fusionists,[40] but these were dissipated. However, certain [old] members of the Central Committee came out in opposition. This grieved me deeply. Thus, the question of power has been posed for a long time. Couldn't we now renounce it because of the disagreement on the part of Zinoviev and Kamenev? The insurrection was [objectively] necessary. Comrades Zinoviev and Kamenev began to agitate against the insurrection, and we began to look upon them as strikebreakers. I even sent a letter to the Central Committee with a proposal to expel them from the party.

I expressed myself sharply in the press when Kamenev made his speech in the All-Russian Central Executive Committee of the Soviets.* I should not like [now, after the victory] to assume a severe attitude toward them. I take a favorable attitude toward Kamenev's negotiations in the Central Executive Committee with a view to conciliation because we are not opposed to it in principle.†

However, when the Social Revolutionists declined to participate in the Government, it was clear to me that they did so after Kerensky rose up in [armed] opposition. Some delay occurred in Moscow (*i.e.*, the seizure of power in Moscow). Our [Rights] became pessimistic. Moscow, if you please, is incapable of taking power, and so on. And so they raised the question of conciliation.

The insurrection poses new tasks. Other forces, other qualities are required. In Moscow, for instance, there were

---

* On August 4 (17), 1917, Kamenev made a speech at a session of the All-Russian Central Executive Committee of the Soviets on the subject of his arrest. On August 6 (19), he also spoke on the subject of the Stockholm International Socialist Conference, which the Conciliationists proposed to convene in the summer of 1917 for the purpose of expediting the conclusion of peace by the Socialist parties exerting pressure upon their respective Governments.

On August 6 (19), Kamenev spoke in his own name in favor of participating in the Conference despite the decision of the Central Committee of the party not to participate in the Stockholm Conference.—L.T.

† Neither Lenin nor I objected at the outset to the negotiations for a coalition with the Mensheviks and the Social Revolutionists on the condition that the Bolsheviks were assured of a stable majority, and that these parties were to recognize the Soviet state, the land decrees, the peace decree, and so on. We were convinced that nothing would come of the negotiations. But an objective lesson was needed.—L.T.

many cases of cruelty on the part of the Junkers, shootings of captive soldiers, etc. The Junkers, sons of the bourgeoisie, understood that with the advent of the people's rule, the rule of the bourgeoisie came to an end, for even at the Conference we outlined a number of such measures as the seizure of the banks, and so on. The Bolsheviks, on the contrary, were often much too soft. Now if the bourgeoisie had triumphed, it would have acted as it did in 1848 and 1871. Who was there that believed that we would not meet with sabotage on the part of the bourgeoisie? This was clear even to an infant. We, too, must apply force. We must arrest bank directors and others. Even brief arrests of these people have already yielded very good results.

This hardly surprises me, for I know how little capable they are of doing any fighting themselves. The most important thing in their eyes is to safeguard their cozy posts. In Paris, they [the revolutionists] used the guillotine while we will only take away the food cards of those who fail to obtain them from the trade unions. Thereby we fulfill our duty. And now, at such a moment, when we are in power, we are faced with a split. Zinoviev and Kamenev say that we will not seize power [in the entire country]. I am in no mood to listen to this calmly. I view this as treason. What do they want? Do they want to plunge us into [spontaneous] knifeplay? Only the proletariat is able to lead the country. . . .

As for conciliation, I cannot even speak about that seriously. Trotsky long ago said that unification is impossible. Trotsky understood this, and from that time on there has been no better Bolshevik.

Zinoviev says that we are not the Soviet power. We are, if you please, only the Bolsheviks, left alone since the departure of the Social Revolutionists and the Mensheviks, and so forth and so on. But we are not responsible for that. We have been elected by the Congress of the Soviets. This organization is something new. Whoever wants to struggle enters into it. It does not comprise the people, it comprises the vanguard whom the masses follow. We go with the masses—the active and not the weary masses. To refrain now from extending the insurrection [is to capitulate] to the weary masses, but we are with the vanguard. The Soviets take shape [in struggle]. The Soviets are the vanguard of the proletarian masses. And now we are being invited to wed the City Duma—how absurd!

We are told that we want to "introduce" socialism—how absurd! We do not intend to institute peasant socialism. We are told that we must "halt." But that is impossible. Some even say that we are not the Soviet power. Then who are we? We are certainly not those who intend to unite with the Duma. We shall have next the proposal to coalesce with the *Rumcherod*[41] and the *Vikzhel.*[42] This is horse-trading. Perhaps we should also unite with General Kaledin? First conciliate with the Conciliators and then they will put a spoke in the wheels. That would be miserable horse-trading and not a Soviet power. That is precisely how we must pose the question at the Conference. 99% of the workers follow us.

If you want a split, go ahead. If you get the majority, take power in the Central Executive Committee and carry on. But we will go to the sailors.

We are in power. Who is capable of deserting now to the *Novaya Zhizn*?[43] [Only] spineless, unprincipled people who are today with us and tomorrow with the Mensheviks. They say that we will be unable to maintain power alone, and so on. But we are not alone. The whole of Europe is before us. We must make the beginning. Only a socialist revolution is possible now. All these vacillations and doubts [conciliations] are a piece of nonsense. When I spoke [at a mass meeting] and said let us fight [the saboteurs] with food cards, the faces of the soldiers lit up. [The Rights] declare that the soldiers are incapable of fighting. But we get reports from speakers [who address the masses] that they have never before seen such enthusiasm. Only we can create a plan of revolutionary work. Only we are capable of waging a struggle. As for the Mensheviks, they will not follow us. At the coming Conference we must put the question of the future course of the socialist revolution. We are confronted with Kaledin, we have not yet conquered [finally]. When we are told [by the *Vikzhel* and the saboteurs and others] that "there is no [central] power," then we must put them under arrest, and we'll do it. Then they can talk all they please about the horrors of the dictatorship of the proletariat. Now, if we were to place the members of the *Vikzhel* under arrest—I could understand that. Let them howl about the arrests. The delegates from Tver* said at the Congress of the Soviets, "Arrest them all"—here is something I can understand. Here you have a man who understands the dictatorship of the proletariat. Our present slogan is: No compromise, *i.e.*, for a homogeneous Bolshevik Government.

LUNACHARSKY: I should like to share with you my impressions of the masses who have done the fighting. I was very much astonished to hear Vladimir Ilyich say in his speech that Kamenev supposedly fails to recognize the revolution as a socialist revolution. But who holds power now? The Bolsheviks. That fact alone speaks for itself. I am unaware that Kamenev holds a Menshevik point of view. Our influence is growing. The peasants are coming

---

* The peasant delegate from Tver demanded at the Congress of the Soviets on October 25 (November 7) the arrest of Avksentiev and other conciliationist leaders of the then Peasant Alliance.—L.T.

over to our side. . . . The city worker, too, is beginning to understand that the question of land is not a matter of indifference to him. We have adopted the S.R. resolution as the basis for the land decree. We have introduced it into the program of our activities, we can likewise introduce it in appointing the government.* We [the Right Wing Opposition] insist that a homogeneous socialist government is necessary. We say: Not a single place to the Constitutional-Democrats [the Cadets].[44]

We have, furthermore, pointed out the necessity of workers' control, the necessity of regulating production by the factory and shop committees. The other parties are agreed on this. We will compel everybody to accept this point. This plus the Soviet power exhausts our program. Does this imply that we reject City Dumas? Why, it is our own people who are seated in them. If these Dumas attempt to seize [power], we will crush them. But does it mean that we aim to give the Dumas a little slice of power? No. [We mean to give them] simply representation [in the Soviet Government]. Is it really possible that we would continue the civil war over this issue? No, we can't do it. Having re-elections for the Dumas—that is another matter. Here we are already eight days in power, but we still do not know whether the peace decree has been made known to the people. . . . Who is responsible for it? The technical personnel which is bourgeois or petty bourgeois. They sabotage us. If the City Duma were to demand a change in the main political line—that would be another matter. But if they demand only representation

* Lunacharsky develops the following idea in his argument: Since the Bolsheviks have included in their land decree a peasant measure permeated with the SR spirit, therefore, the Bolsheviks must also share the state power with the Social Revolutionists.—L.T.

in the government, then there is no need even to discuss it. We cannot manage with our own forces. Famine will break out. If we do not have with us those who are sabotaging, *i.e.*, the technical apparatus, then even our agitation will not be read abroad, and we will not be able to manage anything. Of course, we can resort to terror—but why? Where is the need for it?

We will strive for conciliation. But should they try to hold our hands, we are sufficiently resolute people to give them the proper answer. . . . At the present moment we must above all take possession of the entire apparatus. This implies acting along the line of least resistance, and not taking each post by a bayonet charge. Otherwise we won't achieve anything. That is the first stage. We must conquer the first rung on the ladder in order to climb the next one. It is impermissible to make leaps, we must proceed gradually by stages.* We must consolidate our position as quickly as possible. We must put the entire state apparatus in order, and then proceed. Whoever pulls a string too tightly will end by breaking it. It will burst. The party representative in the Navy Committee said just now that the majority of the sailors are in such a mood that they are ready to go to Smolny[45] and announce that they refuse to wage a civil war over the question whether the Bolsheviks should have more power or less. This emergency situation cannot long continue. To prolong it is to bleed to death, without the support of the technical apparatus.

I was amazed to hear Vladimir Ilyich's remark about

* We have here, from the lips of Lunacharsky, the formula which provides the *leitmotif* for the entire activity of Stalin. In defending for Germany (in 1923) the self-same policy of conciliationism and temporization that Lunacharsky defended in 1917, Stalin kept invariably repeating: "It is impermissible to make leaps, we must proceed gradually step by step."—L.T.

negotiating with General Kaledin,* because, you know, the latter represents a real force, whereas the Mensheviks represent a mythical one. But this mythical force is capable of moving troops from the front and of provoking battle near Vinnitsa, and of preventing the Latvian riflemen from arriving here. We are automatically prevented from achieving anything on the position we have assumed. We have become very fond of war, as if we were not a workers' party but a party of the soldiery, a party of war. It is necessary to create, but we are doing nothing. We continue to polemicize in the party, and we'll keep on polemicizing, until only one man remains—a dictator.†

We cannot possibly handle the situation by means of arrests. It is impossible to attack the technical apparatus, it is too big. The people are reasoning as follows: Our program must be fulfilled, provided the arms remain in the hands of the workers. We can get a breathing spell on this basis. But we cannot set to work now, because there is no apparatus. Such a condition cannot long continue. We must show that we are capable of constructive work, instead of saying only: "Keep on fighting! Keep on fighting!" To clear our path with bayonets—that will get

* Lenin, as is evident from the context, said that if we are to enter into negotiations in order to liquidate the civil war, then we ought to negotiate with Kaledin and not with the Mensheviks. The official editors of the *Istpart,* as their explanatory remarks show, completely missed the meaning of this purely Leninist argument.—L.T.

† These words were greeted by applause (there is further reference to this in Trotsky's speech). The fact is that during the negotiations for a coalition government composed of all Soviet parties, the Conciliationists put forward the demand to "conclude" the civil war, and, in order to attain this, to eliminate Lenin and Trotsky from the government. Sometimes, Lenin alone was mentioned. The Rights were willing to accept this.—L.T.

us nowhere. It is much easier to compel people who are working badly to do their work better, than to coerce a man to work by force. In the face of all these difficulties I consider conciliation desirable. None of your arguments relating to the Mensheviks will convince the masses. I am firmly convinced that it is impermissible to work as we are now working. It is impermissible from the standpoint of principle, and, moreover, it is impermissible to risk innumerable lives.

Do not sow dissension. There is enough dissension as it is, and the masses are becoming very restive.

TROTSKY: We are told that we are incapable of building up. In that case we should simply surrender power to those who were correct in struggling against us. But we have already performed a great labor. We are told that we cannot sit on bayonets. But neither can we manage without bayonets. We need bayonets *there* in order to be able to sit *here*. One should imagine that the experience we have already gone through has taught us something. There has been a battle in Moscow. Yes, there was a serious battle with the Junkers[46] there. But these Junkers owe allegiance neither to the Mensheviks nor the *Vikzhel*. Conciliation with the *Vikzhel* will not do away with the conflict with the Junker detachments of the bourgeoisie. No. A cruel class struggle will continue to be waged against us in the future as well. When all these middle-class lice, who are now incapable of taking either side, discover that our Government is a strong one, they will come to our side, together with the *Vikzhel*. Owing to the fact that we crushed the cossacks of [General] Krasnov beneath Petersburg, we were showered on the very next day with telegrams of congratulation. The petty bourgeois masses are seeking that force to which they must submit themselves. Whoever fails to understand this, cannot have the slightest comprehension of anything in the universe and, least of all, in the state apparatus. Back in 1871, Karl Marx said that a new class cannot simply make use of the old apparatus.[47] This apparatus engenders its own interests and habits which we must run up against. It must be smashed and replaced; only then will we be able to work.

If that were not so, if the old Czarist apparatus suited our new purposes, then the entire revolution would not be worth an empty eggshell. We must create such an apparatus as would actually place the common interests of the popular masses above the proper interests of the apparatus itself.

There are many in our midst who have cultivated a purely bookish attitude towards the question of the classes and of the class struggle. The moment they got a whiff of the revolutionary reality, they began to talk a different language (*i.e.*, of conciliation and not struggle).

We are now living through the most profound social crisis. At present the proletariat is effecting the demolition and the replacement of the state apparatus. The resistance on their part reflects the processes of our growth. No words can moderate their hatred of us. We are told that their program is presumably similar to ours. Give them a few seats and that will settle everything. But why do they give aid to Kaledin, if they have the same program as we? No. The bourgeoisie is aligned against us by virtue of all its class interests. And what will we achieve as against that by taking to the road of conciliation with the *Vikzhel*? . . . We are confronted with armed violence which can be overcome only by means of violence on our own part. Lunacharsky says that blood is flowing. What to do? Evidently we should never have begun. Then why don't you openly admit that the biggest mistake was committed not so much in October but towards the end of

February when we entered the arena of future civil war.

We are told that conciliation with the *Vikzhel* will help us against Kaledin. But why, then, do they fail to support us now if they are closer to us? Because they understand that however bad the counter-revolution may be for them, it will, nevertheless, give the tops of the *Vikzhel* more than the dictatorship of the proletariat. For the moment they are preserving a neutrality which is not friendly to us. They are letting through the shock troops and Krasnov's cossacks. The *Vikzhel* forbade me personally to communicate by direct wire with Moscow in order to report that we are progressing in our struggle against Krasnov. Because, if you please, this "might raise the morale there," and the members of the *Vikzhel,* mind you, are neutral.

To conciliate with them is to continue the policies of Gotz, Dan and the rest. We are told we have no calico and no petroleum, therefore we must have conciliation. But I ask for the thousand and first time: Just how will conciliation with Gotz and Dan give us petroleum?

Why are all the Chernovs against us? They protest because they are bourgeois through and through in their psychology. They are incapable of applying any serious measures against the bourgeoisie. They are against us precisely because we are putting into effect drastic measures against the bourgeoisie. Nobody can tell now what harsh measures we may yet be compelled to apply. The sum total of what the Chernovs can contribute to our work is: vacillation. But vacillation in the struggle against our enemies will destroy our authority among the masses.

What does conciliation with Chernov mean? It does not mean that we have a heart-to-heart talk with him and the matter ends there. No. It means an alignment with Chernov. This would be treason. For that we should all deserve to be shot immediately.

It grieved me to hear in this assembly the applause that greeted [Lunacharsky's] reference to the dictatorship of a single individual. Why and on what grounds do they seek to behead the party that has seized power in battle, in bloodshed, by demanding the removal of Lenin? Miliukov, for example, was driven from the Government—but when? When the proletariat placed its knee on the chest of the Cadets. But now? Who is holding his knee on our chest? Nobody. We have held power for eight days. We are basing our tactics upon the revolutionary vanguard of the masses. We are told by the champions of conciliationism that unless we conciliate the Baltic Fleet will not give us even a rowboat. Nothing of the sort happened. They tried to scare us by insisting that the workers would balk. Meanwhile, the Red Guards are facing death bravely. No. There is no returning to half-way policies, to conciliationism. We will put the dictatorship of the proletariat into effect. We will compel these people to work. How did it happen that society existed and the masses worked under the former terror of the minority? With us it is not the terror of a minority but the organization of the class violence against the bourgeoisie.

What are they scaring us with today? With the self-same thing that the Mensheviks and the Social Revolutionists sought to scare us yesterday. As soon as we undertake the socialist revolution [said they], we shall see that the Junkers take to shooting, that blood begins to flow, the bourgeoisie forges conspiracies, the functionary resorts to sabotage, the army committees resist. . . . Of course! But these are only the tops. Had we the bourgeoisie with us, there would be no civil war—nobody could gainsay that.

The army committees are hated by the masses of the soldiery but in many cases the masses are unable to undertake anything against them as yet. In a whole number of army divisions, however, Military Revolutionary Committees have already been elected and they have placed under arrest the officers, the old committees and the entire commanding staff. This has already been done in about one-fourth of the Army. To fraternize with the old army committees is to rouse the workers against us.

The prejudices of Lunacharsky are a heritage of the petty bourgeois psychology. Naturally, that is also, in part, inherent in the masses, being the heritage of their slavery of yesterday. But should the counter-revolution threaten, even the backward masses will take up arms. The nethermost rank and file are placed in such a position as will make them resort to arms. It is otherwise with the *Vikzhel,* the army committees, the Social Revolutionists, the Mensheviks and all other tops.

Lunacharsky says: We must halt—we must wait. . . . No. We must drive ahead. When you come out against us at the moment of sharp struggle, you weaken us. Conciliation with Chernov will provide nothing. What we need is organization and this we must attain. Chernov is in fear lest the people press too hard against the bourgeoisie, and take away from the bourgeoisie the money it has plundered. Chernov is an auxiliary lever in the hands of the bourgeoisie. He will merely weaken us by his petty bourgeois vacillations, nothing more.

We must tell the workers simply and intelligibly that we do not aim to build a coalition with the Mensheviks and the others but that the crux of the matter lies in a program of action. We already have a coalition. Our coalition is with the peasants—the soldiers who are now fighting for the Bolshevik power. The All-Russian Congress of Soviets transmitted power to a certain party. You seem to forget this.

Is it permissible to share power with those elements

who have heretofore even sabotaged the Soviets and who are today fighting from the outside against the proletarian state? All those who are ready to do so forget to ask themselves whether those with whom they are willing to share power are capable of carrying out our program. They do not even mention that. Are the Conciliationists capable of carrying out the policy of economic terror? No. If after taking power we are incapable of realizing our own program, then we ought to go to the soldiers and workers and declare ourselves bankrupt. But nothing whatever can come of merely leaving a few Bolsheviks in a coalition government. We have taken power; we must also bear the responsibilities.

[*Motion to limit speakers to 15 minutes.*]

NOGIN: The question as to the nature of our revolution has been settled. There is no need to talk about it now that our party has gained power. But can we propose to spill blood together but not rule jointly? Can we deny power to the soldiers? The civil war will last for many years. In our relations with the peasantry, we can't make much headway with bayonets. With respect to capitalist industry—we face one problem. With respect to the peasantry we must have a different tactic.

The word "conciliation" grates altogether too much upon the ears of our comrades. The crux of the matter is not in a conciliation but in the question how to manage if we push aside all the other parties? The Social Revolutionists left the Soviets after the revolution; the Mensheviks did likewise. But this means that the Soviets will fall apart. Such a state of affairs in the face of complete chaos in the country will end with the shipwreck of our party in a very brief interval. We should not bombard swallows with artillery. The famine conditions will provide fertile soil for Kaledin who is now advancing against us. By a single telegram to the railway employees informing them of our intention to deprive them of their food cards we would lay the basis for a mighty wave of protest.

GLEBOV: The situation is rendered serious not because the shock troops are advancing. Power is in our hands and we shall be able to deal with them. But we have the beginning of sabotage within our own party and matters have almost reached the point of an official split. An end must be put to this. Sabotage is effective only to the extent that we pursue a line of conciliation with it. So long as I was conciliatory, the functionaries mocked at me. But as soon as I took decisive measures, I was able to adjust a great many things. With regard to the Department of Posts and Telegraphs, the important thing is that it has passed a resolution in our favor. . . .

They must reckon with us. In Ivanovo-Voznesensk the proletariat has adopted a decisive resolution. They arrested and jailed the saboteurs and when the latter came out they were like lambs. To the comrades who have begun to waver, we must say: "We must part company. Stop interfering with us. Otherwise, if we vacillate, we shall lose everything."

We are told that the government will be responsible to the Parliament. What sort of Parliament *will* it be? Will it by any chance resemble the Pre-Parliament? No. We are for the Soviets. There is no other way. The crux of the matter is not in the seats that we must assign to other parties but in that they will not carry out our policy. Nothing else remains, except to say: "We must part company."

SLUTSKY: The question has been adequately clarified by Trotsky and Lenin. During the July days, from July 3 to July 5, when it seemed as though the counter-revolution had defeated us, we were in reality the victors. The days of the insurrection have proved that we have a coalition with the masses. The peasants and the workers stand shoulder to shoulder.

But the hammer of revolution, while consolidating the masses, has chipped away the Mensheviks, the Defensists, and the Social Revolutionists. We have seen how the Conciliationists worked against consolidation. Now, after we have conquered, an attempt is being made to lead us on the road of conciliationism. Conciliation with these people is a masked retreat from power. Hitherto the parties of conciliation with the bourgeoisie have stood at the helm of power but now we stand at the helm without conciliation. I regard as superfluous comrade Lunacharsky's remarks about there being no harm in giving the City Dumas fifty seats [in the All-Russian Central Executive Committee]. What does giving 50 seats imply? Surely we are not taking them in so as to furnish the premises. We stand for the Soviet power. I, too, should like to ask how petroleum will come pouring to us through faucets by the name of Kamkov? Just how will the doors of granaries open to us through the medium of the Social Revolutionists? In all this, there is an utter lack of principle. Why not give them 60 seats? Why not 25 or 35? The revolutionary masses will not follow this call.

BOKI: Several mentions have been made here of a Conference. This is too high-sounding a name for it. It will be hard to call a full session tomorrow. Let us call together here, tomorrow at 7 o'clock in the evening, a session of the Committee plus local representatives in the Petersburg Committee.

TROTSKY: We have had rather profound differences in our party prior to the insurrection, within the Central Committee as well as in the broad party circles. The same things were said; the same expressions were used then as now in arguing against the insurrection as hopeless. The old arguments are now being repeated after the victorious insurrection, this time in favor of a coalition. There will be no technical apparatus, mind you. You lay the colors on thick in order to frighten, in order to hinder the proletariat from utilizing its victory. It is true [that the apparatus is not ours]. We have had to waste so much time with Kerensky's miserable detachments because we lacked a technical apparatus. But under the given conditions we have already created a magnificent apparatus. At present we are victorious both here and in Moscow. Petrograd is now secure against any surprises of a military nature.

I repeat that we shall be able to draw the petty bourgeoisie behind us only by showing that we have in our hands a material fighting force. We can conquer the bourgeoisie only by overthrowing it. This is the law of the class struggle. This is the guarantee of our victory. Then and only then will the *Vikzhel* follow us. The same might be said about other technical branches. The apparatus will place itself at our service only when it sees that we are a force.

The October Revolution does not consist in setting the old apparatus in motion again. Our task is to rebuild the entire apparatus from top to bottom. For our proletarian tasks to become a living reality, we need our own apparatus, made up of the flesh and blood of our own class. We created such an apparatus of our own against Kerensky and against Krasnov beneath Petrograd. You keep repeating that we cannot sit on bayonets. But in order for us to carry on these discussions with you here it is indispensible to have bayonets at Tsarskoye Selo.

All government is based on force and not conciliation. Our government is the force exercised by the majority of the people against the minority. This is beyond dispute. This is the A.B.C. of Marxism. They prevented me from communication with Moscow by direct wire and then they let through the shock troops. They betray us in the most acute moments of the struggle. And it is proposed to us, now that we have conquered, that we admit them into the very stronghold of the government.

[*Motion: To limit the speakers to 10 minutes.*]

NOGIN: We, Bolsheviks, recognize that our revolution is not a bourgeois revolution. But we will conquer not alone but together with the peasants. It is for this reason that they must possess jointly what has been jointly gained by the blood of workers and soldiers. That is to say, power. Our party must be the most disciplined party in the world.

Session adjourned.

Stalin, Bukharin, and Ordjonikidze. Bukharin, formerly a “Left Communist” (pp. 54–55, 112, 371), joined with Stalin in promulgating the doctrine of “socialism in a single country.” He replaced Zinoviev as head of the Communist International in 1926 and was the Stalin regime’s most prominent ideologist of the right-wing course carried out from 1925 to 1928. The agricultural crisis of 1928 led to his downfall as Stalin initiated an ultraleft course in place of his former opportunist one. Bukharin was killed in the purges of 1938.

Ordjonikidze, a close associate of Stalin, chaired the party trial of Trotsky and Zinoviev. He was scored by Lenin for his action in the Georgian case (pp. 102-3).

Two speeches at the session of the Central Control Commission

The plan to remove Trotsky from the leadership was conceived back in the period of Lenin's first illness, namely in 1922. Throughout the following year, 1923, the preparatory work proceeded in full swing. Toward the end of the year the campaign was brought into the open. This work was under the guidance of the "triumvirate": Stalin, Zinoviev and Kamenev. In 1925, the triumvirate fell apart. Zinoviev and Kamenev found themselves caught in the wheels of the machine they had created against Trotsky. Henceforth the Stalinist faction set itself the task of completely transforming the leading staff by removing from posts all those who had directed the party and the Government under Lenin. At the joint plenary session of the Central Committee and the Central Control Commission,[48] in July 1926, Trotsky read a declaration which quite accurately foretold the future measures the Stalin faction would apply in order to substitute the Stalinist leadership for the Leninist. In the course of the next few years that program was carried through by the Stalinists in amazing conformity with the predictions made.

The most important step on that path was to place Trotsky on trial before the Praesidium of the Central Control Commission on charges of these two crimes: (1) making "factional" speeches at the Plenum of the E.C.C.I.; (2) participating in a farewell demonstration to Smilga, a member of the Central Committee, who, a short time previously, had been sent to the city of Khabarovsk in the Far East as punishment for being in the Opposition. Zinoviev was likewise charged with similar crimes. The proposed penalty was to remove both of them from the Central Committee.

We print below the two speeches by Trotsky at the Praesidium of the Central Control Commission which sat as the court of trial. The author has considerably condensed his two speeches wherever questions of minor importance were concerned. In other respects the speeches are reprinted as they were delivered except for minor corrections in style.

THE FIRST SPEECH

TROTSKY: Before proceeding with my speech—and I am in doubt whether I speak here as the defendant or the accuser—I must insist on the removal of comrade Janson from the judges' bench on the ground that he is disqualified by his entire previous activity. All of you are, of course, well aware of the fact that since 1924 there has existed a factional "septemvirate" composed of all the members of the Political Bureau, with the exception of myself. My own place was taken by your former chairman, Kuibyshev, who, as was his duty, should have been the foremost guardian of party statutes and morals but who was in fact their foremost violator and corruptor. This septemvirate constituted an illegal and anti-party institution which disposed of the fate of the party behind its back. Comrade Zinoviev in one of his speeches at the session of the Central Committee named Janson as one of those who had participated in the functioning of the anti-party septemvirate. Nobody has refuted this statement. Janson himself has kept mum. Although there are others equally guilty of the same crime, in Janson's case we have recorded testimony. At the present moment Janson is about to sit in judgment upon me for anti-party conduct. I demand the removal of Janson from the judges' bench.

CHAIRMAN ORDJONIKIDZE: That is impossible. You are doubtless joking, comrade Trotsky.

TROTSKY: It is not my custom to joke in important and serious questions. I realize that the Praesidium may possibly be placed in a somewhat awkward position by my proposal, because I am afraid that among the personnel of the Praesidium there may be others who likewise participated in the work of the septemvirate. But it was never my intention to turn my proposal into a joke. The fact is that I, a member of the Political Bureau, knew nothing of these meetings at the time, even if they did take place under the guise of "drafting notices." At these meetings were elaborated the ways and means of conducting the fight against me. In particular, it was there decided and made binding upon members of the Political Bureau not to polemicize against each other, but for all to polemicize against Trotsky. The party was not informed of it. Neither was I. This went on for a long time . . . I did not say that comrade Ordjonikidze was a member of the septemvirate, but that he participated in the work of this factional septemvirate.

ORDJONIKIDZE: It may have been Janson, but not Ordjonikidze. Aren't you making a mistake?

TROTSKY: I beg your pardon, although I do believe that the mistake is purely of a formal character. I did in fact refer to Janson. I did not say that comrade Janson was a member of the septemvirate itself. No, but he did participate in the work of this factional septemvirate, for which there is no provision made in the party statutes, and which functioned against the statutes and the will of the party—otherwise it would have had no reason for hiding. Should it prove that other comrades present here participated like Janson in the work of this factional septemvirate, then I humbly ask that my request for removal be extended to include them also.

[*The proposal to remove Janson from the judges' bench is instantly rejected by the Praesidium.*]

TROTSKY: The comrades wish to picture matters as if it is necessary to remove us from the Central Committee because of the incident at the Yaroslav railway station, because of Zinoviev's speech over the radio, and my "conduct" at the E.C.C.I.[49] All this might have seemed very plausible, but not in the light of our declaration which we, the Opposition, presented to the Central Committee as far back as *the beginning of last July.* In this declaration we forecast with complete clarity and in detail all the paths of your struggle against us. We predicted that you would seize upon the slightest pretext in order to achieve the program of reconstructing the party leadership, conceived by your factional tops long ago, even prior to the July Plenum, prior to the Fourteenth Party Congress.

You have brought me up on two charges. First—my speech at the E.C.C.I. I have maintained, and still maintain, that the Central Control Commission can in no case sit in judgment upon me for a speech I delivered at the Plenum of the E.C.C.I., which is a higher body. If this still remains incomprehensible to comrade Janson, he should ponder the matter and re-read the statutes of the Communist International and the statutes of our party. He would then understand that I am right, just as I would be absolutely right in denying a District Control Commission the right to sit in judgment upon me for any speech I may have made as a member of the Central Committee of the party.

The second charge—the farewell demonstration to Smilga at the Yaroslav railway station. You banished Smilga to Khabarovsk. Once again I make an urgent request that you at least agree among yourselves upon a uniform explanation for this exile. In the Commission, Shkyratov shouted: "There is work to be done in Khabarovsk, too!" If Smilga was sent, as a matter of normal procedure, to work in Khabarovsk, then you cannot dare claim that our collective farewell was a demonstration against the Central Committee. However, if this is an administrative exile of a comrade, who is at the present moment needed at responsible posts, that is, at fighting Soviet posts, then you are duping the party. You are guilty of duplicity. Are you going to repeat again that Smilga was sent to Khabarovsk as a normal assignment of work? And at the same time are you going to accuse us of demonstrating against the Central Committee? Such politics are double-dealing.

But I wish to pass from these calumnies presented as charges to the fundamental political question.

On the war danger. In the declaration which we presented last July, we said: "The paramount condition for the defense of the Soviet Union and, therefore, for the maintenance of peace is the indissoluble tie between the ever growing and ever more powerful Red Army and the toiling masses of our country and of the entire world. All economic, political and cultural measures which tend to raise the rôle of the *working class* in the state, which strengthen the ties of the *working class* with the *agricultural laborers* and the *poor peasants,* and its alliance with the *middle peasants*—thereby strengthen the Red Army, assure the inviolability of the land of the Soviets and reënforce the cause of peace."

Here is adequate proof that a year ago we called upon you to concentrate on the question of the war danger and the internal dangers in the U.S.S.R. during war-time. These are not special questions. They are questions of our class policy, of our entire course. When Kalinin, the formal head of the State, the Chairman of the All-Russian Central Executive Committee of the Soviets, delivers a speech in Tver to the effect that we need stalwart and strong soldiers, and that only a middle peasant can make a stalwart and strong soldier, and that the poor peasants cannot provide such soldiers because there are many puny ones among them, then we have here nothing else than an open orientation towards the strong "middle peasant," a label which serves to camouflage none other than the kulak, or a candidate for kulakdom. Kalinin forgets our having accomplished the October Revolution in which the puny and the thin conquered the tall and the strong. Why were they able to conquer? Because there existed and still exist many more of them than of the others. You will say, "The honorable Mikhail Ivanovich [Kalinin] is given to saying a lot of things!" But did you curb him? No, you did not, you curbed us instead when we criticized his line which deprecates the poor peasant and encourages the kulak—the self-same kulak whom Yakovlev is covering up with his statistical tricks. It is Yakovlev who should be up on trial, but instead Yakovlev is about to pass judgment on us.

The war danger is now being exploited by you in order to hound the Opposition and to prepare for its physical annihilation. Of all the labors of the E.C.C.I., where we discussed the question of the war danger, the question of the British labor movement and especially the question of the Chinese Revolution, you have issued for the information of the party only this little red pamphlet, which I hold in my hand, and which you have issued against the Opposition. Moreover, even in this case—how shall I say?—you pilfered my speech from the minutes on the pretext that I had not yet "corrected it." This means precisely that you are exploiting the war danger primarily against us.

We declare that we shall continue to criticize the Stalinist régime so long as you do not physically seal our lips. Until you clamp a gag on our mouths we shall continue to criticize this Stalinist régime which will otherwise undermine all the conquests of the October Revolution. Back in the reign of the Czar there were patriots who used to confound the fatherland with the ruling administration. We have nothing in common with them. We will continue to criticize the Stalinist régime as a worthless régime, a régime of back-sliding, an ideologically emasculated, narrow-minded and short-sighted régime.

For one year we tried to hammer into your heads the meaning of the Anglo-Russian Committee.[50] We told you that it was ruining the developing revolutionary movement of the English proletariat. In the meantime, all your authority, the entire accumulated experience of Bolshevism, the authority of Leninism—all this you threw on the scales in support of Purcell. You will say, "But we criticize him!" This is nothing else than a new form of support to opportunism by backsliding Bolsheviks. You "criticize" Purcell—ever more mildly, ever more rarely—and you remain tied to him. But what is he enabled to say in reply to revolutionists in his own country when they brand him as the agent of Chamberlain? He is able to say, "Now look here! Tomsky himself, a member of the Political Bureau and Chairman of the All-Russian Central Council of the Trade Unions who sent money to the English strikers, has made criticisms of me but nevertheless we are working hand in hand. How dare you call me the agent of imperialism?" Would he be right or wrong? He would be right. In a devious way you have placed the entire machinery of Bolshevism at the disposal of Purcell. That is what we accuse you of. This is a very grave accusation—far graver than bidding Smilga farewell at the Yaroslav station. What have you done to Bolshevism? What have you done in the space of a few years to all the authority of Bolshevism, all its experience, and the entire theory of Marx and Lenin? You have told the workers of the world, and above all our Moscow workers, that in the event of war the Anglo-Russian Committee would be the organizing center of the struggle against imperialism. But we have said and still say that in the event of war the Anglo-Russian Committee will be a ready-made trench for all the turn-coats of the breed of the false, half-way friends of the Soviet Union, and for all the deserters to the camp of the enemies of the Soviet Union. Thomas gives open support to Chamberlain. But Purcell supports Thomas, and that is the main thing. Thomas maintains himself upon the support of the capitalists. Purcell maintains himself by deceiving the masses and lends Thomas his support. And you are lending support to Purcell. You accuse us of giving support to Chamberlain. No! It is you yourselves who are linked up with Chamberlain through your Right wing. It is you who stand in a common front with Purcell who supports Thomas and, together with the latter, Chamberlain. That is the verdict of a political analysis and not a charge based on calumny.

The devil only knows what is already being said about the Opposition at meetings, particularly at meetings of workers' and peasants' nuclei. Questions are raised as to the "resources" used by the Opposition to carry on its "work." It may be that illiterate and unconscious workers, or your own plants, are sending up such questions as are worthy of the Black Hundred.[51] . . . And there are scoundrels acting as reporters who have the audacity to give evasive answers to such written questions. If you were really a Central Control Commission, you would be duty-bound to put an end to this dirty, abominable, contemptible and purely Stalinist campaign against the Opposition. We, on the other hand, are not preoccupied with spreading calumny. We present an open political declaration: Chamberlain and Thomas are in a common front; they are supported by Purcell, without whose support they are ciphers; but you are supporting Purcell and thereby weakening the U.S.S.R. and strengthening imperialism. This is an honest political declaration! And you yourselves are feeling the weight of it at this very moment.

If you were seriously mindful of the war danger, as you claim, how could there possibly have been the wild internal party repressions which are now becoming more and more unbridled? How can you at the present time discard first class military workers who are being removed from military activity because, although they are ready and able to fight for the Socialist fatherland, they consider the present policy of the Central Committee false and ruinous? Have you many such military workers as Smilga, Mrachkovsky, Lashevich and Bakayev? I have heard that it is your intention to remove Muralov from Military Inspection because he was a signatory to the Declaration of 83.[52] You are as one with Purcell and other "fighters against war" of the same stripe, but you want to remove

Muralov from Military Inspection. [*Commotion in the hall. Shouts: "Who gave you that report?"*] No one "reported" it to me, but there is widespread talk of it.

ORDJONIKIDZE: You anticipate too much.

TROTSKY: That was well put, indeed! I am stating 48 hours ahead of time what you will do a little later,* just as last July we presented you beforehand with the entire itinerary of your struggle against us. A new stage of development is now in order.

What about the students in the Military Academy and in the Academy of the Air Corps? You are expelling the best students for being in the Opposition. I have succeeded in obtaining brief biographies of the four students whom you expelled the other day on the eve of their graduation from the Military Academies. The first biography is that of Okhotnikov; the second—Kuzmichev; the third—Broidto; the fourth—Kapel. Here is the first: *Okhotnikov,* born in 1897; father and mother, peasants (from Bessarabia); they possessed no land of their own, but worked on that of the landlord. He received only an elementary education. Until 1915, worked for his father and hired out as a truckman. From 1915, served as a soldier in the Czarist army. During the February Revolution was in the city of Ekaterinoslav; elected delegate from the reserve artillery to the Soviet of Soldiers' Deputies, but was transferred in May to the 4th Army at the front because of Bolshevik tendencies, and was there a delegate from the 14th Artillery Brigade to the divisional and corps committee. During the

* Muralov, one of the most outstanding leaders of the Red Army, was shortly thereafter not only removed from Military Inspection but expelled from the party and exiled to Siberia where he is at present.—L.T.

Muralov was executed as a "Fascist agent" on February 1, 1937, following the conviction of the 17 defendants in the trial of Radek, Piatakov, *et al.,* in January 1937.—Ed.

October Revolution, having been wounded in battle, he was convalescing in a hospital. Upon leaving the hospital in December 1917, he organized, acting under the leadership of the Bolshevik party, a partisan detachment and fought against the Roumanian occupation troops. In 1918, he joined the underground organization in Bessarabia. Served as chairman of the underground Revolutionary Committee of Teletsk district, and as commander of the partisan detachment. For his activities he was tried twice by the Roumanian court martial and was sentenced to death, but escaped. In 1919, he came with the partisans to the Ukraine, where he joined the 45th Red Division. Served in various commanding posts. Throughout the war remained at the front, and at the conclusion of the war repeatedly took part in the struggle against the White bandits. In 1924, he entered the Military Academy and was assigned to a preparatory course in view of his not having had a general schooling. He graduated from the first course to the second *cum laude*. He was first brought up on charges in the party for Oppositionist views in February 1927. Expelled from the Academy for participating in the "farewell to Smilga."

Thus far I have in my possession four biographies which do not differ from each other in any fundamental respect. They are all soldiers of the revolution, soldiers of the party, wounded in battle, honored with certificates by the All-Russian Central Executive Committee of the Soviets, recipients of the medals of the Red Banner, tempered revolutionists who will remain faithful to *October,* who will fight to the end for *October*—but whom you are driving out of the Military Academies. Is that the way to prepare for the military defense of the revolution?

We are accused, as is well known, of *pessimism* and *lack of faith*. How did the accusation of "pessimism" originate?

This foolish and contemptible word was put in circulation, I believe, by Stalin. But a good deal more faith than most of you have in the international revolution is required to swim *against the current.* What is the origin of the accusation of lack of faith? It is the notorious theory of building socialism in one country. We refuse to believe in this theory of Stalin's.

ZINOVIEV: In 1925, Ordjonikidze told me that I must write against Stalin.

TROTSKY: We refused to believe in this revelation which tends to distort fundamentally Marx and Lenin. We did not believe in this revelation and therefore we are pessimists and men of little faith.

But do you know who was the precursor of Stalin, "the optimist"?

I have brought with me and, if you wish, will deliver into your hands an important document. It is an article written in 1879 by Vollmar, who later became famous as a German social-patriot. This article is entitled, "The Isolated Socialist State."[53] It ought to be translated and sent to all members of the Central Committee and the Central Control Commission and, indeed, to all members of the party.

The German social democrat Vollmar developed the theory of national socialism back in 1879, whereas his epigone Stalin set about creating his "original" theory only in 1924. Why in 1879? Because that was the time of reaction, the period of a widespread decline in the European labor movement. The French Commune was crushed in 1871. Up to 1879 there was no revolutionary movement in France. In England, liberal trade unionism and liberal-labor policies triumphed all along the line. This was the time of the most profound decline in the English and continental revolutionary movement. Meanwhile, in Germany, the social democracy was developing quite rapidly. In consequence of that contradiction, Vollmar arrived at his original theory of socialism in one country. And do you know how Vollmar ended? He ended by becoming an extreme Right wing Bavarian social democrat, a chauvinist. You will say that the situation today is different. Of course, the general situation today is different. But the proletariat in European countries has suffered major defeats during the last few years. Hopes are deferred today for an international revolution, for its *immediate victory* as was the hope in 1918–1919, and some of the "optimists" in the majority have lost this hope altogether and are therefore driving to a conclusion that we can get along without an international revolution. Precisely therein lies the prerequisite for the opportunistic back-sliding to the narrow nationalistic Vollmarism, beginning with his theory of socialism in one country.

You accuse us of pessimism and lack of faith both in connection with this theory and without any connection with it. We, the Opposition, are a "tiny clique" of pessimists and men of little faith. The party stands united and in it all are optimists and men of great faith. Isn't this much too simple a picture? Permit me to put the question in the following manner: Will a careerist, *i.e.*, a man seeking personal advancement, now join the Opposition? Certainly not, unless he is such a wily fellow as will join only to withdraw immediately in order to be at once enrolled among the "best representatives" of our party and our country. But these are, so to speak, supremely contemptible exceptions. If you were to take the average careerist, then, I ask, will such an individual seek his career through the Opposition under the present conditions? You yourselves know that he will not. Will a self-seeker join the Opposition under present conditions when worker-Bolsheviks are being driven, for Opposition activity, from factories and mills and into the ranks of the unemployed—all of whom will fight no worse when the need arises than all those now assembled here? The self-seeker will not join. The example of the worker-Oppositionists is proof that despite the repressions, there are still men left in the ranks of the party who have the courage to fight for their opinions. The prime quality of every revolutionist is the ability to dare swim against the current, the ability to struggle for his opinions even under the most adverse conditions. I ask once again: Will the man-about-town, the functionary and the self-seeker join the Opposition? No, they will not. Will the workers with large families, who have grown weary and have become disillusioned in the revolution and who remain in the party out of inertia, go into the Opposition? No, they will not. They will say: "The régime is, of course, bad, but let them do whatever they please, I am not the one to butt in." What are the qualities a man requires to join the Opposition under the present conditions? He must have a very firm faith in his cause, *i.e.*, the cause of the proletarian revolution—a genuine revolutionary faith. But you demand only faith in a protective coloration; the faith to vote as the authorities vote, to identify the Socialist fatherland with the district committee and to emulate the secretary. If you are a manager or an administrator, you must insure yourself through the district committee or through the secretary of the regional committee.

How is your great faith tested? Through 100% votes. Whoever does not wish to participate in such compulsory voting seeks on occasion to sneak out. But the secretary will not allow it—he must vote, and he must vote as per instructions, and the names of those who abstain are noted down. Do you think you can hide all this from the proletariat? What are you trifling with? I repeat: What are you trifling with? You are trifling ominously with yourselves, with the revolution and the party! The man who always votes 100% with you, the man who "smeared" yesterday Trotsky, today Zinoviev, and who will tomorrow "smear" Bukharin and Rykov, will never make a staunch soldier in the difficult hours of the revolution. But the Opposition gives proof of its loyalty and courage precisely because it does not surrender in the most difficult period of back-sliding and repression, but gathers around itself the most valuable fighting elements who can be neither bribed nor brow-beaten.

JANSON: There are careerists and self-seekers among the Oppositionists as well.

TROTSKY: Name them! You need only name them, and then we, together with you, will drive them out. Where are they? The main nucleus of the Opposition is composed of elements who can be neither bribed nor brow-beaten.

The party régime stifles, chokes and chains the party; and it camouflages the profound class processes taking place in the country, with which we are confronted at the very first rumors of the war danger and which will confront us still more sharply at the outbreak of the war.

The present régime effaces the vanguard of the proletariat because it allows no opportunity for stating openly and honestly whence the danger threatens—and the proletariat is threatened with danger from the side of the non-proletarian classes. The entire past period consists in this, that the proletariat is being politically shrivelled up while the other classes are unfolding.

Bound up with this is the question of the workers' state. One of the many scandalous lies that are being disseminated systematically through *Pravda* is the allegation that I said that our state is not a workers' state. This is done by employing a falsified interpretation of an uncorrected speech of mine in which I merely developed Lenin's attitude towards the Soviet state, counterposing it to the Molotov position. Lenin said that we had taken over many of the worst things from the Czarist apparatus. But what are you saying now? You are making a *fetish* of the workers' state, and are seeking to sanctify the given state as a special sort of state "by divine dispensation." And who is the most accomplished theoretician of such sanctification? It is Molotov. That is his contribution. I shall again read you what he said. You have suppressed my criticism of Molotov, while *Pravda* has distorted it. But here is what Molotov said against Kamenev at the Fourteenth Party Conference of the Moscow district: "Our state is a workers' state. . . . But we are being offered a formula according to which it would be more correct to say that the working class must be drawn still closer to our state. . . . What is this? We must set ourselves the task of drawing the workers closer to our state, but what is our state—whose is it? Is it not that of the workers themselves? Is it not the state of the proletariat? How is it possible then to draw closer to the state, *i.e.*, to draw the workers themselves closer to the working class which is in power and which is controlling the state?" (*Pravda,* Dec. 13, 1925.) These are Molotov's words. This, comrades, is the most dull-witted criticism of the Leninist concept of a *given* workers' state which can become genuinely and completely a workers' state only with the accomplishment of a colossal work of criticism, correction and improvement. But according to Molotov, the given state is something absolute which it is no longer possible to draw closer to the masses. It is to this bureaucratic fetishism that my refutation, or rather my exposition of the Leninist analysis of the Soviet state, applies. [*Shouts.*]

You say here, "What must be done?" If you really are of the opinion that there is nothing to be done against the phenomena I have indicated, then it means that you concede the revolution is bound to perish. Because, on the present path, it must perish. It means that you are the real pessimists, even if you are smug. Yet it is entirely possible to remedy the situation with a change of policy. But before we can decide *what to do,* we must say *what is;* we must specify the direction in which the processes are moving. If you were to consider such an acute problem as the housing question, you would discover that two processes are occurring here, reflected in statistics that you can easily verify: The proletariat is undergoing a shrinkage in living quarters while the other classes are expanding. I am not even referring to the village, where construction is proceeding apace. Of course it is not the poor peasants who are building, but the tops, the kulak and the strong middle peasant. But what have we in the cities? The so-called "*kustari*" [handicraft workers], *i.e.,* the petty bourgeoisie, the small business men, the traders and the specialists—all of them occupy this year more cubic feet per person. But there is less space per worker this year than last year. Before there is any talk of what to do, we must honestly state the facts. Just as in the housing question, so in every-day life, in literature, in the theatre and in politics—the non-proletarian classes are expanding, getting elbow room, while the proletariat is being squeezed and is shrinking. I repeat: Just as the bourgeois classes are expanding in the material sphere—you can observe this on the streets, in the stores, in the trolleys and in the apartments—just so in politics; the proletariat as a whole is being shrunk, while *our party régime strengthens this class shrinkage of the proletariat.* This is the fundamental fact. The blow threatens from the Right—from the side of the non-proletarian classes. Our criticism must be aimed to rouse the proletariat to take cognizance of the impending danger, and not to permit the proletariat to think that power has been conquered irrevocably and for all time, regardless of the conditions; and that the Soviet state is presumably an absolute which remains a workers' state always and under all conditions. It is important that the proletariat should understand that in a certain historical period, especially with a false policy of the leadership, the Soviet state may become an apparatus through which power may be shifted from the proletarian base and drawn to the bourgeoisie, which would subsequently discard completely the Soviet covering and transform its power into a Bonapartist rule. With a *false* political line such a danger is quite real.

Without an international revolution, socialism cannot be built. Without correct policies, calculated on the international revolution and not on supporting Purcell, you will not only fail to build socialism, but you will doom the Soviet power itself. It is urgent that the proletariat understand this. The fault of the Opposition, our crime, lies in the fact that we refuse to lull ourselves, and "optimistically" to shut our eyes to the dangers confronting our revolution.

The real danger is from the Right, not from the Right wing of our party—the Right wing of our party serves only as a transmitting mechanism—the real, basic danger comes from the side of the bourgeois classes who are raising their heads, whose ideologist is Ustrialov, that wise and far-seeing bourgeois to whom Lenin used to listen and against whom he warned. You all know that Ustrialov is not supporting us; he supports Stalin. In the autumn of 1926, Ustrialov wrote: "What we need now is a new manoeuvre, a new impulse, to put it figuratively, a *Neo-Nep*. From this standpoint, it must be recognized that a number of actual concessions recently made by the party to the Opposition cannot fail to inspire serious apprehension." Further: "All hail to the Political Bureau if the declaration of repentance on the part of the leaders of the Opposition is the result of their *one-sided* and *unconditional* capitulation. But woe to it, if it is the fruit of a compromise with them. If the latter is the case, the struggle must inevitably flare up again. . . . The victorious Central Executive Committee must acquire an inner immunity against the decomposing poison of the Opposition. It must draw all the necessary conclusions from the defeat of the Opposition. . . . Otherwise, it will be a calamity for our country. . . . It is thus [continues Ustrialov] that the cause must be approached by the Russian intelligentsia within the country, by the business elements and the specialist circles, the ideologists of evolution and not of revolution." Ustrialov draws the conclusion: *"That is why we are now . . . definitely in favor of Stalin."* And what is your reply to that? You seek to remove the Opposition from the Central Committee—for the time being only from the C.C. Ustrialov is a bourgeois who is acquainted with the history of the great French bourgeoisie, indeed, very well acquainted with it. And this spokesman for the moods of the new bourgeoisie understands that only the back-sliding of the Bolsheviks themselves can prepare the power for the new bourgeoisie least painfully. Supporting the Stalinist C.C., Ustrialov writes that it is necessary to safeguard (what?) against the decomposing poison of the Opposition. In consequence he also is in agreement with you that the Opposition is—a decomposing poison; that it is necessary to destroy this poison, otherwise "it will be a calamity for our country." That is what Ustrialov says. That is why he is not only against me, but also why he supports Stalin. Reflect on this. You are dealing here not with ignorant people, the unconscious or the duped who think that the Opposition carries on its activity with English money—no, Ustrialov is a very class-conscious man, he knows what he is saying and whither he is going. Why then does he support you? What is he defending together with you?

I was recently informed that comrade Soltz, in the course of a conversation with one of the comrades who had signed the declaration of the Opposition, drew an analogy with the French Revolution. Now I am of the opinion that this method is a correct one—I believe that a factual exposition and a Marxian interpretation of the Great French Revolution, especially of its last period, should be now reprinted for the benefit of the party. Comrade Soltz is present here, he knows better than I do what he said, and if I quote him erroneously, he will correct me. "What does the Declaration of 83 mean?" said Soltz. "What does it lead to? You know the history of the French Revolution,—and to what this led: to arrests and to the guillotine." Comrade Vorobiev, with whom comrade Soltz was talking, asked him, "So then, is it your intention to guillotine us?" To which Soltz replied by going into a lengthy explanation, "In your opinion, wasn't Robespierre sorry for Danton when sending him to the guillotine? And then Robespierre had to go himself. . . . Do you think he was not sorry? Sure he was, but he had to do it. . . ."

That was the substance of the conversation. I repeat that we must at this time at all costs refresh our knowledge of the Great French Revolution—it is absolutely indispensable. We might begin even with Kropotkin, who was not a Marxist but who understood better than Jaurès the national and class subsoil of the Revolution.

During the Great French Revolution, many were

guillotined. We, too, had many people brought before the firing squad. But in the Great French Revolution there were two great chapters, of which one went like this [*points upward*] and the other like that [*points downward*]. We must understand this. When the chapter headed like this—upwards—the French Jacobins, the Bolsheviks of that time, guillotined the Royalists and the Girondists. We, too, have had a similar great chapter when we, the Oppositionists, together with you, shot the White Guards and exiled the Girondists. And then there began another chapter in France, when the French Ustrialovs and semi-Ustrialovs—the Thermidorians and the Bonapartists from among the Right wing Jacobins—began exiling and shooting the Left Jacobins—the Bolsheviks of that time. I should like comrade Soltz to think his analogy through to the end and, first of all, to give himself an answer to the following question: In accordance with which chapter is Soltz preparing to have us shot? [*Commotion in the hall.*] This is no jesting matter; revolution is a serious business. None of us is scared by firing squads. We are all old revolutionists. But the thing is to know *whom to shoot, and in accordance with which chapter.* When we did the shooting we were firm in our knowledge as to the chapter. But, comrade Soltz, do you clearly understand in accordance with which chapter you are now preparing to shoot? I fear, comrade Soltz, that you are about to shoot us in accordance with the Ustrialov, *i.e.*, Thermidorian chapter.[54]

When the term "Thermidorian" is used among us, it is taken for a term of abuse. It is thought that the Thermidorians were arrant counter-revolutionists, conscious supporters of the monarchic rule, and so on. Nothing of the kind! The Thermidorians were Jacobins, with this difference, that they had moved to the Right. The Jacobin organization—the then Bolsheviks—under the pressure of class contradictions, shortly arrived at the conviction that it was necessary to destroy the Robespierre group. Do you think that on the very next day after the 9th of Thermidor they said to themselves: We have now transferred power into the hands of the bourgeoisie? Nothing of the kind! Refer to all the newspapers of that time. They said: We have destroyed a handful of people who disrupted peace in the party, but now, after their destruction, the revolution will triumph completely. If comrade Soltz has any doubts about it. . . .

SOLTZ: You are practically repeating my own words.

TROTSKY: So much the better. If we are agreed on this, comrade Soltz, then it will help us considerably to decide the question as to what chapter you are preparing to open by the physical annihilation of the Opposition. One thing must be firmly understood: Unless we undertake to rectify the class line of the party, as it should be done, the line indicated by Ustrialov will have to be pursued inevitably inside the party, *i.e.*, the line of a ruthless struggle against the Opposition.

I shall read you what was said by Brival, who was a Right Jacobin, one of the Thermidorians, when he reported about the session of the Convention during which Robespierre and the other Jacobins were handed over to the Revolutionary Tribunal: "Intriguers and counterrevolutionists covering themselves with the toga of patriotism sought the destruction of liberty; the Convention decreed to place them under arrest. These representatives were: Robespierre, Couthon, Saint-Just, Lebas and Robespierre the Younger. The chairman asked what my opinion was. I replied: Those who had always voted in accordance with the spirit of the principles of the Mountain both in the Legislative Assembly as well as in the Convention, those voted for the arrest. I did even more than that, for I am one of those who proposed this measure. Moreover, as secretary, I made haste to sign and to transmit this decree of the Convention." That is how the report was made by a Soltz or a Janson of that time. Robespierre and his associates—those were the counter-revolutionists. "Those who had always voted in accordance with the spirit of the principles of the Mountain" signified in the language of that time, "those who had always been Bolsheviks." Brival considered himself an old Bolshevik. "As secretary, I *made haste* to sign and to transmit this decree of the Convention." Today, too, there are secretaries who make haste "to sign and to transmit." Today, too, there are such secretaries. . . .

Listen further to the Manifesto of the Convention to France, to the country and to the people, after the annihilation of Robespierre, Saint-Just and the others: "Citizens, amid the brilliant victories over the foreign enemies, the Republic is threatened by a new danger. . . . The work of the Convention will prove barren, and the courage of our armies will lose all meaning, if the French citizens vacillate in their choice between the *Fatherland and a few isolated individuals*. . . . Obey the call of the Fatherland, do not join the ranks of the evil-minded aristocrats and the enemies of the people and you will once again save the Fatherland."

They reckoned that in the path of the triumph of the revolution stood the interests of "a few isolated individuals." They did not understand that these "isolated individuals" reflected the nethermost revolutionary elemental forces of that time. These "few individuals" reflected the elemental forces that were against the "Neo-Nep" and against Bonapartism. The Thermidorians thought that the issue involved a change of individuals and not a class shift. "Obey the call of the Fatherland, do not join the ranks of the evil-minded aristocrats." The friends of Robespierre—these were the "aristocrats." And did we not hear today the very same cry "Aristocrat!" from the lips of Janson addressed to me?

I could quote you any number of articles wherein the revolutionary Jacobins are referred to as the agents of the Chamberlain of that time, who was Pitt. The analogy is truly startling! In Chamberlain you have the modern pocket edition of Pitt. Take Aulard's history [of the French Revolution]. "The enemies were not content with killing Robespierre and his friends; they calumniated them, picturing them in the eyes of France as *Royalists and as men who had sold themselves to foreigners."* That is the literal wording of the passage. And today, does not *Pravda's* article entitled "The Path of the Opposition" swerve into a similar path? Whoever is familiar with the last leading article of *Pravda* cannot possibly miss the odor. The odor of the "second chapter" assails one's nostrils. The odor of this second chapter is Ustrialovism, which is already penetrating through the official institutions of our party, and which is disarming the revolutionary vanguard of the proletariat at a time when the party régime stifles everyone who struggles against Thermidor. In the party the mass worker has been stifled. The rank and file worker is silent.

You desire a new "purge" in the name of silence. Such is the party régime. Recall the history of the Jacobin clubs. They had two chapters of purges there. When the wave went like this [*upwards*], the moderates were ejected. When the line began to curve downwards, the revolutionary Jacobins began to be ejected. What did this do to the Jacobin clubs? An anonymous régime of terror was instituted, for silence was made compulsory, 100% votes and abstention from all criticism were demanded, thinking in accordance with orders from above was made obligatory, and men were compelled to unlearn to think that the party is a living, independent organism and not a self-sufficing machine of power. The then Central Control Commission—there were likewise institutions at that time which fulfilled your functions—together with the revolution as a whole, went through two chapters. In the second chapter it disaccustomed the members of the party from thinking, and compelled them to accept blindly everything from above. The Jacobin clubs, the crucibles of revolution, became the nurseries of future functionaries of Napoleon. We should learn from the French Revolution. But is it really necessary to repeat it? [*Shouts.*]

This was not said in factional jesting. No one would risk for the sake of trifles and trash such great things as are at stake between us. I do not know whether this is my last opportunity to express myself on these questions before this body. I do not know how quickly you will effect in the future the itinerary to which I referred in the beginning of my speech. But I sought to use the eighty minutes allotted to me not to refute the miserable petty charges you have presented against me but to pose the basic questions in dispute.

What to do in order to avoid a split? Is it possible to avoid one? If we were living under the conditions of the period prior to the imperialist war, prior to the revolution, under the condition of a comparatively slow accumulation of contradictions, I believe that a split would be far more likely than the preservation of unity. It would be criminal to have any illusions about the profundity of our differences. But we have a different situation now. Our differences have sharpened frightfully, the contradictions have become very great. During the most recent period, in the course of the Chinese Revolution, the differences have again increased in the extreme. But at the same time we have, in the first place, a gigantic revolutionary potential in the party, we possess gigantic ideological wealth of accumulated experience in the works of Lenin, in the program of the party, in the traditions of the party. You have squandered a great deal of this capital, you have substituted for a lot, the cheap surrogates of the "modern school" which prevails now in the party press. But a good deal of pure gold still remains. In the second place, we have the present historical period of abrupt turns, gigantic events, colossal lessons from which one can and must learn. There are stupendous facts, which provide the test for the two lines. But you must not dare hide these facts. Sooner or later they will become known anyway. You cannot hide the victories and defeats of the proletariat. It is possible to make it easier or more difficult for the party to familiarize itself with these lessons and to assimilate them. You make it more difficult. That is why it is we, and we alone, who are the optimists. We say that we are rectifying the policies of the party, without a split. We are fighting and will continue to fight for the line of the October Revolution. We are now so profoundly convinced of the correctness of our line that we have no doubt that this line will make its way into the consciousness of the proletarian majority of our party.

What then is the duty of the C.C.C. under these conditions? It seems to me that the duty of the C.C.C. under these conditions should be to create, for this sharp and critical period, a more healthy and flexible régime in the party so as to enable the gigantic events to provide the test for the antagonistic lines without any convulsions. It is necessary to secure for the party the possibility of ideological self-criticism on the basis of the great events. If this is done, I am certain that, in a year or two, the course of the party will be rectified. There is no need to rush, there is no necessity for adopting such decisions as cannot be later remedied. Beware lest you are compelled to say: We parted company with those whom we should have preserved, while preserving those from whom we should have parted.

THE SECOND SPEECH

TROTSKY: I am pleased to take note of comrade Ordjonikidze's declaration that in his opinion, as well as in mine, bureaucratism has grown during the past year. It is not a question of the mere number of functionaries. It is a question of the régime, of the course, of the attitude of the rulers towards the ruled. At a secret and select regional membership meeting where Yakovlev, the regional secretary, delivered a factional report against the Opposition, a working woman took the floor and said substantially the following: "I agree with everything that was said here. It is necessary to make short shrift of the Opposition, but the whole trouble is that when a man who happens to be dressed a little cleaner, comes to the Regional Committee, he is immediately directed where he needs go; but when a working woman comes, somewhat more drab and dirty, she has to wait a long time in the hall-way." That was said by a working woman, a member of the Regional Committee. Such voices are to be heard more and more often. They signify not only that the number of bureaucrats has increased, but also the fact that the ruling circles are becoming more and more fused with the upper layers of the Soviet-Nep society; and that two floors are being created, two forms of life, two kinds of habits, or, to use the more fully expressive words, *elements* are being created *of dual power in daily life* which upon further development may become transformed into political dual power. Now, political dual power would already constitute a direct threat to the dictatorship of the proletariat. An enormous layer of the urban party-Soviet personnel leads the lives of functionaries until 3 p.m. after three o'clock, they live like men-about-town, taking the attitude of liberals toward the Central Committee, while on Wednesdays, after six o'clock, they condemn the Opposition for being men of little faith. This type of party member bears a considerable resemblance to the Czarist functionary who used to profess privately the theory of Darwin, and who, when the need arose, presented credentials of holy communion.

Comrade Ordjonikidze has proposed to us that we aid him in the struggle against bureaucratism. Why then does he remove Oppositionists from their posts? I maintain that the overwhelming majority of Oppositionists are removed not for performing their work badly or for failing to work in keeping with the directives of the C.E.C., but as punishment for their convictions. They are removed as Oppositionists. They are removed as punishment for so-called "Trotskyism."

I should like to avail myself of at least a single opportunity to express myself briefly on the subject of Trotskyism, *i.e.*, the lie that has been passing under the guise of my political biography, especially from the lips and pen of Yaroslavsky, who is present here in the capacity of a judge, and others like himself. I have stated more than once, as is well known to all old party members, that on many most important questions I at one time fought against Lenin and the Bolshevik party, but I was not a Menshevik. If by Menshevism is understood a political class line—and that is the only way to understand it—then I was never a Menshevik. I broke organizationally and politically with what was to become Menshevism in the middle of 1904, *i.e.*, from the moment when it began to take shape as a political tendency. I broke on the question of the attitude towards the liberal bourgeoisie,[55] with the publication of Vera Zasulich's article, and the article by Axelrod in which he presented his plan of supporting the Zemstvo* liberals, etc. On the question of the rôle of the classes in the revolution I was never in agreement with Menshevism. And this was the fundamental question. All the Yaroslavskys are duping the party and the International not only with respect to the last ten years, but also with respect to the more distant past when I stood outside both of the main factions of the then social democracy.

In May 1905, the Bolshevik Congress adopted a resolution on the question of the armed insurrection and the Provisional Government. At the Congress comrade Krassin introduced a major amendment, which was, in reality, a separate resolution, which was referred to by Lenin at the Congress in the most laudatory manner.[56] This resolution presented by Krassin was written entirely by me in Petrograd—I have proof of this, namely, a note written by Krassin to me during one of the sessions. The most important resolution of the first Congress of the Bolshevik Party on the question of the armed insurrection and the Provisional Government, contained the central portion—consult the protocols!—that was written by me, and I am proud of it. Have any of my critics perhaps something similar to list among their assets?

In 1905, a whole number of proclamations issued in Baku in the underground Bolshevik printshop were written by me: the one to the peasants on the occasion of

---

* Provincial and county council elected by a limited franchise and having only economic and cultural functions.

January 9; another on the Czarist agrarian laws, and so on. In 1905, in November, *Novaya Zhizn,* under the editorship of Lenin, solidarized itself with my articles in *Nachalo*[57] on the nature of our revolution. And I was expounding in them the so-called theory of the permanent revolution.

ORDJONIKIDZE: Nevertheless you happened to be with *Nachalo* and not *Novaya Zhizn.* Isn't that so?

TROTSKY: But you have apparently forgotten that at that time the Bolshevik C.E.C. headed by Lenin unanimously adopted a resolution in favor of unity between the Bolsheviks and Mensheviks. Within a few weeks, *Nachalo* was merged with *Novaya Zhizn,* and the latter wrote in warm praise of my articles on more than one occasion. This was the period of the tendency toward unification. You hide the fact that I worked hand in hand with the Bolsheviks in the 1905 Soviet. You hide the fact that in 1906 Lenin published in *Novaya Volna* my pamphlet "Our Tactics" which defined our attitude toward the peasantry in the revolution. You hide the fact that at the London Congress in 1907, Lenin referred favorably to my attitude towards the bourgeoisie and the peasantry.[58] I maintain that my differences with Bolshevism were never greater than those of Rosa Luxemburg and Karl Liebknecht upon those questions on which they also differed from Bolshevism. Let anyone dare assert that they were Mensheviks!

I was not a Bolshevik at that time. But I was never guilty of such monstrous blunders as the preservation of the Anglo-Russian Committee, or the subordination of the Chinese Communist Party to the Kuomintang.

KRYVOV: What about the Vienna platform?

TROTSKY: Are you referring to the bloc[59] in August 1912?

KRYVOV: Yes.

TROTSKY: That was the fruit of conciliationism. I had not yet lost hope at the time of the possibility of uniting the Bolsheviks and the Mensheviks. But let not Ordjonikidze, Yaroslavsky and the others forget that they themselves participated in 1917—not in 1912, mind you, but in 1917—in joint organizations with the Mensheviks. The Vienna Conference was one of the attempts at conciliationism. It was not at all my intention to make a bloc with the Mensheviks against the Bolsheviks. I still had hopes of reconciling the Bolsheviks with the Mensheviks, and sought to unite them. In this as in all other instances, Lenin refused to have anything to do with such an artificial unification. As a result of conciliationist policies, I found myself formally in a bloc with the Mensheviks. But the struggle between us flared up instantly, almost on the very next day; and the outbreak of the war found us irreconcilable opponents. Incidentally, Stalin, throughout this period, was himself rather a vulgar conciliationist and, moreover, during the most acute moments. In 1911, Stalin wrote concerning the struggle between Lenin and Martov that it was "a tempest in a teapot." This was written by a member of the Bolshevik party. In March 1917, Stalin was in favor of unity with Tseretelli. In 1926, Stalin was in favor of a bloc with Purcell, Chiang Kai-shek and Wang Ching-wei. My mistakes are trifling indeed when compared with these mistakes. My activity from 1914 to 1917, *i.e.*, during the war, is being distorted ruthlessly, after the easy manner of that simon-pure social democrat Kuusinen, and especially by those gentlemen who were either patriots or followers of Kautsky at the time. Let me remind you that at the beginning of the war I wrote a pamphlet entitled *War and the International* concerning which Zinoviev—who was not and could not have been favorably disposed toward me—wrote that it posed the question correctly on all fundamental issues.

SHKLOVSKY: That was in 1914!

TROTSKY: Very true, that was in 1914. This pamphlet became a weapon in the hands of extreme Left wingers in Germany, Austria and Switzerland. I was a revolutionary internationalist, even though I was not a Bolshevik. In France, I collaborated with a group of comrades, socialists and syndicalists, who later joined the Communist International, and who were among its founders. I was deported from France as a revolutionary internationalist. I was deported from Spain as a revolutionary internationalist. In New York, I worked on the editorial board of *Novy Mir,* together with Volodarsky and Bukharin. In February and March 1917, I wrote articles in *Novy Mir* which were written in the same spirit as Lenin's Geneva articles, at a time when Stalin came out in *Pravda* as a semi-Menshevik and semi-defensist. In a Canadian concentration camp at Amherst, I organized the German sailors who were followers of Liebknecht, and who later fought on the side of the Spartacists.

ORDJONIKIDZE: You have four minutes left, comrade Trotsky.

TROTSKY: I have not yet touched on the answer to the fundamental question that you posed in reference to the "decline" of our revolution.

ORDJONIKIDZE: Why did you dwell so long on your biography?

TROTSKY: I think that an accused man has a right to speak of his biography, and it is not within the province of a chairman to restrict him on such occasions. At any rate, I was not the one who first brought up the question of my biography. Nothing was further from my mind. There are enough questions as it is. But it is precisely the Stalinist faction that has substituted the question of my biography for all political questions. And I reply to fictions with irrefutable facts. I appeal to the Praesidium to grant me 15 minutes in order to reply on the question of the destiny of our revolution.

ORDJONIKIDZE: You will speak the remaining four minutes, and then we shall take up the question of extending your time.

TROTSKY: Ordjonikidze upbraided me for drawing an analogy with the Great French Revolution. One must not talk, you see, of prisons, guillotines and the perspectives of decline, etc. It is a superstition that harm can come from words. Harm can come from facts, from actions, from false policy. I must say, however, that the question itself was not raised on my initiative at all. I made reference to Soltz's words. They motivated me to pose the question of the different stages of the revolution, its waves of rise and fall, either temporary or final.

Temporary or final—herein is the crux of the question, comrade Ordjonikidze. Before dwelling on this question, I must state that in all the nuclei preparations are being made at the present time to draw further and further conclusions—preparations for precisely that line which you, comrade Ordjonikidze, so lightly and bureaucratically dismiss, namely, the path of expulsions and repressions. Yes, I repeat, you do so lightly and bureaucratically, shutting your eyes to what is taking place in the party and above the party. In all nuclei, the reporters, especially rehearsed beforehand, pose the question of the Opposition in such a manner as makes some worker rise—most often on instructions—and say: "Why are you bothering with them? Is it not high time to shoot them?" Then the reporter, with a hypocritically mild mien, objects, "Comrades, there is no need to be hasty." This has already become a routine in the party. The question is always being posed behind the backs of the Oppositionists, with insinuations, with filthy implications, with rude, dishonest and purely Stalinist distortions of the Opposition's platform and of the revolutionary biographies of the Oppositionists, who are being pictured as the enemies of the revolution, as the enemies of the party—all this in order to arouse a wild reaction on the part of the duped audience, on the part of the raw young party members with whom you are artificially loading the party ranks; so that you will later have the opportunity to say, "Now look! We are ready to be patient, but the masses are insisting." This is the specific strategy of Stalin, you yourselves are to a greater or lesser degree the organizers of this campaign, and when the backwash engulfs you, you say, "The party demands it, and I can do nothing about it. . . ."

The second rebuke launched by comrade Ordjonikidze against me is a political rebuke of a more general nature. He says that my comparison with the Great French Revolution precisely expresses my "pessimism." Trotsky, you see, thinks the revolution has perished. If I thought the revolution had perished why should I struggle against you? On this issue you are never consistent. If I do not believe in the construction of socialism, as you assert, why should I propose to "plunder the peasant" as you likewise assert? Is it perhaps out of my personal hostility toward the peasant? If I do not believe in the revolution, why should I engage in a struggle? It would then be best to swim with the tide. Please, try to understand this! Whoever thinks that the revolution has already perished anyway, would not engage in a struggle. Comrades, you have once again failed to put two and two together.

The October Revolution has not perished. I never said it has. I do not believe it has. But I did say that it is *possible* to ruin the October Revolution, if one really undertakes to do so—and that you have already accomplished a few things to that end. Your entire thinking on this question, comrade Ordjonikidze, is not dialectical but formal. You ignore the question of the conflict of living forces, the question of the party. Your thinking is utterly permeated with fatalism. You differentiate between optimism and pessimism as if they were two immutable categories independent of conditions and politics. According to your way of thinking, one can be only either an "optimist" or a "pessimist," *i.e.*, either think that the revolution has completely perished or that it will not perish under any circumstances no matter what we did. The one and the other are false. Has not the revolution already passed through a number of ups and downs? Didn't we have a stupendous upswing in the period of the October overturn, and didn't we hang suspended by a hair in the period of the Brest-Litovsk peace? Recall to your minds what Lenin said during the struggle against the Left Communists—that it is extremely difficult to control the automobile of power in the epoch of revolution, because it is necessary to keep making sharp turns all the time. Brest-Litovsk was a retreat. The N.E.P., after the Kronstadt uprising, was a retreat. And did not each wave of retreat engender in its turn opportunist moods? It is clear as noonday that when these movements of retreat and of downward swings in the revolution are prolonged for a year, or two and three years, they engender a more profound drop in the moods of the masses and of the party as well. Comrade Ordjonikidze, you are a native Caucasian and you know that a road that leads up the mountain, does not go straight upward, but winds and zigzags, and often after a steep rise, it is necessary to descend two or three *versts** in order then to resume the upward march—but the road itself leads nevertheless up the mountain. While making a partial downward descent, I must keep aware that the

* A Russian measure, app. 2/3 of a mile.

road will turn and again mount upwards. But if I, for the sake of "optimism," altogether ignore these upward and downward zigzags, then my wagon will fly off into the abyss on one of the turns. I say that at the present time your road leads to the right and downwards. The danger lies in the fact that you do not see this, *i.e.*, that you shut your eyes to it. And it is dangerous to ride up the mountain with one's eyes shut.

In the autumn of 1923, we had a stupendous upsurge in the party, parallel with the lift in the German revolution. But after its defeat we, too, suffered an ebb-tide. Out of this ebb-tide grew the Stalinist theory of socialism in one country, a theory of decline, which is in radical contradiction with the fundamentals of Marxism. In 1926, during the Chinese Revolution, simultaneously with the improvement of our international situation, there was a powerful upward surge. Then followed an intensified ebb-tide—after the defeat of the Chinese Revolution. One must take the curve of the historical movement in all of its concreteness. From 1923 on, we have had a series of major defeats. Only a miserable coward would lose heart because of that. But he is blind, and a dullard and a bureaucrat, who cannot differentiate between the right foot and the left, between the upsurge of the revolution and its ebb. When I had a discussion with Brandler in January 1924, after the defeat, he said to me, "In the autumn of 1923, I was not in agreement with you because you were over-optimistic; now you are too pessimistic and I am again in disagreement with you." I replied, "Comrade Brandler, I fear that you will never make a revolutionist, because you cannot distinguish between the face of the revolution and its other extremity."

Comrade Ordjonikidze approaches the question of the victory or defeat of the revolution independently of any connection with the dialectic process, *i.e.*, independently of the mutual interaction between our policies and the objective conditions. He poses the question in the following manner: either the inevitable victory of the revolution or its inevitable defeat. Now, I say: If we proceed to make real and thorough mistakes, then we can doom the revolution. But if we apply all our forces to rectify a false line, then we shall triumph. But to assert that no matter what we may do—either in relation to the kulak, in relation to the Anglo-Russian Committee, or in relation to the Chinese Revolution—it can do no harm to the revolution; that the revolution must triumph "anyway"—is to reason in the manner that only indifferent bureaucrats are capable of doing. And so far as they are concerned, it is precisely they who are capable of ruining the revolution.

Wherein does our revolution differ from the French?

In the first place, with respect to the economic and class foundation of the respective epochs. In France, the leading rôle was played by the lower sections of the urban petty bourgeoisie. In our country—by the proletariat. It was owing to this alone that the bourgeois revolution could grow over into a socialist revolution in our country, and develop as such—with great obstacles and dangers remaining as yet. This is the first point of difference.

The second point of difference: France was surrounded by feudal countries—more backward in the economic and cultural sense than France herself. We, on the other hand, are surrounded by capitalist countries more advanced than we are with respect to technology and industry, and with a more powerful and cultured proletariat. We may expect revolutions in these countries in a comparatively near future. In consequence, the international position of our revolution, despite the fact that imperialism is mortally hostile to us, is in a wide historical sense far more favorable to us than was the case in France toward the end of the 18th century.

Finally, the third point of difference. We live in the epoch of imperialism, in the epoch of the greatest international and internal upheavals—and this creates the great rising revolutionary curve upon which our policies are based. But it is impermissible to think that this "curve" will carry us through under *any and all* conditions. This is false! He understands nothing who believes that we can build socialism even in the event capitalism is able to crush the proletariat for several decades to come. This is not optimism but the stupidity of national-reformism. We can be victorious only as an integral section of the world revolution. We must hold on until the world revolution, even if the latter is deferred for a number of years. In this respect, the trend of our policy is of decisive importance. By means of a correct revolutionary course, we shall intrench ourselves for a number of years, we shall intrench the Communist International, move ahead along the socialist path and achieve our being taken in tow by the great historical tugboat of the international revolution.

Our present party course is the main danger. It stifles the revolutionary power of resistance. What does your course consist of? You put your stake on the strong peasant and not on the agricultural laborer and the poor peasant. You steer toward the bureaucrat and the functionary and not the masses. You place far too much faith in the apparatus. In the apparatus you have tremendous internal support for each other, and mutual insurance for yourselves—that is why Ordjonikidze is unable to succeed even in reducing the staffs. Independence from the masses creates the system of mutual concealment and shielding. And all this is considered as the main prop of power. In the party, reliance is now placed on the secretary and not on the rank and file member. You rely now on Purcell and not on the rank and file proletarian. You rely not on the revolutionary miner but on Purcell who has betrayed the miners. In China, you steer a course toward Chiang Kai-shek and Wang Ching-wei and not toward the Shanghai proletarian, not the coolie who drags cannon on his shoulder, and not the insurgent peasant.

You have placed on the order of the day the question of expelling us from the Central Committee. Assuredly, each one of us will carry out his work regardless of his position, as a rank and file party member. But this will not solve the question; you will have to draw further conclusions. Life itself will compel you to make these conclusions. You had better pause instead and change your course.

The war danger—the defense policy and the Opposition

Speech at the Joint Plenary Session of the Central Committee and the Central Control Commission (August 1, 1927)

The Praesidium of the Central Control Commission which met in June 1927 to take up the question of the expulsion of Trotsky and Zinoviev from the Central Executive Committee of the party failed to arrive at any decision. The question had not yet been given sufficient "preparation." The principal art of Stalinist strategy consists in cautiously apportioning the doses in which blows are dealt to the party. Throughout June and July a tireless hounding of the Opposition ensued. The question of the expulsion of Oppositionists from the highest bodies of the party was carried before the joint plenary session of the Central Committee and the Central Control Commission which convened at the end of July and the beginning of August. At this Plenum, the question of the war danger was deliberately interlaced with the question of the Opposition so as to envenom to the highest possible degree the subsequent struggle against the latter. However, even the joint Plenum was unable to decide upon the expulsion of

Trotsky and Zinoviev from the Central Committee. The Stalin faction had to gain a few more weeks in order to develop its agitation against the Opposition as the "ally" of Chamberlain.

We print below the speech delivered by the author of this book on August 1, 1927, on the subject of the war danger and the defense policy.

TROTSKY: You have allotted me 45 minutes. I will summarize as concisely as possible in view of the very wide scope of the subject under consideration. Your theses assert that the Opposition allegedly holds some sort of Trotskyist formulation on the questions of war and defeatism. New fictions! Paragraph 13 of your theses is entirely devoted to this twaddle. So far as the Opposition as a whole is concerned, it can in no way be held accountable for my former differences with Lenin, differences which, upon these questions, were altogether secondary in character. So far as I am personally concerned, I can make here a brief reply to the silly insinuations. Back in the time of the imperialist war, the appeals to the international proletariat—all of them dealing with war and the struggle against war—were written by me in the name of the first Council of People's Commissars and in the name of the Central Committee of the party. I wrote the war section of our party program, the main resolution of the Eighth Party Congress and the resolution of a number of Soviet Congresses, the manifesto of the First World Congress of the Comintern, a considerable portion of which is devoted to war, and the programmatic manifesto of the Second World Congress of the Comintern which devotes considerable space to the evaluation of war, its consequences and future perspectives. I wrote the theses of the Third

World Congress of the Comintern on the question of the international situation and the perspectives of war and revolution. At the Fourth World Congress I was assigned by the CC of the party to give the report on the perspectives of the international revolution and war. At the Fifth World Congress (1924) I wrote the manifesto on the occasion of the tenth anniversary of the imperialist war. There were no disputes whatever in the Central Committee over these documents, and they were adopted not only without any controversy, but virtually without any corrections. I ask: How is it that my "deviation" failed to manifest itself throughout my entire long and rather intensive activity in the Communist International?

Now it suddenly appears, after my rejection of "economic defeatism" in 1926—an absurd and illiterate slogan advanced by Molotov for the English workers—that I had presumably parted company with Leninism. Why then did Molotov hide his silly slogan in his back-pocket after my criticism of it?

MOLOTOV: There was no slogan at all.

TROTSKY: That's what I say. There was nonsense, but no slogan. That's just what I say. [*Laughter.*] Why then was it deemed necessary to exaggerate rudely old differences which, moreover, were liquidated long ago? For what purpose? For the purpose of covering up and camouflaging the actual palpable and current differences. Is it possible to pose seriously the question of a revolutionary struggle against war and of the genuine defense of the U.S.S.R. while at the same time orienting toward the Anglo-Russian Committee? Is it possible to orient the working-class masses toward a general strike and an armed insurrection in the course of a war while simultaneously orienting towards a bloc with Purcell, Hicks and other traitors? I ask: *Will our defensism be Bolshevik or trade unionist?* That is the crux of the question!

Let me first of all remind you of what the present leadership has taught the Moscow proletariat during the whole of the last year. Everything centers round this point. I read you the verbatim directives of the Moscow Committee: "The Anglo-Russian Committee can, must and undoubtedly will play a tremendous rôle in the struggle against all types of intervention directed at the U.S.S.R. It [the Anglo-Russian Committee!] will become the organizing center for the international forces of the proletariat in the struggle against all attempts of the international bourgeoisie to start a new war."

Molotov has made here the remark that "through the Anglo-Russian Committee we disintegrated Amsterdam." It is as clear as noon-day that even now he has grasped nothing. We disintegrated the Moscow workers together with the workers of the entire world, deceiving them as to where their enemies were, and where their friends.

SKRYPNIK: What a tone!

TROTSKY: The tone is suited to the seriousness of the question. You consolidated Amsterdam, and you weakened yourselves. The General Council is now more unanimously against us than ever before.

It must be said, however, that the scandalous directive I just read expresses much more fully, clearly and honestly the actual standpoint of those who favored the preservation of the Anglo-Russian Committee than does the scholastic hocus-pocus of Bukharin. The Moscow Committee taught the Moscow workers and the Political Bureau taught the workers of the entire Soviet Union that in the event of a war danger our working class would be able to seize hold of the rope of the Anglo-Russian Committee. That is how the question stood politically. But this rope proved rotten. Saturday's issue of *Pravda,* in a leading article, speaks of the "united front of traitors" in the General Council. Even Arthur Cook, Tomsky's own beloved Benjamin, keeps silent. "An utterly incomprehensible silence!" cries *Pravda*. That is your eternal refrain: "This is utterly incomprehensible!" First you staked everything on the group of Chiang Kai-shek; I mean to say Purcell and Hicks, and then you pinned your hopes on "loyal" Wang Ching-wei, that is, Arthur Cook. But Cook betrayed even as Wang Ching-wei betrayed two days after he had been enrolled by Bukharin among the loyal ones. You turned over the Minority Movement[60] bound hand and foot to the gentlemen of the General Council. And in the Minority Movement itself you likewise refuse to counterpose and are incapable of counterposing genuine revolutionists to the oily reformists. You rejected a small but sturdier rope for a bigger and an utterly rotten one. In passing across a narrow and unreliable bridge, a small but reliable prop may prove one's salvation. But woe to him who clutches at a rotten prop that crumbles at a touch—for, in that case, a plunge into the abyss is inevitable. Your present policy is a policy of rotten props on an international scale. You successively clutched at Chiang Kai-shek, Feng Yu-hsiang, Tang Cheng-chih, Wang Ching-wei, Purcell, Hicks and Cook. Each of these ropes broke at the moment when it was most sorely needed. Thereupon, first you said, as does the leading article in *Pravda* in reference to Cook, "This is utterly incomprehensible!" in order to add on the very next day, "We always foresaw this."

What about China?

Let us take the entire tactical, or rather strategical line in China as a whole. The Kuomintang is the party of the liberal bourgeoisie in the period of revolution—the liberal bourgeoisie which draws behind it, deceives and betrays the workers and peasants.

The Communist party, in accordance with your directives, remains throughout all the betrayals within the Kuomintang and submits to its bourgeois discipline.

The Kuomintang as a whole enters into the Comintern and does not submit to its discipline, but merely utilizes the name and the authority of the Comintern to dupe the Chinese workers and peasants.

The Kuomintang serves as a shield for the landlord-generals who hold in their grip the soldier-peasants.

Moscow—at the end of last October—demands that the agrarian revolution be kept from developing so as not to scare away the landlords in command of the armies. The armies become mutual insurance societies for the landlords, large and small alike.

The landlords do not raise any objection to their military expeditions being called national revolutionary, so long as the power and the land remain in their hands. The proletariat, which composes a young revolutionary force in no wise inferior to our own proletariat in 1905, is driven under the command of the Kuomintang.

Moscow offers counsel to the Chinese liberals: "Issue a law for the organization of a *minimum* of workers' detachments." This, in March 1927! Why the counsel to the tops—Arm yourselves to the minimum? and why not a slogan to the rank and file—Arm yourselves to the maximum? Why the minimum and not the maximum? In order not to "scare away" the bourgeoisie, so as not to "provoke" a civil war. But the civil war came inevitably, and proved far more cruel, catching the workers unarmed and drowning them in blood.

Moscow came out against the building of Soviets in the "army's rear"—as if the revolution is the rump of an army!—in order not to disorganize the rear of the very same generals who two days later crushed the workers and peasants in their rear.

Did we reënforce the bourgeoisie and the landlords by compelling the communists to submit to the Kuomintang and by covering the Kuomintang with the authority of the Comintern? Yes, we did.

Did we weaken the peasantry by retarding the development of the agrarian revolution and of the Soviets? Yes, we did.

Did we weaken the workers with the slogan of "minimum arming"—nay, not the slogan but the polite counsel to the bourgeois tops: "Minimum arming," and "No need for Soviets"? Yes, we did. Is it to be wondered at that we suffered a defeat, having done everything that could have made victory difficult?

Voroshilov gave the most correct, conscientious and candid explanation for this entire policy. "The peasant revolution," he says, "might have interfered with the Northern Expedition of the generals." You put a brake on the revolution for the sake of a military expedition. That is exactly how Chiang Kai-shek viewed the matter. The development of the revolution might, you see, make an expedition difficult for a "national" general. But, after all, the revolution itself is indeed an actual and a real expedition of the oppressed against the oppressors. To help the expedition of the generals, you put a brake on the revolution and disorganized it. Thereby the expedition of the generals was turned into a spearhead not only against the workers and the peasants but also—precisely because of that—against the national revolution.

Had we duly secured the complete independence of the Communist party, assisted it to arm itself with its press and with correct tactics; had we given it the slogans "Maximum arming of the workers!" "Extend the peasant war in the villages!" the Communist party would have grown, not from day to day, but from hour to hour, and its cadres would have been tempered in the fires of revolutionary struggle. The slogan of Soviets should have been raised from the very first days of the mass movement. Everywhere, wherever the slightest possibility existed, steps for the actual realization of Soviets should have been taken. Soldiers should have been drawn into the Soviets. The agrarian revolution would have disorganized the pseudo-revolutionary armies but it would have likewise transmitted the infection to the counter-revolutionary armies of the enemy. Only on this foundation could it have been possible to forge gradually a real revolutionary, *i.e.*, workers' and peasants' army.

Comrades! We have heard here a speech made not by Voroshilov, the People's Commissar for Army and Navy, but by Voroshilov, a member of the Political Bureau. This speech, I say, is in itself a catastrophe. It is equivalent to a lost battle.

[*Shouts from the Opposition benches: "Correct!"*]

TROTSKY: Last May, during the Plenum of the E.C.C.I., when after finally assigning Chiang Kai-shek to the camp of reaction, you put your stakes on Wang Ching-wei, and then on Tang Cheng-chih, I wrote a letter to the E.C.C.I. It was on May 28. "The shipwreck of this policy is absolutely inevitable." What did I propose? Here is literally what I wrote. On May 28, I wrote: "The Plenum would do the right thing if it buried Bukharin's resolution, and replaced it with a resolution of a few lines. In the first place, peasants and workers should place no faith in the leaders of the Left Kuomintang but they should, instead, build their Soviets jointly with the soldiers. In the second place, the Soviets should arm the workers and the advanced peasants. In the third place, the Communist party must assure its complete independence, create a daily press, and assume the leadership of creating the Soviets. Fourth, the land must be immediately taken away from the landlords. Fifth, the reactionary bureaucracy must be immediately dismissed. Sixth, perfidious generals and counter-revolutionists generally must be summarily dealt with. And finally, the general course must be towards the establishment of a revolutionary dictatorship through the Soviets of Workers' and Peasants' Deputies." Now, compare this with: "There is no need for a civil war in the villages," "Do not alarm the fellow travellers," "Do not irritate the generals," "Minimum arming of the workers," and so on. This is Bolshevism! While our position is called in the Political Bureau . . . Menshevism. Having turned yourselves inside out, you have firmly resolved to call white, black. But your misfortune is that international Menshevism—from Berlin to New York—approves of the Chinese policy of Stalin-Bukharin, and being fully cognizant of the issue, solidarizes with your political line on the Chinese question.

Please try to understand that in question here is not the individual betrayals of the Chinese members of the Kuomintang, or of the Right and Left Chinese army commanders, or English trade unionists, and Chinese or English communists. When one rides in the train, it is the earth that appears to be in motion. The whole trouble lies in the fact that you placed hopes on those who were not to be relied upon; you underestimated the revolutionary training of the masses, the principal requirement for which is inoculating the masses with mistrust towards reformists, vague "Left" Centrists, and all vacillators in general. The fullest measure of this mistrust is the supreme virtue of Bolshevism. Young parties have still to acquire and assimilate this quality. Yet, you have acted and are acting in a diametrically opposite direction. You inoculate young parties with the hopes that the liberal bourgeoisie and the liberal labor politicians from the trade unions will move to the Left. You hinder the education of the English and Chinese Bolsheviks. That is the source whence come these "betrayals" which each time catch you unaware.

On 'centrism,' and the policy of rotten ropes

The Opposition warned that the Chinese Communist Party under your leadership would inevitably come to Menshevist policies—for which the Opposition was at the time mercilessly condemned. It is with certainty that we now warn you that the British Communist Party, under the influence of the policies that you are foisting on it, is becoming inevitably poisoned by Centrism and conciliationism. If you do not turn the helm sharply, the consequences with respect to the British Communist Party will not be any better than those with respect to the Chinese party. The same thing applies to the Comintern as a whole.

It is high time to understand that the Centrism of Bukharin-Stalin is unable to withstand the test of events. The greatest events in the history of mankind are revolution and war. We have put the Centrist policy to the test on the Chinese Revolution. The revolution demanded decisive conclusions from vacillating directives. The Chinese Communist Party found itself compelled to draw these conclusions. That is why it has arrived—and it could not have failed to do so—at Menshevism. The unprecedented collapse of your leadership in China demands that you finally repudiate the policy which compelled you under the most difficult conditions to clutch at rotten ropes.

Next to the revolution the greatest historical test is war. We say beforehand: There will be no room during the events of war for the Stalinist and Bukharinist policy of zigzags, side-stepping and subterfuges—the policy of Centrism. This applies to the entire leadership of the Comintern. Today, the only test put to the leaders of the foreign communist parties is the question: Are you ready to vote night and day against "Trotskyism"? But war will confront them with far weightier demands. Meanwhile, the policy with respect to the Kuomintang and the Anglo-Russian Committee has obviously made them turn their eyes towards the Amsterdam and social-democratic tops. No matter how you squirm—the line of the Anglo-Russian Committee was the line of relying upon the rotten rope of the Amsterdam bureaucracy, whose worst section at the present time is the General Council. In the event of war you will have to stumble time and again over "surprises." The rotten ropes will fall apart in your hands. War will cause a sharp differentiation among the present tops of the Comintern. A certain section will go over to the Amsterdam position under the slogan: "We want to defend the U.S.S.R. seriously—we do not wish to be a handful of fanatics." Another section of the European communists—we firmly believe they will be in the majority—will stand on the position of Lenin, on the position of Liebknecht that we are defending. There will be no room for the intermediate position of Stalin. That is why, permit me to say this frankly, all this talk of a handful of Oppositionists, of generals without an army, and so forth and so on, seem utterly ludicrous to us. The Bolsheviks have heard all this more than once—both in 1914 and in 1917. We foresee tomorrow all too clearly, and we are preparing for it. Never before did the heart of the Opposition beat with such an immutable conviction of its correctness. Never before was there such unanimity as now prevails.

ZINOVIEV AND KAMENEV: Absolutely correct!*

TROTSKY: Nor will there be any room for the gradual Centrist back-sliding with respect to *internal policies* under the conditions of war. All the controversies will congeal, the class contradictions will become aggravated, the issues will be posed point-blank. It will be necessary to give clear and precise answers.

Which do we need during war-time: *"Revolutionary unity"* or *"Union sacrée"*? The bourgeoisie has devised for the period of war and war danger a special political condition under the name of "civil peace" or *"Union sacrée."* The meaning of this purely bourgeois concept is this, that the differences and squabbles of all bourgeois parties, including the social democracy, as well as internal disagreements within all parties must, you see, be silenced for the duration of the war—in the aim of the best possible befuddlement and deception of the masses. *"Union sacrée"* is the highest form of the conspiracy of the rulers against the ruled. Needless to say, if our party has nothing to hide in the political sense from the working class during peacetime, then this is all the more true during war-time when the purity and clarity of the political line, the profundity of the ties with the masses are life-and-death questions. That is why, under the incomparably greater centralization of our party, as compared with any bourgeois party, we permitted ourselves in the heat of the civil war to discuss in the sharpest possible way and to resolve in a democratic party way, all the fundamental questions of political leadership. This was the inevitable overhead expense by means of which the party worked out and reënforced a correct line, and fortified its revolutionary unity. There are—or rather it would be more correct to say, only

* Zinoviev and Kamenev, as is well known, did not hold out for long.—L.T.

yesterday we still had—comrades who thought that after the death of Lenin, the absolute correctness of the leadership among us was assured to such an extent that it no longer required to be checked upon by the party. We, on the other hand, think just the contrary: Today the leadership requires a check-up and a change more than ever before in the entire history of our party. What we need is not a hypocritical *"Union sacrée"* but honest revolutionary unity.

The shilly-shallying Centrist policy cannot hold its own during wartime. It must turn either to the Right or to the Left, *i.e.*, take either the Thermidorian road or the road of the Opposition. [*Commotion in the hall.*]

Is victory in war possible on a Thermidorian path? Generally speaking, such a victory is not excluded. As the first step, repeal the monopoly of foreign trade. Give the kulak the opportunity of doubling the export and the import. Enable the kulak to squeeze the middle peasant. Compel the poor peasant to understand that without the kulak there is no other road. Raise and reënforce the importance of the bureaucracy, of the administration. Cast aside the demands of the workers as so much "guildism." Restrict the workers politically in the Soviets, reëstablish last year's election decree and gradually extend it in favor of the property owners. That would be the road of Thermidor. Its name is—*capitalism on the installment plan.* Then at the head of the army would stand the lower commanding staff of kulaks, and the high commanding staff of intellectuals and bourgeoisie. On this road victory would signify the acceleration of the switch to the bourgeois rails.

Is victory possible on the revolutionary proletarian path? Yes, it is possible. Nor is that all. The entire world situation bespeaks the fact that victory is most assured in the event of war precisely on this path. But for that, we must first dispel the political twilight in which all cats appear to be gray. The kulak on the Right—is an enemy. The agricultural laborers and poor peasants on the Left—are friends. Through the poor peasant lies the road to the middle peasant. We must create a political environment which makes it impossible for the bourgeoisie and the bureaucracy to give free play to their elbows and to push the workers aside, while saying, "This is not the year 1918, my boy!" It is necessary that the working class itself be able to say: "In 1927, we are not only better fed, but politically we are greater masters of the state than in 1919." Along this road, victory is not only possible, but is most surely secured, for only on this road will we have the support of the lower classes among the people of Poland, Roumania and the whole of Europe. . . .

Can the Stalinist Centrist course give victory? The course which vacillates between both camps, which promises first to comfort the kulak, to adopt his son and to cherish his grandson, and then irresolutely passes to the creation of the groups of poor peasants; which alters the electoral decrees from year to year, *i.e.*, the Soviet constitution, first to the side of the kulak, and then against him, and then once again in his favor as was done in Northern Caucasus; which orients itself toward Chiang Kai-shek and Wang Ching-wei, Purcell and Cook, the perfidious tops, while confusing the rank and file—can this course give victory? This course has dictated to our Political Bureau the unbelievable decree of October 29, 1926, in relation to China which made it prohibitory to introduce the civil war into the Chinese village, which made it binding not to drive away the fellow travellers or the bourgeoisie, the landlords and the generals; or that other directive with the appeal to the liberal bourgeoisie to give the workers a minimum (!!!) of arms. This course irritates or dampens the ardor of some while it fails to win over the others; it loses the "friend" Wang Ching-wei and confuses the Communists. This course signifies constant clutching at rotten ropes. During peace-time such a course might persist for an indefinite period of time. Under the conditions of war and revolution, Centrism must turn the helm sharply either to the Right or to the Left. It is already splitting into a Right and a Left wing, both of which are incessantly growing at the expense of the center. This process will be inevitably speeded up; and the war, if it is thrust upon us, will invest the process with a feverish character. The Stalinist Center will inevitably melt away. Under these conditions the Opposition will be needed by the party more than ever before, in order to aid the party in rectifying the line, and at the same time preventing the disruption of revolutionary unity, and preserving the party cadres, its basic capital, from being dismembered. Because the overwhelming majority of the genuinely Bolshevik proletarian cadres—with a correct policy, with a clear line, and under the compulsion of objective conditions—will be able to reconstitute the policies, and steer a firm revolutionary course, not out of fear, but from conviction. It is this, and this alone, that we are striving to achieve. The lie of conditional defensism, the lie of the two parties, and the most despicable lie of an uprising—these lies we fling back into the faces of the calumniators.

[*A voice from the Opposition benches: "Hear! Hear!"*]

TROTSKY: But does not the criticism of the Opposition reflect upon the authority of the U.S.S.R. in the international labor movement?

We would never think of even posing such a question. This very posing of the question of authority is worthy of the papal church, or feudal generals. The Catholic Church demands an unquestioning recognition of its authority on the part of the faithful. The revolutionist gives his support, while criticizing, and the more undeniable is his right to criticize, all the greater is his devotion in struggling for the creation and strengthening of that in which he is a direct participant. The criticism of the Stalinist mistakes may, of course, lower the "indisputable" and puffed-up Stalinist authority. But that is not the mainstay of the revolution and of the republic. Open criticism and actual correction of mistakes will give evidence to the entire international proletariat of the inner strength of the régime, which under the most adverse conditions is able to find internal guarantees for the assurance of the correct road. In this sense, the criticism of the Opposition, and the consequences already arising from it, and which will arise to a greater degree on the morrow, in the last analysis, raises the authority of the October Revolution and strengthens it not with a blind but with a revolutionary trust of the international proletariat—and thereby raises our capacity for defense on an international scale.

The draft resolution of the Political Bureau says: "The preparation for war against the U.S.S.R. signifies nothing else but the reproduction on an extended base of the class struggle between the imperialist bourgeoisie and the victorious proletariat."

Is that correct? Absolutely correct. But the resolution goes on to add: "Everyone who, like the Opposition in our party, casts doubt on this character of the war, . . . etc." Does the Opposition cast doubt on this general class significance of the war? Nonsense! It does not. There is not even a hint of it. Only those can assert the contrary who have themselves become completely lost in a maze, and seek to entangle others. Does this mean, however, that the general class meaning, undeniable to all of us, should serve as a cover for any and every blunder, and backsliding?

No, it does not mean this. It provides no such cover. If we take for granted *a priori* and forevermore that the given leadership is the only conceivable and born leadership, then every criticism of the incorrect leadership will appear as a denial of the defense of the socialist fatherland, and a call to an uprising. But such a position is a pure and simple denial of the party. According to you, in the event of war, the party will serve only for the purpose of defense. But how the defense should be carried out, will be told the party by somebody else. Or again, to put it more succinctly and plainly: Do we, the Opposition, cast any doubts on the defense of the socialist fatherland? Not in the slightest degree. It is our hope not only to participate in the defense, but to be able to teach others a few things. Do we cast doubts on Stalin's ability to sketch a correct line for the defense of the socialist fatherland? We do so and, indeed, to the highest possible degree.

In his recent article in *Pravda,* Stalin poses the following question: "Is the Opposition really opposed to the victory of the U.S.S.R. in the coming battles with imperialism?" Allow me to repeat this: "Is the Opposition really opposed to the victory of the U.S.S.R. in the coming battles with imperialism?" We leave aside the brazen impudence of the question. We do not intend to dwell now on Lenin's carefully weighed characterization of Stalinist methods—of Stalin's rudeness and disloyalty. We will take the question as it has been posed, and give an answer to it. Only White Guards can be "opposed to the victory of the U.S.S.R. in the impending battles with imperialism." The Opposition is *for* the victory of the U.S.S.R.; it has proved this and will continue to prove this in action, in a manner inferior to none. But Stalin is not concerned with that. Stalin has essentially a different question in mind, which he does not dare express, namely, "Does the Opposition really think that the leadership of Stalin is incapable of assuring victory to the U.S.S.R.?" Yes, we think so.

ZINOVIEV: Correct!

TROTSKY: The Opposition thinks that the leadership of Stalin makes victory more difficult.

MOLOTOV: And what about the party?

TROTSKY: The party has been strangled by you. The Opposition thinks that the leadership of Stalin makes the victory more difficult. The Opposition insisted on that with regard to the Chinese Revolution. Its warnings have been confirmed by events, to a frightful extent. It is necessary to effect a change in policy without waiting for a similar catastrophic test from within. Every Oppositionist, if he is a genuine Oppositionist and not a fraud, will assume in the event of war whatever post, at the front or behind the lines, that the party will intrust to him, and carry out his duty to the end. But not a single Oppositionist will renounce his right and his duty, on the eve of war, or during the war, to fight for the correction of the party's course—as has always been the case in our party—because therein lies the most important condition for victory. To sum up. For the socialist fatherland? Yes! For the Stalinist course? No!

A contribution to the political biography of Stalin

Eight post-Leninist years of struggle, eight years of struggle against Trotsky, eight years of the régime of the epigones—first the *"troika"* [triumvirate], then the *"semerka"* [septemvirate] and, finally, "the one and only"—this entire highly important period of the *downward sweep* of the revolution, its ebbings on an international scale, and the decline in revolutionary theory, have brought us to a most crucial point. In the bureaucratic triumph of Stalin a great historical zone is summarized and, at the same time, the impending inevitability of the defeat of the bureaucracy is signalized. The attainment by the bureaucracy of its culmination is the harbinger of its crisis, which may prove far more rapid than was its growth and rise. The régime of national-socialism, together with its hero, is subject to the blows, not only of inner contradictions, but also of the international movement. The world crisis will impart to the latter a number of new impulsions. The proletarian vanguard will be unable, and will refuse to suffocate, in the vise of a Molotov leadership. The personal responsibility of Stalin is committed beyond evasion. Doubt and alarm have crept into the hearts of even those who are best schooled. But Stalin cannot give more than he has. The downfall in store for him may prove all the more precipitate, the more artificial the nature of his rise.

In the following pages, we aim to provide certain materials for Stalin's political biography. Our materials are very incomplete. We have selected the most essential data from among our archives. But our archives still lack many essential and, it may be, most important materials and documents. From among the archives of the police department, which for decades intercepted and copied the letters of revolutionists, documents, etc., Stalin has been assiduously gathering during the past years those materials which would enable him, on the one hand, to keep a tight rein on his insufficiently reliable friends and to cast a shadow on his opponents, while, first and foremost, securing himself and his associates against the publication of any one of the excerpts or episodes which are injurious to the false "monolithism" of the artificially manufactured biographies. We do not possess these documents. In evaluating the materials published below, the reader should bear in mind the extreme incompleteness of our information.

1. On December 23, 1925, the closest friends of Stalin published in the party newspaper *Zarya Vostoka* the following police report, dating back to 1903:

> "According to the recent information received by me from our agents, Djugashvili [Stalin] was known in the organization under the nicknames *Soso* and *Koba;* since 1902, he has been active in the social democratic party organization first as a Menshevik, and then as a

> Bolshevik, as the propagandist and leader of the first [railway] region."

No refutations of this police report on Stalin made public by his partisans have appeared anywhere, so far as we know. It appears from the report that Stalin began his activities as a *Menshevik*.

2. In 1905, Stalin was a member of the Bolsheviks and took an active part in the struggle. What were his views and actions in 1905? What were his views as to the character of the revolution and its perspectives? To our knowledge, there are no documents in circulation on this score. No articles, speeches or resolutions by Stalin have been reprinted. Why? Evidently because a republication of Stalin's articles or letters for that period could only damage his political biography. There is no other explanation for the stubborn oblivion that enshrouds the past of the "leader."

3. In 1907, Stalin took part in the "expropriation" of the Tiflis bank. The Mensheviks, in the wake of bourgeois philistines, have expressed no little indignation at the "conspiratorial" methods of Bolshevism, and its "anarcho-Blanquism." We can have only one attitude toward this indignation, namely, *contempt*. His participation in a bold, even if a partial, blow dealt to the enemy can only do honor to the revolutionary resoluteness of Stalin. One can only be astonished, however, as to why this fact has been deleted in a cowardly manner from all the official biographies of Stalin? Was it done, perhaps, in the name of bureaucratic respectability? We venture to think not. The reasons are most probably political. For, while participation in an expropriation cannot in itself in any way compromise a revolutionist in the eyes of revolutionists, a false political evaluation of the then existing situation does compromise Stalin as a politician. Partial blows to the institutions

of the enemy, including "treasuries," are compatible only with a mass offensive, *i.e.,* the upsurge of the revolution. With the masses in retreat, partial, isolated and partisan blows inevitably degenerate into adventures and lead to the demoralization of the party. In 1907, the revolution was receding, and the expropriations degenerated into adventures. In any case, Stalin gave proof even in that period that he was incapable of distinguishing the ebb-tide from the flood-tide. He was to reveal this incapacity to orient himself politically on a broad scale more than once in the future (Esthonia, Bulgaria, Canton, the "Third Period").

4. From the time of the first revolution, Stalin led the life of a professional revolutionist. Jail, exiles, escapes. But for the entire period of reaction (1907–1911) we do not find a single document containing Stalin's formulation of his own estimate of the situation and its perspectives. It is impossible for them not to have been preserved, even if only in the archives of the police department. Why have they not appeared in print? The reason is as clear as noonday: They are of such nature as renders it impossible to strengthen the silly characterization of theoretical and political infallibility that the apparatus is creating for Stalin, *i.e.,* for itself.

5. Only a single letter pertaining to that period has appeared through an oversight in the press—and it wholly confirms our hypothesis.

On January 24, 1911, Stalin wrote from exile to his friends, and this letter, that had been intercepted by the police department, was reprinted on December 23, 1925, by the selfsame editorial board of *Zarya Vostoka,* none too rational in its zeal. Here is what Stalin wrote:

> "We have of course heard from abroad of the 'tempest in a teapot' there; the blocs between Lenin-Plekhanov,

> on the one hand, and between Trotsky-Martov-Bogdanov, on the other. The attitude of the workers towards the first bloc is, so far as I know, favorable. But the workers are generally beginning to look with disdain on what's going on abroad: Let them climb the walls to their heart's content. So far as we ourselves are concerned, whoever holds dear the interest of the movement, will keep on working, the rest will take care of itself. This, in my opinion, is for the best."

This is not the place to dwell on how correctly Stalin had defined the composition of the blocs. That is not in question here. Lenin was waging a desperate struggle against the legalists, liquidators and opportunists, for the perspective of the second revolution. All the groupings abroad at that time were fundamentally determined by that struggle. But how did the Bolshevik, Stalin, evaluate these battles? Like the most inept empiricist: "A tempest in a teapot; let them climb the walls; keep on working, the rest will take care of itself." Stalin welcomes the mood of indifference to theory and the presumed superiority of myopic "practicals" over revolutionary theorists. "This, in my opinion is for the best," he writes with reference to those moods which were characteristic of the period of reaction and decline. Thus, in the person of Stalin, the Bolshevik, we have not even political conciliationism—for, conciliationism was an *ideological* tendency, which attempted to create a *principled* platform—we have blind empiricism, verging on complete disregard of the principled problems of the revolution.

It is not difficult to imagine the lashing the hapless editors of *Zarya Vostoka* received for the publication of this letter; and the measures that were taken on an "All-Union scale" to prevent any further publication of such letters.

6. In his report at the Seventh Plenum of the E.C.C.I. (1926), Stalin characterized the party's past in the following manner:

> ". . . If we take the history of our party from the moment of its inception in the shape of the Bolshevik group in 1903, and if we follow its subsequent stages down to our own day, then we can say without exaggeration that the history of our party is the history of the conflict of the contradictions within the party. There is not, and there cannot be a 'middle' line in questions of a principled character. . . ."

These momentous words were directed against ideological "conciliationism" toward those against whom Stalin was waging his struggle. But these abstract formulae of ideological irreconcilability are in complete contradiction with the political physiognomy and the political past of Stalin himself. As an empiricist he was a congenital conciliationist, but precisely because he was an empiricist he gave no principled expression to his conciliationism.

7. In 1912, Stalin participated in *Zvezda,* the legal newspaper of the Bolsheviks. The Petersburg editorial board, in a direct struggle against Lenin, issued this paper at first as a conciliationist organ. Here is what Stalin wrote in a programmatic editorial article:

> ". . . It will be a source of satisfaction to us, if our newspaper succeeds, *without falling into the polemical infatuation of the different factions,* in defending ably the spiritual treasures of consistent democracy which are being impudently encroached upon both by the open enemies and the false friends." (*The Revolution and the CPSU—Materials and Documents,* Vol. V, pp. 161*f*.)

The phrase referring to the "polemical infatuation of the different [!] factions" is aimed entirely against Lenin, against Lenin's "tempest in a teapot," and his constant readiness to "climb the walls" due to some sort of "polemical infatuation."

Thus, Stalin's article is completely in harmony with the vulgar conciliationist tendency expressed in his above-quoted letter of 1911, and is in complete contradiction with his latter-day declaration as to the impermissibility of a middle line in questions of a principled character.

8. One of Stalin's official biographies reads: "In 1913, he was once again exiled to Turukhansk, where he remained until 1917." The Stalin jubilee issue of *Pravda* similarly stated that "Stalin spent 1913–1914–1915–1916 in exile in Turukhansk" (*Pravda,* Dec. 21, 1929). That is all! These were the years of the imperialist war, of Zimmerwald and Kienthal, of the collapse of the Second International, of the profoundest ideological struggle in the ranks of socialism. What part did Stalin take in this struggle? These four years of exile should have been the years of intense intellectual activity. The exiles, under such conditions, keep diaries, write treatises, elaborate theses, platforms, exchange polemical letters, etc. It is hardly conceivable that Stalin did not write anything during four years of exile on the basic problems of war, the International and the revolution. Yet one would seek in vain for any traces of Stalin's intellectual labors during those four amazing years. How could this have happened? It is all too obvious that had a single line been found in which Stalin had formulated the idea of defeatism or had proclaimed the need for a new International, this line would have long since been printed, photographed, translated into all languages, and endowed with learned commentaries by all the academies and institutes. But no such line was ever found. Does this mean

that Stalin wrote nothing at all? No, it means nothing of the sort. That would be utterly improbable. But it does mean that among everything he had written during the four years there is nothing, literally nothing, that could be utilized today to reënforce his reputation. Thus, the years of the war, when the ideas and slogans of the Russian Revolution and of the Third International were being hammered out, prove to be only a void in the ideological biography of Stalin. It is very likely that during this time he said and wrote: "Let them climb the walls there, and busy themselves with stirring up a tempest in a teapot."

9. Stalin arrived with Kamenev in Petrograd in the middle of March 1917. *Pravda,* under the editorship of Molotov and Shliapnikov, was vague and primitive, but, nevertheless, "Left" in character, antagonistic to the Provisional Government. Stalin and Kamenev removed the old editorial board, as being too far to the Left, and assumed an utterly opportunist position in the spirit of the Left Mensheviks: (a) support of the Provisional Government, "in so far as"; (b) military defense of the revolution (*i.e.,* the bourgeois republic); (c) unification with the Mensheviks of the Tseretelli type. The position of *Pravda* of that time is truly a scandalous page in the history of the party and in the biography of Stalin. His articles of March 1917, which were the "revolutionary" conclusions of his deliberations in exile, wholly explain why from the works of Stalin pertaining to the epoch of war not a single line has appeared to this day.

10. We reprint below Shliapnikov's account of the overturn effected by Stalin and Kamenev, who, at that time, were united on a common position:

> "The day of the first issue of the 'transformed' *Pravda*—the 15th of March—was a day of rejoicing for the

> defensists. The whole Tauride Palace, from the jobbers in the State Duma Committee to the very heart of the revolutionary democracy, the Executive Committee of the Soviets, buzzed with a single piece of news: the victory of the moderate and reasonable Bolsheviks over the extremists. In the Executive Committee itself we were met with venomous smiles. This was the first and only occasion on which *Pravda* met with the approval of even the staunch defensists of the Lieber-Dan stripe. When this issue of *Pravda* reached the factories, it there aroused utter dismay among our party members and our sympathizers, and caustic gratification among our opponents. Inquiries poured into the Petersburg Committee, the Bureau of the CC and the editorial board of *Pravda*—What happened? Why has our newspaper renounced the Bolshevik line and taken the path of defensism? But the Petersburg Committee, as well as the entire organization, was caught unawares by this *coup*. There was general indignation and the Bureau of the CC was blamed for this incident. The indignation in the local districts was enormous, and when the workers found out that PRAVDA *had been seized by three former editors of* PRAVDA *arriving from Siberia, they demanded their expulsion from the party"* [The third member was the former deputy, Muranov.] (Shliapnikov, *The Year 1917,* Bk. 2, 1925).

We must add the following to the above: (a) Shliapnikov's account was altered and modulated in the extreme under the pressure of Stalin and Kamenev in 1925 (the "troika" was still in power at the time!); (b) no refutations of Shliapnikov's account appeared in the official press. Indeed, how could it have been refuted? The issues of *Pravda* for that period were then readily available.

11. Stalin's attitude to the problem of revolutionary power was expressed by him in a speech made at a party Conference (the session of March 29, 1917). Said Stalin:

> "On the other hand, the government has in fact taken the rôle of fortifier of the conquests of the revolutionary people. The Soviet of Workers' and Soldiers' Deputies mobilizes the forces, and exercises control, while the Provisional Government—balking and muddling, takes the rôle of fortifier of those conquests of the people, which they have already seized as a fact. Such a situation has disadvantageous, but also advantageous sides. It is not to our advantage at present to force events, hastening the process of repelling the bourgeois layers, who will in the future inevitably withdraw from us."

Stalin is afraid of "repelling the bourgeoisie"—the principal argument of the Mensheviks from 1904 on.

> "In so far as the Provisional Government fortifies the steps of the revolution, to that extent we must support it; but, in so far as it is counter-revolutionary, support to the Provisional Government is not permissible."

That is exactly what Dan said. After all, what other words can be used to defend a bourgeois government in the eyes of the revolutionary masses?

Further, we read in the minutes:

> "Comrade Stalin reads the resolution on the Provisional Government adopted by the Bureau of the Central Committee, but states that he is not in complete agreement with it, and is rather in accord with the

The first Provisional Government under Prince Lvov: counterclockwise, Prince G.E. Lvov, A.I. Konovalov, A.F. Kerensky, A.I. Guchkov, V.N. Lvov, P.N. Miliukov, M.I. Tereshchenko, F.I. Rodichev (not a member of the government), N.V. Nekrasov, A.A. Manuilov, A.I. Shingarev, and I.V. Godnev.

In his report to the March Party Conference of the Bolsheviks, Stalin asserted that the Lvov government had "in fact taken the role of fortifier of the conquests of the revolutionary people" and that it must be supported "in so far as [it fortified] the steps of the revolution" (pp. 291–92). Lenin, arriving at the end of the conference, in his *April theses* said that the Bolsheviks should give "no support whatever to the Provisional Government. We must explain the utter falsity of all of its promises" (p. 351).

resolution of the Krasnoyarsk Soviet of Workers' and Soldiers' Deputies."

We quote the most important points of the Krasnoyarsk resolution:

> "To make entirely clear that the only source of the power and the authority of the Provisional Government is the will of the people who have accomplished this revolution, and to whom the Provisional Government is obliged wholly to submit. . . ."
>
> "To support the Provisional Government in its activities only in so far as it follows a course of satisfying the demands of the working class and the revolutionary peasantry in the revolution that is taking place."

The reference here is to the Government of Prince Lvov-Miliukov-Guchkov.

Such was the position of Stalin on the question of power.

12. We must particularly underscore the date of the above, namely, *March 29, 1917*. Thus, more than a month after the beginning of the revolution, Stalin still spoke of Miliukov as an ally: The Soviet conquers, the Provisional Government fortifies. It is hard to believe that these words could have been pronounced by a reporter to the Bolshevik Conference at the end of March 1917! Even Martov would not have posed the question in this manner. This is the theory of Dan expressed in its most vulgar form: The democratic revolution viewed as an abstraction, within the framework of which function the more "moderate" and the more "resolute" forces, among whom there is a division of labor—the resolute conquer, the moderate fortify. Nevertheless, Stalin's speech was not accidental. We have in it the pattern of the entire Stalinist policy in

China from 1924 to 1928.

Lenin, who had managed to arrive in time for the last session of this same Conference, castigated the position of Stalin with an indignation that was impassioned despite all its restraint.

> "Even our Bolsheviks [he said] show confidence in the Government. That can be explained only by intoxication incidental to revolution. That is the death of socialism. You, comrades, place confidence in the government. If that's your position, our ways part. I prefer to remain in the minority. One Liebknecht is worth more than 110 defensists of the type of Steklov and Chkheidze. If you are in sympathy with Liebknecht and extend even a finger [to the defensists]—this will be a betrayal of international socialism." (The March 1917 Party Conference. Session of April 4. "Report by comrade Lenin.")

It should be borne in mind that Lenin's speech, as well as the protocols as a whole, have been kept hidden from the party to this day.

13. How did Stalin pose the war question? In the same way as Kamenev. It is necessary to arouse the European workers, but in the meantime we must fulfill our duty towards the "revolution." But how arouse the European workers? Stalin's reply is contained in his article for March 17, 1917.

> ". . . We have already indicated one of the most serious methods of doing so. It consists in this, that we compel our own government to put itself on record not only against all plans of conquest . . . but also openly to formulate the will of the Russian people,

> immediately begin negotiations for universal peace on the basis of a complete renunciation of all conquests by both sides, and on the basis of the rights of all nations to self-determination."

Thus, the "pacifism" of Miliukov-Guchkov was to have served as the means for arousing the European proletariat.

On April 4, the day after his arrival, Lenin indignantly declared at the Party Conference:

> "*Pravda* demands from the *Government* that it renounce annexations. To demand from the government of the capitalists that it renounce annexations—Nonsense! Flagrant mockery of. . . ." (The March 1917 Party Conference. Session of April 4. "Report by comrade Lenin.")

These words were directed wholly against Stalin.

14. On March 14, the Menshevik-S.R. Soviet issued a manifesto on war to the toilers of all nations. The manifesto represented a hypocritical, pseudo-pacifist document in the spirit of the entire policy of the Mensheviks and the S.R.'s who were urging the workers of other countries to rise against their bourgeoisie, while they themselves remained yoked to the imperialists of Russia and of the whole Entente. How did Stalin evaluate this manifesto?

> "In the first place, it is indubitable that the bare slogan 'Down with War!' is absolutely worthless as a practical path. . . . It is impermissible not to hail yesterday's manifesto of the Soviet of Workers' and Soldiers' Deputies in Petrograd to the peoples of the whole world, summoning them to compel their own governments to terminate the slaughter. This manifesto, if

> it reaches the broad masses, will undoubtedly recall hundreds and thousands of workers to the forgotten slogan: 'Workers of the World, Unite!' "

How did Lenin evaluate the manifesto of the defensists? In his April 4 speech, from which we have already quoted, he said: "The manifesto of the Soviet of Workers' Deputies—there isn't a word in it imbued with class-consciousness. There is nothing to it but phrase-mongering." (The March 1917 Party Conference. Session of April 4. "Report by comrade Lenin.")

These words are directed entirely against Stalin. That is why the protocols of the March Conference are kept hidden from the party.

15. Since he was carrying through the policy of the Left Mensheviks in relation to the Provisional Government and the war, Stalin had no reason whatever for rejecting unification with the Mensheviks. Here is how he expressed himself on this question at the self-same March 1917 Conference. We quote the protocols verbatim:

> "*Order of the day*—Tseretelli's proposal for unification.
>
> "STALIN: We ought to go. It is necessary to define our proposals as to the terms of unification. Unification is possible along the lines of Zimmerwald-Kienthal."

At this, even Molotov expressed his doubts; to be sure, not very articulately. Stalin replied in refutation:

> "There is no use running ahead and anticipating disagreements. There is no party life without disagreements. We will live down trivial disagreements within the party." (The March 1917 Party Conference. Session of April 1.)

These few words speak louder than volumes. They serve to establish the thoughts upon which Stalin fed during the war years and they attest with juridical precision that Stalin's Zimmerwaldism was of the same brand as Tseretelli's Zimmerwaldism. Here, once again, there is not even a hint of that ideological irreconcilability, which was put on by Stalin as a false mask several years later, in the interests of the apparatus struggle. On the contrary, Menshevism and Bolshevism appear to Stalin at the end of March 1917 as shades of thought that could abide in a single party. Disagreements with Tseretelli Stalin calls "trivial," which can be "lived down" in the framework of a single organization. We can gather from this how becoming it is for Stalin to condemn in retrospect Trotsky's conciliationist attitude to the Left Mensheviks . . . in 1913.

16. With such a position, Stalin, in the nature of things, could not counterpose anything serious to the S.R.'s and the Mensheviks in the Executive Committee of the Soviet, which, on his arrival, he entered as a representative of the party. There has not remained in the minutes or in the press a single proposal, declaration or protest in which Stalin in any distinguishable manner counterposed the Bolshevik point of view to the flunkeyism of the "revolutionary democracy" toward the bourgeoisie. One of the chroniclers of that period, the non-party semi-defensist Sukhanov, the author of the above-mentioned manifesto to the toilers of the whole world, says in his *Notes on the Revolution:*

> "Among the Bolsheviks, besides Kamenev, there appeared in the Executive Committee of the Soviets in those days Stalin. During the time of his modest activity in the Executive Committee [he] gave me the impression—and not only me—of a drab spot which would

sometimes emit a dim and inconsequential light. There is really nothing more to be said about him." (*Notes on the Revolution,* Bk. 2, pp. 265*f*.)

17. Lenin, who had finally managed to break through from abroad, raged and thundered against the "Kautskyist" *Pravda* (the term is Lenin's). Stalin withdrew to the sidelines. At the time when Kamenev manned the defenses, Stalin remained silent. Gradually he slid into the new official groove made by Lenin. But we do not find emanating from him a single independent idea or generalization on which it is worth while dwelling. Whenever the occasion arose, Stalin stepped in between Kamenev and Lenin.

Let us take the most acute moment of the inner-party struggle on the eve of the October insurrection. Kamenev and Zinoviev came out in the non-party press against the insurrection. Lenin in a letter to the Central Committee branded their action as "infinitely vile," and raised the question of expelling them from the party. Lenin was particularly indignant at the fact that in all their open declarations, Zinoviev and Kamenev, without ceasing to agitate against the insurrection, covered their violation of the decision of the party with hypocritical and diplomatic formulae. Meanwhile, on that very same day, October 20, there appeared to the astonishment of the Central Committee the following declaration in the central organ of the party:

"*Statement by the Editorial Board.* We on our part express the hope that the matter will be considered as closed with the statement made by comrade Zinoviev (and also comrade Kamenev's statement in the Soviet). The sharp tone of comrade Lenin's article does not alter the fact that we are fundamentally in agreement." (*Protocols of the C.C. of S.D.L.P.R.,* Aug. 1917–Feb. 1918. State Publishers, 1929,

p. 137.) Thus, where Lenin spoke of an "infinitely vile" behavior, covered up by diplomatic subterfuges, the editorial board, basing itself on these subterfuges, spoke of "agreement."

The editorial board consisted at the time of Stalin and Sokolnikov. "Comrade Sokolnikov announced that he had had no part in the declaration of the editorial board with regard to the letters of Zinoviev, and that he regarded this declaration as erroneous." (*Idem.,* p. 128.) Thus, it was made clear that Stalin on *his own responsibility* supported—against Lenin, against the Central Committee, and against the other member of the editorial board—Kamenev and Zinoviev at the most critical moment, four days prior to the insurrection; and did so through an official declaration which could not but confuse the entire party. There was universal indignation. The protocol reads: "Comrade Stalin presents a statement that he is withdrawing from the editorial board." (*Idem.,* p. 129.) Rather than aggravate an already rather difficult situation, the Central Committee did not accept Stalin's resignation.

But, after all, how explain the astounding declaration of Stalin in *Pravda*? Like a number of other steps taken by Stalin during the period from April to October, the declaration cannot be understood unless we take into consideration the fact that Stalin was under the influence of his Menshevik policy during March and the first days in April. What had occurred only yesterday was still so fresh in the minds of everyone. Stalin up to April 4 had marched so closely in step with Kamenev. The turn in party policy after April 4 was so sharp that Stalin found himself all this time in a condition of acute political infirmity: he squirmed, kept mum, allowed others to commit themselves, but once in a while he would burst out against Lenin, in the spirit of the above-quoted editorial declaration.

18. For a number of years, Stalin and all his Kuusinens have been broadcasting throughout the world the version alleging that Trotsky had willfully and against the decision of the C.C. decided not to sign the peace treaty at Brest-Litovsk. Stalin even undertook to prove this in the press. We have now the official evidence as presented in the published protocols of the Central Committee for the year 1917. (State Publishers, 1929.)

> "Session of January 24, 1918. Comrade Trotsky moves the following formula to a vote: We terminate the war, but we do not conclude peace. The vote is taken. Carried: 9—for; 7—against." (*Idem.*, p. 207.)

That seems clear enough.

19. What was Stalin's attitude to the formula of Trotsky? Here is what Stalin had to say one week after the session at which this formula had been adopted by a vote of 9 to 7.

> "Session of February 1 (January 19), 1918. Comrade STALIN: . . . the way out of the difficult situation was provided us by the middle point of view—the position of Trotsky." (*Idem.*, p. 214.)

We cannot but express our astonishment at how these words of Stalin ever came to be preserved in the protocols, despite the all-seeing eye of Saveliev, the editor. For these words leave no stone unturned in exposing the latter-day agitation of many years' standing on the subject of the Brest-Litovsk peace. It now appears that on January 19 (February 1), 1918, Stalin considered that the position of Trotsky provided the party with a "way out of the difficult situation." Stalin's words will become fully comprehensible, if we bear in mind that throughout this entire critical period the overwhelming majority of the party organizations and of the Soviets were in favor of a revolutionary war and that, in consequence, Lenin's position could have been carried through only by means of an overturn in the party and in the government (which was, of course, utterly out of the question). Thus Stalin was not at all mistaken, but was only stating an incontrovertible fact when he said that Trotsky's position was the *only conceivable way out* for the party at that time.

20. But what was Stalin's own position?

> "Session of February 23, 1918. Comrade *Stalin:* We need not sign but we must begin peace negotiations.
>
> "Comrade *Lenin:* . . . Stalin is wrong in saying that we need not sign. These conditions must be signed. If you do not sign them, you will sign the death sentence of the Soviet power within three weeks.
>
> "Comrade *Uritsky,* in refuting Stalin, states that the conditions must be either accepted or rejected, but that it is impossible to continue negotiations." (*Idem.,* p. 249.)

Anyone who is familiar with the situation at that moment, can clearly perceive the hopeless muddle in which Stalin found himself, arising from his lack of any thoroughly thought-out position. By the 18th of February the Germans had already captured Dvinsk. Their offensive was developing with extraordinary speed. The policy of stalling and pulling wires had been exhausted. Stalin proposes on February 23 not to sign the peace treaty, but . . . to carry on negotiations.

During the Brest-Litovsk negotiations Stalin had no independent position. He would vacillate, side-step and keep silent. At the last moment he would vote for Lenin's motion. The muddled and impotent position of Stalin during that period is characterized quite clearly, though not fully, even in the officially "improved" minutes of the C.C.

21. During the period of the Civil War, Stalin was opposed to the principles upon which the creation of the Red Army was based, and inspired behind the scenes the so-called "military opposition" against Lenin and Trotsky. The facts that pertain to this are in part dealt with in Trotsky's autobiography. (*My Life,* "The Military Opposition," Ch. 36. See also Markin's article in this volume.)

22. At the time when Lenin was ill and Trotsky away on a leave of absence, Stalin carried through in the Central Committee, under the influence of Sokolnikov, a decision undermining the monopoly of foreign trade. Owing to the decisive attack of Lenin and Trotsky this decision was revoked. (See "Letter to the *Istpart.*")

23. During the same period, Stalin assumed a position on the national question which Lenin condemned for its bureaucratic and chauvinistic tendencies. Stalin on his part accused Lenin of national liberalism. (See "Letter to the *Istpart.*")

24. What was Stalin's conduct on the question of the German Revolution in 1923? He was here once again compelled, as in March 1917, to orient himself independently on a major question. Lenin was ill, a struggle was being waged against Trotsky. Here is what Stalin wrote to Zinoviev and Bukharin in August 1923 on the situation in Germany.

> "Should the Communists strive (at the given stage) to seize power without the Social Democrats? Have they sufficiently matured for that?—that's the question as I see it. Upon our taking power, we had in

> Russia such reserves as (a) peace; (b) land to the peasants; (c) the support of the vast majority of the working class; (d) the sympathy of the peasants. The German Communists have at present nothing of the sort. They have, of course, contiguous to them the land of the Soviets, which we did not have, but what can we give them at the present moment? Should the power in Germany, so to speak, drop now, and should the Communists catch it up, they'll fall through with a crash. That's 'at best.' But if it comes to the worst—they will be smashed to pieces and beaten back. The gist of the matter does not lie in Brandler's desire to 'teach the masses'; the gist of the matter is that the bourgeoisie plus the Right Social Democrats would surely convert the practice-demonstration into a general battle (they still have all the odds on their side for that) and would crush them. The Fascists, of course, are not napping, but it is to our advantage to let the Fascists attack first: this will fuse the entire working class around the Communists (Germany is not Bulgaria). Moreover, the Fascists, according to all reports, are weak in Germany. In my opinion the Germans should be restrained and not encouraged."

Thus, in August 1923, when the German Revolution was knocking at all doors, Stalin reckoned that Brandler must be restrained and not encouraged. Stalin bears the main responsibility for letting slip the revolutionary situation in Germany. He supported and encouraged the weaklings, the skeptics and the temporizers in Germany. He did not accidentally assume an opportunist opposition on this question of world-historic importance: he was in essence only continuing the policy that he had followed in Russia in March 1917.

25. After the revolutionary situation had been doomed by passivity and irresolution, Stalin for a long time defended against Trotsky the Brandlerite CC, thereby defending himself. In so doing Stalin brought, of course, the argument from "exceptionalism." Thus, December 17, 1924—a year after the shipwreck in Germany—Stalin wrote:

> "One must not forget for an instant this peculiarity. It must especially be borne in mind in analyzing the German events in the Autumn of 1923. It must especially be borne in mind by comrade Trotsky, who draws a wholesale [!] analogy [!!] between the October Revolution and the revolution in Germany and who incessantly keeps lashing the German Communist Party." (*Problems of Leninism,* 1928, p. 171.)

Accordingly, Trotsky was guilty in those days of "lashing" Brandlerism and not of patronizing it. It is quite evident from the above to what extent Stalin and his Molotov are of service in the struggle against the Rights in Germany!

26. The year 1924 is the year of the great turn. In the Spring of that year, Stalin was still repeating the old formulae of the impossibility of building socialism in one country, especially in a backward country. In the Autumn of that same year, Stalin broke with Marx and Lenin on the fundamental question of the proletarian revolution, and constructed his "theory" of socialism in one country. Incidentally, Stalin has nowhere developed this theory in a positive form, nor has he even expatiated on it. The entire foundation for it comes down to two quotations from Lenin that have been deliberately given a false interpretation. Stalin has made no reply to a single objection. The theory of socialism in one country has an administrative and not a theoretical foundation.

27. In that same year, Stalin created the theory of "bi-composite," *i.e.,* two-class worker and peasant parties for the Orient. This constitutes a break with Marxism and with the entire history of Bolshevism on the fundamental question of the class nature of the party. Even the Communist International found itself compelled in 1928 to draw back from this theory which has doomed the communist parties of the Orient for a long time to come. But this great discovery continues even today to grace the Stalinist *Problems of Leninism.*

28. In that same year, Stalin carried through the subordination of Chinese communism to the bourgeois party of the Kuomintang, passing the latter off as a "worker and peasant" party of the type he had himself invented.

The Chinese workers and peasants, on the authority of the Comintern, were politically enslaved to the bourgeoisie. Stalin organized in China the "division of labor" which Lenin prevented him from organizing in Russia in 1917: the Chinese workers and peasants did the "conquering" while Chiang Kai-shek did the "fortifying."

Stalin's policy was the direct and immediate cause of the shipwreck of the Chinese Revolution.

29. Stalin's position and his zigzags on the questions of Soviet economic life are too fresh in the memory of the entire world, and, therefore, we shall not dwell on them here.

30. In conclusion, we shall merely recall once again Lenin's "Testament." In question here is not a polemical article or speech, where one may with some justification presuppose inevitable exaggerations from the heat of the struggle. No, in the "Testament," Lenin, calmly weighing every word, offered his last counsel to the party, evaluating each one of his collaborators on the basis of his entire experience with them. What has he to say of

Stalin? That Stalin is (a) rude, (b) disloyal, (c) inclined to abuse power. Conclusion: Remove Stalin from the post of General Secretary.

A few weeks later Lenin also dictated a note to Stalin in which he announced that he was "breaking off all personal and comradely relations with him." This was one of the final expressions of Lenin's will. All these facts are recorded in the protocols of the July 1927 Plenum of the Central Committee.

❖

Here are a few milestones in the political biography of Stalin. They provide a sufficiently distinct portrait of a man in whom energy, will and resoluteness are combined with empiricism, myopia, an organic inclination to opportunist decisions in great questions, personal rudeness, disloyalty and a readiness to abuse power in order to suppress the party.

How the October insurrection actually took place

The schema of the October overturn in the official delineation has undergone, as is well known, interminable changes in obedience to the political needs of the ruling group. The final version now set forth may be briefly formulated in the following words: Lenin demanded that the insurrection be expedited in every possible way. Zinoviev and Kamenev came out against the insurrection. Trotsky sought to defer the question of the insurrection to the Congress of the Soviets on October 25 (November 7). Lenin implacably fought against the "constitutional illusions" of Trotsky, who placed the question of the material seizure of power in dependence upon the Congress of the Soviets. The Central Committee, under the leadership of Stalin, supported the position of Lenin, and only thus was the October victory assured.

The exposition of the actual course of events in my *History of the Russian Revolution* did not leave, I venture to believe, a stone unturned in exposing this historical falsification. I am now compelled to say that I could have been far more sparing of proofs, had I in my possession, when working on the *History,* the document which I succeeded in locating only later.

On the 23rd of April 1920, the Moscow organization celebrated Lenin's fiftieth birthday, in the absence, to be sure, of the guest of honor who was not fond of such projects. One of the orators at the celebration was Stalin who, as we shall see presently, missed a wonderful opportunity to remain silent. The Moscow Committee published the jubilee speeches in a booklet on grayish paper (the year, 1920!) which has since become a bibliographical rarity. This tiny book has been forgotten by everybody, and those who are informed dare not mention it: An unseasonable reminder of historical facts can nowadays cost a man his head.

In a very short and incoherent speech, Stalin set himself the task of pointing out "one trait [of Lenin's] about which no one has as yet spoken; namely, modesty, the admission of his mistakes." The orator adduced two examples: the first, relating to the boycott of the State Duma in 1905; the second, relating to the method and the date for the October insurrection. Let us quote literally Stalin's story of this second "mistake" of Lenin:

> "In 1917, in July, under Kerensky, at the moment the Democratic Conference was convoked and when the Mensheviks and the Social Revolutionaries were building up the new institution—the Pre-Parliament which was to have set the rails for a switch to the Constituent Assembly—now, at that very moment it was decided among ourselves in the Central Committee to go forward on the road of reënforcing the Soviets; convene the Congress of the Soviets; launch the insurrection

and proclaim the Congress of the Soviets as the organ of state power. Ilyich, at the time in hiding, was not in agreement and wrote that this garbage [the Democratic Conference] must be dispersed and arrested. We understood that the matter was not quite so simple, knowing full well that the Conference consisted one-half or at least one-third of delegates from the front, and that by arresting and dispersing we could only spoil the whole business and worsen the relations with the front. All the gullies, pits and ravines in our path were more easily to be seen by us. But Ilyich is great [?]; he is not afraid [?!] of either pits, hollows, or ravines in his path; he does not fear threats [?] and says: 'Begin and go straight ahead.' But our faction saw that it was not to our advantage at the time to act in this way; that it was necessary to walk around these obstacles in order to take the bull by the horns. And despite all the demands of Ilyich, we proceeded along the road of reënforcement and came up [?] on October 25 before the picture [?] of the insurrection. Ilyich, smiling, looking at us slyly, said: 'Yes, you were right.' This again astonished us. At times, Comrade Lenin, in questions of immense importance, admitted his failings [?]. . . ." (*The Fiftieth Anniversary of V.I. Ulianov-Lenin,* 1920, 27*ff*.)

Stalin's speech has not entered into any collection of his "works." Yet it is instructive to the highest degree. In the first place, it leaves no stone unturned of the latter-day legend alleging that the Central Committee, under the leadership of Lenin, smashed the "constitutional illusions" of Trotsky with regard to the date and the method of the insurrection. According to Stalin—according, that is, to the Stalin of 1920—it follows, on the contrary, that upon this question the Central Committee supported Trotsky *against* Lenin.

In my recollections of Lenin published in 1924, I related how Lenin, when he arrived at the Smolny on the night of the 25th, said to me: "Well, well—it can be done that way too. Just take the power." The "historian" Yaroslavsky in 1930 indignantly denied the authenticity of this story. For, you see, the overturn had been accomplished by the Central Committee in accord with Lenin—and against Trotsky; how then could Lenin have said: "It can be done that way too"? Yet, from Stalin we learn that the Central Committee "despite all the demands of Ilyich" pursued its line oriented upon the Congress of the Soviets and "came up on October 25 before the picture of the insurrection"; while Lenin on arriving at the Smolny announced: *"Yes, you were right."* Is it possible to imagine a more convincing, even if involuntary, confirmation of my story and a more crushing refutation of all the latter-day fictions?

However, the actual plan of the Central Committee was delineated inaccurately by Stalin even in 1920: "to go forward on the road of reënforcing the Soviets; *convene the Congress of the Soviets; launch* the insurrection and proclaim the Congress of the Soviets as the organ of state power"—this constitutes, after all, that very same mechanistic schema which was not unjustifiably stigmatized by Lenin because of its "constitutional illusions." To call in advance the Congress of the Soviets in order only *later* to summon the insurrection would have meant to facilitate for our opponents the opportunity for dealing a blow at the Congress of the Soviets *before* the insurrection. Involuntarily the question arises: Were not Lenin's fears a result of one of his meetings with Stalin? As a matter of fact, the plan conducted and realized by me in action consisted in this: that in the process of mobilizing the masses under the slogan of the Congress of the Soviets as the supreme organ in the country, *and under the cover of this legal campaign,* we prepare the insurrection and strike the blow at a propitious moment, proximate to the Congress of the Soviets but by no means necessarily *after* the opening of the Congress.

Whoever reads carefully the chapters in my *History* treating of the disagreements in the party on the eve of the October overturn will without difficulty ascertain that Stalin in his speech depicts the divergence between the Central Committee and Lenin far more sharply than was done by me. And this for the very reason that the differences and controversies of that period found their reflection only partially and, moreover, indirectly in letters and other documents. In my presentation, I meticulously avoided personal recollections, unless I was unable to substantiate them through other sources. I was doubly cautious inasmuch as it was a question of a tactical disagreement with Lenin on which the subsequent course of events confirmed the correctness of my own position. I might point out that Stalin's speech at the jubilee meeting of 1920 was not and could not have been contradicted by anybody there. If the speech, in conformity with the general mental equipment of the orator, tends to simplify the question, then it all the more weightily refutes that version which was concocted with the participation of Stalin during the most recent period.

Leon Trotsky
MARCH 3, 1937.

Trotsky and the staff reviewing the 2nd Red Army, Zarapul, 1919.

APPENDIX

Stalin and the Red Army

by N. Markin

Under the heading, "Stalin and the Red Army," *Pravda* has printed a jubilee article by Voroshilov whose avowed aim is to "refresh the memories of the comrades" about the past. This article has been republished in pamphlet form, in an edition of 100,000. It is worth while to dwell in some detail upon this piece of creative writing. It sets a record in the quantity of fictions and discrepancies, even against the background of the articles written by all the Yaroslavskys. It may be said without exaggeration that this article does not contain a line of truth—*not even a single line.* We shall try as briefly as possible to reëstablish the truth by citing actual facts and genuine documents, some of which have never been published. (We have utilized a section of comrade Trotsky's archives.)

Tsaritsin

In his autobiography, comrade Trotsky has dealt in considerable detail with the history and the roots of the

"Tsaritsin Opposition."[61] This opposition had one of its roots in a peasant's hatred—and not that of a proletarian—of *"spetzes"* [specialists], which hatred in no way hindered every Tsaritsinite from having close at hand his "own *spetz,* only of an inferior grade." The telegrams of Stalin which are cited by Voroshilov illuminate to the utmost this "spetzophobia" of the Tsaritsinites and their "ideologist" Stalin. After the Eighth Party Congress (March 1919), the question of the *"spetzes"* was settled in principle. Ten years later we learn "officially," with Voroshilov's assistance, that Stalin was among those elements who were able to grasp the question of the military specialists only after a considerable time and with considerable difficulty. These elements held the supreme manifestation of revolutionism to be "the stupid taunting of military specialists" (Trotsky). Voroshilov, who remains today on the Tsaritsin level, instead of seeking to hide more securely Stalin's mental lapses of 1919, obliges us with exemplars of this "stupid taunting":

". . . Had not our military 'specialists' (shoemakers) been sleeping and loafing, the line would not have been broken; and should the line be restored it will not be due to the military gentry but despite them."

And more of the same, in the self-same spirit of wholesale taunting and cheap boasting. Therein is all their wisdom. These telegrams—today—in the light of the experience of the civil war, compromise their author to such an extent that we shall confine ourselves merely to confronting them with the remarks made by comrade Trotsky in another connection, but which directly apply in this instance:

". . . This is the worst type of commander. They remain ever ignorant, but they ever refuse to learn. For their failures—how could they possibly gain successes?—they always seek explanations in somebody else's betrayal. . . . Tenaciously hanging on to their posts, they react with hatred to the very mention of military science. For them, the latter is synonymous with treason and betrayal." (L. Trotsky, *How the Revolution Armed Itself,* Vol. I, pp. 172*f*.)

Later on in his article, Voroshilov, with undisguised approbation, almost in ecstasy, quotes the following from the White Guard turncoat, Nossovich:

"What particularly characterized this breach was the attitude taken by Stalin to the telegrams with instruction from the center. When Trotsky, in alarm at the disruption of the regions he had with such great difficulty organized, sent a telegram pointing out the necessity of leaving the Staff and Commissariat as they were, and of giving them an opportunity to function, Stalin would make a categorical and very significant notation on the telegram: 'Disregard this.'

"So the telegram was disregarded, and the entire artillery staff, together with a part of the leading staff, would remain sitting on a barge in Tsaritsin."

Voroshilov puts his signature to these words; he adopts them, as it were. Until now, we must confess, it would have never even entered our mind to give any credence to Nossovich. But we are compelled to take the word of both Voroshilov and Nossovich. "What particularly characterized" Stalin's attitude toward telegrams with instructions from the center was: "disregard." Stalin's worst enemy could not have caused him greater injury than did Voroshilov by appending his seal of approval to the characterization of the White Guard, Nossovich.

It is not difficult to judge what sort of discipline prevailed in the Tenth Army under these conditions. The orders of the Military Revolutionary Council were being violated in a deliberately demonstrative manner. Stalin's "resolution" was made common knowledge to Nossovich, to the army itself, while the center alone was kept in ignorance. Observe, gentlemen, here is an example for you of how to "cover up." If the instructions of the center were incorrect from the standpoint of local conditions, there was always the opportunity of revoking or changing them through the normal channels. The Military Council maintained a practical discipline and not an officious one. Especially characteristic of Stalin is his manner of not fulfilling orders, without the knowledge of the Military Council, behind the latter's back, and with a special display of "independence." It must be stated candidly that had one-fifth or even one-tenth of the responsible leaders of the army displayed the above-mentioned "characteristic trait" of Stalin, the Red Army would have never gained its victories, and the revolution would have been massacred. And it was precisely owing to this "characteristic trait," and for no other reason, that first Stalin and then Voroshilov were removed from Tsaritsin by the decision of the Political Bureau.

Stalin's indiscipline and disloyalty were likewise clearly made evident in his direct relations with the Military Council itself. It was of course impossible in this case to reply "I disregard this," but there were other methods of expressing the notorious "characteristic trait." We shall give a few such examples, together with Lenin's attitude to them.

In transmitting to Trotsky one of Stalin's telegrams (No. 02583, May 29, 1920), Lenin, who was well aware of Stalin's disloyalty, appended the following note in his own handwriting:

"Comrade Trotsky: If you have not received this telegram as well as *all* decoded telegrams to the Secretariat of the Vice-Chairman, then you should immediately send Stalin the following code telegram *with my signature:* 'Forward all military dispatches also to Trotsky, otherwise dangerous delay. Lenin'." (Lenin's emphasis throughout. The Secretariat of the Vice-Chairman refers to Sklyansky, Trotsky's alternate in the Military Council.—N.M.)

The gist of the matter is clear without any commentaries.

Another instance. Transmitting (during one of the sessions) Stalin's telegram—No. 4620, June 4, 1920—to Trotsky, Vladimir Ilyich added the following note:

"Comrade Trotsky: It is necessary to get in touch with the Chief Commander and to demand their conclusions. After receiving their opinion, send me your own conclusions to the session of the Council of Defense. We shall talk (if it is not too late) on the telephone." (The note is in Lenin's handwriting.)

"I do not understand this system: why does not Yegorov (in command of the Southern Front) report directly to the Chief Commander as he was ordered to do—this roundabout way disrupts all stability of communications." (This notation is in Trotsky's handwriting.)

"Some capriciousness here, no doubt . . . ," replied Lenin on the same note.

In concluding his Tsaritsin recollections, Voroshilov writes: "Stalin worked with a colossal energy." But Voroshilov passes over in silence the end to which this energy was in the main directed, and the conclusion of this Tsaritsin epic (which had its sequel in the Ukraine). The reason for his silence can be easily gathered from documents we print below.*

Telegram

"Moscow. To the Chairman of the CEC of the Soviets; copy, Moscow: To *Lenin,* Chairman of the Council of People's Commissars. From Tambov.

"I insist categorically on Stalin's recall. Tsaritsin front in a bad way, despite the abundance of troops. Voroshilov qualified to command a regiment, but not an army of 50,000. Nevertheless I shall leave him in command of the Tenth Tsaritsin Army on condition of obedience to Sytin, the commander of the Southern Army. The Tsaritsinites have failed to date to transmit to Kozlov even reports of operations. I ordered them to transmit twice a day reports of operations and reconnoitering. If this is not done tomorrow, I will commit Voroshilov and Minin to trial, and announce this in an order to the Army. In so far as Stalin and Minin remain in Tsaritsin, they, in accordance with the constitution of the Military Council, possess only the rights of members of the Military Council of the Tenth Army. Very little time left for an offensive before the roads become impassable either by foot or by horse. Without coördinating activities with Tsaritsin, serious steps are impossible. No time left for diplomatic negotiations. Tsaritsin must either submit or be removed. We possess a colossal superiority in forces but there is complete anarchy among the tops. This can be overcome within 24 hours provided your support is firm and

* In order not to overburden the text, we give a number of these documents in an abbreviated form, omitting the military and technical sections.

> decisive. In any case, this is the only way out that I see personally.
>
> "October 4, 1918. No. 552.
> *"Trotsky."*

The next day Trotsky sent another telegram:

> "Moscow. To the Chairman of the CEC [of the Soviets]. Copy to the Chairman of the Council of People's Commissars, *Lenin.*
>
> "I have received the following telegram: 'Stalin's military order number 118 must be canceled. I have issued all necessary orders to the commander of the Southern Front, Sytin. Stalin's actions are destroying all my plans. . . . No. 01258, Commander in Chief, Vatsetis. Member of the Military Council, Danishevsky.' Trotsky. Kozlov, Oct. 5, 1918."

Stalin was removed from Tsaritsin. It became easier to "manage" Voroshilov without Stalin. Trotsky also agreed to allow Voroshilov to remain, in an attempt to adjust the situation. However, Voroshilov, too, had shortly to be removed, for Stalin continued to direct him in the former spirit from Moscow. In the Ukraine, where Voroshilov was next appointed, he sought to continue the "Tsaritsin line," which resulted in the following telegrams from Trotsky:

> "Moscow. To the Chairman of the CEC, Sverdlov:
>
> "Did not find the Ukrainians in Kursk. In consequence, carried on no negotiations. Must state categorically that the Tsaritsin line, which led to the complete disintegration of the Tsaritsin Army, cannot be tolerated in the Ukraine. . . . The Ukrainians are in chaos. There

> is a clique struggle due to the absence of responsible and authoritative leaders. Okulov is leaving for Moscow. Propose that you and comrade Lenin give utmost attention to his report on Voroshilov's work. The line of Stalin, Voroshilov and Rukhimovich spells ruin for our entire cause. Chairman of the Military Council, Trotsky. Jan. 10, 1919. Gryaz."

The following day, in reply to a (missing) telegram from Lenin, Trotsky transmitted by direct wire:

> "To comrade Lenin:
>
> "Compromise is of course necessary but not a rotten one. As a matter of fact, all the Tsaritsinites have now foregathered in Kharkov. What the Tsaritsinites are you can gather from the report of Okulov which contains solely factual material and reports of Commissars. I consider Stalin's patronage of the Tsaritsin tendency a most dangerous ulcer worse than any treason or betrayal by military specialists. If not for the prospects of the Anglo-French front in the Ukraine one might remain indifferent to the question of the commanding staff. But we shall have to carry on serious operations there. Rukhimovich is only an alias for Voroshilov. Within a month we shall have to swallow the Tsaritsin mess, having against us this time not the Cossacks but the Anglo-French. Rukhimovich is not alone. They firmly hang on to each other, raising ignorance into a principle. Voroshilov plus the Ukrainian partisan methods plus the low cultural level of the population, plus demagogy—this cannot be accepted under any conditions. Let them appoint Artem, but not Voroshilov or Rukhimovich.
>
> "Am immediately leaving for Balashov, because of

certain alarming developments there. If you are unable to arrange matters with the Ukrainians by correspondence, I shall summon them to Voronezh. Greetings.

"Once again I urge a careful reading of Okulov's report on the Tsaritsin Army and how Voroshilov demoralized it with the assistance of Stalin. Trotsky. Jan. 11, 1919 (Balashov)."

Lenin during that period was still inclined toward a compromise with the Tsaritsinites. But the situation became worse and worse. It is quite possible that under the influence of Lenin's "lashing" Voroshilov "pulled himself together" a little in the beginning. That is how we are inclined to explain the fact that for a period of almost five months Trotsky did not raise the "question" of Voroshilov. But in June, it all started up again. This time Lenin no longer counted on a compromise but made a sharp rebuff to Voroshilov and Co.

We reprint a telegram by Trotsky and two telegrams by Lenin in reply.

"From Kantemirovka. To Moscow. To Sklyansky. To Lenin.

"Insistent demands of certain Ukrainians to merge the Second, Thirteenth and Eighth Ukrainian Armies under Voroshilov are utterly indefensible. What we need is not an operative unity on the Donetz scale but a general unity against Denikin. The disgraceful condition of food supplies in the Donetz basin are a result in the first place of inadequate deliveries and secondly of the absence of a civil supplies apparatus. The idea of the military and food dictatorship by Voroshilov is the result of the Donetz 'separatism', directed against Kiev and the Southern Front. Melnichansky has failed completely to take this into consideration. I have no doubt that the realization of this plan would only aggravate the chaos, and completely kill military leadership. Please demand of the CC that Voroshilov and Mezhlauk carry out the wholly real task set them: the creation of a strong Second Ukrainian Army. Expect tomorrow or the next day to summon to Izyum, the central junction, the commanders of the Eighth, the Thirteenth, and the Second Armies, *i.e.,* Voroshilov (together with Mezhlauk and Podvoisky) and the supply-men in order to effect a union of all that should be united, without in any way creating a Donetz Military Republic. June 1, 1919. No. 79/c. Chairman of the Military Council, Trotsky."

The same day, Lenin sent a reply to the "Ukrainians":

"Kharkov. To Mezhlauk. To Voroshilov.
To Melnichansky. To Artem. To Kaminsky.

"It is absolutely imperative that all agitation be stopped immediately, and that all work be placed on a military basis. You must appoint without fail individual who will be responsible for carrying out strictly specified tasks. After all, we must have military discipline. The Commander of the Second Army and the Military Council of the Second Army must consult on all things with their direct superior command, *i.e.,* Gittis. Drop all plans of separate groups and any similar attempts at restoring the Ukrainian front in a disguised manner. The equipment and the arms in the Ukraine and at the disposal of Gittis will suffice. If *chaos, agitation and bickerings as to priority* are done away with, you will be able to obtain everything. Send detailed information as to the fulfillment of specific orders, such as

> the arrival of military detachments at the appointed place, the collection of arms, etc.
>
> *"June 1, 1919. No. 350. Lenin."*

> "Kharkov. To Mezhlauk. To Voroshilov. Copy to Melnichansky, Artem and Kaminsky.
>
> "The Political Bureau of the CC met on June 1 and in complete agreement with *Trotsky* decisively rejected the plan of the Ukrainians to unite the Second, Eighth and Thirteenth Armies and to create a separate Donetz unit. We demand that *Voroshilov* and *Mezhlauk* carry out their immediate task of creating a strong Ukrainian Army. Tomorrow or the next day *Trotsky* will call you to Izyum and issue more detailed orders. Send more precise, adequate and strictly factual accounts of how much war material *Voroshilov* took from *Grigoriev,* and elsewhere. By the instruction of the Bureau of the C.C. *Lenin."*

We observe from these two telegrams that the Tsaritsin experiment did not pass without leaving a trace, and that Lenin was considerably worried by the situation. The second of Lenin's two telegrams, sent a few hours after the first, is "bolstered" up with the words, "By the instruction of the Bureau of the C.C." That is how matters really stood with the "Tsaritsinites" and "Tsaritsinism," with Stalin and Voroshilov!

Perm

First of all, we shall demonstrate Voroshilov's manner of quoting documents (unfortunately we have not at our disposal *all* the documents and therefore we are unable to expose textually all the "refreshing"). Here is what Voroshilov writes:

> "Lenin telegraphed to the then Chairman of the Military Council: Received a number of party reports from Perm concerning the catastrophic condition of the army, and of drunkenness. I thought to send Stalin—I fear Smilga will be soft with . . . who according to rumors drinks himself and is not in a position to restore order."

We shall now quote from the actual text of the telegram, which reveals what Voroshilov did to Lenin's text:

> "To Kozlov. Forward to the Chairman of the Military Council, Trotsky. Moscow, December 31, 1918. No. 6684.
>
> "Received a number of party reports from beneath Perm concerning the catastrophic condition of the army, and of drunkenness. *Sending them to you. They request that you go there.* I thought to send Stalin, I fear Smilga will be soft with . . . who, according to rumors, drinks himself and is not in a position to restore order. *Wire your opinion.* Lenin."

The italicized words were swallowed by Voroshilov who did this without choking, without so much as placing the all-saving dots. The psychology and the reasons behind that are clear.

Trotsky replied to Vladimir Ilyich from Voronezh on January 1, 1919:

> "From the reports of the operations of the Third Army I concluded that complete confusion existed among the tops there, and proposed a change of command. The decision was delayed. Consider now that change unpostponable. Completely share your fears about the extreme softness of the comrade assigned there. Agree

> to Stalin's going with plenipotentiary powers from the party and the Military Council.
>
> *"Chairman of the Military Council, Trotsky."*

Voroshilov of course does not mention this at all for these two telegrams as well as any scores of others reveal only too vividly the nature of the collaboration between Lenin and Trotsky.

Now as to the trip itself. The assignment of Stalin and Dzerzhinsky to Vyatka was purely for the purpose of inspection. This is quite evident from the decision of the C.C. itself ("To appoint a party investigating committee composed of the following members of the C.C.: Stalin and Dzerzhinsky, in order to make a detailed investigation into the reasons for the surrender of Perm, and the latest defeats on the Ural front; and also to elucidate all the circumstances surrounding the above facts, etc."). In the telegrams of Dzerzhinsky and Stalin from Vyatka, quoted by Voroshilov, they constantly demand reënforcements, failing which, in their opinion, "Vyatka is doomed." Voroshilov then proceeds to do some "refreshing" on his own account, and does it in a deliberately equivocal manner so as to create the impression that he is only re-stating official documents. It appears that one of the reasons for the surrender of Perm was "the criminal methods of managing the Front by the Military Council of the Republic." Let us for a moment allow that Voroshilov is right. The question arises: Why did the party tolerate Trotsky and the entire Military Council of that time? Why was not Trotsky removed during the years of the civil war? Furthermore: Why were victories gained on all fronts under the leadership of the *"then"* Military Council? After all, Military Councils are intended for war and not peace! Why were neither Stalin nor Voroshilov called upon to lead the army, but, on the contrary, removed time and again from difficult sectors? By their declarations the Stalinists compromise only the party, the Central Committee and Lenin. If the myths the Stalinists record were true, it would mean that the C.C. was guilty of the gravest crimes towards the revolution. For it must be borne in mind that all these things took place in the period of cruel civil war and not in peace-time when all the Voroshilovs are freely able to "refresh."

But that is not all. Summarizing the "historic" trip of Stalin to Vyatka, Voroshilov writes: "In consequence of all these [?] measures [of Stalin-Dzerzhinsky] not only was the further offensive of the enemy halted, but in January 1919 . . . Uralsk was captured." Here is a zeal truly excessive! "In consequence" of Stalin's having safely visited Vyatka in January 1919, *a thousand kilometers away*—one thousand!—from Vyatka, Uralsk was captured. . . . In the month of January, *i.e.,* at the very moment when Stalin-Dzerzhinsky arrived in Vyatka there could not have been any results even in Vyatka itself. ("Results"—that is easier written than done.) Or is it perhaps precisely for that reason that Voroshilov had to go to Uralsk to excavate them?

We shall not dwell in detail on Voroshilov's next chapter entitled "Petrograd," we confine ourselves merely to three points.

1. We shall not undertake to judge the extent to which Stalin was instrumental in recapturing Krasnaya Gorka (it had been evacuated without any cause, and was "retaken" four days later without any difficulty). Voroshilov confines himself to vague generalities. But this particular episode is entirely insignificant.

2. The Krasnaya Gorka episode pertains to *June* 1919.

At that time, Stalin, according to his apologist, "liquidated a most dangerous situation beneath Petrograd." Yet the advance of Yudenich and the collapse of the Seventh Army (in which Stalin functioned) began precisely *after* the above-mentioned "liquidation," attaining its most critical stage in October 1919. From June to October the situation of the Red Army beneath Petrograd became worse and worse. Under these circumstances, to say that Stalin had "liquidated" the danger is, to put it mildly . . . risky. Stalin did very little beneath Petrograd, and indeed there was probably not much that he could have done: this front was at that time temporarily neglected. But in that case why is Stalin depicted with the halo of a "savior"?

3. The point, however, is that Voroshilov is here resorting to juggling with words. The entire and most transparent trick lies in the use of the word "Petrograd." In the history of the civil war there is only one decisive "liquidation of the most dangerous situation beneath Red Petrograd"—and that is the victory over Yudenich in October 1919, which took place four months after Stalin's excursion to Petrograd. This is not a matter of common knowledge, but, on the other hand, everybody is acquainted with the fact that Yudenich was liquidated. That is precisely the foundation upon which Voroshilov's trick is built: "To assign" to Stalin the actual liquidation of the danger, *i.e.,* that danger with which Stalin had absolutely no connection.

Incidentally, Stalin himself in his own time appraised his journeys with much less assurance—and that is hardly to be wondered at, since it was ten years ago! Here, for example, is what he wired in reply to a proposal of the C.C. that he go to the Southwestern Front: "February 4th, 1919. To the C.C. of the Party. To comrades Lenin and Trotsky.

My own profound conviction is: No change in the situation can possibly be effected by my trip. . . ."

Or, are we perhaps to seek the causes for that in another "characteristic" trait of Stalin—his "capriciousness" (Lenin)? In any case, these are the facts. And facts are stubborn things.

The Southern Front

Following in the footsteps of Voroshilov, we now pass to the central and most important question, that of the Southern Front. Here, in addition to an immense pile of all sorts of petty insinuations, we find two "general" falsifications (although, perhaps, falsification is much too mild an expression).

The first "general" falsification. This is how Voroshilov describes the autumn of 1919, *i.e.,* the most crucial period of the civil war (Denikin threatens Tula; Yudenich threatens Petrograd). "The situation had to be saved, so the C.C. sent comrade Stalin to the Southern Front in his capacity as a member of the Military Council. It is now [!] no longer necessary to hide [!] that prior to his appointment comrade Stalin put three main conditions to the C.C.: 1) Trotsky must not interfere in the affairs of the Southern Front and must not trespass the lines of demarcation set. . . . These conditions were completely accepted."* *This is a lie from beginning to end.* It does not even contain that grain of truth which is occasionally contained even in a lie. Why has the time for this latest disclosure arrived only "now"? After all, since the year 1924

---

* According to Voroshilov, the second and third conditions consisted of a change in a number of responsible workers and the appointment of new ones (he gives no names—is it perhaps the Tsaritsinites who are hidden under the pseudonym "new ones"?).—N.M.

everything has been "disclosed" that could have been "disclosed." Why was it necessary to wait before making the latest disclosure which is by far less sensational than scores of others made in 1929? It is not for nothing that Voroshilov once again resorts to a free rendition "in his own words." If such a decision of the C.C. really existed, why wasn't it quoted? And why refrain in general from precise reference to facts and documents? The reason is quite apparent. Every fact, every document is in flagrant contradiction with this invention. It ought, by the way, to be remarked here that it is not Voroshilov himself who invented this history. He recounts only that which Stalin in sheer affectation announced during one of the sessions of the Political Bureau back in 1927. Rumors of it penetrated into the party even at that time, arousing indignation among some comrades (those who were well informed), and among others, complete bewilderment. We must also add that during the session of the Political Bureau at which Stalin spoke, minutes were taken which were meant for publication, as is always the case in such procedure. At this session N.I. Muralov, present in the capacity of a member of the Central Control Commission, gave an annihilating answer in rebuttal to Stalin. The recorded minutes were then placed under lock and key and never made public to the party, despite the insistence of the Opposition. Comrade Trotsky at that time (in his "letter to the *Istpart*" and since then in his autobiography) refuted this absurd fiction with documents in hand. Neither Stalin nor anybody else either at that time or since then brought any semblance of excerpts or proofs. Neither Stalin nor anybody else, either at that time or since then, has had a single word to say in reply to the irrefutable documents cited by Trotsky. Moreover, they were compelled to keep silent. Today, three years later, Voroshilov once again raises this ridiculous piece of gossip. But let us give the floor to the documents:

"MOSCOW, JULY 5, 1919.

"The Communist Party of Russia (B.)
"Central Committee
"Kremlin.

"The Organization Bureau and the Political Bureau of the Central Committee, after considering the statement of comrade Trotsky and discussing it in full, have come to the unanimous conclusion that his resignation cannot be accepted, being entirely out of question.

"The Organization Bureau and the Political Bureau of the Central Committee will do all that they can to make more convenient for comrade Trotsky, and more fruitful for the Republic, that work on the Southern Front which comrade Trotsky himself has chosen and which is the most difficult, the most dangerous and the most important at the present moment. In his position as People's Commissar for War and Chairman of the Military Council, comrade Trotsky is also fully empowered to act as a member of the Military Revolutionary Council of the Southern Front with the Commissar of the Southern Front (Yegorov) whom he himself proposed and whom the Central Committee has confirmed.

"The Organization Bureau and the Political Bureau of the Central Committee give comrade Trotsky full authority by every means whatsoever to achieve what he considers a necessary correction of policy on the military question and, if he so desires, to expedite the Congress of the party.

"Firmly convinced that the withdrawal of comrade Trotsky at the present moment is absolutely impossible, and that it would cause the greatest injury to the Republic, the Organization Bureau and the Political Bureau of the Central Committee emphatically suggest to comrade Trotsky not to raise this question again and to fulfill his functions in the future, if he so desires, *concentrating them in the maximum on his work at the Southern Front.*

"In view of this the Organization Bureau and the Political Bureau of the Central Committee reject both the resignation of comrade Trotsky from the Political Bureau and his withdrawal from the post of the Chairman of the Military Council of the Republic (People's Commissar for War).

"Lenin
"Kamenev
"Krestinsky
"Kalinin
"Serebriakov
"Stalin
"Stassova.

"CHECKED BY SECRETARY OF THE CENTRAL COMMITTEE, HELENA STASSOVA."

This document neither requires any commentaries nor does it allow of any false interpretations. Comrade Trotsky has dealt in his autobiography with the reasons which impelled him to take this serious step (*My Life,* pp. 594–97 [2009 printing]). We shall in passing take the opportunity to indicate how the Central Committee reacted when Stalin sought to "threaten" resignation. We cite an excerpt from the session of the Political Bureau, November 14th, 1919:

"(Present: Lenin, Trotsky, Kamenev, Krestinsky.) To inform comrade Stalin that the Political Bureau regards as absolutely impermissible any attempt to reënforce practical demands with ultimatums and declarations of resignation."

Thus, the entire Central Committee sustained comrade Trotsky's decision that he concentrate his work on the Southern Front, as the decisive front. This document alone crumbles to dust the Voroshilov construction. But one could adduce scores of other proofs that Trotsky spent most of his time at the Southern Front. For example, one need only examine the orders of Trotsky to the Red Army for the year 1919 in order to become convinced that the overwhelming majority of them not only apply to the Southern Front but were issued at the very front itself (in connection with another question we shall later deal more fully with this). In particular, the entire decisive preparatory stage which preceded the advance against Denikin was spent by Trotsky at the Southern Front, with the exception of October and the beginning of November when he directed the defense of Petrograd.

It seems to us that we have dealt amply with this question above. But what sloppiness and what disrespect for the party are needed in order to put in circulation the Voroshilov twaddle!

The second "general" falsification. This time we have apparently an independent (and, indeed, for the first time expressed) invention of the "refresher" himself. We have in mind the question of the two strategic plans for the Southern Front. In accordance with the plan of the Chief Command the decisive blow was to have been dealt to Denikin from the Balashov-Kamishin Front at Nizhni Don. This plan was based on the idea of annihilating Denikin's Cossack base, even at the cost of our own retreat in the direction of Moscow. Trotsky from the very beginning (July 1919) considered this plan erroneous and fought against its confirmation by the Central Committee. He considered that this plan would only assist in uniting two absolutely heterogeneous social formations, *i.e.,* the

Cossacks with the volunteer army. On the contrary, by dealing a blow along the line Voronezh-Kharkov-Donbass, the Red Army would move in a socially friendly milieu (the Kharkov and Donetz proletariat and peasantry), the Cossacks would be cut off from Denikin, on whom would fall the entire force of the blow. Nevertheless, the plan of the Chief Command was accepted, with the direct assistance of Stalin and against the sharp opposition of Trotsky. (The episode of Trotsky's handing in his resignation is intimately linked up with the question of the Southern strategic plan.) There followed serious failures at the front (all this can be easily checked up chronologically). Trotsky characterized the situation in September 1919 (and not ten years later as Voroshilov is doing) in his letter to the Central Committee of the party as follows:

> "The plan of operations on the Southern Front which was worked out *a priori* has proved false to the core. The failures at the Southern Front are to be explained first and foremost by the falseness of the basic plan. . . . Therefore the reasons for the failures must be sought entirely in the plan of operations."

And Trotsky goes on to explain how and why this erroneous plan came to originate:

> "The erroneousness of this plan is now so self-evident, that the question arises: How could it have originated at all? Its origin is to be explained historically. When Kolchak threatened the Volga, the chief threat was in the junction between Denikin and Kolchak. In a letter to Kolchak, Denikin set Saratov as the meeting place. Hence the task as proposed even by the old command was the creation of a powerful wedge in the

> Tsaritsin-Saratov area. . . ." (*How the Revolution Armed Itself,* Vol. 2, Bk. 1, pp. 300*f*. This document was published more than six years ago. Voroshilov, it is obvious, counts—not without some justification—on the fact that all of Trotsky's books had been removed from circulation.)

Shortly prior to the writing of this document, comrade Trotsky had succeeded at the front in convincing Lashevich and Serebriakov of the correctness of his plan. The result of this agreement was their joint code telegram which we quote in full:

> "Moscow. To the Chief Command; copy to the C.C.
>
> "Consider it necessary to draw your attention to the following questions:
>
> "The efforts to liquidate Mamontov have thus far brought almost no results. Motorized machine gun detachments have not been created because of nonreceipt of machine guns for even the small number of available automobiles. Mamontov is clearly headed through the Kursk front to effect a junction with his allies. Our weak and dispersed infantry detachments hardly harass him. Lashevich's command is being paralyzed by lack of a contact apparatus. Mamontov's successfully effecting unification may be considered almost assured. The danger of the front being broken in the Kursk-Voronezh area becomes self-evident. Lashevich's most pressing task comes down to following the enemy in order to attempt to fill up the breach that the latter will make. The attempt to harass Mamontov with partisan activities will be made. *The center of gravity of the struggle on the Southern Front has shifted entirely in the direction of Kursk-Voronezh where we have no reserves.*

The destruction of the road prevents the transfer of troops from the Tsaritsin sector to Kursk. Yet the situation imperiously demands the transfer of reserves to the West. Possibly the cavalry corps of Budenny may be able to march there. It is also necessary to add that the situation is being aggravated in the extreme by the complete breakdown of the front line apparatus. The practical tasks seem to us to be the following:

"1) The immediate appointment of Selivachev as the Commander of the Southern Front.

"2) Selivachev's post must be assumed by Yegorov, the assistant Commander of the Southern Front.

"3) Rush reserves including the 21st Division towards Kursk, in the footsteps of Mamontov.

"4) Deploy the Ninth Army from the Novorossisk sector towards Starobelsk.

"5) If possible, to transfer Budenny's corps to the right center.

"6) Rush effective replacements and supplies for the Eighth and Thirteenth Armies.

"Number 364. September 6, 1919.

"Trotsky, Serebriakov, Lashevich."

In other words, Trotsky made the effort to obtain the acceptance of his plan, no longer *a priori* but on the basis of the experience of two to three months of fighting.

Here is the reply of the Political Bureau, undersigned by Lenin:

"Orel. To Trotsky, Serebriakov, Lashevich.

"The Political Bureau having considered the telegram of Trotsky, Serebriakov and Lashevich has confirmed the reply of the Chief Command and expresses its surprise at the attempts to reconsider the adopted basic

> strategic plan. September 6, 1919. By the instructions of the Political Bureau, Lenin."

As we see, the C.C.—and where was Stalin at the time?—even in that period still supported the operating plan of the Staff. It was only the subsequent failures (the surrender of Orel, and the threat to Tula) that forced a review of the plan, in the sense of transferring the main blows in the Donetz direction. In this period, *i.e., when experience had already demonstrated the erroneousness of the old plan* which was renounced even by the Staff itself, Stalin, too, grasped the mistake that had been committed.

Voroshilov quotes Stalin's letter but omits the date it was sent. That was, of course, done deliberately. Had he given the date, Voroshilov would have been unable to ascribe the plan to Stalin. As we shall shortly prove, Stalin's letter was sent several months after the question of the two plans had first arisen. Voroshilov writes: "As regards operating directives, he [Stalin] was offered the *old plan* (that of *September*) of dealing the main blow, etc. . . ." With this statement Voroshilov exposes himself completely. In the first place, if during the period of Stalin's creative work on "planning" at the Southern Front, the "September" (?) plan was already an "old" plan, then it is quite self-evident that all of the above took place after September, *i.e.,* already after Trotsky had raised the question of reconsidering the plan for the second time (see document on p. 277). In the second place, the erroneous plan was adopted not in September but two months earlier, so that there had never existed such a thing as the "September" plan. In September there was only a *reaffirmation* of the previously adopted plan of the Chief Command (see Lenin's reply to the telegram of Trotsky, Lashevich and Serebriakov). As we have already stated, Trotsky fought against the adoption of the plan of the Chief Command as early as July and August, at a time when Stalin was with the majority of the Political Bureau. Furthermore, at the beginning of September, Trotsky tried again—this time on the basis of a number of conclusions drawn from experience itself—to obtain reconsideration of the plan. Stalin remained as hitherto in favor of—the erroneous plan. And it was only later that Stalin proceeded to the "re-valuation of values." There is an indirect proof that the date of Stalin's letter must be assigned to *October* or November 1919, namely, Stalin concludes his well-publicized letter with "threats" of resignation. We have already cited above the reply of the C.C. on this score ("absolutely impermissible," etc.). This reply is dated *November 14;* therefore the deduction is that Stalin must have written his letter of criticism, sometime early in November, and hardly prior to that time, *i.e.,* after a delay of some three or four months. Voroshilov, on the other hand, after a delay of ten years, asserts on the basis of this letter that "Stalin's [??] plan was accepted by the Central Committee." That is how history is being "refreshed"!

Having disposed of the two "general" falsifications, we pass on to the petty falsifications of Voroshilov.

Citing the telegram of the Military Council of the Southern Front for November 11, 1919, to the Supreme Military Council of the Republic with the request to affirm the organization of the First Cavalry Army, Voroshilov adds the following comment: "The Cavalry Army was created despite and even against the center." In the first place, what "center" is this? Always equivocations! Is it the Political Bureau? or the Chief Command? or Lenin? or Trotsky? In the second place, if the "center" was against the organization of the First Cavalry, why did it have to affirm the decision of the Military Council of the Southern Front?

So far as Trotsky is personally concerned, if we take the question in its broadest aspects, *i.e.,* the timely realization of the rôle of cavalry in the manoeuvre-operations of a civil war, then it is sufficient to refer to a slogan, popular in its time, which was raised by comrade Trotsky (incidentally, long before the telegram adduced by Voroshilov): "Proletarians, to horse!" Under this same title, comrade Trotsky published an article which likewise posed the question of large scale bodies of cavalry. One of the main tasks of the "armored train" (of the Chairman of the Military Council) in that period was the creation of the cavalry. It would not be inappropriate to recall that the closest collaborator of Trotsky's secretariat, I.M. Poznansky, formed fighting mounted detachments during that period. But Poznansky himself cannot say anything, because he is kept under lock and key by Stalin-Voroshilov.

Further on, as one of the instances of Stalin's "rescue" expeditions to the "most dangerous places," Voroshilov informs us of Stalin's journey to the Caucasian front *which never took place.* Ludicrous as it may seem, this is a fact! Stalin, you see, did not take the trip only because of "illness." Illness is a weighty reason, but we are rather inclined to think that "capriciousness" had something to do with this incident, and for the following reason: A week after Stalin's trip, which "rescued" even though it never took place, Stalin sent the following telegram in reply to Lenin's demand that he take emergency measures in order to speed up the transfer of two divisions to the Caucasian Front:

> "Moscow. Kremlin. To Lenin; copy to the C.C. of the Party.
>
> "I am not quite clear as to why the chief concern about the Caucasian Front falls primarily upon me. The strengthening of the Caucasian Front properly and

> entirely falls upon the Military Council of the Republic, the members of which, according to my information, are in good health; it is their concern and not that of Stalin who is overburdened with work as it is. Number 970. February 20, 1920. Stalin."

Here is what Lenin replied to him:

> "The concern of speeding up the arrival of reënforcements from the Southwestern Front to the Caucasian Front has been placed on you. It is generally necessary to give all possible assistance and not to bicker about departmental jurisdiction. No. 37/3. Lenin."

How characteristic of Stalin is this tone of petty intrigue and personal grievance! How characteristic of Lenin is his tone of restrained indignation! The documents speak for themselves. And we observe how eloquent is their language.

It goes without saying that the man whom the party *always* really did send to the most difficult sectors (as a matter of fact that was really his "job") was not at all Stalin. Here are a few brief excerpts from Lenin's telegrams:

> "August 22, 1918. Sviazhsk. To Trotsky. Treason on the Saratov Front, though discovered in time, has nevertheless produced extremely dangerous vacillations. We consider your going there at once absolutely indispensable, for your appearance at the front has an effect on soldiers and the entire army. . . . Lenin, Sverdlov."

> "April 10, 1919. To Trotsky. Nizhni Novgorod.
>
> "In view of the extremely grave situation on the Eastern Front I think it is most expedient for you to remain there. Lenin."

"May 7, 1919. Shikhrana. To Trotsky. I have just consulted the Political Bureau of the C.C., and in agreement with the Bureau I am in favor of your immediate and speediest departure to Kharkov, where it is urgent to put an end to disorganization and to give immediate aid to the Donetz Basin. Lenin."

"May 15, 1919. Kupyansk. To Trotsky.

"Extremely pleased by the energetic measures by which the uprising was crushed. . . . Lenin."

"May 21, 1919. . . . I would insist personally on your going to Bogachur once again, in order to complete the crushing of the uprising, otherwise there is no hope for victory. Lenin."

(24 hours later) "May 22, 1919. . . . I insist again on your going without fail a second time to Bogachur and putting an end to the matter, because it is obvious that Sokolnikov cannot handle the situation. Lenin."

And here is Trotsky's reply:

"Kharkov-Lugansk (*en route*). To Moscow. To Sklyansky for Lenin. Leaving for Bogachur, and will try to bring the matter to an end there. Trotsky. May 22, 1919."

Such are the facts. Similar *facts* can be adduced to any number! That Voroshilov today has to "refresh" inventions only proves that despite everything these facts are still too fresh in the memory of the party.

The March 1917 party conference

FOREWORD

The All-Russian Conference of the Soviets of Workers' and Soldiers' Deputies was convened at the end of March 1917. Simultaneously with this Conference the Bureau of the Bolshevik Central Committee issued a call for the All-Russian Conference of party workers for March 28, the first one held after the February revolution.

The agenda planned for the Conference was as follows:

1) Local reports.

2) Report of the Bureau of the Central Committee.

3) S.D.L.P.R. and the Soviet of Workers' and Soldiers' Deputies.

4) The attitude towards the Provisional Government.

5) The attitude to the war.

6) The organization of the counter-revolutionary forces and the struggle against the counter-revolution.

7) Preparation for the Constituent Assembly.

8) The Agrarian question.

9) The Eight-Hour day.

The following organizations and comrades took part in the Conference:

Organizations	**Names of Delegates**
1) Archangel—	Maryan Verzhbitsky*
2) Alexandrovsk-Gruschevsk—	P.V. Novov-Okhlonin*
3) Almaznaya—	Daineko
4) Baku—	Ter-Gabryelan*
5) Voronezh—	Komissarov
6) V. Volochek—	V.F. Sokolov*
7) Vitebsk—	J. Abolin
8) Vologda—	Shalva Zurab Eliava
	Ivan A. Sammer
9) Vyborg—	Panshin*
10) Gomel—	P.N. Sevruk*
11) Helsingfors-Sviborg—	S.A. Garin*
12) Grozny—	Bogdanov*
	H.E. Bugai*
13) Ekaterinodar—	A.A. Limansky*
14) Ekaterinoslav—	G.V. Golovko*
15) Ekaterinburg—	L.S. Sosnovsky
	P. Bykov*
16) Enakievo (Petrovsky mines and mills)—	Speransky*
	K.P. Susenkov*
17) Ivanovo-Voznesensk—	Vera A. Korovaikova
18) Irkutsk—	Peter I. Starostin*
	Robert J. Dukur*
19) Kiev—	Maximilian A. Saveliev*
	Alexandrov

20) Kostroma—	Leonid P. Serebriakov*
	Vassili A. Krapivin
	Nicolai I. Vorobiev
21) Kursk—	Alexander N. Grigoriev
22) Kenavino—	S. Levitt
23) Kronstadt—	Uliantsev
24) Krasnoyarsk—	Teodorovich*
25) Lozovaya—	Teploukhov*
26) Lysivensky Factory—	Savchenko*
	Danilenko
27) Moscow—	Victor P. Nogin*
	E.N. Ignatov*
28) Minsk—	Boris P. Pozern*
	Yakhontov
29) Novgorod—	Ionov
30) Morshansk—	Nicolai A. Skrypnik*
31) Minyarsk (Ufa Goubernia)—	Vakhterov*
32) Nikolayev—	Nicolai M. Mandelstam*
	Alexander G. Ovchinnikov*
33) Novo-Nikolayevsk—	S.I. Kanatchikov*
	Adolf Klepner*
34) Nikitovka—	Jacob Grosfin*
	N. Akimov*
35) Odessa—	Ochkanov*
36) Omsk—	Peter A. Kravtsov
37) Poltava—	Drobnis
38) Revel—	I.E. Kuzmin*
	A. Balevsky
39) Rostov-on-the-Don—	Vassilchenko

40) Samara—	N. Teplov*
	Gersimov*
	Robert Bauza
41) Saratov—	M.I. Vassiliev*
	V.P. Miliutin
	K.I. Plaxin
42) Syzran—	N.D. Vozdvizhensky*
43) Sormovo—	Nicolai E. Miroshin
44) Simferopol—	T. Fedoseyev*
	T. Kravchenko*
45) Tomsk—	Ivan N. Smirnov*
	Nakhanovich*
46) Taganrog—	Paul M. Berman*
47) Tula—	Nikita G. Brigadirov
48) Ufa—	Boris M. Eltsin*
49) Kharkov—	Gregory A. Romanovich*
50) Kherson—	Ivan F. Sorokin
51) Tsaritsin—	Weinzweig*
	Sergei K. Minin
	D.A. Sagareishvili
52) Chelyabinsk—	S.M. Tsvilling
53) Scherbinovka—	Nahum Dubovoi*
54) Yuriev—	A.K. Rozov
55) Yaroslavl—	Ivan I. Korotkov
56) Stavropol-Kavkaz—	Vassili F. Tolstov
57) Petropavlovsk—	Alexander M. Povolotsky
58) 180th Regiment—	Kutuzov

In addition to those listed above, the following organizations

* The asterisk denotes those participants who were delegates to the Soviet Conference.

whose delegates failed to report to the Secretariat participated in the Conference:

1) Kamyshlova
2) Valka
3) Petrovska
4) Narvy
5) 1st Reserve Infantry
6) 112th Infantry Regiment
7) 729th Infantry Regiment

Present from the Central Committee were—
Stalin
Vyacheslav M. Molotov
Peter A. Zalutsky
Helena D. Stassova
Shliapnikov

Participating personally were—
Ivan T. Smilga
G.F. Fedorov
M.S. Olminsky
A.I. Elizarova
Stuchka, member of the Latvian Central Committee
Kollontai, member of the Finnish CC

Present from the Petrograd Committee were—
Leon M. Mikhailov
Vladimir N. Zalezhsky
(Sergei) Bagdatiev
Boki
Shagov
Goloschekin
Badayev
Yakovlenko
Enukidze
Epstein
Krestinsky

The sessions were first held at the Kshesinskaia Palace and later transferred to the Tauride Palace, in the gallery.

The original protocols were destroyed by Kerensky's gangs during the July days in a raid on the Kshesinskaia Palace, at that time the headquarters of the Central Committee of our party.

Fortunately, I have preserved the original drafts of the protocols and the records of the sessions, with the exception of the sessions for March 27 and March 28, when the war question was under discussion. From these documents it was possible to restore the protocols of the sessions.

These records do not of course represent stenographic minutes—our small party, poor in resources, did not even dare dream of such luxury at that time. These are merely notes as taken down during the sessions; and they are more or less complete, depending upon the individual peculiarities of the particular speaker (the speed and lucidity of his delivery, etc.). In any case, there is nothing in them that is "personally interpolated." Everything in the notes represents an exact, even though incomplete, reproduction of what the speakers said.—L.T.

SESSION OF MARCH 29, 1917

Chairman: comrade Nogin.

Secretaries: comrades Boki and Drabkina.

The order of the day: The question of the attitude toward the Provisional Government.

After the session was called to order, all the delegates of the Conference were divided into sections in accordance with the projected Conference of the Soviet of Workers' and Soldiers' Deputies.

Soldiers' Section: comrades Pozern, Borisov, Shashkin,

Vengerov, Panshin, Verzhbitsky, I.N. Smirnov, Ter-Gabryelan, Klepner, Syrkin, Shklovsky, Paderin, Garin, Serebriakov.

Workers' Section: comrades Starostin, Vassiliev, Kanatchikov, Kravtsov, Okhlonin, Ter-Gabryelan, Speransky, Sosnovsky, Yakhontov, Romanovich, Nakhanovich, Sammer, Sorokin.

Organizational Section: comrades Sevruk, Saveliev, Skrypnik, Pozern, Mandelstam.

Section of Local Affairs: comrades Dukur, Teploukhov, Tsvilling, Drobnis.

Agrarian Section: comrades Romanovich, Miliutin, V.P. Lebed.

Mandate Commission: comrades Sevruk, Skrypnik.

The resolution of the Praesidium of the Soviet Conference dealing with the manner in which the work would be divided was read: At 6 P.M. elections to the Mandate Commission; division into sections; report by Tseretelli.

Reporters: On War—Tseretelli; On the Organization of Power—Steklov.

DELEGATE: Has an agreement been reached on the question of reporters?

NOGIN: Proposes that the representatives of the various sections come to an agreement on the question of the speakers.

SKRYPNIK: Proposes to suggest to the representatives of all factions that they insist on co-reports.

ON THE ATTITUDE TO THE PROVISIONAL GOVERNMENT

Report by Comrade Stalin

STALIN: The Russian Revolution unfolded not under ordinary circumstances, but against the background of the imperialist war. This fact has left a peculiar mark on the development of the revolution. Due to the fact of the war, the revolutionary crisis, aggravated by a food crisis, was resolved very rapidly. Owing to the war, the army has played a rôle which it never played in any other revolution due to the fact that the entire adult population was mobilized and that the army joined the insurrectionary people. Due to the fact of the war, Czarism has been isolated even from imperialist bourgeois circles. Czarism, by its betrayals, repelled the bourgeoisie from itself. Even the imperialist circles of the West, England and France, turned their backs on Czarism, because they wanted to have at the head of the Russian government people capable of waging the war to the end. There are four forces in the revolution. The two basic ones are the workers and the soldiers. And, in addition, there are two secondary ones: the imperialist circles, both our own and the Anglo-French. These forces, having united, prepared the soil for such an easy and rapid overthrow of Czarism. But since the forces are heterogeneous, therefore their aims are likewise heterogeneous. The tops, the bourgeoisie, both our own and those of Western Europe, have united in order to effect a change in the decorative scenery; they have united in order to replace one Czar by another. They wanted an easy revolution, like the Turkish, with very little freedom, so as to wage the war. A tiny revolution for a big victory. But the lower ranks—the workers and the soldiers—have deepened the revolution, having destroyed the props of the old system. Thus, it is as if we had two currents—one from below, the other from above—which have brought forward two governments, two forces: 1) the Provisional Government, supported by Anglo-French capitalism; 2) the Soviet of Workers' and Soldiers' Deputies. The power has been divided between two organs, of which neither one possesses full power. There is and there ought to be friction and struggle between them. The rôles have been divided. The Soviet of Workers' and Soldiers' Deputies has in fact taken the initiative in effecting revolutionary transformations. The Soviet of Workers' and Soldiers' Deputies is the revolutionary leader of the insurrectionary people; an organ of control over the Provisional Government. On the other hand, the Provisional Government has in fact taken the rôle of fortifier of the conquests of the revolutionary people. The Soviet of Workers' and Soldiers' Deputies mobilizes the forces and exercises control, while the Provisional Government, balking and muddling, takes the rôle of the fortifier of those conquests by the people which they have already seized as a fact. Such a situation has disadvantageous, but also advantageous sides. It is not to our advantage at present to force events, hastening the process of repelling the bourgeois layers, who will in the future inevitably withdraw from us. It is necessary for us to gain time by putting a brake on the splitting away of the middle-bourgeois layers so that we may prepare ourselves for the struggle against the Provisional Government. But such a situation will not endure endlessly. The revolution is deepening. From the political questions there will be a transition to the social questions. The social demands will cause the middle-bourgeois layers to split away. It is silly to think that it will be possible to bring the revolution to its completion without a split with the bourgeoisie. When that time comes, in so far as the split grows, the Provisional Government will become transformed from an organ for fortifying the conquests of the revolution into an organ for organizing the counter-revolution. A struggle is already being conducted against the Soviet of Workers' and Soldiers' Deputies; an agitation is being carried on against it among the troops. Clashes are beginning to occur over the questions of the [loyalty] oath, the democratization of the army, the change of the Supreme Commanding Staff. The mobilization of the counter-revolutionary forces has as its banner: "War to a victorious conclusion!" This offensive is being carried on not only from within but also from without—from the side of England and France. Their semi-official organs have launched a veritable offensive against the revolution. The offensive against dual power has begun, and in proportion as the revolution develops the Provisional Government must (it must objectively) become transformed into the bulwark of counter-revolution, not a Czarist counter-revolution—we face no danger from that side—but an imperialist counter-revolution. To prepare for repelling it—that is our task. In view of this, the question becomes more complex. The question of support—let us even allow that support is not permissible. In so far as the Provisional Government fortifies the steps of the revolution, to that extent we must support it; but in so far as it is counter-revolutionary, support to the Provisional Government is not permissible. Many comrades who have arrived from the provinces ask whether we shouldn't immediately pose the question of the seizure of power. But it is untimely to pose the question now. The Provisional Government is not so weak. The strength of the Provisional Government lies in the support of Anglo-French capitalism, in the inertia of the provinces and in the [widespread] sympathy for it. It is being showered with telegrams [of congratulation]. We must bide our time until the Provisional Government exhausts itself, until the time when in the process of fulfilling the revolutionary program it discredits itself. The only organ capable of taking power is the Soviet of Workers' and Soldiers' Deputies on an All-Russian scale. We, on the other hand, must bide our time until the moment when the events will reveal the hollowness of the Provisional Government; we must be prepared, when the time comes, when the events have matured, and until then we must organize the center—the Soviet of Workers' and Soldiers' Deputies—and strengthen it. Therein lies the task of the moment.

Comrade Stalin reads the resolution on the Provisional Government adopted by the Bureau of the Central Committee, but states that he is not in complete agreement with it, but is rather in accord with the resolution of the Krasnoyarsk Soviet of Workers' and Soldiers' Deputies.

The resolution of the Bureau of the Central Committee

"The Provisional Government, brought forward by the moderate bourgeois classes of our society and linked through all its interests with Anglo-French capitalism, is incapable of solving the tasks posed by the revolution. Its resistance to the further development and deepening of the revolution is being paralyzed only by the growth of the revolutionary forces and their own organizations. The focal point for their consolidation must be the Soviet of Workers' and Soldiers' Deputies in the cities and the Soviet of Peasants' and Farmhands' Deputies in the country, which, as the embryos of revolutionary power, are prepared, in the course of the further development and at a given moment in the development of the revolution, to realize in full the power of the proletariat in an alliance with the revolutionary democracy, so that the demands of the insurrectionary people may be wholly put into effect.

Even at the present moment these Soviets should exercise the most decisive control over all the actions of the Provisional Government and its agents both in the center and in the provinces; and they should themselves assume a number of functions of state and of an economic character arising from the complete disorganization of economic life in the country and from the urgent necessity to apply the most resolute measures for safeguarding the famine-stricken population whom war has ruined. Therefore the task of the day is: The consolidation of all forces around the Soviet of Workers' and Soldiers' Deputies as the embryo of revolutionary power, alone capable both of repelling the attempts on the part of the Czarist and bourgeois counter-revolution as well as of realizing the demands of revolutionary democracy and of explaining the true class nature of the present government.

"The most urgent and important task of the Soviets, the fulfillment of which will alone guarantee the victory over all the forces of counter-revolution and the further development and deepening of the revolution, is, in the opinion of the party, the universal arming of the people, and, in particular, the immediate creation of Workers' Red Guards throughout the entire land."

Resolution of the Krasnoyarsk Soviet of Workers', Soldiers' and Cossacks' Deputies

"Whereas:

"1) the revolutionary overturn has been achieved by the working class and the Army representing the revolutionary peasantry,

"2) the Provisional Government expresses the demands of the Russian imperialist belligerent bourgeoisie and not the demands of the proletariat and the revolutionary peasantry,

"3) the clash between the demands of the imperialist bourgeoisie and the demands of the working class and the peasantry in the revolution is inevitable in the future inasmuch as the bourgeoisie will seek to defend its own interests against the interests of the working class and the revolutionary peasantry,

"The Krasnoyarsk Soviet of Workers', Soldiers' and Cossacks' Deputies resolves:

"1) to recognize as urgent that it be made clear to the broad layers of the working class, the Army and the peasantry that the Provisional Government in its composition expresses the interests of the imperialist bourgeoisie and not those of the people; that it is incapable of coöperating in carrying the present revolution through to the fulfillment of the basic demands of the proletariat and the revolutionary peasantry;

"2) to make entirely clear that the only source of the power and the authority of the Provisional Government is the will of the people who have accomplished this revolution and to whom the Provisional Government is obliged wholly to submit;

"3) to make likewise clear that the submission of the Provisional Government to the basic demands of the revolution can be secured only by the unrelaxing pressure of the proletariat, the peasantry and the revolutionary Army, who must with unremitting energy maintain their organization around the Soviets of Workers' and Soldiers' Deputies born out of the revolution, in order to transform the latter into the terrible force of the revolutionary people;

"4) to support the Provisional Government in its activities only in so far as it follows a course of satisfying the demands of the working class and the revolutionary peasantry in the revolution that is taking place."

❖

The resolution of the Moscow District Committee is next read. It was not among the documents.

❖

VOITINSKY (CO-REPORTER): Leaving aside the contradictions, all three resolutions express one and the same view of the Provisional Government: The monarchist Guchkov arrests the monarch; the monarchist Miliukov becomes a member of the republican Provisional Government. Among the members of the Provisional Government there is not a single supporter of the Constituent Assembly with the exception of Kerensky—but notwithstanding this, it organizes the Constituent Assembly. While being counter-revolutionary to the core, being counter-revolutionary in all respects—in the program of the parties represented in it, and in their aims—it is nevertheless revolutionary in its activities. The contradiction between its counter-revolutionary nature and its revolutionary activities is a basic contradiction. The reporter has called our attention to the support of Anglo-French capitalism. But that is absolutely wrong. Recall the almost threatening tone of Buchanan's speech: We will support you only to the extent that you fulfill the promises of the Czarist government. Recall the speeches of Bonar Law and others in the House of Commons. Anglo-French capitalism is protesting, of course, not against Miliukov and not against the Government but against its *activities*. They are in sympathy with the Government but they are opposed to its activities and they demand that "an end be put to agitation," in the guise of the Soviet of Workers' and Soldiers' Deputies.

All the sympathies of the parties that have formed the Provisional Government were inclined not to the side of participating in the revolution but of resisting it. The Octobrists[62] and the Cadets took no part in the revolution, remaining counter-revolutionists, till the moment when the revolution conquered. The Provisional Government received the power from the hands of the people. The Soviet of Workers' and Soldiers' Deputies could have refused to recognize it—and it would never have come into existence. But I ask, why then are the counter-revolutionary forces fulfilling the work of the revolution? Why didn't the revolutionary democracy take power into its own hands instead of passing it into the hands of the moderate and liberal bourgeoisie? The answer to the second question will at the same time provide an answer to the first.

It is as clear as noonday that to take the power into our own hands at the moment when it was possible to realize the dictatorship of the democracy would have meant to ruin the bourgeois democratic revolution. The proletariat would have been unable to cope with the anarchy. The revolutionary proletariat halted at the threshold and transferred the power into other hands. We had no revolutionary democratic bourgeois parties in our country. It was impossible for the socialists to take the power into their own hands. Only one thing remained—to hand the power over to the moderate elements, but on the condition that they fulfill a revolutionary program inimical to themselves. The Cadet-Monarchists were attached to the republican Government. They are fulfilling, with hatred towards us, and without disguising their hatred, our revolutionary program. It was thus that there arose this incongruity between the activities and the inner essence of the Provisional Government which we are now witnessing. The Government is in its majority comprised of moderate bourgeois layers, but it received the power from the hands of the revolutionary people, after it had pledged to the latter to fulfill the revolutionary program of the people—to destroy the monarchy, to convene the Constituent Assembly, to democratize autonomous local rule, etc. But precisely because of this internal contradiction there must be control on the part of the Soviet of Workers' Deputies. So long as this control exists, it [the Government] will put the program into effect. It [the Government] does not want to solve, but under the control of the revolutionary democracy it is able to solve problems of the revolution. The Cadets and the Octobrists turned to the Soviet of Workers' Deputies with the request: "Give us Ministers." It is objectively inevitable for the power to pass from the less revolutionary into the more revolutionary hands, but this transfer will be effected gradually, through the resignation of the more moderate Ministers and their replacement by more radical ones, but not in a revolutionary way through their violent overthrow. I ask you to consider attentively the following detail: Miliukov came with the slate of Ministers to the Soviet of Workers' Deputies for confirmation; the threat of resignation was likewise submitted to the Soviet, that is to say, they turned to the Soviet in very much the same way as is usually done in the case of monarchs in the countries of constitutional monarchy. It is not true that the Soviet is an embryo of power. The Soviet is the power, dictating its own terms, while the Provisional Government is a clerk of the Soviet. It is impossible for us to take the power entirely into our own hands under the bourgeois system.

While recognizing the counter-revolutionary essence of the Provisional Government we must at the same time recognize that it is fulfilling revolutionary work. We must support each and every revolutionary step on its part and fight against any of its attempts to evade control, viewing that as a betrayal of and as mutiny against democracy. But in the meantime our task is to organize the forces, to prepare for the transfer of power into our own hands. Therefore not the Red Guard, but the attraction to us of the Army, the fulfillment of the socialist program, the preparation for the transfer of power into our hands—these are our immediate tasks.

Introduces a resolution. [Not in the records.—L.T.]

SAVELIEV: Comrade Stalin has pointed out absolutely correctly the meaning of the rôle of the bourgeoisie in the present war and of the position occupied by the proletariat. It is impossible to agree with comrade Voitinsky that Anglo-French capitalism has played no rôle. To be sure, it did not expect the revolution to attain such a sweep. The revolutionary democracy mixed all the cards. The paths of the imperialist bourgeoisie and of the revolutionary democracy momentarily crossed each other. Due to entirely different reasons, to entirely different motives, the two forces criss-crossed in such a manner as to coincide during the moment of the overthrow of the autocracy. In any case, having crossed, having taken to this path, the Russian bourgeoisie has had to follow in the wake of the proletariat, *i.e.,* it found the path already closed to any compromise with the autocracy that was in process of liquidation. It made the pretense of joining the insurrectionary people. But why did we get such a situation? Because the relation of forces in the country was not such as would allow the dictatorship of the proletariat.

Comrade Saveliev moves the following resolution for adoption:

> "1) Whereas the Provisional Government brought forward by the moderate bourgeois classes had to take

upon itself the fulfillment of a number of demands advanced by the insurrectionary people;

"2) this Provisional Government is incapable of solving all the tasks which have been posed by the present revolution;

"3) the concentration of the revolutionary forces and the focal point of their consolidation are the Soviets of Workers' and Soldiers' Deputies—in the cities, together with the Soviets of Peasants' and Farmhands' Deputies now being organized in the villages—as the organs of revolutionary power;

"4) in the subsequent development of the process, and at a certain point of this development, the revolution will realize the full measure of the power of the proletariat in an alliance with the democratic section of the peasantry and the revolutionary Army for the full realization of the demands of the insurrectionary people,

"We *recognize* that at the present moment it is necessary:

"1) to maintain unrelaxing control over the Provisional Government and to conduct a struggle against all inclinations on its part to manifest its counter-revolutionary tendencies;

"2) to consolidate all the forces around the Soviets of Workers' and Soldiers' Deputies—as the organs of revolutionary power which are alone capable both of repelling the attempts of the Czarist and bourgeois counter-revolution as well as of realizing the demands of the revolutionary democracy; and

"3) to clarify the true class nature of the present Government."

GARIN: I do not believe, comrades, that there is anybody here who would agitate for undermining the confidence in the Provisional Government in so far as its activity is directed toward the benefit of the people. But naturally we must issue a declaration to the effect that the revolution has been accomplished by the people, that the Provisional Government has given the people an I.O.U. which it must pay. But if it should fail to fulfill its obligations, then the people will demand not only full payment, but collect the interest too.

The Helsingfors Committee of the S.D.L.P.R. has adopted the following resolution:

> "To support the Provisional Government, in so far as it fulfills its obligations as proclaimed to the whole nation, and so long as the Provisional Government is inclined to follow the path of the revolutionary conquests for the benefit of Free Russia. While so doing, we, social democrats, must use all means to eliminate among the people those trivial demands which prior to the convocation of the Constituent Assembly might raise a wall between the people and the Provisional Government."

MILIUTIN: We are all agreed that the Provisional Government is counter-revolutionary in essence. Then why are there disagreements on the question of our attitude toward it? Voitinsky says that the Provisional Government is bourgeois, but that it received the power from the hands of the people and is carrying through the people's program. The power is in our hands and we must give active support to the Government in carrying through the measures aimed to fortify the conquests of the revolution. Stalin, on the other hand, speaks of the broadening of the tasks of the revolution. The difference lies not in the conclusions but in the tactics. We proceed from different basic assumptions. Voitinsky has caught the technical side but missed the socio-political side. The fact that the Provisional Government submitted the ministerial slate is meaningless. Our revolution is not only a political but also a social revolution. A government consisting of the representatives of the bourgeoisie is therefore counter-revolutionary. The most important things that the Provisional Government must realize are: the war question, the social questions. In this sphere we can place no confidence in it. We must extend and fortify the conquests of the revolution but not solidarize with the steps of the Provisional Government.

STAROSTIN: Voitinsky has missed the social side of the revolution, but he has grasped the political side. What has compelled the Provisional Government to take the power into its hands? The fear lest it lose the possibility of attaining its imperialist plans. On the other hand, the working class was unable at that time to advance its own slate, and we ourselves didn't know what was going to happen. Petrograd could not sit and wait for a number of Vendées. Had we known here that the whole of Russia would join in, then perhaps we might have taken power into our own hands.

An offensive against democracy is already in progress. *Novoye Vrema* writes that the soldiers have to stay in the trenches 24 hours at a stretch, but the workers are introducing the eight-hour day. In some places, outright pogrom agitation is being conducted. It is necessary to make a definite declaration as to the extent of our support to the Provisional Government. The speaker is not in agreement with the point on the "Red Guard." This might be construed as mistrust of the Red Army and engender discord. If the revolutionary Army does not back us up, then dozens of Red Guard detachments will not be able to accomplish anything. Our task therefore must be to do our utmost to strengthen our influence on the revolutionary Army.

GOLOSCHEKIN: Should the Provisional Government take revolutionary steps—for instance, proclaim the confiscation of the lands—we will support it. But we cannot vote it complete confidence. Everybody is agreed that the Provisional Government is counter-revolutionary both in its personnel and in its essence. Under the pressure of the masses it is accomplishing revolutionary tasks, and to this extent, it intrenches itself. We must not overlook that the masses are saying that the Provisional Government has done everything. Voitinsky envisions a parliamentary method of the struggle for power! The government will depart of its own accord, and no struggle for power will be necessary. We forget that for the time being it is hiding its claws, and we ourselves are strengthening it. If we want to struggle against the counter-revolution, we must aim for the seizure of power, but without forcing events. How? By grouping around the Soviet of Workers' and Soldiers' Deputies so that gradually the Soviet assumes all functions, and dominates all spheres of activity. It is necessary to teach the people to see that they are getting everything from the Soviet.

The speaker concludes with a proposal to proclaim an All-National Militia.

VASSILIEV: We all have the same attitude to the Provisional Government. But that is not the task of the moment. On the agenda is the creation of a revolutionary provisional government. Having accomplished the revolution, the people have created the Provisional Government, but this government is non-revolutionary not because Miliukov and Guchkov sit in it—no; even if they should go away—the others likewise will not prove any more revolutionary.

Our task, therefore, is to prepare a revolutionary government. All government consists of executive and controlling power. We have an organ of revolutionary control in the Soviet of Workers' and Soldiers' Deputies, but the executive power has not yet been created among us. The longer it exists, the more powerful the Provisional Government will become, for at its disposal are enormous resources, the entire state machinery. Our task is the formation of a provisional revolutionary parliament which will put forth executive power. There must be created as quickly as possible a permanent organ comprised of the representatives of the proletariat and of the revolutionary Army of all Russia which would function as the provisional revolutionary parliament up to the convocation of the Constituent Assembly. The Provisional Government must be viewed as the executive organ of the Provisional Revolutionary Parliament. It must not initiate a single important measure without the knowledge and approval of the Provisional Revolutionary Parliament. The Provisional Revolutionary Parliament must be empowered to issue, in agreement with the Provisional Government, decrees on all vital questions.

Such a correlation between the Provisional Government and the Provisional Revolutionary Parliament would decisively do away with the question of dual power.

Will we go there?—In 1905, we said that we will participate in a revolutionary government. There can be talk not of giving support but of subordinating the Provisional Government to the Provisional Revolutionary Parliament.

The speaker proposes the following draft resolution.

> "1) Placing above all else the international solidarity of the working class, we heartily hail and support the Manifesto of the Petrograd Soviet of Workers' and

Soldiers' Deputies to the people of the whole world, and its appeal to all proletarians that they put an end to imperialism and to the debauch of predatory passions in their own respective countries, and that they coöperate with might and main for the most rapid termination of the bloody slaughter. Only the peoples themselves can conclude an honest and a stable peace.

"2) Revolutionary democratic Russia does not seek an inch of foreign soil, or a penny of foreign property. But not an inch of our own soil or a penny of our own property can be taken away from us. The fate of disputed regions, the fate of oppressed nationalities in all belligerent countries and in the entire world must be left to the free decision of the subject nationalities. No annexations, no contributions, and the free self-determination of all nations—that is our platform of peace!

"3) Considering that the European war, which has convulsed the socio-economic life of the entire terrestrial globe, has been engendered by the predatory urge of the rulers in all countries; and that the earliest possible termination of this war which is ruining the best forces and the culture of the states involved in it will be in the interests of the proletariat and the democracy of the whole world, we urge the Provisional Government to turn both to the Allies as well as their foes with a proclamation to open peace negotiations on the above-stated basis.

"4) But so long as peace is not concluded we must stand fully armed; and in guarding the interests of new democratic Russia we must increase tenfold our efforts, for we are now defending our budding liberties. The revolutionary army must be powerful and unconquerable. It must be provided by the workers and by the Provisional Government with everything necessary

> to strengthen its forces. Discipline in the ranks, being the necessary condition of an army's strength, must be sustained not out of fear but out of free will, and based upon mutual confidence between the democratic officer staff and the revolutionary soldiers.
>
> "5) If the summons of the Petrograd Soviet of Workers' and Soldiers' Deputies, and our revolution find an echo in the midst of the European proletariat and democracy, if in Western Europe a revolution breaks out against predatory capitalism, we will support our international comrades with all our might, and we will struggle for a social revolution."

SKRYPNIK: What is understood by the term "support"? So far as I was able to gather, everybody said that the Provisional Government has been undertaking these or those revolutionary measures under the pressure of the revolutionary proletariat. But this is not the support of the Government but of those measures which we ourselves demanded and which it has been putting into effect. On the other hand, the question of support obviously has another meaning, namely not the support of measures, but a declaration of confidence in it [the Government] before the eyes of Russia, and the rest of the world. We cannot extend such confidence to it. The Government is not fortifying but checking the course of the revolution. For instance, let us take the replacement of the old power. The Government has replaced it, but in a half-hearted manner in order to restrain the further development of the revolution. It has transferred power to the local city administrations and the representatives of Zemstvos, entrusting power not to the revolution but to those elements that were mobilizing for counter-revolution. On the war question, it has prepared a loop-hole for itself; on the agrarian question—it has not solved it, but declares that it is preparing measures for its solution. In view of this, we will support the measures introduced by the Government in the interests of the revolution, but we will not declare confidence in it.

YAKHONTOV: In speaking of the Provisional Government, it is necessary to bear in mind the Government as it exists at the present moment. We should not prejudge what it will become. Comrade Stalin is correct in saying that the Provisional Government fortifies the conquests of the revolution. We are accustomed to look at events objectively. From the objective standpoint—it [the Government] is revolutionary. It is the captive of the revolution. While being counter-revolutionary in essence, it convokes the Constituent Assembly, it replaces the old ruling power, in short, it clears the path for the revolution. Everybody speaks of the counter-revolutionary nature of the Government but nobody adduces facts to prove its counter-revolutionary activity. In speaking of the attitude to the Government, we are concerned not with an expression of confidence but with the support of measures aimed to fortify the conquests of the revolution.

Those who talk about the immediate replacement of the Government forget one thing. The war has called forth devastation, and there are no objective forces able to direct the mechanism. Had the democracy taken power in its own hands, it would have meant the defeat of the revolution. The democracy must strive to this, that it prepare itself for the moment when it will take power into its own hands. But striving toward this new power, it must support the Provisional Government.

SEVRUK: Comrade Miliutin has correctly pointed out that the divergence between the resolutions presented by the Bureau and by comrade Voitinsky is conditioned upon different principled postulates. In the resolution of the Bureau no mention is made of the support of the Provisional Government. But what does it generally say about the attitude to the Provisional Government? It speaks of what not to do; the conclusions must be read between the lines; but that is not enough for a political program. Some say: How to support the Government? The answer to that is contained in our party program: "To support every oppositionist step directed to . . . etc." I agree with Miliutin that Voitinsky has overlooked the socio-political side. The final point in Voitinsky's resolution must be amplified in two directions: (1) to mobilize the forces around the Soviet, unfolding the agitation for the struggle against the counter-revolutionary propaganda aimed at the Soviet; (2) to organize the agitation among the troops on the agrarian question.

KANATCHIKOV: If, as comrade Voitinsky says, the provinces lagged behind at the moment when the Government was formed in Petrograd, then it follows logically that when the provinces have become organized, the executive power which does not correspond to the demands of the country must withdraw. In such a moment as demands the maximum exertion of forces, the power not only fails to organize but it even puts a brake on the development of the revolution. The executive power must be brought into harmony with the mood of the country. In the further development of the revolution the power must pass to the Soviet of Workers' and Soldiers' Deputies which must be precisely the one to put forth the executive power.

KRESTINSKY: As to practical action there is no disagreement between Stalin and Voitinsky. We will not immediately overthrow the Provisional Government. How do I envisage the current situation of the Provisional Government?

The Provisional Government is the clerk of the Soviet. At the apex of the revolution the supreme organ of power will be the Soviet of Workers' Deputies and Peasants' or Army Deputies. As yet—the Soviets are only embryos of power. So long as that power is not organized we will tolerate the Provisional Government, even if it parts company with us. What will happen then? It is schematically possible, that the Provisional Government by renewing its personnel will faithfully serve us. Then we will not replace it. The most probable initiator of the clash between the present Government and the revolutionary people will not be ourselves but the Provisional Government itself, and then we shall have to take power into our own hands. Finally, there is a third possible course. When our strength grows and we know that the provinces are with us and that they remain uninfluenced by the lure of names, we will ourselves assume the offensive. And it is for that moment that we must prepare ourselves. The resolution of Voitinsky is far too mild, it does not point out the inevitability of a clash. It is strange to talk of supporting one's own clerk. We must underscore in our resolution that the Provisional Government and ourselves represent two hostile forces.

SVERDLOV: Introduces a motion to close the discussion, elect a committee and give the floor to the reporters for summaries.

VOITINSKY: Speaks against the motion, inasmuch as he fears that the same thing will happen as with the resolution on war.

Sverdlov's motion is carried.

The discussion is closed. The reporter and co-reporter are given the floor to sum up.

VOITINSKY: Comrades have said that in my resolution I paid too much attention to the political side of the Government's activity and missed the social side. But those who argued against me overlook that at the present moment special legislation is being energetically introduced not in the shape of legal enactments but in the shape of agreements with the Soviet and that here the Government under our pressure is doing not what it would have liked to do, and that here, too, it is putting our program into effect. A vote of confidence [from the party] cannot be given, but support to it can be shown. We must not forget that on various questions the Government will be unable to cope with a whole number of tasks facing it. A defeat on the food supply question would be not only a defeat for the Government but also a defeat for us, because we, too, will be unable to cope with the disruption of the transport system. We need the Government as a technical clerk. We must prepare the apparatus; by entering into all the organs, into all the departments. If Petrograd or the Army are left without bread, the indignation will be directed not against the Provisional Government but against us. Without our support the Government will be unable to cope with a number of technical tasks. If you say that you will support certain measures—then you must express this in the resolution. You must point out that the moment that the Provisional Government steps from under our control and takes counter-revolutionary steps, we will go head on against it. But when it fulfills our program, we support it. We will come out against it because it betrays the revolution. The people must know that we are revolutionary not for the sake of revolution, that we have our own program. . . .

STALIN: I will speak on the first point which has aroused disagreement. Up to now the revolutionary initiative has come from the Soviet. The Soviet of Workers' Deputies has issued declarations, broached issues and made threats, while the Provisional Government has balked, struggled only finally to agree. In such a situation can one speak of supporting such a Government? One can rather speak of the Government supporting us. It is not logical to speak of the support of the Provisional Government, on the contrary, it is more proper to speak of the Government not hindering us from putting our program into effect.

The speaker proposes that a resolution which does not support the Provisional Government be accepted as a basis. The Government is organizing the army, it is arousing the hostility of the soldiers against the workers, and leaning on the strength of Anglo-French capitalism, it is already organizing the counter-revolution.

VOITINSKY: Speaks in favor of theses being prepared for the Committee. Is it not necessary to point out in the resolution that we give support to steps directed toward the development of the revolution?

(For—33; against—26.)

Election of a committee to draft the resolution.

The following elected: Voitinsky, Miliutin, Stalin, Sammer, Sevruk, Krestinsky, Kamenev, Eliava, Teodorovich.

SESSION OF MARCH 30

Chairman: Nogin.

Secretaries: Comrades Boki and Drabkina.

KAMENEV: Reports that he has entered into negotiations with the internationalist S.R.'s and Mensheviks. Inasmuch as it is clear that an absolutely inacceptable resolution of the Executive Committee [of the Soviets] will be passed, it is necessary to counterpose to it a joint resolution of the internationalists. The S.R.'s (22) are a national minority. They will not vote against the resolution of the

Bolsheviks and will withdraw their resolution. The Mensheviks are seeking to introduce a single resolution and are for uniting on a joint resolution. Should factional discipline be imposed to compel the minority to submit to the majority, the internationalists will come out in favor of our resolution.

The plan of action is as follows: If we do not obtain a majority, then at least to constitute a compact internationalist minority. And to vote against the resolution of the Executive Committee. After the adoption of the resolution of the Executive Committee, to introduce the following four amendments:

1) The Executive Committee demands of the Provisional Government as its next step that it proclaim openly to the whole world the readiness of the peoples of emancipated Russia to enter into peace negotiations on the basis of the right of all nations to self-determination without annexations and contributions.

2) The Conference, rejecting all hopes in the secret diplomatic game of the imperialist governments that plunged the world into war, proclaims that the only ally of revolutionary Russia in her struggle for the liquidation of the imperialist war is the international proletariat.

3) Demands from the Provisional Government that it break with secret diplomacy and make public the treaties of Czarism, concluded behind the back of the people.

4) Rejects the principle of class peace, advantageous only to the bourgeoisie and the landlords who make profits out of the war.

The amendments are intended not for the purpose of improving the resolution but to demonstrate a point of view. In Tseretelli's resolution there is no mention of peace, hence insertion: 1) the Conference demands from the European governments the open assumption of peace negotiations; 2) makes no mention of the only ally in the struggle for peace—the international proletariat; 3) to insert: "Demands a break with secret diplomacy"; 4) to add at the end—"Rejects. . . ."

VOITINSKY: Considers that the amendments are unquestionably acceptable but proposes that they be first introduced in the Executive Committee, and that all measures be taken to have them accepted there. All the comrades who are in agreement with it should vote for the resolution of comrade Kamenev.

KRASSIKOV: The gist of the matter is not in the amendments and not in a demonstrative presentation of social democratic slogans, but in the current moment. If we recognize the Soviets of Deputies as the organs that express the will of the people, then the question before us is not the consideration of what concrete measures must be taken on this or that issue. If we think that the time has now come to realize the dictatorship of the proletariat, then we ought to pose the question that way. We unquestionably have the physical force for a seizure of power. I believe that we will have sufficient physical force both in Petrograd as well as in other cities. [Commotion in the hall. Shouts: "Not true."] I was present. . . .

THE CHAIRMAN (INTERRUPTING): The question under discussion involves the practical steps for today. The question of the dictatorship of the proletariat is not under discussion.

KRASSIKOV (CONTINUES): If we do not pose the question that way then ought we to take steps in relation to the Provisional Government which. . . .

THE CHAIRMAN deprives him of the floor.

NOGIN: Comrade Voitinsky's declaration that we should act contrary to the customary procedure of party organizations is not subject to discussion. We consider our sessions as party sessions, the decisions of which are binding on all.

SEVRUK: Moves that a vote be taken first on the amendments and then on the resolution. If the resolution as amended is adopted, then the other resolutions will not be read. To safeguard against this, and to have the battle take place, I propose that the Bureau of the internationalists comes to an agreement with the Praesidium, that the vote is taken first as to which one of the resolutions is accepted as the basis.

As to the question of being bound—all those present are duty bound to submit [to the majority].

BAGDATIEV: If the amendments are not accepted then what will we do? Will we vote for? [KAMENEV: Against!] Is that the opinion of comrade Kamenev, or is it the opinion of all the internationalists? [KAMENEV: The question was not discussed.]

SKRYPNIK: Moves to vote on the amendments drafted by the Committee and if they meet with no objections, to proceed to a vote without a discussion.

ELTSIN: So far as the party statutes are concerned, those who are in the minority may abstain at the Conference but they cannot vote against the decision.

A vote is taken as to whether this question should be discussed. Defeated by all votes against three.

Comrade Kamenev's amendments are put to a vote.

BAGDATIEV: It is necessary to discuss whether we should introduce the amendments at all.

The majority is against discussion.

Amendment 1 is voted on.

VOITINSKY proposes an amendment to the amendment.

SKRYPNIK: Opposed to amendments as we have before us a compromise platform and any changes would require a reconsideration of the whole.

Motion to accept amendments adopted.

QUESTION: Who has amendments to introduce?

DELEGATE: Proposes to close the list of speakers and to designate individuals representing all factions.

SAVELIEV: Moves that the matter be put in such a way as would not create the impression that we are in agreement with the resolution. Therefore, I propose that the amendments are not introduced officially in the name of our faction.

KAMENEV: The speakers will make that clear. Ought we go to the meeting with the Mensheviks?

KRESTINSKY: It is meaningless to go to such a meeting.

NOGIN: We ought to discuss and seek to arrive at an agreement but it is impermissible to arrange such meetings on personal initiative.

THE JOINT SESSION OF THE BOLSHEVIKS AND THE MENSHEVIKS

Time: 3:30 A.M.

Present: In addition to the Bolshevik faction—Khinchuk, Rozanov, Ehrlich, Lieber, Ermansky, Kopelinsky, N.D. Sokolov.

Comrade Khinchuk is added to the Praesidium, and he takes the chair to conduct the meeting.

NOGIN: At a gathering which represents the party Conference, it has been decided to discuss jointly the question of the attitude to the war.

KHINCHUK: What is of importance is not to determine upon whose initiative this was done but the attitude to the war. There are three resolutions—that of the Executive Committee, that of the Mensheviks and that of the Bolsheviks.

KAMENEV: At a private conference between the Bolsheviks and the Mensheviks we arrived at an agreement about the resolution. But the Bolsheviks have been elected to this Conference, while the Mensheviks have not. That is why it is necessary for this meeting to approve this draft.

EHRLICH: We ought not only discuss the resolution on the attitude toward the war, but also decide the tactical question as to our attitude toward the text of the manifesto drafted by the Executive Committee. If we consider the draft inacceptable to us, then we should declare our own point of view; but if it is acceptable, then we should make our viewpoint known without sharpening the issue.

KHINCHUK: Is the draft final in character or can changes be introduced?

EHRLICH: Does the Executive Committee consider it possible to introduce changes?

SEVRUK: All the faction conferences held up to now have made clear that within both tendencies there are two points of view: 1) the anti-defensist or, as it is called, the internationalist viewpoint; and 2) the viewpoint of revolutionary defensism. To the extent that these viewpoints exist in the conferences, to the same extent they will manifest themselves at the Soviet Conference too. I believe that when comrade Tseretelli put the question of the social democrats' supporting the position of the Executive Committee, he took as his starting point the fact that everybody was in fundamental agreement with the position of the Executive Committee. It is therefore necessary to clarify the question as to whether the social democratic delegation will vote for or against the draft of the Executive Committee. It is necessary to clarify the position of the majority and then to decide the question of the minority. I move that each group elaborate its own resolution and come out at the Conference in the name of the majority and of the minority. I welcome this meeting because instead of four points of view, we will have two: that of the majority and that of the minority.

KAMENEV: To pose here the question of defensism and anti-defensism is to repeat the discussion which we have already had. We have come to the conclusion that it is impermissible to vote for the resolution of the Executive Committee. It is not a socialist resolution. The Executive Committee assumes in it the viewpoint of Henderson and Thomas. It is impossible to vote for a resolution which says nothing about peace, about the abrogation of the secret treaties left over from Czarism. Another resolution must be counterposed to it. Our task is to fuse the socialist-internationalists around the resolution. [*Reads the resolution.*]

ROZANOV: I take part in this private conference, empowered by nobody. At the present time, in many places in the provinces, there is taking place the spontaneous unification of the masses of Bolsheviks and Mensheviks. Every time that party activity is revived, such a unification takes place. I consider this to be a sign of a healthy instinct on the part of the working-class masses who strive with all their might for the creation of a *united* social democratic party. I consider it necessary that whenever possible all public statements generally should be made in solidarity. And I appeal to all those comrades who are not satisfied with the resolution to make concessions. In particular, I appeal to those comrades who are defensists and who are dissatisfied with the resolution. Comrades, do not stress the disagreements, for this will cause a split.

As regards the text of the resolution, it underscores, as has already been said at the Menshevik conference, that the Provisional Government is not revolutionary in itself, that the proletariat of all countries has a common basis for solidarity, and that it is necessary to exert all our strength to reënforce this basis of solidarity. The masses lacked this basis, so long as the revolution did not break out. Only when the democratic idea triumphed, did this solidarity manifest itself.

With respect to the last point, I foresee objections on the part of the defensists. The compromise will satisfy neither the comrades Bolsheviks nor the comrades Defensists. But, nevertheless, both sides can arrive at an agreement. After all, it is impossible to satisfy at one and the same time both sides, because we have two different viewpoints here, and it is impossible not to fool anybody and to have a single resolution. The appeal to remain at the posts cannot be interpreted as primitively as is being done by some soldiers, namely: Neither to advance nor retreat. While the defensists do not look upon the Bolsheviks and the internationalist-Mensheviks as people upon whom one could spit—and I hope there is nothing of the sort here—you should consider whether or not it is expedient, while remaining socialists, to cause a large section of the party to split off, merely because this does not correspond to the mood of the soldier and peasant masses—and all the more so, of the bourgeoisie! [*Applause.*]

To us you are valuable as representatives of the working-class masses, and you defensists will be drawn into a single socialist party. For the sake of this future, I call upon you to unite on the resolution.

Motion is made to have two reporters for the second tendency: Lieber and Voitinsky.

LIEBER: Comrade Rozanov is absolutely wrong in posing the question of the prospects of our future party structure in dependence upon the attitude on the question of defensism. As far as I know, within the Bolshevik tendency there is taking place the same struggle around the question of the attitude to defensism. In consequence, we must do away with the old division between Bolsheviks and Mensheviks, and speak only of our attitude toward the war. Comrade Rozanov correctly said that precisely at the moment when the question of the unity of the social democracy is especially vital, we are being threatened with a split in the party. But he forgot another great danger: That the proletariat may become isolated from the rest of the democracy at such a moment as we are now living through, and the social democracy in its turn may become isolated from the proletariat. And I appeal to you not to forget the enormous task facing us, and not to substitute for this problem, the dominant rôle of the social democracy.

Every attempt to evade giving an answer to the question of our attitude to defensism is doomed to failure, because the bourgeoisie is conducting a forthright agitation. It is politically more advantageous to renounce defensism altogether than to come out with a compromise. For we cannot face unarmed the bourgeoisie which is conducting an agitation. In the resolution we speak of: Soldiers, Workers. But up to now it has been our habit to operate with the class. Where is the place of the class? Where is its post? [VOICE: *"Remain at your post!"*]

The formula of the resolution, you must agree, is not an answer, but an evasion. It is inacceptable both to you and to ourselves. For the sake of the urgent need of the unity of the proletarian front, in order that the victory of the revolution may be made secure, and bearing in mind that we have not yet conquered—we ought to remember that we cannot adopt a resolution which isolates the proletariat from the democracy, while isolating the social democracy from the proletariat. The delegates from the provinces report that the moods locally are quite different from the mood prevailing here. If we do not stand in a majority on a position opposed in principle to that of the Executive Committee. . . .

KAMENEV: We do so stand. . . .

LIEBER: . . . then there was no need to carry on any discussion. But we are facing an abyss, not a party, but an abyss into which we are plunging the proletariat. Can the social democracy permit itself the luxury of digging an abyss between itself and the workers and the soldiers who have gathered for the Conference? If the question involved the triumph of the chauvinist moods expressed at the Conference by a few soldiers, then of course I would be in favor of an abyss, because this mood of the soldiery can lead the proletariat into the abyss. But the question is whether we should strive to break away the more conscious section of the delegation, or repel them towards the less conscious. This, of course, does not do away with the necessity of advancing those sides which we think necessary to advance. The line of conduct, dictated by political tact, speaks for the necessity of uniting the majority of the Conference on a platform which, though less illuminating, will be acceptable to all. We will vote for the resolution of the Executive Committee, but this will not hinder us from coming forward with our own, more illuminating declaration.

VOITINSKY: I am ready to put my signature to every word of comrade Lieber. In both factions there are both tendencies. There are two viewpoints that are far removed from each other. The representatives of both factions are on the Executive Committee. The entire work of the Soviet has been conducted under our banner. If we engage in a battle over the resolution, we will discredit our representatives on the Executive Committee not only at the present session but in the future as well. The Executive Committee must be far more cautious in its actions than a political party. It is impermissible to thrust socialist views upon this body. This is the business of parties, but as the representatives of factions and parties we are duty bound to come out independently with a demonstrative declaration of our own point of view. Kamenev has made such a declaration, and we must continue to do likewise in the future. Our public appearance must be a fighting, not a theoretical one, but adapted to the level of the understanding of the masses; for this reason we must cede certain theoretical postulates in return for practical effects. Our coming out with an independent resolution would weaken the forces of the Executive Committee, and thereby deal a heavy blow to the cause of revolution. We must announce that the resolution does not satisfy us, but when it comes to voting on the resolution, then we must vote unanimously [*applause*] in favor of the resolution, without introducing any amendments, and without raising any objections.

ERMANSKY: Comrade Lieber has declared that the resolution gives only a negative answer, and not a positive one. This is not true. The resolution does give an answer: Peace on an international scale.

What has happened to make the comrades who previously stood on the internationalist viewpoint, speak now of the necessity of changing our attitude toward the war?—1) The Russian Revolution; 2) The proclamation of the Provisional Government. But in essence there has been no change in the situation, and therefore there are no reasons for a change of attitude toward defensism. Has the imperialist content of the war actually changed because of the fact that Russia has become a republic? After all, France and America are republics too, and this notwithstanding, they are conducting imperialist policies. As regards the proclamation of the Provisional Government, only the Russian Government has renounced annexations; everything else depends on what England and France say.

I am certain nothing will come of it. We know that a government headed by Miliukov, who did not resign, knows that France and England who have invested colossal resources in the enterprise called war, will not allow this. The intent of the proclamation is to weaken German imperialism by disrupting civil peace. If we change our attitude to the war before there is a change in the situation itself—what will be said abroad? That we are utilizing a superficial pretext in order to conduct an imperialist war under the cover of beautiful slogans. Within certain limits we are falling into the position which is being taken by the semi-official organs. We conduct the war only in order to defend the country.

The soldiers will understand the slogan if we develop it. After all, the Germans can say that they have long stood for peace, that their government has even come out with peace proposals, but that our coalition has replied with a refusal.

KAPELANSKY: The question must be discussed on two planes: What is our principled attitude to the resolution of the Executive Committee, and what is our own resolution. If we were to come out in the sense of not supporting the resolution of the Executive Committee—this would weaken the Executive Committee and the Soviet, who have great work ahead of them, and thereby we would cause enormous harm. The resolution of Kamenev is not an internationalist resolution. What does it mean: "Remain at your posts"? We must give a clear answer to the soldier as to what he must do until the time when an insurrection breaks out in Western Europe.

Discussion closed.

The following motions are put to a vote:

> "1) To come out with an absolutely independent joint compromise resolution.

"2) To announce that we support the resolution of the Executive Committee, and make a demonstrative declaration of our own resolution.

"3) To introduce amendments to the resolution of the Executive Committee.

"4) To try to come to an agreement beforehand with the Executive Committee on the amendments.

"5) To discard all resolutions and wholly to adhere to the appeal of the Executive Committee."

NOGIN: There are two sharply different lines: To adhere to the resolution of the Executive Committee, or to accept Kamenev's resolution as the basis.

KROKHMAL: Moves that the following be put to a vote: 1) To accept the appeal of the E.C.; 2) Whether to introduce amendments.

KRESTINSKY: Who is eligible to vote? In the Bolshevik conference only delegates with decisive votes could vote.

KHINCHUK: The same holds true for the Mensheviks. The decision is not unconditionally binding because the faction Conference has still to take place.

SEVRUK: Inasmuch as the question discussed is the collective position to be taken at the Conference, I move that we allow only those elected to the Conference to vote.

CHAIRMAN: Those will vote who voted at the faction Conference.

The vote is taken.

Motion 5 is put to a vote. (Defeated by all votes against 29.)

Motion 1 is put to a vote. (After three ballots: For—74; against—66.)

The motion to come out against the resolution of the Executive Committee is adopted. (*Commotion in the hall. Shouts.*)

Motion 4 is put to a vote. (For—62–63; against—66–70.)

Motion carried: To come out with an independent resolution, taking as the basis the text of the Executive Committee.

Election of conciliationist committee.

Elections to this committee to be according to tendencies.

The following elected: Kamenev, Voitinsky, Lieber, Ermansky.

This committee is also entrusted to carry on negotiations with the Executive Committee.

The Mensheviks leave for a faction session to discuss the question of their future conduct.

THE SESSION OF THE BOLSHEVIKS (CONTINUED)

Chairman: Nogin.

KRESTINSKY: If no agreement is reached, what will we do?

VOITINSKY: Proposes that the Bolsheviks who disagree with Kamenev's resolution leave and vote with the Menshevik-Defensists.

Seven men leave the hall, among them: Voitinsky, Sevruk, Eliava, Yakhontov.

LUGANOVSKY: Moves that a joint plan of action be worked out, for instance, that they abstain during the voting. Moves to call back those who left and try to come to an agreement with them.

GOLOSCHEKIN: Speaks against, in view of the fact that negotiations have been carried on with the defensists for several days already, and have brought no agreement. It is useless to keep this game up.

SVERDLOV: Agrees with Philip. We must have party discipline.

TSVILLING: That's a false interpretation. Nobody knew that the Mensheviks and the S.R.'s have the same disagreements as there are among ourselves. It is necessary to call them back.

TER-GABRYELAN: Announces that his mandate binds him to fight for unification.

SKRYPNIK: We did not cause the split, and it was not we who walked out. There is no reason whatever for placing the blame for the split on our shoulders.

POZERN: Announces that he belongs to the tendency of revolutionary defensism but that he did not walk out because he considers himself bound by the Conference. He reserves the right to abstain.

ZALUTSKY: Moves that those who left be invited to return and that it be proposed to them that they abstain.

TEPLOV: Announces that he had always been a Bolshevik, and feels now obliged to declare that if things go on this way, the Army will be left without a staff. The Samara resolution differs fundamentally from the one adopted here.

A vote is taken on the motion to invite those who walked out. (The majority in favor.)

Voitinsky on his return is informed of the proposal to abstain.

VOITINSKY: Will there be objections made to the resolution?

CHAIRMAN: Yes.

VOITINSKY: In that case I refuse to abstain. Delegates Dan and Lieber have announced that they are withdrawing their resolution, and even though they are not at all points in agreement with the resolution of the Executive Committee, they will support it. Voitinsky declares in the name of the group of the Bolsheviks, that they too will support it.

SESSION OF MARCH 31

Chairman: Nogin.

Secretaries: Comrades Boki and Drabkina.

STALIN: Inquires whether it is permissible to allow the

defensists who split last night to be present.

MILIUTIN: The question of the splitter must be settled at a general conference of the faction.

The question is tabled until there is a fuller attendance of the faction.

The question of the Provisional Government.

MILIUTIN: Reports that the Committee of Eight, actually of five, assigned to draft a resolution on the attitude to the Provisional Government was unable to arrive at any agreement. On the first point: Voitinsky remained on his original position that the Provisional Government is revolutionary, and is ours, and that therefore we have to support it. We, on the other hand, proceeded from the standpoint that the Government is not ours, but bourgeois, and strives to confine the development of the revolution. For this reason we were unable to arrive at any agreement. We will support the measures in so far as they are directed toward fortifying the conquests of the revolution. We support the revolution but we do not support the Provisional Government as such.

In the last analysis, Voitinsky's resolution comes down to a vote of confidence.

He reads the resolution of Voitinsky* and the resolution of Kamenev-Stalin, which is appended [see pages 359–60].

VASSILIEV: Cannot understand why an agreement was not reached. After all, the majority has already expressed itself in favor of supporting the measures aimed to further the development of the revolution. In essence, I am in agreement with the second text, but am unable to see any difference between the two. After all, in question here is not the support of the Government, but of certain

* Not among the documents.

measures—the support and strengthening of steps taken by the Provisional Government.

KAMENEV: Inquires whether the question has been settled of counterposing his resolution to Steklov's resolution.

NOGIN: We must first formulate our own opinion.

KAMENEV: In Steklov's resolution the point dealing with support is absolutely inacceptable. It is impermissible to have any expression of support, even to hint at it. We cannot support the Government because it is an imperialist government, because, despite its own declaration, it remains in an alliance with the Anglo-French bourgeoisie. In the *Communist Manifesto* there is a statement to the effect that we give support to the liberal bourgeoisie, but only in the event of its being attacked. But from Steklov's report it is obvious that it is not they who are being attacked, but rather it is they themselves who are attacking the Soviet of Workers' Deputies. In yesterday's amendments to the resolution we stated that support at the present time is impossible. In view of the dual power, the will of the revolutionary people is embodied not in the Provisional Government but in the Soviets of Workers' Deputies; and also that the latter must be strengthened and that they must come to a clash with the Provisional Government. Our task is to point out that the only organ worthy of our support is the Soviet of Workers' Deputies. The task of the Congress is to proclaim to all Russia that the sole expressor of the will of the revolutionary people is the Soviet of Workers' and Soldiers' Deputies, and that we must strengthen and support them and not the Provisional Government.

At the Conference, all the Bolshevik speakers must point out that our task is to support the Soviets. Whether or not we should introduce our own resolution or major amendments to the resolution of the Executive Committee—that is the question which we ought to discuss here.

FEDOROV: The cardinal issue is the question of our attitude to the Provisional Government. In order to express our attitude to the Provisional Government we must first know what it represents. At the head of the Government are the representatives of the landlord class and of the big bourgeoisie. The policy of these classes is the exploitation of the proletariat and the peasantry and the pursuance of imperialist aims in the war. But whether or not the Government puts this policy into effect—that depends on the relation of forces. In order that this relationship of forces be favorable to the proletariat and the peasantry, it is necessary to strengthen the Soviets of Workers' and Soldiers' Deputies. It is impermissible to support and place our confidence in a Government which does not merit it. Life itself demands a clear-cut answer. It is necessary that the proletariat and the peasantry be informed of our attitude to the Provisional Government. For this reason we must say that we do not *oppose* it. If it will fortify the revolution we shall not oppose it; but as soon as counter-revolutionary machinations are begun behind the backs of the people, we shall proclaim a decisive struggle against it.

MILIUTIN: Nobody on the committee will protest if the point on support is deleted from the resolution. But the majority of the Conference has decided to include the point on support. Should the present session find it possible to change its decision, it will undoubtedly take a progressive step. If after our resolution on war and the speech made by Steklov, the meeting should decide to reconsider, we would welcome this step. On points 1, 3 and 4, there was agreement reached in the committee, but on point 2, the committee felt unable to say that the Provisional Government is a revolutionary government, and we remained intransigent. I move that we exclude the point on support.

❖

NOGIN: For those who have held the viewpoint against support, the speech of Steklov has introduced one new thought: It is clear that we ought not now talk about support but about *resistance.*

SKRYPNIK: Since yesterday's speech* many things have changed. There can be no more talk of supporting the Government. There is a conspiracy of the Provisional Government against the people and the revolution, and it is necessary to prepare for a struggle against it. We must present a separate resolution. The reporter speaks of danger, of the organization of the counter-revolution, but the resolution speaks of support. At the present moment we must take one of the resolutions as the basis and proceed to a vote.

NOGIN: Moves the election of a committee consisting of three people.

STALIN: Moves to instruct the committee to change the point on support.

Comrade Stalin's motion is voted on.

Adopted by a majority of all votes against four. The point on support is deleted from the resolution. Elections to the committee to draft the resolution: Miliutin, Kamenev, Stalin, Teodorovich.

NOGIN: Shall we introduce our own separate resolution?

Unanimously adopted: To introduce a separate resolution.

NOGIN: There are almost 100 speakers already on the list. The list is being made up chaotically; the order is being violated. We succeeded only with difficulty in getting Kamenev placed on the list.

---

* The report delivered by Steklov.—Trans.

Our names which were among the first to be presented were found, after considerable difficulty, on the bottom. The members of the Executive Committee will speak against Steklov (Sukhanov is a co-reporter). It would be well for the committee to prepare not only the resolution but also amendments.

POZERN: Did the Mensheviks draft a resolution?

NOGIN: Proposes that we get information about the Menshevik resolution.

(*Shouts: "They tricked us. Don't bother!"*)

NOGIN: This evening a solemn session will be held. I move that we propose Kamenev as a reporter. If we are refused—we do not go.

STUCHKA: (*Special announcement.*) In the agrarian section I am the only social democrat, the remaining fifteen are all S.R.'s. Other comrades must come in.

A motion is introduced to draft a resolution on the agrarian question. The following are elected on the committee to draft this resolution: Stuchka, Pozern, Teodorovich, Miliutin, Skrypnik.

Nogin reads the resolution of the Moscow Regional Conference: "On the organizational tasks in the village." [Not among the documents.—L.T.]

NOGIN: The resolution contains a proposal to organize the seizure of lands without waiting for the Constituent Assembly. The S.R.'s did not dare to raise such a slogan, but proposed rather to wait for the Constituent Assembly. Upon learning of the decision of the Moscow Conference they said, "Woe to us! Now the peasants will elect the Bolsheviks."

SESSION OF APRIL 1

Chairman: Comrade Teodorovich.

Secretaries: Comrades Boki and F.I. Drabkina.

Order of the day: Tseretelli's proposal for unification.

STALIN: We ought to go. It is necessary to define our proposals as to the terms of unification. Unification is possible along the lines of Zimmerwald-Kienthal.

LUGANOVSKY: The Kharkov Committee is carrying on negotiations precisely along these lines.

MOLOTOV: Tseretelli wants to unite heterogeneous elements. Tseretelli calls himself a Zimmerwaldist and a Kienthalist, and for this reason unification along these lines is incorrect both politically and organizationally. It would be more correct to advance a definite internationalist socialist platform. We will unite a compact minority.

LUGANOVSKY (in refuting comrade Molotov) says: At the present time we are unaware of any disagreements. The Mensheviks abstained in the Soviet and spoke more strongly than did . . . the Bolsheviks who came out against. Many disagreements have been outlived. It is out of place to underscore tactical differences. We can have a joint Congress with the Mensheviks, the Zimmerwaldists and Kienthalists.

SKRYPNIK: This debate is purely a verbal one. Unification is possible only with those who reject revolutionary defensism and who share our attitude toward the Provisional Government.

ZALUTSKY: If we enter into negotiations with the Mensheviks, we must put forward our own views. We proceed from a definite position. Only a petty bourgeois and not a social democrat can proceed from a mere desire for unification. There is disagreement between us on the following questions: 1) the attitude to war; 2) the evaluation and rôle of the capitalist forces in the revolution. If we now slur over them, we will have a split within a week just the same. It is impossible to unite on the basis of a superficial Zimmerwald-Kienthal token. Teplovsky's argument that the "provinces will compel us to go to the Right"—is wrong. He is a poor social democrat who will allow himself to become dissolved in the mass. It is necessary to lead the masses behind us. It is necessary to advance a definite program.

LAZURKINA: On the order of the day is the question whether or not we go to the meeting.

TEODOROVICH: There is nothing for us "to go with."

STALIN: There is no use running ahead and anticipating disagreements. There is no party life without disagreements. We will live down trivial disagreements within the party. But there is one question—it is impossible to unite what cannot be united. We will have a single party with those who agree on Zimmerwald and Kienthal, *i.e.,* those who are against revolutionary defensism. That is the line of demarcation. We must inform the Mensheviks that our desire is only the desire of the group meeting here and that it is not binding upon all Bolsheviks. We ought to go to the meeting, but not advance any platforms. Within the framework of what we desire is the convocation of a Conference on the basis of anti-defensism.

The discussion is closed.

The motions of comrades Stalin and Molotov are voted upon.

The motion of comrade Stalin:

"1) To announce that we can unite only with those who hold the standpoint of Zimmerwald and Kienthal, i.e., anti-defensism;

"2) That the meeting be informative in character. Those participating in it are expressing the views of the group of the Bolsheviks, and is not binding on all."

The motion of comrade Molotov:

"1) It is necessary to come out with a platform;

"2) Same as comrade Stalin's."

Passed unanimously:

"1) To go to the meeting.

"2) To recognize the meeting as informative."

LUGANOVSKY: Speaks in favor of creating a committee for the organization of a unity Congress.

MILIUTIN: Moves the creation of a Bureau for contact with the centers.

STALIN: Moves that we elect no Bureau for the convocation of a Conference of internationalists but instead propose to the Central Executive Committee that it communicate with the leaders of the internationalist-Mensheviks on the question of calling such a conference.

The motion of comrade Stalin is adopted by a majority of all votes against one.

LUGANOVSKY: Moves to convene a joint meeting of the Zimmerwaldists. (For—14; against—13.)

The following committee to carry on negotiations is elected: Comrades Stalin, Kamenev, Teodorovich, Nogin.

Comrade Stalin is assigned to make the report at the joint session.

SESSION OF APRIL 2

Chairman: Comrade Shliapnikov.

Secretaries: Comrades G.E. Boki and F.I. Drabkina.

The session opens with a discussion on the question of prolonging the Conference. The comrades from the provinces speak in favor of their earliest possible departure, since matters locally "have been left to the whim of fate." The decision as expressed by the vote is to continue the Conference until the close of the Soviet Conference.

The agenda is next discussed: Which should be considered first—the questions involving the agenda as published in *Pravda,*[*] or the questions which are being taken up at the Conference of the Soviets of Workers' and Soldiers' Deputies, and in particular the question of the coalition government.

STASSOVA: Reports that Buryanov had sent telegrams far and wide with a proposal to demand the inclusion of Plekhanov in the ministry.

SHLIAPNIKOV: There is no need for us to occupy ourselves with a question raised by Buryanov.

The agenda is put to a vote.

Decided to take up first the questions that are being discussed at the Soviet Conference.

I. The organization question.
The organization of the revolutionary forces and the struggle against counter-revolution.

MANDELSTAM: The section has narrowed down the scope of its work and has taken up the question of the organization of the Soviets and of calling the Congress [of the Soviets].

In the section, the question was posed in the following manner: At the second sitting, Voitinsky reviewed the discussion and proposed the following plan for the organization of the Soviet of Workers' and Soldiers' Deputies.

1) A merged organization of soldiers and workers in the Soviet of Workers' and Soldiers' Deputies. (Voitinsky insisted on changing the name from "Soldiers'" to "Military" because the latter name corresponds more closely to the actual make-up of the Soviets, but the majority was not in agreement with this.) The merger must take place all along the line of activities. The separation of activities can be made only on special questions of soldiers'

* See the Foreword.—Trans.

and workers' life. But their political work must be carried out only jointly.

2) Regional organizations through Regional Congresses, and the creation of a Regional Bureau of the Soviet of Workers' and Soldiers' Deputies.

3) The All-Russian Congress.

The first Congress to be called on April 25.

Voitinsky has proposed joint representation for workers and soldiers. As regards the officer staff, the question was raised whether a separate officers' organization ought to exist alongside of the workers' and soldiers' organization. This question was settled negatively: the progressive officers must enter into the existing Soviets, as is already being done locally. The Army organizations will have representation as small district organizations, and then as central organizations, but in the large working-class centers a close tie-up between them and the workers' organizations is desirable. The peasant organizations are to be created on the initiative of the peasantry, but in the district organs there must be the participation of peasant organizations.

The delegates of the local Soviets of Workers' and Soldiers' Deputies and the organizations of toiling peasantry are to participate in the regional Congresses.

The Congress.

Voitinsky proposed representation on the basis of 1 to 25,000; Bogdanov, proportional representation. The following decision was adopted: Up to 100,000, one representative for each 25,000; five from 150,000; above 200,000, six. In addition, the Congress will include the representatives of the organizations of the toiling peasantry from among the socialist parties. Voitinsky proposed to convene the Congress for the Russian May 1, but the representatives of the Army objected, feeling it desirable to arrange a demonstration on that day. It was decided that the Congress must be convened before the close of the season of bad roads, so that the Army is organized for the beginning of military activities. The Congress will elect an All-Russian Center which will be supplemented from time to time at the regional conferences. It is possible that a permanent body will be established—the Executive Committee. The composition of this Executive Committee has not been decided beforehand, the decision is left to the Congress. The calling of the Congress is entrusted to the Executive Committee of the Petrograd Soviet of Workers' and Soldiers' Deputies, which is to be supplemented with 10 delegates from the present Conference (Voitinsky insists on 5). This Organization Bureau is instructed to draw up the agenda and to transmit it to the organizations. Up to the convocation of the Congress, the Bureau will perform all the political work. This Bureau represents at the present time the entire revolutionary democracy.

I should like to explain the question of binding mandates.

The Army representatives have arrived with binding mandates, which hinders the work. I consider this impermissible. I had a conversation with Voitinsky who considers this a debatable question. He is personally of the opinion that it is permissible.

DROBNIS (*supplementary report*): At the last session of the organizational section, the following question arose: Inasmuch as the Government heads the democratic revolutionary Russia, the question arises that this Government should reflect the opinion of all Russia. A desire was expressed that those who are elected to the Central Executive Committee take up this question. In addition, a desire was expressed that the Executive Committee be supplemented with representatives from the *oblasts*.* The army representatives expressed the desire that representatives from each army should be included (all told, about 20 men); others were in favor of representatives from each front (since there are four fronts, that would be 4 men). The question was left open.

TSVILLING: Is it the opinion of the section that representatives of officers should be elected?

MANDELSTAM: There must be no separate representatives from the officers. Should an officer be elected by the soldiers, he will be seated; otherwise, no.

NEVSKY: It has been decided that the Executive Committee will direct the political work in the country. But how?

MANDELSTAM: This question was raised and settled in the sense that the Petrograd Soviet of Workers' Deputies, as represented by the Executive Committee, is deserving of complete confidence.

KOROVAIKOVA: Was the question of the reorganization of the Soviets of Workers' Deputies raised? For instance, in Ivanovo-Voznesensk are seated representatives of coöperatives, of the committee for literacy and other non–working-class organizations. As a result, in the Ivanovo-Voznesensk Soviet the workers are in a minority.

DELEGATE: Was the question raised of a *goubernia*† organ?

MANDELSTAM: Not of a *goubernia* organ, only of an *oblast* organ.

ANOTHER DELEGATE: Our faction should introduce a motion to reorganize the Soviets of Workers' Deputies. Since the majority regards the scope of the revolution as an embryo of the international revolution, was the question

---

* A province.

† A governmental district.

raised of inviting the representatives of the international proletariat?

MANDELSTAM: No.

TSVILLING: I am entirely unable to agree with the decision of the section that the officers' collective has no right to delegate its own representatives to the Congress. This may arouse friction in the provinces. In Chelyabinsk the officers were allotted one-fifth of the seats. If this decision is enforced, there will not be a single representative of the officers in the Soviet.

I move that we support another point of view, namely, that of giving the officers the right to elect directly into the Soviet of Deputies. Such a situation is being created as will compel the officers to organize their own Soviet of Deputies, which will be worse. In Chelyabinsk has been formed a Committee for Social Security. When it began to issue resolutions contrary to the decisions of the Soviet of Workers' Deputies, the latter resolved not to permit it in its midst. There is no need to make enemies.

ZELIGSON: There are inadequacies in the plan. The organization is along *goubernia* lines at the present time. Our plan of organization should be made to correspond to that. In the provinces, within the *goubernia* committees, it is not we who function but absolutely alien elements. This can be overcome only in the event that the revolutionary democracy is organized in *goubernias*. The organization must begin not with the *oblast* but with the *goubernia*.

KOMISSAROV: It seems to me that people here are unacquainted with the structure in the provinces. An important question has been overlooked: the inclusion of representatives from the provinces, and this is very important. The legislative organ is—the Soviet of Workers' Deputies of Petrograd. Since our Soviet of Workers' Deputies represents a legislative organ for ourselves and for the Provisional

Government to which it prescribes the laws, it is necessary to include in it the representatives from the provinces.

SMIRNOV (IVAN N.): In the military commission the opinion also prevailed that the officers should be seated in the Soviet of Soldiers' Deputies. The speaker is against the participation of the officers in the Soviet of Workers' and Soldiers' Deputies. Let them organize themselves separately. Owing to this, in Tomsk the Soviet of Soldiers' Deputies plays the decisive rôle. The Soviet consists of social democrats. Among the officers there are not more than 20 socialists. We have introduced the election of the representatives among the detachments. No orders are valid without the signature of the representatives of the soldiers. Among us the Soviets of Workers' and Soldiers' Deputies have taken all the power. Things are being managed magnificently. The Soviet of Workers' and Soldiers' Deputies decided to release 12,000 men for work in the fields, having calculated beforehand how many could be sent. When the head of the Omsk Military District began to put a spoke in the wheels, the Soviet demanded categorically that not a single order touching local conditions, should be issued without the sanction of the Soviet of Soldiers' Deputies. It turned out that he was entirely uninformed about local conditions. The officers might be formed into special sections in party organizations and through them the entire remaining mass might be influenced. The Soviet of Soldiers' Deputies decided not to send out companies into the field until discipline was established. The officers were in favor of sending them; despite this, the head of the military district revoked the order, pending special disposition.

Unfortunately the question of separating out the officers will not be passed at the Conference. And yet, observing the officers at the Congress, it is necessary to state:

Who is a chauvinist?—The officer. Who is an opportunist?—The officer.

In Siberia, at the beginning of April, elections took place to the city Dumas on the basis of *4-khvostki.* We managed to get for the soldiers the right of participating in the elections on equal rights with the rest of the population. In Omsk for example there are 70,000 soldiers to the 50,000 adult population. Thus, in the Duma the soldiers turned out in majority.

As for the proposal to call the Congress on April 25, the speaker expresses himself in opposition. We will hardly manage to get back when we shall have to prepare for the All-Russian Congress. Why is this called for? The need to fortify the organization? This can be done without a Congress. This will create a bad impression on the provinces and the disorganization will be aggravated.

VOZDVIZHENSKY: I also conclude from practical experience, although among us the officers are socialists, that it is necessary to separate out the officers. If we are to elect one to every 25,000, why should they, a minority, be specially allotted one-fifth of the seats? There are separate military committees into which officers also enter.

OKHLONIN: Is in favor of giving the officers a vote on an equal footing with the soldiers. If the officers are revolutionary, the soldiers themselves will elect them. Sees no reason for separating out the officers into a special caste.

As regards the date set for the calling of the Congress, it should be postponed: Russia is an enormous country and it is impossible to get a congress together quickly. The provinces will underscore that the Petrograd Soviet of Workers' Deputies deserves confidence and this will fortify its influence. If there is a postponement for two weeks or a month, we shall be able to determine whether it is feasible to hold a Congress.

Motion: To close the speakers' list on the general discussion.

DELEGATE: I move that discussion on this question be closed and that we proceed to the general political discussion on the attitude to the Provisional Government.

SKRYPNIK: Our attitude to the Soviet of Workers' Deputies is expressed in the resolution which we adopted.

TEODOROVICH: At the Congress the organizational question will be discussed. It is therefore necessary to close discussion and take up the resolution of the organizational section, take it up article by article, and introduce changes and amendments.

Discussion on the agenda closed.

The following two motions are put to a vote: 1) To open the discussion on the question of the attitude of the party to the Soviet of Workers' Deputies; or 2) to refer these general discussions to the question of the organization of the struggle against the counter-revolutionary forces and to proceed with the reading of the resolution article by article.

The second motion is carried.

The resolution of the Organizational Section.

Article 1.

MANDELSTAM: This question is closely bound up with the question of the participation of the officers. The officers are undoubtedly opportunist and reactionary. If they are allowed to organize separately, they will organize into a hostile organization. If organized jointly with the Soviet of Soldiers' Deputies, their influence will be nullified by the influence of the class-conscious elements.

TSVILLING: I emphatically disagree with comrade Smirnov. In the nature of things, if there is a separate officers' organization, a Soviet of Officers' Deputies alongside of the Soviet of Soldiers' Deputies, it will engender friction.

I do not know why the officers are a reactionary element. These are the self-same service men and not a special caste. The officers, of course, are not the proletariat, but neither are the soldiers. It is stated that among the officers there are opportunists. But there are any number of opportunists among other groups as well. If we were to come to Chelyabinsk with such a decision, the representatives of the party would have to leave the Soviets. In most of the cities, in the provinces, the same mood prevails. The formal argument that this is a Soviet of Soldiers' Deputies and that therefore the officers have no place there, is unsound. It is necessary to give the officers the right to delegate their representatives to the Soviets.

Motion: One speaker for, one speaker against, on each amendment.

Motion carried.

SMIRNOV: The more officers there will be, the more opportunist will be the Soviets. In our Bolshevik Conference there is not a single officer but many soldiers. The conciliationist moods will predominate. It is necessary to play on the democratic feelings of the officers—they must not be given a special number of seats.

TEODOROVICH: We ought not to raise the question of a separate organization of officers. New directives for reconstruction in the provinces ought not to be issued.

TSVILLING: Introduces a motion that the officers send in delegates according to a fixed proportion.

For—2.

SMIRNOV: The officers send delegates on an equal basis.

For—13.

Against—12.

TEODOROVICH: Moves that the matter be left as is in article 1.

For—11.

Against—15.

Article 1 is put to a vote and is adopted by a majority.

KOROVAIKOVA: Moves for the reorganization of the Soviet of Workers' Deputies in such a manner as will not allow the representatives of non-proletarian elements more seats than the workers, in the Soviet of Workers' Deputies.

TOLSTOV: In favor of this motion because in Stavropol a resolution was passed against giving socialists seats on the ground that they obstruct the work and that there are many provocateurs among them. Comrade Tolstov moves to instruct the center to work out a definite plan, and to effect reorganization in accordance with this plan.

MANDELSTAM: Opposed to closing the doors to the representatives of non-proletarian organizations inasmuch as the Soviets of Workers' and Soldiers' Deputies are the organs of revolutionary democracy.

Korovaikova's motion is withdrawn.

Article 2 is adopted unanimously.

Article 3.

ZELIGSON: Proposes an amendment: To create *goubernia* Soviets of Workers' Deputies. It will then be possible to exert an influence on the goubernia organs.

For—3; against—6. Rejected.

Article 3 is adopted.

Article 4.

TEODOROVICH: Introduces an amendment: Small organizations numbering less than 25,000 members are combined during elections.

Amendment adopted.

Article 4 adopted.

Article 5 is adopted with the following amendment: To call the Congress not later than May 15, and not earlier than May 1.

Article 6.

VASSILCHENKO: Introduces an amendment: "This Executive Committee is to act in close contact with the central bodies of the socialist parties."

TEODOROVICH: Is opposed to the amendment, not because I disagree with it in essence, but because such things are carried out in practise but not made public. To broadcast such a declaration is to give grist to the mill of all those who are conducting an agitation against the Soviets.

The amendment is rejected.

Article 6 is adopted.

Article 7 is adopted.

Article 8.

OKHLONIN and MANDELSTAM: Move that we fight for increasing the number of representatives from the provinces—even if only up to 15. For example, to include the representatives of the oblast organizations.

TEODOROVICH: Moves to elect a Committee entrusted with carrying on negotiations in the name of the faction with the Praesidium of the Conference as to the number and composition of the representatives from the provinces.

Teodorovich's motion adopted.

Article 8 adopted.

Article 9 adopted with the following amendment: "Immediately and in agreement with the Petrograd Soviet of Workers' Deputies."

SMIRNOV: Introduces a supplementary amendment: "That a central organ of the Soviets be issued by the Bureau."

We are electing a Bureau to serve for a whole month, but we have no organ. "The Petrograd *Izvestia* of Soviet of Workers' Deputies" is not authoritative.

TSVILLING: The composition of the Conference is an accidental one and we might get an accidental editorial board; therefore it is possible that undesirable views might be advanced.

The amendment is rejected.

The draft as a whole is accepted.

A committee is elected to negotiate with the Praesidium: Stalin, Skrypnik, Teodorovich.

A question is raised concerning the candidates to the Organization Committee for convoking the All-Russian Congress of Soviets of Workers' and Soldiers' Deputies. Candidates to be elected from each oblast, and two representatives from each party.

LUGANOVSKY: Moves that we fight for tabling the election to the next day, when the organizational centers will be selected, and not to have elections now.

SAVELIEV: Moves that the representatives of the oblasts be left to designate their own candidates.

STASSOVA: The Bureau of the Central Committee proposes to designate two comrades representing the oblasts and one candidate—comrade Teodorovich.

ELIAVA: I can understand a proposal to elect two representatives from the provinces. But I do not understand how we can elect representatives from the oblast.

TEODOROVICH: The organizational section has worked out a draft of a resolution to be presented to the Conference of the Soviet Deputies. The articles have been discussed and adopted as a whole. We are interested in the last article: The organizational section proposes to elect from the Conference a body of ten to enter into the Executive Committee and to participate in the calling of the Congress, to direct its convening, and to strengthen its influence. The question is how many and whom to elect. We are entitled to two places out of ten (the Bolshevik faction represents one-fourth of the Congress). We must designate these two. We have already decided that the Committee of 3 that has been elected will insist on elections not taking place on an oblast basis. But even should elections take place according to oblasts, the candidates will in every case be from some oblast. Right now the immediate task is to designate two candidates. The same committee will try to increase the number of representatives from 10 to 15; we will then have 4 seats.

The following are elected: Teodorovich, Serebriakov.

SESSION OF APRIL 4

On the order of the day: The Question of Unification and Report of comrade Lenin.

Chairman: Comrade Zinoviev.

Secretaries: I.I. Boki and F.I. Drabkina.

LENIN: My report and the question of unification may be combined. I apologize for coming late.

AVILOV: The general meeting of the social democrats is scheduled for one o'clock. It is therefore necessary to set the minimum time for the session of the Bolshevik faction.

(*Shouts: "Up to three o'clock."*)

DELEGATE: The delegates from the provinces have especially remained to be present at this session which will either unite or disunite.

ZINOVIEV: Moves to get in touch with the organizers of the joint meeting.

VOITINSKY: Moves to refer the report to the joint meeting.

Comrade Teodorovich is designated to get in touch with the organizers of the joint meeting.

Report by comrade Lenin.

I have outlined several theses which I will supply with some brief comments. I was unable, because of the lack of time, to prepare a thorough and systematized report.

The fundamental question is our attitude to the war.

The essential thing that confronts one when reading the papers in Russia and observing conditions here, is the triumph of defensism, the victory of the traitors to socialism, the deception of the masses by the bourgeoisie. One is hit between the eyes by the fact that here in Russia the same situation exists in the socialist movement as in other countries: defensism, "the defense of the Fatherland." The difference is this, that nowhere is there the degree of freedom we have, and upon us, therefore, falls the responsibility before the whole international proletariat. The new Government, like the preceding one, is imperialist, despite the promise of a republic. It is imperialist through and through.

Thesis I. In our attitude to the war, which on Russia's part, even under the new Government of Lvov and Co., unconditionally remains a predatory imperialist war, owing to the capitalist nature of this Government, it is impermissible to make the slightest concession to "revolutionary defensism."

The conscious proletariat may give its assent to a revolutionary war actually justifying revolutionary defensism only under the following conditions: a) the transfer of power into the hands of the proletariat and its ally, the poorest section of the peasantry; b) the renunciation of all annexations in deeds and not merely in words; c) a complete break, in practise, with all interests of capitalism.

In view of the indubitable honesty of the mass of the rank and file representatives of revolutionary defensism who accept the war only out of necessity and not for the sake of conquests, in view of their being duped by the bourgeoisie, it is necessary with *especial* detail, persistence and patience, to explain to them their mistake, to explain the indissoluble tie between capitalism and imperialist war, to prove that, without the overthrow of capitalism, it is impossible to conclude the war with a really democratic, non-oppressive peace.

This view must be widely propagated among the army units in the field.

Fraternization.

In our attitude toward the war even under the new Government, which remains an imperialist government, it is impermissible for us to make the slightest concession to defensism. The masses regard this thing from a practical, not a theoretical, standpoint. They say: "We want to defend the Fatherland, but not to seize foreign territory." When may we consider a war as our own? When there is a complete renunciation of annexations.

The masses approach this question not theoretically but practically. Our mistake lies in our theoretical approach. The class-conscious proletariat may give its consent to a revolutionary war that really justifies revolutionary defensism. To the representatives of the mass of the soldiers the question must be put in a practical way, for there is no other way. We are not at all pacifists. But the fundamental question is: Which class is waging the war? The capitalist class, tied to the banks, cannot wage any but an imperialist war. The working class can. Steklov, Chkheidze, have forgotten everything. In reading the resolution of the Soviet of Workers' Deputies, one is amazed that people who call themselves socialists could have adopted such a resolution.

What is peculiar in Russia is the gigantically swift transition from savage violence to the most delicate deceit. The fundamental condition is *the renunciation of annexation not in words but in action. Rech* is yowling over the declaration of the *Sotsial-Demokrat* that the incorporation of Courland into Russia is annexation. But annexation is the act of incorporating any country distinguished by national peculiarities, every incorporation of a nation against its will, regardless of whether it has a language of its own, so long as it feels itself to be a distinct nation. This is a prejudice of the Great-Russians, cultivated for centuries.

The war can be terminated only through a complete break with international capitalism. The war was caused not by separate individuals but by international finance capital. To break with international capitalism is no easy matter, but neither is it an easy matter to put an end to the war. It is infantile and naïve to suppose that the war can be stopped at will by one side. . . . Zimmerwald, Kienthal. . . . Upon us more than upon anybody else devolves the duty of defending the honor of international socialism. The difficulty of the approach. . . .

In view of the unquestionable prevalence of defensist moods among wide layers of the masses who accept the war *only out of necessity* and not for the sake of conquests, we must explain to them in special detail, patiently, insistently, that it is impossible to terminate the war by a non-oppressive peace, unless capitalism is overthrown. It is necessary to develop this idea widely, in broadest possible scope. The soldiers demand a concrete answer to the question—how to end the war. But to promise the people that we can end the war solely through the good intentions of a few individuals—that is political charlatanism. We must warn the masses. The revolution is a difficult thing. Mistakes are unavoidable. Our mistake is that we have not exposed revolutionary defensism to its very roots. Revolutionary defensism is treason to socialism. It is not enough to limit ourselves to. . . . The mistake must be admitted. What to do? We must explain. How give . . . to those who do not understand what socialism is. . . . We are no charlatans. We must base ourselves only on the consciousness of the masses. Even if it is necessary to remain in a minority—so be it. It is a good thing to give up for a time the position of leadership; we must not be afraid to remain in the minority. When the masses announce that they do not want conquests, I believe them. When Guchkov and Lvov say they do not want conquests, they are deceivers! When a worker says that he wants the defense of the country, what speaks in him is the instinct of the oppressed.

Thesis II. The peculiarity of the present moment in Russia consists in the *transition* from the first stage of the revolution, which gave power to the bourgeoisie on account of the inadequate organization of the proletariat, to its *second* stage, which must give power to the proletariat and the poorest layers of the peasantry.

This transition is characterized, on the one hand, by a maximum of legality (Russia is now the freest of all the belligerent countries in the world); and, on the other hand, by the absence of oppression of the masses, and finally, by their trusting and not class-conscious attitude to the government of the capitalists, the worst enemies of peace and socialism. This peculiarity of the present moment demands of us an ability to adapt ourselves to the *special* conditions of party work among the unprecedently vast masses of the proletariat just awakened to political life.

Why didn't you seize power? Steklov says it was because of this and that, and something or other. That's nonsense. The reason is that the proletariat is not sufficiently conscious and sufficiently organized. That we have to acknowledge. The material force is in the hands of the proletariat, but the bourgeoisie was conscious and ready. That is the monstrous fact. But it is necessary to acknowledge frankly, and say to the people straight out that we did not seize power because we were unorganized and not conscious.

Millions are being impoverished; millions killed. The most advanced countries are perishing, and in consequence they will be confronted with the question. . . .

The transition from the first stage to the second—the transition of power to the proletariat and the peasantry is characterized, on the one hand, by a maximum of legality (Russia is now the freest, the most advanced country in the world); and, on the other, by a trusting and not conscious attitude of the masses toward the Government. Even our Bolsheviks show confidence in the Government. That can only be explained by intoxication incidental to revolution. That is the death of socialism. You, comrades, have confidence in the government. If that's your position, our ways part. I prefer to remain in the minority. One Liebknecht is worth more than 110 defensists of the Steklov and Chkheidze type. If you are in sympathy with Liebknecht and extend even a finger to the defensists—this will be a betrayal of international socialism. We must speak to the people without using Latin words. We must speak simply, intelligibly. They have the right . . . we must adapt ourselves . . . we must make the transition . . . but we must do it. Our line will prove right. If we draw away from these people, all the oppressed will come to us, because the war will bring them to us. They have no other way out.

Thesis III. No support whatever to the Provisional Government. We must explain the utter falsity of all its promises, particularly its renunciation of annexations. There must be exposure instead of the impermissible illusion-breeding "demand" that this Government, the government of the capitalists, cease being imperialistic.

Pravda demands of the *Government* that it renounce annexations. To demand of the government of the capitalists that it renounce annexations—nonsense! Flagrant mockery of. . . .

From the scientific standpoint, it is such a fog of deceit, which the entire international proletariat, the entire. . . . It is high time to admit the mistake. Have done with greetings and resolutions! It's time to get down to business. We must proceed with a business-like, sober. . . .

Thesis IV. Recognition of the fact that in the majority of the Soviets of Workers' and Soldiers' Deputies our party constitutes a minority, and as yet a weak minority, in the face of the bloc of all the petty bourgeois opportunist elements, from the Populist socialists and the S.R.'s down to the Organization Committee—Steklov, etc., etc. (Chkheidze, Tseretelli, etc.)—who have yielded to the influence of the bourgeoisie, and have been extending this influence to the proletariat.

We must explain to the masses that the Soviet of Workers' Deputies is the *only possible form* of revolutionary government; and that, therefore, our task is, while this Government is submitting to the influence of the bourgeoisie, a patient, systematic and persistent *explanation* to the masses of the error of their tactics, an explanation especially adapted to the practical needs of the masses.

So long as we remain in the minority, we carry on the work of criticism and of explaining errors, advocating all along the necessity of transferring the entire state power to the Soviets of Workers' Deputies, so that the masses may learn from experience how to rid themselves of their errors.

We Bolsheviks are in the habit of adopting a maximum of revolutionism. But that is not enough. It is necessary to analyze. . . . The real government is the Soviet of Workers' Deputies. To think otherwise is to lapse into anarchism. It is conceded that in the Soviet our party is in the minority. We must explain to the masses that the Soviet of Workers' Deputies is the only possible government, never seen in the world before, except for the Commune. What if the majority in the Soviet of Workers' Deputies holds the defensist point of view? That cannot be helped. For us there remains only to explain patiently, insistently, systematically the error of their tactics.

So long as we are in the minority, we carry on the work of criticism, in order to free the masses from deceit. We do not want the masses to believe us just on our say-so; we are not charlatans. We want the masses to be freed by *experience* from their mistakes.

The Manifesto of the Soviet of Workers' Deputies—there isn't a word in it imbued with class-consciousness. There is nothing to it but phrases. The one thing that can ruin everything revolutionary is the phrase—this flattery of the revolutionary people. All of Marxism teaches us not to succumb to the revolutionary phrase, especially at the moment when it is particularly current.

Thesis V. Not a parliamentary republic—a return to it from the Soviet of Workers' Deputies would be a step backward—but a Republic of Soviets of Workers', Farmhands' and Peasants' Deputies, from top to bottom.

Abolition of the police, the army* and the officialdom.

Salaries of all functionaries not to exceed the average wage of a competent worker; all functionaries to be elected and to be subject to recall at any time.

This is the lesson taught us by the French Commune, a lesson forgotten by Kautsky, but taught by the workers in the years 1905 and 1917. The experience of these years teaches us that . . . we must not permit the reëstablishment of the police, we must not permit the reëstablishment of the old army. We must change our program; it is antiquated. The Soviet of Workers' and Soldiers' Deputies

* *I.e.,* the replacement of the standing army by the universal arming of the people.—Lenin's note.

is a step toward socialism. No police, no army, no officialdom. The Constituent Assembly must be convoked—but by whom? Resolutions are written to be filed or scrapped. I would be glad to see the Constituent Assembly convened tomorrow, but it is naïve to believe that Guchkov will convoke the Constituent Assembly. All this prattle about compelling the Provisional Government to convoke the Constituent Assembly is hollow, wholesale deception. There were revolutions in the past, but the police has remained; there were revolutions in the past, but all the functionaries and the rest have remained. Therein lies the reason for the ruin of revolutions. The Soviets of Workers' Deputies is the only government that can convoke this Assembly. We have all embraced the Soviets but we have failed to grasp their meaning. From this form of government we are pulling back to the International, which drags at the tail of the bourgeoisie.

A bourgeois republic cannot solve the question [of war], because the latter can be settled only on an international scale. We do not promise to emancipate, but we say that only under this form (Soviets of Workers' and Soldiers' Deputies) can this be done. No other government but that of the Soviet of Workers' and Farmhands' Deputies. If we talk about the Commune, we will not make ourselves understood. But if we say: Replace the police by the Soviets of Workers' and Farmhands' Deputies, learn how to rule, there is no one to stop you—(this will be understood). The art of ruling cannot be gleaned from any books. You must experiment, make mistakes and learn how to rule.

Thesis VI. In the agrarian program—the center of gravity must be shifted to the Soviets of Farmhands' Deputies. The confiscation of all landlord estates. Nationalization of all lands in the country. The management of the lands to be in the hands of the local Soviets of Farmhands' and

Peasants' Deputies. Creation of Soviets of Deputies from among the poorest peasantry. Creation of model establishments out of large estates (from 100 to 300 *dessiatins,*[*] depending on local and other conditions and in accordance with the estimates of local institutions) under the control of the Soviet of Farmhands' Deputies and at public expense.

What is the peasantry? We do not know. There are no statistics, but we do know that it is a force.

If they take the land, rest assured that they will not give it up to you, nor will they ask your permission. The axis of the program has shifted. The center of gravity is the Soviets of Farmhands' Deputies. If the revolution is not settled by the Russian peasant, it will be settled by the German worker.

The mouzhik from Tambov. . . .

No payment for one *dessiatin;* one rouble for the second; two roubles for the third. We will take the land, and the landlord will never be able to get it back.

Agriculture on a communal basis.

It is necessary to create separate Soviets of Deputies from among the poorest peasants. There is the mouzhik, the middle peasant and the agricultural laborer. Even if the latter is given land, he will be unable to build up a farm anyway. It is necessary to create model establishments out of large estates, run on a communal basis, with the management in the hands of the Soviets of Farmhands' Deputies.

There are large estates. . . .

Thesis VII. Immediate merger of all the banks in the country into one general national bank, over which the Soviet of Workers' Deputies must have control.

---

* A land measure equivalent to 2.7 acres.

"A bank is a form of social accounting" (Marx). The war teaches economics. Everybody knows that the banks plunder the national forces. Banks are the nervous system, the focal point of national economic life. We cannot take the banks into our own hands, but we advocate their merger under the control of the Soviet of Workers' Deputies.

Thesis VIII. Not the "introduction" of socialism as our immediate task, but the immediate placing of social production and the distribution of goods under the *control* of the Soviets of Workers' Deputies.

Life and the revolution are pushing the Constituent Assembly into the background. It is not important who writes the laws down on paper, but it is important who puts them into effect. A dictatorship of the proletariat exists, but nobody knows what to do with it (Marx . . . only that which has matured into actuality). Capitalism has become state capitalism.

Thesis IX. The party tasks:

1. Immediate party Congress.

2. Change the party program, chiefly:

a) on imperialism,

b) on the attitude to the state, and our demand for a "Commune-State,"*

c) amend our outdated minimum program.

3. Change the party name.†

Thesis X. Rebuilding of the International.

We must take the initiative in the creation of a

---

* *I.e.,* a state the model for which we had in the Paris Commune.—Lenin's note.

† Instead of "social democracy," the official leaders of which have betrayed socialism the world over by going over to the bourgeoisie ("the defensists" and the vacillating Kautskyans), we must call ourselves the Communist Party.—Lenin's note.

revolutionary International, an International against the social-chauvinists and against the "center."*

Summary.

The Soviet of Workers' Deputies has been created; it wields enormous influence. Everyone instinctively sympathizes with it. In this instinct there is more revolutionary thought than in all the revolutionary phrases. If the Soviets of Workers' Deputies prove able to take the reins into their own hands—the cause of freedom is secure. Even if you write the most ideal laws—who will execute them? The self-same functionaries, but they are connected with the bourgeoisie.

We must not say to the masses "realize socialism," but "adopt" socialism. Capitalism has advanced; war capitalism is different from pre-war capitalism.

On the basis of tactical conclusions it is necessary to turn to practical measures. It is necessary to call a party Congress immediately; it is necessary to revise the program. A great deal in it is antiquated. It is necessary to change the minimum program.

Personally and speaking for myself alone, I propose that we change the name of the party, that we call it the *Communist Party.* The people will understand the name "Communist." The majority of the official social democrats have betrayed socialism. Liebknecht is the only social democrat. You are afraid to go back on your old memories? But to change our linen, we've got to take off the dirty shirt and put on a clean one.

---

* The "Center" is the name given to the tendency in the international social democracy which vacillates between chauvinists ("defensists") and internationalists, namely: Kautsky & Co. in Germany, Longuet & Co. in France, Chkheidze & Co. in Russia, Turati & Co. in Italy, MacDonald & Co. in England, etc.—Lenin's note.

Why reject the entire experience of the world struggle?

The majority of the social democrats all over the world have betrayed socialism and have gone over to the side of their governments (Scheidemann, Plekhanov, Guesde). What to do to get Scheidemann to agree? This point of view is the death of socialism. To send a radio telegram to Scheidemann [proposing] the termination of the war . . . is deceit.

The name social democrat is inaccurate. Don't hang on to an old name which is rotten through and through. Have the will to build a new party . . . and all the oppressed will come to you.

In Zimmerwald and Kienthal the Center, *Rabochaya Gazeta,* predominated. We shall prove to you what the entire experience has shown. We declare that we have formed a left and have broken with the center. Either you talk of the International, and then you must carry on . . . or you. . . .

The Left Zimmerwald tendency exists in all countries of the world. The masses must realize that socialism has split throughout the world. The defensists have renounced socialism. Liebknecht alone . . . the future is his.

I hear that in Russia there is a trend toward unification. Unification with the defensists—that is a betrayal of socialism. I think that it is better to stand alone like Liebknecht—one against a hundred and ten.

BAGDATIEV: Proposes not to open discussion but to settle the question of the meeting that is now taking place, and if it is decided not to go, then the meeting can continue.

SKRYPNIK: The report of comrade Lenin must provide the answer to the question as to whether we should go there or not.

VOITINSKY: In the report of comrade Lenin a mass of questions were touched upon that were not touched at the conference of the Bolsheviks. A discussion is taking place both among the Bolsheviks as well as among the Mensheviks; it would be interesting therefore to place the theses for discussion before the joint meeting. I propose that we go to the joint meeting, which binds nobody.

The discussion is of importance to the delegates from the provinces.

The proposal is adopted.

The faction proceeds to the meeting hall in the Tauride Palace.

APPENDIX TO PAGE 326

The resolution on the Provisional Government.

"Whereas the Provisional Government is composed of the representatives of moderate bourgeois classes, bound up with the interests of Anglo-French imperialism;

"The program it has proclaimed is being only partially realized by it and only under the pressure of the Soviets of Workers' and Soldiers' Deputies;

"The organizing forces of the counter-revolution, covering themselves with the banner of the Provisional Government, with the open toleration on the part of the latter, have already launched an attack against the Soviets of Workers' and Soldiers' Deputies;

"The Soviets of Soldiers' and Workers' Deputies are the only organs of the will of the revolutionary people;

"The Conference calls upon the revolutionary democracy:

"1) To exercise a vigilant control over the activities of the Provisional Government in the center and in the provinces, urging it on toward a most energetic struggle for the complete liquidation of the old régime;

"2) To fuse around the Soviets of Workers' and Soldiers' Deputies, the only ones capable, in an alliance with other progressive forces, of repelling the attempts of Czarist and bourgeois counter-revolution, and of intrenching and extending the conquests of the revolutionary movement."

Explanatory notes

1. The Panama scandal occurred in France towards the end of the last century. Having plundered the savings of countless small investors, the Society for the Building of the Panama Canal sought permission for a lottery loan from the Chamber of Deputies in order to save itself from bankruptcy. Permission was granted, but only after the bribing of cabinet ministers and some 150 deputies. After numerous beginnings at an investigation which never went through due to the bribing of the judges, the scandal was finally disclosed—involving the reactionary followers of General Boulanger, who were the Society's directors, as well as their political opponents, the bourgeois republicans in government office.—Alfred Dreyfus, Lieutenant of the General Staff, was the victim of a frame-up which made French history. In 1894, he was tried, condemned, and banished to Devil's Island on the charge of espionage for Germany. The perpetrators of the frame-up were the military clique and the reactionary politicians, who made Dreyfus the symbol of the Jewish financial interests and on that basis, conducted a violent anti-Semitic and anti-democratic campaign. The revelation of the frame-up by the "revisionists" (those for "revising" the Dreyfus trial), among them Emile Zola, made public the depravity of wide sections of the French ruling class.—The Oustric affair became public at the end of 1930, when the banks of the swindler-financier of that name collapsed. Resulting investigations revealed the intimate connection between Oustric and leading statesmen and government officials of the day, who had secretly and handsomely profited from his swindles. The cabinet of André Tardieu, who had been connected with Oustric, as had numerous associates, fell on December 4, 1930, as a result of the scandal.—*Le Temps,* roughly the equivalent of the New York or London *Times,*

is a leading reactionary journal of Paris, and almost always the semi-official voice of the government. It is owned by the *Comité des Forges* (the steel trust of France) and associated interests. Its lofty moral probity may be judged from such facts as that its founder, Senator Adrien Hebrard, received 1,769,415 francs in blackmail money for his silence about the Panama Scandal, and that it was secretly and lavishly subsidized (together with most of the other "reputable" French periodicals) with vast sums by the Czarist Government, through its agent, Raffalovich, secret counselor of the Russian Ministry of Finances at Paris, for years before the war.—P. 19.

2. The "American comrade, F." referred to here is Louis C. Fraina. The collection of articles appeared under the title, *The Proletarian Revolution in Russia,* by N. Lenin and Leon Trotsky. Edited with an Introduction, Notes and Supplementary Chapters by Louis C. Fraina. New York, The Communist Press, Publishers. 1918.—P. 28.

3. Most of the self-styled "Old Bolsheviks" who sat in judgment upon Trotsky played a lamentable rôle during the war and especially upon the outbreak of the revolution of February (March), 1917. Thus, the Bolshevik Duma fraction and their guide, Kamenev, upon being tried for treason when war broke out, repudiated Lenin's theses on the war which were introduced in evidence against them and which called for the transformation of the imperialist war into a civil war. After the February revolution and before Lenin's arrival in Russia, most of the Bolshevik leaders merely adopted a radical democratic, but by no means proletarian, revolutionary position. Many, like Stalin, inclined strongly to defense of the fatherland (under Kerensky) in the war and to political support of the government. Interesting details are given in Leon Trotsky's *History of the Russian Revolution,* Vol. I, Chaps. XV and XVI.—P. 28.

4. Lenin's theses, drawn up immediately after his arrival in Russia in April, 1917, were aimed to orient the Bolshevik party towards leading the workers and peasants to the seizure of power independently of the bourgeoisie. For the

relations between Lenin's theses and Trotsky's theory of the permanent revolution, see the latter's *The Permanent Revolution,* New York, 1931, and his *The History of the Russian Revolution,* Vol. III, Appendix III.—P. 29.

5. The German edition of Lenin's collected works describes the *Mezhrayontsi* as follows in an annotation (p. 573*ff.*) to the first book of Vol. XX, published in 1928: "'Inter-District Organization of the United Social Democrats,' called 'Mezhrayontsi' in brief.—The organization arose in Petrograd during the war and existed until the Sixth Congress of the Bolsheviks in July, 1917, when it fused with the Bolshevik party. The organization officially bore an extra-factional character; up to the February Revolution it numbered some 200 organized workers; it distributed leaflets and also published two numbers of an illegal periodical, *Vperyod* [Forward]. In its attitude towards the war, the 'Mezhrayontsi' defended an internationalist standpoint and in its tactics it stood close to the Bolsheviks. In the summer of 1917, Trotsky, Lunacharsky, Volodarsky, Uritsky, and others belonged to the 'Mezhrayontsi' organization. The conference of the 'Mezhrayontsi' at which the question of unification was dealt with took place on May 23 (10), 1917. The Bolshevik Central Committee was represented at the conference by Lenin, Zinoviev and Kamenev. The conference rejected the resolution proposed by Lenin and adopted the Trotsky resolution."—P. 30.

6. A letter written by Trotsky from Vienna, on April 1, 1913, to N.S. Chkheidze, then chairman of the Menshevik fraction of the Duma, in which Lenin is sharply attacked for what Trotsky considered his divisive activities in the Bolshevik organ, which had been launched by Lenin in that period under a name, *Pravda* [Truth], similar to the name of the popular revolutionary organ founded shortly before by Trotsky in Vienna. In the same letter, Trotsky warns Chkheidze against the liquidationist tendencies of the (Menshevik) parliamentary organ, *Luch* [Ray]. As was the case with many, if not most of the political documents, and even private letters, of that period of intense factional struggle,

the language employed by Trotsky in the letter to Chkheidze was extremely sharp.—P. 34.

7. Corporal Ermolenko, who was used in the reactionary period of the "July days" in 1917, for the purpose of helping to frame-up Lenin and Trotsky as agents of the Kaiser's General Staff. Ermolenko testified that the German General Staff had given him a sum of money for its agents, the Ukrainian separatists and Lenin, so that the latter might continue their agitation for the separation of the Ukraine from Russia. Among the other tasks of "Lenin and his followers" as "agents of the General Staff," according to Ermolenko, were espionage, blowing up bridges, etc. The aim of the whole frame-up, as perpetrated by Kerensky and the Czarist prosecutors and military men who continued to function under the Provisional Government after the February, 1917, Revolution, was to discredit the revolutionary Bolshevik leaders as common criminals and paid foreign spies. The whole miserable affair was speedily exposed by the Bolsheviks, but not without the story that Lenin and Trotsky were "German agents" continuing to be disseminated from interested quarters for a long time afterwards. It is interesting to note the similarity in patterns between Kerensky's frame-up of the Bolsheviks in 1917 and Stalin's frame-up of Trotsky and other defendants in the Zinoviev-Kamenev-Radek-Piatakov trials of 1936–1937.—P. 34.

8. The "Wrangel officer" was an agent introduced by the G.P.U. into the ranks of the Left Opposition towards the end of 1927. In September of that year, the G.P.U. announced that a raid on a number of party members' homes had revealed the existence of a secret printing press and also of a conspiracy of the Trotskyist Opposition with military men, including a former officer of the army of General Baron Peter Wrangel, for the purpose of overturning the Soviet government. This abominable story acquired wide currency, despite the fact that it was officially established, only a few days after the G.P.U. raids, that the "secret printing press" consisted of a mimeographing machine and a typewriter on which the documents of the Opposition had been

copied, and that the "Wrangel officer," whose name was never made public, had been sent by the G.P.U. as a provocateur to some of the Oppositionists, or more accurately, to men claiming sympathy with the Opposition. For full details of the Wrangel officer frame-up, see *The New International,* Vol. I, No. 4, November, 1934, p. 120*ff*.—P. 35.

9. The question of the "Pre-Parliament" marked an important stage in the development of the Bolsheviks towards the seizure of power. The "Pre-Parliament," or Council of the Republic, was set up by the Democratic Conference which came together during the days of the struggle against the Kornilov uprising. The "Pre-Parliament" was conceived by the bourgeois and social democratic elements not so much as a preliminary to the Constituent Assembly whose convocation was constantly postponed, and in reality as a substitute for it, but above all for the purpose of distracting attention from the Soviets as instruments of power. The Right wing of the Bolsheviks, Zinoviev, Kamenev, Nogin and others, were just as much in favor of Bolshevik participation in the "Pre-Parliament" as they had been of staying in the Democratic Conference, which Lenin had urged that the Bolsheviks quit in protest. The Right wing argued that the Bolsheviks should stay in the "Pre-Parliament" as its radical section, just as revolutionists participate in any regular parliamentary body. The Left wing, headed by Lenin and Trotsky (the former still in hiding, the latter openly active), urged the boycott of the "Pre-Parliament" as a final demonstration of the Bolshevik rupture with all forms of bourgeois and coalitionist rule and of their orientation towards the seizure of power by the Soviets. In the meeting of the Bolshevik fraction of the Democratic Conference, Trotsky's proposal for a boycott was at first voted down. Lenin cordially and vigorously endorsed Trotsky's position and, under their joint pressure, combined with such instructive events as the growth of Bolshevik influence in the Soviets throughout the country, the vote was finally altered and a majority expressed itself for the boycott. On October 23, the Bolsheviks withdrew from the "Pre-Parliament" after the reading of a declaration by Trotsky in their name, and

six days later the Petrograd Soviet created the Military Revolutionary Committee which guided the insurrection that took place on November 7, 1917.—P. 37.

10. The "special position" of Kamenev, shared by Zinoviev, and by the Right wing of the Bolshevik party which they represented in the period prior to the Bolshevik insurrection, consisted essentially in opposition to Lenin's orientation, set forth in the famous April Theses, towards the overthrow of the bourgeois government and the establishment of the dictatorship of the proletariat in the form of a Soviet republic. Kamenev and Stalin followed a policy of compromise with the bourgeois government prior to Lenin's return to Russia; Kamenev opposed the April Theses; Kamenev opposed withdrawal from the Democratic Conference and boycott of the "Pre-Parliament"; together with Zinoviev and others, he opposed the November 7 insurrection of the Bolsheviks; finally, with a whole group of other party leaders, he resigned from the Bolshevik government because Lenin and Trotsky carried their proposal to vote down the Right wing demand for the inclusion of all the other Soviet parties (i.e., the Mensheviks and Social Revolutionaries) in the government.—P. 40.
11. For the full text of the minutes of the November 14, 1917, meeting of the Petrograd Committee, see p. 141*ff*.—P. 43.
12. The records of the March Party Conference are contained in an appendix to this volume, beginning with page 273. The conference started under the political direction of Stalin and Kamenev, and took a position which was sharply condemned by Lenin, who arrived towards the end to present his own position, formulated in what came to be known as the April Theses.—P. 44.
13. The "defensists" or *"Oborontsi"* were those who stood for the defense of the fatherland. Specifically, in the situation existing after the overthrow of Czarism and the establishment of the Provisional Government, "defensists" was the name applied to those who, whatever their position may have been on this question during the reign of the Czar, were now in favor of continuing the war against Germany

and defending the fatherland on the ground that it was now revolutionary and deserving of defense. The "defensists" included the leaders of the Menshevik and Social Revolutionary Parties, as well as Plekhanov and his small *Yedinstvo* [Unity] group. Lenin, Trotsky and most of the other Bolsheviks, especially after the return to Russia of these two leaders, called for an end to the war, for peace with Germany—a general peace if possible and a separate peace otherwise—and were vigorously opposed to any defense of the fatherland under a capitalist government (Lvov or Kerensky) which continued to pursue imperialist aims.—P. 44.

14. In the German Reichstag meeting in December, 1914, at which the second war credit demanded by the government was being considered, Karl Liebknecht finally broke the discipline of the social democratic fraction to which he belonged and voted against the entire Reichstag membership, including the members of his own party (110). Refusing to cast his vote for the credit demanded, he made a flaming attack upon the government and the war as imperialistic. He was subsequently expelled from the party fraction. Other members, who were also opposed to voting the war credits, nevertheless submitted to the decisions of the patriotic majority and voted with it in the plenary sessions of the Reichstag.—P. 45.

15. Zimmerwald and Kienthal are the two Swiss towns where the most important conferences of the anti-war socialists were held during the World War. The Zimmerwald Conference, in September, 1915, was initiated by the Swiss and Italian Socialist parties, and was attended by their representatives as well as by delegates from other anti-war parties and groups, including the Bolsheviks, who organized the Zimmerwald Left out of the extreme radical section of the conference. The Zimmerwald Manifesto condemned the war as imperialistic on both sides, rejected civil peace and voting for war credits, and called for a struggle against the war and for socialism. The defeated Left wing resolution sharply denounced the social patriots and the International

Bureau and called openly for civil war in place of civil peace. The Kienthal Conference, in April, 1916, was a more radical gathering, in which the influence of Lenin and the Left wing showed its growth over that of the Centrists. The International Socialist Bureau was attacked for the first time and the "utopian demands of bourgeois and socialist pacifism" rejected. Lenin continued to urge the formation of a new International. His views on "the lines of Zimmerwald-Kienthal" as a basis for unification of the Bolsheviks and Mensheviks, as proposed by Stalin early in 1917, at a time when Lenin was fighting for a break with the Centrists who dominated the Zimmerwald Commission, may be deduced from Lenin's letter of June 17, 1917, to Karl Radek for the Foreign Bureau of the Central Committee (Vorovsky, Ganetzky, Radek) which was then located in Stockholm: "If it is true that the miserable Grimm, who has become quite confused (we were right in never trusting this ministerial good-for-nothing), has handed over all the Zimmerwald affairs to the Left Swedes, and that the latter are going to convene a Zimmerwald Conference in a few days, then I should like—speaking for myself personally (I write this solely on my own account)—urgently to warn against getting involved in Zimmerwald. 'It would be a good thing, however, to capture the Zimmerwald International now,' said Gregory [Zinoviev] today. In my opinion, this is an arch-opportunist and harmful tactic. 'Capture' Zimmerwald? This means taking over the dead weight of the Italian Party (the Kautskyans and pacifists), the Swiss Greulich and Co., the American Socialist Party (still worse!), the various Pelusos, the Longuetists and the like. This would mean to throw all our principles overboard, to forget everything that we have written and spoken against the Center, to become entangled and to make ourselves ridiculous. No, if the Left Swedes take Zimmerwald into their hands and if they become desirous of running into error, then we must submit to *them* an ultimatum: *either* they declare, on the first day of the Zimmerwald Conference, Zimmerwald to be dissolved and found the Third International, *or* we shall go. In this way or another, we must at any price bury the dirty (very

"Grimmish"), Zimmerwald and found a *real* Third International only of Lefts, *only against the Kautskyans*. Better a little fish than a big black beetle. . . ." (*International Press Correspondence,* Vol. XII, No. 51, p. 1107.)—P. 45.

16. The Okhrana was the Czarist Secret Police, one of whose principal tasks was the hounding of the revolutionary movements.—P 48.

17. Rykov, together with Bukharin and Tomsky, was part of the ruling machine at the time Trotsky wrote his letter to the Bureau of Party History. Together with the Stalin faction, this trio carried through the crushing and, finally, the expulsion of the Left Oppositionists in the party. Trotsky was the first, however, to mark off the political line of the Right wing trio from that of the Stalinist bureaucratic Center, and to foretell, years in advance, the break-up of the Right-Center bloc into its constituent parts. The quotation from Lenin against Rykov, which Trotsky refers to here, was only one part of the "ideological preparation" in Stalin's campaign to liquidate his Right wing allies in the struggle against "Trotskyism." Early in 1929, this campaign began to take on flesh and blood and by the end of the year, Rykov had been removed as Chairman of the Council of People's Commissars, Tomsky as head of the trade unions, and Bukharin as the head of the Comintern and editor of *Pravda*—all on charges of being the channels through which the capitalist restoration, i.e., the counter-revolution, was expressing itself in the country. The trio thereupon capitulated to the Stalin machine and continued to capitulate regularly, upon command, until 1936. Then, Tomsky was driven to suicide or was killed for alleged complicity in the alleged assassination plot against Kirov and others (Zinoviev-Kamenev trial); and Rykov and Bukharin were finally arrested on similar charges.—P. 48.

18. The onerous conditions of peace which the Germans, threatening a constantly deeper invasion of the Ukraine and Russia itself, sought to impose at Brest-Litovsk upon the young Soviet republic, created a violent dispute in the leading circles of the Bolshevik party and in the ranks.

Emphasizing the exhaustion of the Soviet forces and the need of a breathing spell, Lenin stood for signing the proposed peace treaty, even though it meant agreement to Russia's being despoiled of vast territories and forced to pay tribute to the Germans. Bukharin and his group (including Inessa Armand, A. Bubnov, Bela Kun, Alexandra Kollontai, Kuibyschev, N. Muralov, M.N. Pokrovsky, Preobrazhensky, Piatakov, Radek, Uritsky, etc.), opposed the acceptance of the peace terms and advocated a revolutionary war against the Germans. Trotsky, recognizing the exhaustion of the armed forces of the Soviets, proposed that the war be declared at an end, that the peace treaty be not signed, and that if the Germans continued to advance, the terms be accepted "at the point of a bayonet," in order to show the international and especially the German working class that the Soviets had held out against German imperialism till the very last. Trotsky's formula—"Neither war nor peace"—was, for example, exactly the status for years to come of relations between Russia and Roumania. At first Lenin was in a minority in the leadership and the ranks. The principal Soviets in the country (except for Petrograd and Sebastopol) expressed themselves against signing the treaty (thus, Moscow, Ekaterinburg, Kharkov, Kronstadt, etc.). On January 21, 1918, at a conference in Petrograd of active leaders throughout the country, with 63 present, the revolutionary war position received an absolute majority of 32, the Trotsky position ("Neither war nor peace") 16, and the Lenin position 15. At the very last moment, when the Germans had resumed their advance and given their final ultimatum, the Central Committee session carried Lenin's proposal to sign the treaty. At the February 23 meeting, Lenin, Zinoviev, Sverdlov and Sokolnikov voted to sign, with Bukharin, Dzerzhinsky, Uritsky and Lomov voting against. Trotsky stated: "If there were unanimity among us, we could proceed with the organization of the defense and would do a good job of it. . . . But this requires a maximum of unity. But since this unity does not exist, I cannot assume the responsibility for voting in favor of war." The CC thereupon decided by 7 votes to 4, with 4 abstaining (Trotsky's abstention gave Lenin the necessary majority) to accept the German proposal instantly. At this session, it was Stalin who declared: "It is not necessary to sign, but we can begin peace negotiations"—a position which Lenin attacked. The "Left Communists," Bukharin, Lomov, Bubnov, Yakovlev, Piatakov and V. Smirnov thereupon announced their withdrawal from all responsible party and Soviet posts in order to be free to carry on their agitation against the decision in the ranks of the party; in the name of the Moscow Party Committee controlled by them, they issued *Kommunist* as a faction organ in which a violent polemic was conducted for several months against Lenin's course. The signing of the Brest Treaty also had as one of its results the withdrawal of all the Social Revolutionary Commissars from the Soviet Government, followed by an armed uprising of that party against the Bolshevik régime.—P. 54.

19. The N.E.P. (New Economic Policy) was adopted, on Lenin's initiative, by the Tenth Congress of the Communist Party of Russia, early in 1921, and reënforced at the Tenth Party Conference in May of the same year. Not only had the post-war revolutionary wave in Europe subsided, especially after the failure of the Red drive on Warsaw, but relations with the peasantry in Russia had become strained to the breaking point. The extremely rigorous regulations of so-called War Communism (requisitioning and confiscation of grain from the peasant), accompanied by the breakdown of industry consequent upon the ravages of the civil war (in 1920, industrial output was only 18 per cent of the pre-war level; in heavy industry, specifically, the situation was far worse), had brought the alliance of the workers and peasants to extreme tension. The Tenth Congress met during the Kronstadt rebellion, which reflected the intense discontent of the peasants. Lenin proposed a policy of substituting a tax in kind for requisitions; of allowing the peasant to dispose of his surplus within the limits of "local trade"; of allowing the development of capitalist concessions to a delimited extent, and of state capitalism, on the ground that state capitalism was a higher economic form than that

which prevailed in most of agricultural Russia. The retreat sounded by Lenin was to allow a breathing spell during which, while waiting for the decisive aid of the European revolution, Russia could reconstruct her industries, electrify and modernize them, and establish a more harmonious relationship with the mass of her population, the peasantry. Capitalism, in industry and agriculture, was to be allowed a considerable field of possibilities in which to develop, provided, however, that the workers' state retained control of the so-called "commanding heights," namely, the nationalized key industries, state banking, nationalization of the land, monopoly of foreign trade. The N.E.P., despite the inherent dangers of capitalist restoration, greatly facilitated not only the reëstablishment of good relations between worker and peasant, but also the reconstruction of Russia's industrial life.—P. 56.

20. On March 1, 1921, the sailors of Kronstadt, the fortress outside of Petrograd, rose in armed rebellion against the Soviet Government, mainly around the demands for new elections to the Soviets and for eliminating the Communist Party monopoly. Attempts at peaceful negotiations and settlement of differences, proved unsuccessful. The government called upon the Kronstadters to lay down their arms and acknowledge the discipline of the federal government, but the rebels refused. The decisive strategic importance of Kronstadt, the key to Petrograd, made it impossible to allow it to remain in hostile hands for any length of time, and a couple of days after the uprising, it was suppressed by troops led across ice floes from Petrograd. The suppression of the Kronstadt rising was one of the saddest necessities of the Russian Revolution. Unlike the sailors of the November, 1917, revolution, who were drawn largely from the industrial heart of Petrograd, and who were subsequently dispersed to the four corners of Russia during the civil war, the sailors in 1921 were drawn largely from southern ports (like Odessa), usually the sons of Ukrainian peasants (four members of the Kronstadt rebels' committee were Ukrainian, as was their chief, Petrichenko). On furlough in their home towns, they were heavily influenced

by the complaints of the peasants against the strenuous régime of War Communism, and against the Communists who led the régime. In Kronstadt itself, anti-Communist elements—anarchists and Social Revolutionaries—were active in sharpening relations between Kronstadt and Petrograd. Outside of Russia, the reactionary elements regarded the Kronstadt uprising as a rallying pole for the counterrevolution—at first under the war-cry of "Soviets without Communists!"—a bridge to no Soviets at all. The Kronstadt sailors were, for the most part, the unwitting victims of these forces. The uprising did serve, however, to call sharply to the attention of the Bolsheviks the imperative need of putting an end to the War Communism course, which had brought relations with the peasantry, and even with sections of the working class, to a breaking point. The Tenth Congress of the Party, which met during the uprising, was the one that initiated the New Economic Policy.—P. 57.

21. The call of the German Communist Party in March, 1921, for an armed insurrection to seize power, in connection with the struggles in Central Germany, was a direct manifestation of the so-called "theory of the offensive," whose principal inspirers and theorizers in the Comintern were Bukharin and, to a somewhat lesser extent, Zinoviev. The party leadership not only plunged its membership into what was obviously doomed in advance as a futile military action by a small minority of the working class, but after the collapse of the March Action, it declared that it would repeat the action at the first opportunity. These actions, it was stated by the ultra-Leftists, would electrify or galvanize the working class and cause them, each time, to mobilize into an ever greater force which would eventually overthrow capitalist rule. "If it is asked what was actually new about the March Action, it must be answered: precisely that which our opponents reprove, namely, that the party went into struggle without concerning itself about who would follow it." (A. Maslow, *Die Internationale,* Berlin, 1921, p. 254.) "The March Action as an isolated action of the party would be—our opponents are right to this extent—a crime against the proletariat. The March Action

as the introduction to a series of constantly rising actions, a redeeming act." (A. Thalheimer, *Taktik und Organisation der revolutionäre Offensive,* Berlin, 1921, p. 6.) "The slogan of the party can, therefore, be nothing but: offensive, offensive at any cost, with all means, in every situation that offers serious possibilities of success." (Heyder, *Ibid.,* p. 22.) The Third Congress of the Comintern, confronted with this problem, was almost on the verge of a split. The Bukharin wing was supported by the majority of the delegates and leaders, including Pepper (Pogany) and Rakosi, who had really directed the March Action, Bela Kun, Münzenberg, Thalheimer, Frölich, most of the Italians, etc. Lenin, who placed himself demonstratively in the "Right wing of the Congress," threatened it with a split if the supporters of Bukharin and the "offensive" carried the day. Supported by Trotsky, and through the medium of Radek, who played the rôle of a conciliator, Zinoviev and Bukharin were outvoted in the Russian delegation, with the final result that Lenin's views triumphed. The theses of the Third Congress and the slogan "To the masses!" which introduced the broad policy of the united front adopted shortly afterward, was a definite blow at the Leftists and put an effective end for a long period of time to putschist moods in the International.—P. 62.

22. The criticism of the French party by the delegate from the Communist Party of Luxemburg, L. Reiland, dealt with the strike that broke out in March, 1921, in the mining district of his country, that is, on the very frontier of France. The Communist Party of France, then headed by the notorious opportunists, L.-O. Frossard and Marcel Cachin, paid no attention at all to the strike in the columns of the party organ, *l'Humanité,* nor was any protest made when the armed forces of France intervened and helped to crush the strike with the aid of bayonets. Reiland proposed the expulsion from the International of Frossard and Cachin. Coming on the heels of the speech by Maurice Laporte, leader of the French Communist Youth, who proposed that the party should have organized for a struggle against the mobilization of the Class of 1919 "with revolver in hand," Reiland's

criticism was exploited by the ultra-Leftists at the Third Congress and drew the fire of Trotsky and Lenin.—P. 64.

23. Early in 1925, Bukharin, addressing himself to the Russian peasantry, exclaimed: "Enrich yourselves!"—the slogan with which Guizot helped to fortify the French reaction. This was one of the many manifestations of the growing tendency of the ruling Soviet bureaucracy to base itself upon the rich peasants (Kulaks), a tendency which was one of the main causes of the rise of an Opposition in Leningrad, led by Zinoviev, Kamenev and Krupskaya, in 1925, and the merger of the Trotskyist and Zinovievist groups in 1926 into the United Opposition bloc.—Towards the end of 1925, Bukharin made a formal acknowledgment of error in advancing his slogan, but nothing was changed in the main policies of the Stalin-Bukharin régime with regard to the countryside.—P. 65.

24. In a polemic against Radek in 1929, Trotsky wrote concerning his pre-revolutionary conflict with Lenin: ". . . I never endeavored to create a grouping on the basis of the theory of the permanent revolution. My inner-party stand was a *conciliatory* one and when at certain moments I strove for groupings, then it was precisely on this basis. My conciliationism was derived from a certain Social Revolutionary fatalism. I believed that the logic of the class struggle would compel both factions to pursue the same revolutionary line. The great historical significance of Lenin's stand was still unclear to me at that time, his policy of irreconcilable ideological demarcation and when necessary, split, for the purpose of uniting and steeling the backbone of the truly revolutionary party. . . . By striving for unity at all costs, I involuntarily and unavoidably had to idealize the Centrist tendencies in Menshevism. Despite the threefold episodic attempts, I arrived at no common work with the Mensheviks, and I could not arrive at it. Simultaneously, however, the conciliatory line brought me into an all the harsher position towards Bolshevism, since Lenin, in contrast to the Mensheviks, mercilessly rejected conciliationism and could do no different. It is obvious that no faction could

be created on the platform of conciliationism." (*The Permanent Revolution and Results and Prospects,* New York, 1969, pp. 173–74.)—P. 65.

25 Lenin urged the advance on Warsaw in the summer of 1920, in the hope of effecting a juncture with the revolutionary workers of the capital and ensuring the establishment of a Polish Soviet Republic. Trotsky counselled against a further advance, on the ground that the army forces were too exhausted and that they were moving too speedily away from their principal bases of economic as well as military support. With the aid of French imperialism, Pilsudski was able to drive back the Red Army after it had succeeded in coming within a short distance of Warsaw itself. Lenin later acknowledged that Trotsky had been correct in his views.—P. 74.

26. Back in July, 1920, with the whole system a wreck, Trotsky was chosen to restore transportation. One of his first acts was to issue "Order No. 1042," the first serious attempt to introduce long-term planning into Soviet economy. The Order, the first of a series of systematic measures that finally brought order and regularity where chaos and collapse had prevailed before, was based upon a five-year outline of activity.—P. 83.

27. The "original critics" of Trotskyism referred to are Zinoviev and Kamenev, who were the principal initiators of the fight against Trotsky which they opened in 1923 together with Stalin, Bukharin and Rykov. How the entire campaign was conspiratorially and disloyally conceived, is related in the testimony of Radek, Piatakov, Rakovsky, Eltsin and others, printed in this volume in the chapter "The Legend of Trotskyism."—P. 113.

28. The "scissors" was an image employed by Trotsky in dealing with the economic crisis in the Soviet Republic, especially as affecting the peasantry. One blade of the scissors was to represent the high price of manufactured articles, the other the low price for agricultural products and consequently the low purchasing power of the rural masses. The crisis became increasingly acute as the "blades" opened

wider. The crisis would be eliminated, said Trotsky, by closing the "blades," that is, primarily, by lowering the price of industrial products.—P. 118.

29. *Smychka* is the Russian word for alliance or union. In popular Russian political parlance, it refers specifically to the alliance between the workers and the peasants, the firm maintenance of which, the Bolsheviks always insisted, was a precondition to the preservation of the Soviet power—P. 118.

30. Among the earliest differences developing between Trotsky and his supporters on one side, and the leadership of the Russian party and the Comintern, on the other, revolved around the strategy pursued in the German Revolution of October, 1923, the Bulgarian insurrection of September, 1923, and the Esthonian putsch of December, 1924. For a fuller elucidation of the differences, see Leon Trotsky's *The Third International After Lenin,* New York, 1936, specifically the chapter entitled "Strategy and Tactics in the Imperialist Epoch," [2018 printing].—P. 118.

31. *Vperyodism* was the tendency represented by the group calling itself *Vperyod* [Forward], which was formed towards the end of 1909 in exile by a number of ultra-Leftist Bolsheviks, Bogdanov, Lunacharsky, Alexinsky, Pokrovsky, Menzhinsky, Manuilsky and Gorky. The group existed for several years, issuing a number of literary works, and condemning Lenin for having departed from the true traditions of Bolshevism which the *Vperyodists* alone were now defending. The ultra-radicalism of the group, which was displayed in its opposition to utilizing parliamentary participation in the Duma, or active work in the trade unions, was combined with attempts at philosophical revision of Marxism, especially by Bogdanov and Lunacharsky. Lenin devoted an entire volume, *Materialism and Empirio-Criticism,* to the latter aspect of the *Vperyodist* policy.—P. 122.

32. Trotsky refers to Stalin's continual capitulation to the Right wing British trade union leaders, associated with him in the Anglo-Russian Trade Union Unity Committee, during the period from the end of the General Strike in May, 1926, until the dissolution of the Committee a year later.

For a more detailed account of the criticism of Trotsky, see his *The Third International After Lenin,* pp. 152–59, and *Leon Trotsky on China,* New York, 1976, pp. 230–35 [2018 printing].—P. 123.

33. When the entire Left Opposition was expelled from the Communist Party of the Soviet Union by the Fifteenth Party Congress at the end of 1927, the Zinovievist section of the Opposition (Zinoviev, Kamenev, Yevdokimov, Bakayev, etc.), faced with the demand by Stalin's congress that they not only renounce their right to disseminate their political views, but even their right to entertain such views, ended by presenting a statement of complete capitulation. Shortly thereafter, they were re-admitted into the party. Their submission availed them little, for at the end of 1932 they were once more expelled for having had "guilty knowledge" of a secret faction organized by Syrtsov, Lominadze, Shatskin and Sten, and for having failed to inform the party authorities. Once more, Zinoviev and Kamenev presented a statement of recantation, even more humiliating than the first; they were again re-admitted in 1933. From then on, their self-debasing statements continued periodically, until January, 1935, when they admitted "moral complicity" in the assassination of S.M. Kirov in Leningrad, for which they were sentenced, along with a number of their real and alleged political associates, to prison sentences ranging from five to ten years. In August, 1936, they were once more accused of complicity in the assassination of Kirov, but this time of direct responsibility. Less than two weeks after the opening of the tragically farcical trial, they were executed along with fourteen other defendants.—P. 125.

34. The "literary discussion" was launched in 1924 in the Russian party on the pretext of the publication of *The Lessons of October* (Eng. trans. New York, 1937), which examined the problems of revolutionary strategy and tactics in the German Revolution of October, 1923, in the light of the instructive internal disputes which developed in the Bolshevik Party during the year 1917 over the question

of the insurrection which finally occurred in November. Trotsky's work, an introduction to his volume *1917,* was almost universally condemned by the various Communist parties on command from Moscow, but not one person in a hundred called upon to condemn it, ever laid eyes on it. In fact, in the American Communist Party, the press was called upon, at one and the same time, to condemn Trotsky's work and to refrain from publishing it! The Central Executive Committee of the party issued the following decision to all party editors: "You will find attached hereto an English translation of a review of comrade Trotsky's book *1917* entitled 'How One Should Not Write the History of October.' By decision of the Central Executive Committee all party papers are instructed to reprint this *Pravda* review within ten days time. It is the further instruction of the Central Executive Committee that no party paper shall reprint the book *1917* or any chapter thereof in the party press. . . . It is the view of the Central Executive Committee of the Workers [Communist] Party of America that the publication of Trotsky's book in this country would be a detriment to the work of Bolshevizing the Workers Party which is the most important task before our party. The Central Executive Committee regrets to note that the *Volkszeitung* [the party organ in German at that time] has already begun publication of the book serially. It has instructed the *Volkszeitung* to discontinue the publication and further instructs all other party papers that neither the book as a whole nor any chapter thereof is to be reprinted in the party press. . . . Central Executive Committee, W. P. of A., Wm. Z. Foster, Chairman, C.E. Ruthenberg, Executive Secretary." (*Daily Worker,* December 13, 1924.) It was therefore a "detriment to the work of Bolshevizing" the American Communist movement to make available to the membership Trotsky's essay so that they might at least know the contents of what they were instructed to condemn as counter-revolutionary!—P. 126.

35. On October 16, 1926, the recently formed Opposition, faced with the threat of expulsion which would prematurely cut them off from contact with the party membership,

issued a statement to the party in which the pledge is made to cease advocating their views in the intensely sharp factional form which the struggle had assumed by that time. The increasingly repressive and bureaucratic measures taken by the Stalinist leadership, plus the decisive importance of the events in England and especially in China, made it impossible to conduct the struggle against the decadent bureaucracy in the form pledged by the statement.—P. 132.

36. The modern universal calendar, differs from the old Russian by being thirteen days in advance. Thus, the revolution which took place on November 7, 1917, is almost always referred to by the Russians (and often abroad, too), as the "October Revolution" because, according to the old calendar, it took place on October 25, 1917. The meeting of the Petrograd Committee of the Bolsheviks was, therefore, actually held on November 14, 1917, a week after the insurrection.—P. 137.

37. *Rabochi Put* [Worker's Path], the Bolshevik central party organ published in Petrograd after the suppression of its organ *Rabochi* by the Provisional Government. *Rabochi Put* appeared between September 3 and October 26, 1917, and the polemic referred to by Lenin was the one directed at Zinoviev and Kamenev, who had broken party discipline and appeared in the columns of Gorky's paper with an attack on the Bolshevik plan for an insurrection.—P. 146.

38. *Delo Naroda* [People's Cause], the daily organ of the Social Revolutionary party from March 15, 1917, until March 30, 1919. Its editorial board was directed by such men as Zenzinov, Kerensky, Chernov, Gotz, Avksentiev and Sorokin, and it pursued a violently anti-Bolshevik policy both before and after the November Revolution.—P. 146.

39. An English translation of this essay, published in 1932, is available under the imprint of International Publishers. It presented Lenin's arguments in favor of taking power, and set out to prove that the Bolsheviks would take power and would be able to maintain it, on the basis of the program elaborated in the essay itself.—P. 146.

40. The "Internationalist-Fusionists" referred to by Lenin were the former *Mezhrayontsi* (see Note 5) who fused with the Bolsheviks at their Sixth Congress in July, 1917, the latter electing three *Mezhrayontsi,* Trotsky, Joffe and Uritsky, to their Central Committee.—P. 146.

41. *Rumcherod,* a combined term made up of abbreviations of the Joint Executive Committee of the Soviet of the Soldiers of the Roumanian Front, of the Black Sea Coast and of the Odessa Garrison. The Joint Executive was in the hands of the Mensheviks and the Social Revolutionaries who sought to employ it as a battering ram against the Bolshevik government.—P. 149.

42. *Vikzhel,* a combined term made up of abbreviations of the Central Executive Committee of the All-Russian Union of Railwaymen. This body was also controlled by the Mensheviks and Social Revolutionaries, and disposed of a strong and powerful organization throughout the country, whereas the Bolsheviks were just beginning to establish an administrative apparatus of their own. For a time the Bolsheviks were at the mercy of the *Vikzhel* which controlled the movement of trains and would not cooperate until the Bolsheviks consented to organize a government including the Mensheviks and Social Revolutionaries. The sabotage of the *Vikzhel* was finally broken.—P. 149.

43. The "desertions" to *Novaya Zhizn* [New Life], the organ of Gorky, refers to the action taken by Zinoviev and Kamenev, on the eve of the insurrection, in publishing their attack on the Bolshevik plan in the columns of a public organ and, moreover, a violently anti-Bolshevik paper.—P. 149.

44. Cadets, a combined term made up of the initials of the Constitutional-Democrats, or the Party of People's Freedom, the party of the Russian democratic bourgeoisie and "liberal" landowners who, under the Czar, stood for a constitutional monarchy, and later even for a republic. Led by Professor Paul Miliukov, now the leader of a section of the counter-revolutionary *émigrés.*—P. 151.

45. Smolny Institute, formerly a school for young ladies of the nobility, was taken over by the revolutionists and made

the headquarters of the Petrograd Soviet and the Revolutionary Military Committee which directed the Bolshevik uprising.—P. 152.

46. The *Junkers* was the name given to the students at the officers' school. They were used in an attempt to crush the Bolshevik insurrection.—P. 154.

47. In the manifesto on "The Civil War in France," issued on May 30, 1871, in the name of the General Council of the International Workingmen's Association (First International), Marx wrote: "But the working class cannot simply lay hold of the ready-made State machinery and wield it for its own purposes." (*The Paris Commune,* New York, 1920, p. 70.) On April 12, 1871, Marx wrote to his friend Kugelmann: "If you look at the last chapter of my *Eighteenth Brumaire,* you will see that I declare the next attempt of the French Revolution to be: not merely to hand over, from one set of hands to another, the bureaucratic-military machine—as has occurred hitherto—but to *shatter* it; and it is this that is the preliminary condition of any real people's revolution on the Continent. That is just what our heroic Parisian comrades are attempting to do." (*Briefe an Kugelmann,* Berlin, 1924, p. 86.)—P. 155

48. The Central Control Commission is a body, formally distinct from the Central Committee, which presides over the morals and the discipline of the party membership. It is, in theory, supposed to be made up of the most authoritative and unimpeachable party members, so that their decisions shall not be influenced by factional or other extraneous considerations. In Stalin's period, the C.C.C. was converted into a mere factional instrument for the punishment and expulsion of any political opponent or critic indicated by the bureaucracy.—P. 165.

49. The incident at the railway station refers to the gathering of political and personal friends to bid farewell to I.T. Smilga who was being deported from Moscow on the pretext of being sent to do party work in the provinces—an action in direct violation of the party rules, adopted as early as the Tenth Congress on Lenin's motion, providing against

the shifting of members for party work on the grounds of their political views. Zinoviev's speech over the radio was on the occasion of the anniversary of the central party organ, *Pravda;* he was charged with having spoken about inner-party affairs to an audience containing non-party members—at a time when the public press was filled with column upon column of the most violent and slanderous attacks upon the Oppositionists every single day. As for Trotsky's "breach of discipline," he had been condemned by the Stalinist press more than a year before for having failed to appeal his case to the international tribunal, namely, to the Communist International, which is, in theory, a superior body to any committee or assembly of the Russian party, which is only one of its national sections. Trotsky and Vuyovich, as members of the Executive Committee of the Communist International, did exercise their rights as members to appear before the Eighth Plenum of the E.C.C.I. in May, 1927, to present their point of view on the Anglo-Russian Committee, the Chinese Revolution, and the situation in the Soviet Union. For having done so, they were removed from the E.C.C.I. in violation of its statutes.—P. 168.

50. By the time Trotsky was delivering this speech, it was possible to draw a complete balance sheet of the Anglo-Russian Trade Union Unity Committee, which was dissolved by the withdrawal of the British trade union leaders sometime in May, 1927, after they had squeezed out of it every possible political advantage to themselves. See also, Note 32.—P. 171.

51. The Black Hundreds was the name given to the arch-reactionary and monarchistic "Union of the Russian People" which terrorized revolutionists and instigated anti-Semitic pogroms under the rule of the Czar.—P. 173.

52. The "Declaration of 83" was handed to the Central Committee of the Communist Party of the Soviet Union on May 26, 1927 by G. Yevdokimov, G. Zinoviev, I.T. Smilga and L. Trotsky in the name of 83 old revolutionists. The declaration was a summary of the Opposition's point of view on the decisive questions in dispute in the Soviet Party.

Among its signers, the year of whose adherence to the party is given in parentheses, were: Beloborodov (1907), Visnevskaya (1905), Vuyovich (1912), Vassiliev (1904), Vardin (1907), A. Gertek (1902), N. Gordon (1903), Yemelianov (1899), Yevdokimov (1903), Shuk (1904), Zinoviev (1899), Zaks-Gladnev (1906), Kuklin (1903), Kavtaradze (1903), Lizdin (1892), Muralov (1903), Ostrovskaya (1905), Piatakov (1910), Radek (1902), Serebriakov (1905), I.N. Smirnov (1899), Samsonov (1903), Sosnovsky (1903), Ter-Vaganyan (1912), Kharitonov (1905), Sharov (1904), Tsibulsky (1904), Eltsin (1898). The declaration was speedily signed by several hundred names.—P. 173.

53. It is to be found in the *Jahrbuch für Sozialwissenschaft und Sozialpolitik,* published by Dr. Ludwig Richter, Zurich, 1879, pp. 54–75 and is entitled "Der Isolirte Sozialistische Staat" von G. V[ollmar]. In setting forth his view, Vollmar, prominent spokesman for the Right wing of the German social democracy in his time, wrote: "I believe—and shall seek to demonstrate it in the following pages—that the final victory of socialism is not only historically more likely primarily in a single state, but that nothing stands in the road of the existence and prosperity of the isolated socialist state." (p. 55)—P. 176.

54. The "Thermidorian chapter" of the French Revolution opened up on the 9th of Thermidor (July 27, 1794) when the counter-revolution effected its dramatic *coup* by the execution of the revolutionary Jacobins, Robespierre, Saint-Just, Couthon, Lebas and others. The term is applied by Trotsky to conditions socially analogous in the Russian Revolution, meaning the growth of social, economic and political reaction occurring under the old structural forms and banners.—P. 185

55. The Menshevik attitude towards the "liberals," that is, the "progressive bourgeoisie," was fundamentally different from the attitude of the Bolsheviks, or of Trotsky. The Mensheviks saw the basic problem of the coming revolution in Russia as that of the alliance of the proletariat with the bourgeoisie against feudalism and for the establishment of

a democratic, parliamentary bourgeois republic, in which the working class and its party would constitute the Left wing, in approximately the same way as the socialist parties of France, England and Germany functioned in their bourgeois republics or parliaments. The Bolsheviks saw the problem as one of an alliance of the proletariat with the peasantry *against* the industrial bourgeoisie, for the establishment of a "democratic dictatorship of the proletariat and peasantry." Trotsky saw the problem of the *alliance* in exactly the same way as the Bolsheviks, but differed from the latter in his insistence upon a more precise formulation of the nature of the future revolution, arguing that the proletariat once having come to power, in alliance with the rural masses, would be unable to halt at the "democratic" stage and would have to continue to the "socialist stage," i.e., would make the revolution permanent.—P. 193.

56. In defending his (that is, Trotsky's) amendment, Krassin said at the third congress of the Bolsheviks: "As regards the resolution of Comrade Lenin, I see its weak point in its failure to stress the question of the provisional government, and to indicate with sufficient clarity the connection between provisional government and armed uprising. As a matter of fact, the provisional government is established by the popular uprising as its own organ. . . . I further find in the resolution the incorrect opinion that the provisional revolutionary government will appear only *after* the final victory of the armed uprising and after the overthrow of autocracy. No—it arises in the very process of the uprising and takes the most active part in the conduct of the uprising, insuring the latter's victory by its organized action. It is naïve to think that the social democracy will be able to take part in the provisional revolutionary government the moment the autocracy is completely overthrown; when the chestnuts have been removed from the fire by other hands than ours, nobody will ever dream of sharing them with us." In dealing with Krassin's remarks, Lenin said: "Taking it by and large, I subscribe to the opinion of Comrade Krassin. It is natural that as a literary man, I should concentrate my attention on the literary shaping

of the question. The importance of the object of the struggle is pointed out by Comrade Krassin very exactly, and I wholly subscribe to his view. One cannot engage in a struggle without expecting to capture the position for which one is fighting." Commenting on the episode twenty-four years later, Trotsky wrote: "The resolution was correspondingly amended. It may not be superfluous to remark that during the polemics of the last few years, the resolution of the Third Congress on the question of provisional government has been quoted hundreds of times as something opposed to 'Trotskyism.' The 'Red Professors' of the Stalin school have not the ghost of an idea that they are quoting against me, as an example of Leninism, the very lines that I wrote myself." (*My Life,* New York, 1970, p. 254.)—P. 193.

57. In reply to an article in the bourgeois liberal journal, *Nasha Zhizn* [Our Life], which sought to contrast the "reasonable" views of Lenin to the "permanent revolution" of Trotsky, the Bolshevik organ, *Novaya Zhizn* [New Life] replied, on November 27, 1905: "This gratuitous report is of course sheer nonsense. Comrade Trotsky said that the proletarian revolution, without standing still at the first stage, by pressing hard upon the exploiters, can continue on its road, while Lenin pointed out that the political revolution is only the first step. The publicist of *Nasha Zhizn* would like to perceive a contradiction there. . . . The whole misunderstanding comes, first, from the fear with which the name alone of the social revolution fills *Nasha Zhizn,* secondly, out of the desire of this paper to discover some sort of sharp and piquant difference of opinion among the social democrats and, thirdly, in the metaphorical expression of Comrade Trotsky: 'at one fell swoop.' In No. 10 of *Nachalo* [The Beginning], Comrade Trotsky explains his ideas quite unequivocally: 'The complete victory of the revolution signifies the victory of the proletariat,' writes Comrade Trotsky. 'But this victory in turn signifies the further uninterruptedness of the revolution. The proletariat realizes the fundamental tasks of democracy and the logic of its immediate struggle for the safeguarding of political domination causes purely socialist problems to arise at

the given moment. Between the minimum and the maximum program of the social democracy, a revolutionary continuity is established. This is not one "blow," it is not one day and not a month, it is a whole historical epoch. It would be absurd to want to determine its duration in advance.'"—P. 194.

58. At the London Congress in 1907, Lenin said of Trotsky's programmatic speech: "I merely wish to observe that Trotsky, in his book *On the Defense of the Party* emphatically expressed his solidarity with Kautsky, who wrote of the economic community of interests of the proletariat and the peasantry in the present revolution in Russia. Trotsky recognized the admissibility and expediency of a Left bloc [with the peasants] against the liberal bourgeoisie. These facts are enough for me to establish Trotsky's approach to our conception. Independent of the question of the 'uninterrupted revolution,' we have here before our eyes a solidarity in the fundamental points of the question concerning the relationship to the bourgeois parties." (*Collected Works,* Vol. VIII, p. 400. Russ. ed.)—P. 194.

59. In the period of the upswing in the Russian labor movement, Trotsky sought to unify the various socialist groups and took the initiative to call a conference in Vienna of all the contending factions. It met in August, 1912, attended by various Menshevik representatives, Trotsky, and a number of Bolshevik conciliators. Largely because of Trotsky's irreconcilable political differences with the Mensheviks, the bloc formed in Vienna failed to hold together for any length of time. Looking back on the episode, Trotsky later wrote: "Among the Bolsheviks themselves, conciliatory tendencies were then still very strong, and I had hoped that this would induce Lenin also to take part in a general conference. Lenin, however, came out with all his force against union. The entire course of the events that followed proved conclusively that Lenin was right." (*My Life,* p. 316.)—P. 194.

60. The Minority Movement was the Left wing of the British trade union movement, inspired and initiated by the

communists, but enjoying the growing support of hundreds of thousands of non-communist trade union members. By the time the British trade union leaders were prepared to withdraw from the Anglo-Russian Trade Union Unity Committee, the backbone of the Minority Movement was broken and it continued to decline to the point of complete dissolution.—P. 209.

61. See, "The Military Opposition," chap. 36 of *My Life,* by Leon Trotsky, pp. 574–91, for an analysis of the "Tsaritsin" group led by Stalin, Voroshilov, Dybenko and others.—P. 256.

62. The "Octobrists" were those who supported the imperial manifesto of October 1905 which established a Duma. It was the party of the big commercial, industrial and landowning bourgeoisie, head by Guchkov, a Moscow capitalist.—P. 297.

Appendix to the fourth edition

On the suppressed testament of Lenin

APPENDIX TO THE FOURTH EDITION

On the suppressed testament of Lenin

by Leon Trotsky

The postwar epoch has brought into wide currency the psychological biography, the masters of which art often pull their subject up out of society by the roots. The fundamental driving force of history is presented as the abstraction, personality. The behavior of the "political animal," as Aristotle brilliantly defined mankind, is resolved into personal passions and instincts.

The statement that personality is abstract may seem absurd. Are not the superpersonal forces of history really the abstract things? And what can be more concrete than a living man? However, we insist upon our statement. If you remove from a personality, even the most richly endowed, the content which is introduced into it by the

This article, dated December 31, 1932, was first published in English in the July and August 1934 issues of New International *magazine. In 1935 Pioneer Publishers, Pathfinder's predecessor, printed it in pamphlet form. The version published here is based on a slightly revised 1946 translation.*

milieu, the nation, the epoch, the class, the group, the family, there remains an empty automaton, a psycho-physical robot, an object of natural, but not of social or "humane," science.

The causes of this abandonment of history and society must, as always, be sought in history and society. Two decades of wars, revolutions, and crises have given a bad shake-up to that sovereign, human personality. To have weight in the scales of contemporary history, a thing must be measured in millions. For this, the offended personality seeks revenge. Unable to cope with society on the rampage, it turns its back upon society. Unable to explain itself by means of historic processes, it tries to explain history from within itself. Thus the Indian philosophers built universal systems by contemplating their own navels.

The school of pure psychology

The influence of Freud upon the new biographical school is undeniable, but superficial. In essence these parlor psychologists are inclining to a belletristic irresponsibility. They employ not so much the method as the terminology of Freud, and not so much for analysis as for literary adornment.

In his recent work Emil Ludwig, the most popular representative of this genre, has taken a new step along the chosen path: he has replaced the study of the hero's life and activity with dialogue. Behind the answers of the statesman to questions put to him, behind his intonations and grimaces, the writer discovers his real motives. Conversation becomes almost a confession. In its technique Ludwig's new approach to the hero suggests Freud's approach to his patient: it is a matter of bringing the personality to the surface with its own cooperation. But with all this external similarity, how different it is in essence! The fruitfulness of Freud's work is attained at the price of a heroic break with all kinds of conventions. The great psychoanalyst is ruthless. At work he is like a surgeon, almost like a butcher with rolled-up sleeves. Anything you want, but there is not one hundredth of one percent of diplomacy in his technique. Freud bothers least of all about the prestige of his patient, or about considerations of good form, or any other kind of false note or frill. And it is for this reason that he can carry on his dialogue only face-to-face, without secretary or stenographer, behind padded doors.

Not so Ludwig. He enters into a conversation with Mussolini, or with Stalin, in order to present the world with an authentic portrait of their souls. Yet the whole conversation follows a program previously agreed upon. Every word is taken down by a stenographer. The eminent patient knows quite well what can be useful to him in this process and what harmful. The writer is sufficiently experienced to distinguish rhetorical tricks and sufficiently polite not to notice them. The dialogue developing under these circumstances, if it does indeed resemble a confession, resembles one put on for the talking pictures.

Emil Ludwig has every reason to declare: "I understand nothing of politics." This is supposed to mean: "I stand above politics." In reality it is a mere formula of personal neutrality—or to borrow from Freud, it is that "mental censor" which makes easier for the psychologist his political function. In the same way diplomats do not interfere with the inner life of the country to whose government they are accredited, but this does not prevent them on occasion from supporting plots and financing acts of terrorism.

One and the same person in different conditions develops

different sides of his personality. How many Aristotles are herding swine, and how many swineherds wear a crown on their heads! But Ludwig can lightly resolve even the contradiction between Bolshevism and fascism into a mere matter of individual psychology. Even the most penetrating psychologist could not with impunity adopt such a tendentious "neutrality." Casting loose from the social conditioning of human consciousness, Ludwig enters into a realm of mere subjective caprice. The "soul" has not three dimensions, and it therefore lacks the refractory quality common to all other substances. The writer loses his taste for the study of facts and documents. What is the use of this colorless evidence when it can be replaced with bright guesses?

In his work on Stalin, as in his book about Mussolini, Ludwig remains "outside politics." This does not in the least prevent his works from becoming a political weapon. Whose weapon? In the one case Mussolini's, in the other that of Stalin and his group. Nature abhors a vacuum. If Ludwig does not occupy himself with politics, this is not saying that politics does not occupy itself with Ludwig.

Upon the publication of my autobiography some three years ago, the official Soviet historian Pokrovsky, now dead, wrote: "We must answer this book immediately, put our young scholars to work refuting all that can be refuted, etc." But it is a striking fact that no one, absolutely no one, responded. Nothing was analyzed, nothing was refuted. There was nothing to refute, and nobody could be found capable of writing a book which would find readers.

A frontal attack proving impossible, it became necessary to resort to a flanking movement. Ludwig, of course, is not a historian of the Stalin school. He is an independent psychological portraitist. But a writer foreign to all politics may prove the most convenient means for putting into circulation ideas which can find no other support but a popular name. Let us see how this works out in actual fact.

'Six words'

Citing the testimony of Karl Radek, Emil Ludwig borrows from him the following episode:

> After the death of Lenin we sat together, nineteen members of the Central Committee, tensely waiting to learn what our lost leader would say to us from his grave. Lenin's widow gave us his letter. Stalin read it. No one stirred during the reading. When it came to Trotsky the words occurred: "His non-Bolshevik past is not accidental." At that point Trotsky interrupted the reading and asked:
>
> "What does it say there?" The sentence was repeated. Those were the only words spoken in that solemn moment.

And then in the character of analyst, and not narrator, Ludwig makes the following remark on his own account: "A terrible moment, when Trotsky's heart must have stopped beating; this phrase of six words essentially determined the course of his life." How simple it seems to find a key to the riddles of history! These unctuous lines of Ludwig would doubtless have uncovered to me myself the very secret of my destiny if . . . if this Radek-Ludwig story did not happen to be false from beginning to end, false in small things and great, in what matters and in what matters not.

To begin with, the testament was written by Lenin not two years before his death as our author affirms, but one year. It was dated January 4, 1923; Lenin died on January 21, 1924. His political life had broken off completely in March 1923. Ludwig speaks as though the testament had never been published in full. As a matter of fact it has been reproduced dozens of times in all languages of the world press. The first official reading of the testament in the Kremlin occurred, not at a session of the Central Committee, as Ludwig writes, but in the Council of Elders at the Thirteenth Congress of the party on May 22, 1924. It was not Stalin who read the testament, but Kamenev in his then position as permanent president of the central party bodies. And finally—most important—I did not interrupt the reading with an emotional exclamation because of the absence of any motive whatever for such an act. Those words which Ludwig wrote down at the dictation of Radek are not in the text of the testament. They are an outright invention. Difficult as it may be to believe, this is the fact.

If Ludwig were not so careless about the factual basis of his psychological patterns, he might without difficulty have got possession of an exact text of the testament, established the necessary facts and dates, and thus avoided those wretched mistakes with which his work about the Kremlin and the Bolsheviks is unfortunately brimful.

The so-called testament was written at two periods, separated by an interval of ten days: December 25, 1922, and January 4, 1923. At first only two persons knew of the document: the stenographer, M. Volodicheva, who wrote it from dictation, and Lenin's wife, N. Krupskaya.[1] As long as there remained a glimmer of hope for Lenin's recovery, Krupskaya left the document under lock and key. After Lenin's death, not long before the Thirteenth Congress, she handed the testament to the Secretariat of the Central Committee in order that through the party congress it should be brought to the attention of the party for whom it was destined.

At that time the party apparatus was semiofficially in

the hands of the troika (Zinoviev, Kamenev, Stalin)—as a matter of fact, already in the hands of Stalin. The troika decisively expressed themselves against reading the testament at the congress—the motive not at all difficult to understand. Krupskaya insisted upon her wish. At this stage the dispute was going on behind the scenes. The question was transferred to a meeting of the Elders at the Congress—that is, the leaders of the provincial delegations. It was here that the oppositional members of the Central Committee first learned about the testament, I among them. After a decision had been adopted that nobody should make notes, Kamenev began to read the text aloud. The mood of the listeners was indeed tense in the highest degree. But so far as I can restore the picture from memory, I should say that those who already knew the contents of the document were incomparably the most anxious. The troika introduced, through one of its henchmen, a resolution previously agreed upon with the provincial leaders: the document should be read to each delegation separately in executive session; no one should dare to make notes; at the plenary session the testament must not be referred to. With the gentle insistence characteristic of her, Krupskaya argued that this was a direct violation of the will of Lenin, to whom you could not deny the right to bring his last advice to the attention of the party. But the members of the Council of Elders, bound by factional discipline, remained obdurate; the resolution of the troika was adopted by an overwhelming majority.

In order to grasp the significance of those mystical and mythical "six words" which are supposed to have decided my fate, it is necessary to recall certain preceding and accompanying circumstances. Already in the period of sharp disputes on the subject of the October Revolution, certain

"Old Bolsheviks" from the right wing had more than once pointed out with vexation that Trotsky after all had not formerly been a Bolshevik. Lenin always stood up against these voices. Trotsky long ago understood that a union with the Mensheviks was impossible, he said, for example, on November 14, 1917—"and since then there has been no better Bolshevik."[2] On Lenin's lips those words meant something.

Two years later, while explaining in a letter to the foreign Communists the conditions under which Bolshevism had developed, how there had been disagreements and splits, Lenin pointed out that "at the decisive moment, at the moment when it seized the power and created the Soviet Republic, Bolshevism was united and *drew to itself all the best elements in the currents of socialist thought that were nearest to it.*"[3] No current closer to Bolshevism than that which I represented up to 1917 existed either in Russia or in the West. My union with Lenin had been predetermined by the logic of ideas and the logic of events. At the decisive moment Bolshevism drew into its ranks "all the best elements" in the tendencies "that were nearest to it." Such was Lenin's appraisal of the situation. I have no reason to dispute him.

At the time of our two months' argument on the trade union question (winter of 1920–21), Stalin and Zinoviev had again attempted to put into circulation references to the non-Bolshevik past of Trotsky. In answer to this, the less restrained leaders of the opposite camp had reminded Zinoviev of his conduct during the period of the October insurrection. Thinking over from all sides on his deathbed how relations would crystallize in the party without him, Lenin could not but foresee that Stalin and Zinoviev would try to use my non-Bolshevik past in order to mobilize the Old Bolsheviks against me. The testament tries, incidentally, to forestall this danger, too. Here is what it says immediately after its characterization of Stalin and Trotsky: "I will not further characterize the other members of the Central Committee as to their personal qualities. I will only remind you that the October episode of Zinoviev and Kamenev was not, of course, accidental, but that it ought as little to be used against them personally as the non-Bolshevism of Trotsky."

This remark that the October episode "was not accidental" pursues a perfectly definite goal: to warn the party that in critical circumstances Zinoviev and Kamenev may again reveal their lack of firmness. This warning stands, however, in no relation with the remark about Trotsky. In regard to him it is merely recommended not to use his non-Bolshevik past as an argument *ad hominem*. I therefore had no motive for putting the question which Radek attributes to me. Ludwig's guess that my heart "stopped beating" also falls to the ground. Least of all did the testament set out to make a guiding rôle in the party work difficult for me. As we shall see below, it pursued an exactly opposite aim.

'The mutual relations of Stalin and Trotsky'

The central position in the testament, which fills two typewritten pages, is devoted to a characterization of the mutual relations of Stalin and Trotsky, "the two most able leaders of the present Central Committee." Having remarked upon the "exceptional abilities" of Trotsky ("the most able man in the present Central Committee"), Lenin immediately points out his adverse traits: "far-reaching self-confidence" and "a disposition to be too much attracted by the purely administrative side of affairs." However serious the faults indicated may be in themselves, they do not—I remark in passing—bear any relation to "underestimating the peasants" or "lacking faith in the inner forces of the revolution" or any other of the inventions of the epigones in recent years.

On the other side Lenin writes: "Stalin, having become general secretary, has concentrated an enormous power in his hands; and I am not sure that he always knows how to use this power with sufficient caution."

It is not a question here of the political influence of Stalin, which at that period was insignificant, but of the administrative power which he had concentrated in his hands, "having become general secretary." This is a very exact and carefully weighed formula; we shall return to it later.

The testament insists upon an increase of the number of members of the Central Committee to fifty, even to one hundred, in order that with this compact pressure it may restrain the centrifugal tendencies in the Political Bureau. This organizational proposal has still the appearance of a neutral guarantee against personal conflicts. But only ten days later it seemed to Lenin inadequate, and he added a supplementary proposal which also gave to the whole document its final physiognomy: ". . . I propose to the comrades to find a way to remove Stalin from that position and appoint to it another man who in all other respects* differs from Stalin only in superiority—namely, more patient, more loyal, more polite and more attentive to comrades, less capricious, etc."

During the days when the testament was dictated, Lenin was still trying to give to his critical appraisal of Stalin as restrained an expression as possible. In the coming

* We must not forget that the testament was dictated and not corrected; hence stylistic difficulties in places; but the thought is completely clear.—L.T.

weeks his tone would become sharper and sharper right up to the last hour when his voice ceased forever. But even in the testament, enough is said to motivate the demand for a change of general secretary: along with rudeness and capriciousness, Stalin is accused of *lack of loyalty.* At this point the characterization becomes a heavy indictment.

As will appear later, the testament could not have been a surprise to Stalin. But this did not soften the blow. Upon his first acquaintance with the document, in the Secretariat, in the circle of his closest associates, Stalin let fly a phrase which gave quite unconcealed expression to his real feelings toward the author of the testament. The conditions under which this phrase spread to wide circles, and above all the inimitable quality of the reaction itself, is in my eyes an unqualified guarantee of the authenticity of the episode. Unfortunately this winged phrase cannot be quoted in print.

The concluding sentence of the testament shows unequivocally on which side, in Lenin's opinion, the danger lay. To remove Stalin—just him and him only—meant to cut him off from the apparatus, to withdraw from him the possibility of pressing on the long arm of the lever, to deprive him of all that power which he had concentrated in his hands in this office. Who, then, should be named general secretary? Someone who, having the positive qualities of Stalin, should be more patient, more loyal, less capricious. This was the phrase which struck home most sharply to Stalin. Lenin obviously did not consider him irreplaceable since he proposed that we seek a more suitable person for his post. In tendering his resignation, as a matter of form, the general secretary capriciously kept repeating: "Well, I really am rude. . . . Ilyich suggested that you find another who would differ from me *only* in greater politeness. Well, try to find him." "Never mind," answered the voice of one of Stalin's then friends. "We are not afraid of rudeness. Our whole party is rude, proletarian." A drawing-room conception of politeness is here indirectly attributed to Lenin. As to the accusation of inadequate loyalty, neither Stalin nor his friends had a word to say. It is perhaps not without interest that the supporting voice came from A.P. Smirnov, then people's commissar of agriculture, but now under the ban as a Right Oppositionist. Politics knows no gratitude.

Radek, who was then still a member of the Central Committee, sat beside me during the reading of the testament. Yielding with abandon to the influence of the moment and lacking inner discipline, Radek took instant fire from the testament and leaned to me with the words, "Now they won't dare go against you." I answered him, "On the contrary, they will have to go the limit, and moreover as quickly as possible." The very next days of that Thirteenth Congress demonstrated that my judgment was the more sober. The troika were compelled to forestall the possible effect of the testament by placing the party as soon as possible before a fait accompli. The very reading of the document to the local delegations with "outsiders" not admitted, was converted into a downright struggle against me. The leaders of the delegations in their reading would swallow some words, emphasize others, and offer commentaries to the effect that the letter had been written by a man seriously ill and under the influence of trickery and intrigue. The machine was already in complete control. The mere fact that the troika was able to transgress the will of Lenin, refusing to read his letter at the congress, sufficiently characterizes the composition of the congress and its atmosphere. The testament did not weaken or put a stop to the inner struggle, but on the contrary lent it a disastrous tempo.

Lenin's attitude toward Stalin

Politics is persistent. It can press into its service even those who demonstratively turn their backs to it. Ludwig writes: "Stalin followed Lenin fervently up to his death." If this phrase expressed merely the mighty influence of Lenin upon his pupils, including Stalin, there could be no argument. But Ludwig means something more. He wants to suggest an exceptional closeness to the teacher of this particular pupil. As an especially precious testimony Ludwig cites upon this point the words of Stalin himself: "I am only a pupil of Lenin, and my aim is to be his worthy pupil." It is too bad when a professional psychologist operates uncritically with a trite phrase, the conventional modesty of which contains not one atom of intimate content. Ludwig becomes here a mere transmitter of the official legend manufactured during these recent years. I doubt if he has the remotest idea of the contradictions into which his indifference to facts has brought him. If Stalin actually was following Lenin up to his death, how then explain the fact that the last document dictated by Lenin, on the eve of his second stroke, was a curt letter to Stalin, a few lines in all, *breaking off all personal and comradely relations*? This single event of its kind in the life of Lenin, a sharp break with one of his close associates, must have had very serious psychological causes, and would be, to say the least, incomprehensible in relation to a pupil who "fervently" followed his teacher up to the end. Yet we hear not a word about this from Ludwig.

When Lenin's letter breaking with Stalin became widely known among the leaders of the party, the troika having by that time fallen to pieces, Stalin and his close friends found no other way out but to revive that same old story about the incompetent condition of Lenin. As a matter of fact the testament, as also the letter breaking off relations, was written in those months (December 1922 to the beginning of March 1923) during which Lenin in a series of programmatic articles gave the party the most mature fruits of his thinking. That break with Stalin did not drop out of a clear sky. It flowed from a long series of preceding conflicts upon matters of principle and upon practical matters alike, and it sets forth the whole bitterness of these conflicts in a tragic light.

Lenin undoubtedly valued highly certain of Stalin's traits: his firmness of character, tenacity, stubbornness, even ruthlessness, and craftiness—qualities necessary in a war and consequently in its general staff. But Lenin was far from thinking that these gifts, even on an extraordinary scale, were sufficient for the leadership of the party and the state. Lenin saw in Stalin a revolutionist, but not a statesman in the grand style. Theory had too high an importance for Lenin in a political struggle. Nobody considered Stalin a theoretician, and he himself up to 1924 never made any pretense to this vocation. On the contrary, his weak theoretical grounding was too well known in a small circle. Stalin is not acquainted with the West; he does not know any foreign language. He was never brought into the discussion of problems of the international workers' movement. And finally Stalin was not—this is less important, but not without significance—either a writer or an orator in the strict sense of the word. His articles, in spite of all the author's caution, are loaded not only with theoretical blunders and naivetes, but also with crude sins against the Russian language. In the eyes of Lenin, Stalin's value was wholly in the sphere of party administration and machine maneuvering. But even here

Lenin made substantial reservations, and these increased during the last period.

Lenin despised idealistic moralizings. But this did not prevent him from being a rigorist of revolutionary morals—of those rules of conduct, that is, which he considered necessary for the success of the revolution and the creation of the new society. In Lenin's rigorism, which flowed freely and naturally from his character, there was not a drop of pedantry or bigotry or stiffness. He knew people too well and took them as they were. He would combine the faults of some with the virtues of others, and sometimes also with their faults, and never cease to watch keenly what came of it. He knew also that times change, and we with them. The party had risen with one jump from the underground to the height of power. This created for each of the old revolutionists a startlingly sharp change in personal situation and in relations with others. What Lenin discovered in Stalin under these new conditions he cautiously but clearly remarked in his testament: a lack of loyalty and an inclination to the abuse of power. Ludwig missed these hints. It is in them, however, that one can find the key to the relations between Lenin and Stalin in the last period.

Lenin was not only a theoretician and technician of the revolutionary dictatorship, but also a vigilant guardian of its moral foundations. Every hint at the use of power for personal interests kindled threatening fires in his eyes. "How is that any better than bourgeois parliamentarism?" he would ask to express more effectively his choking indignation. And he would not infrequently add on the subject of parliamentarism one of his rich definitions. Stalin meanwhile was more and more broadly and indiscriminately using the possibilities of the revolutionary dictatorship for the recruiting of people personally obligated and devoted to him. In his position as general secretary he became the dispenser of favor and fortune. Here the foundation was laid for an inevitable conflict. *Lenin gradually lost his moral trust in Stalin.* If you understand that basic fact, then all the particular episodes of the last period take their places accordingly, and give a real and not a false picture of the attitude of Lenin to Stalin.

Sverdlov and Stalin as types of organizers

In order to accord the testament its proper place in the development of the party, it is here necessary to make a digression. Up to the spring of 1919 the chief organizer of the party had been Sverdlov. He did not have the name of general secretary, a name which was then not yet invented, but he was that in reality. Sverdlov died at the age of 34 in March 1919 from the so-called Spanish fever. In the spread of the civil war and the epidemic, mowing people down right and left, the party hardly realized the weight of this loss. In two funeral speeches Lenin gave an appraisal of Sverdlov which throws a reflected but very clear light also upon his later relations with Stalin. "In the course of our revolution, in its victories," Lenin said, "it fell to Sverdlov to express more fully and more wholly than anybody else the very essence of the proletarian revolution." Sverdlov was "before all and above all an organizer." From a modest underground worker, neither theoretician nor writer, there grew up in a short time "an organizer who acquired irreproachable authority, an organizer of the whole Soviet power in Russia, and an organizer of the work of the party unique in his understanding." Lenin had no taste for the exaggerations of anniversary or funeral panegyrics. His appraisal of Sverdlov was at the same time a characterization of the task of the organizer: "Only thanks to the fact that we had such an organizer as Sverdlov were we able in war times to work as though we had *not one single conflict worth speaking of."*

So it was in fact. In conversations with Lenin in those days we remarked more than once, and with ever renewed satisfaction, one of the chief conditions of our success: the unity and solidarity of the governing group. In spite of the dreadful pressure of events and difficulties, the novelty of the problems, and sharp practical disagreements occasionally bursting out, the work proceeded with extraordinary smoothness and friendliness, and without interruptions. With a brief word we would recall episodes of the old revolutions. "No, it is better with us." "This alone guarantees our victory." The solidarity of the center had been prepared by the whole history of Bolshevism and was kept up by the unquestioned authority of the leaders—and above all of Lenin. But in the inner mechanics of this unexampled unanimity the chief technician had been Sverdlov. The secret of his art was simple: to be guided by the interests of the cause and that only. No one of the party workers had any fear of intrigues creeping down from the party staff. The basis of this authority of Sverdlov was *loyalty.*

Having tested out mentally all the party leaders, Lenin in his funeral speech drew the practical conclusion: "Such a man we can never replace, if by replacement we mean the possibility of finding one comrade combining such qualities. . . . The work which he did alone can now be accomplished only by a whole group of men who, following in his footsteps, will carry on his service."[4] These words were not rhetorical, but a strictly practical proposal. And the proposal was carried out. Instead of a single secretary, there was appointed a collegium of three persons.

From these words of Lenin it is evident, even to those

unacquainted with the history of the party, that during the life of Sverdlov, Stalin played no leading rôle in the party machinery—either at the time of the October Revolution or in the period of laying the foundations and walls of the Soviet state. Stalin was also not included in the first secretariat which replaced Sverdlov.

When at the Tenth Congress, two years after the death of Sverdlov, Zinoviev and others, not without a hidden thought of the struggle against me, supported the candidacy of Stalin for general secretary—that is, placed him de jure in the position which Sverdlov had occupied de facto—Lenin spoke in a small circle against this plan, expressing his fear that "this cook will prepare only peppery dishes." That phrase alone, taken in connection with the character of Sverdlov, shows us the differences between the two types of organizers: the one tireless in smoothing over conflicts, easing the work of the collegium, and the other a specialist in peppery dishes—not even afraid to spice them with actual poison. If Lenin did not in March 1921 carry his opposition to the limit—that is, did not appeal openly to the congress against the candidacy of Stalin—it was because the post of secretary, even though "general," had in the conditions then prevailing, with the power and influence concentrated in the Political Bureau, a strictly subordinate significance. Perhaps also Lenin, like many others, did not adequately realize the danger in time.

Toward the end of 1921, Lenin's health broke sharply. On December 7, in taking his departure upon the insistence of his physician, Lenin, little given to complaining, wrote to the members of the Political Bureau: "I am leaving today. In spite of my reduced quota of work and increased quota of rest, these last days the insomnia has increased devilishly. I am afraid I cannot speak either at the party congress or the Soviet congress."*

For five months he languishes, half removed by doctors and friends from his work, in continual alarm over the course of governmental and party affairs, in continual struggle with his lingering disease. In May he has the first stroke. For two months Lenin is unable to speak or write or move. In July he begins slowly to recover. Remaining in the country, he enters by degrees into active correspondence. In October he returns to the Kremlin and officially takes up his work.

"There is no evil without good," he writes privately in the draft of a future speech. "I have been sitting quiet for a half year and looking on 'from the sidelines.'"[5] Lenin means to say: I formerly sat too steadily at my post and failed to observe many things; the long interruption has now permitted me to see much with fresh eyes. What disturbed him most, unquestionably, was the monstrous growth of bureaucratic power, the focal point of which had become the Organization Bureau of the Central Committee.

The necessity of removing the boss who was specializing in peppery dishes became clear to Lenin immediately after his return to work. But this personnel question had become notably complicated. Lenin could not fail to see how extensively his absence had been made use of by Stalin for a one-sided selection of men—often in direct conflict with the interests of the cause. The general secretary was now relying upon a numerous faction, bound together by ties which, if not always intellectual, were at least firm. A change of the heads of the party machine had already

* This, like many other letters quoted in the present article, is reproduced from documents in my archives.—L.T. [This letter is printed in *The Trotsky Papers*, ed. by Jan M. Meijer (The Hague: Mouton, 1971), vol. 2, p. 647.—Ed.]

become impossible without the preparation of a serious political attack. At this time occurred the "conspiratorial" conversation between Lenin and me in regard to a combined struggle against Soviet and party bureaucratism, and his proposal of a "bloc" against the Organization Bureau—the fundamental stronghold of Stalin at that time. The fact of this conversation as well as its content soon found their reflection in documents, and they constitute an episode of the party history undeniable and not denied by anyone.

However, in only a few weeks there came a new decline in Lenin's health. Not only continual work, but also executive conversations with the comrades were again forbidden by his physicians. He had to think out further measures of struggle alone within four walls. To control the backstage activities of the secretariat, Lenin worked out some general measures of an organizational character. Thus arose the plan of creating a highly authoritative party center in the form of a Control Commission composed of reliable and experienced members of the party, completely independent from the hierarchical viewpoint—that is, neither officials nor administrators—and at the same time endowed with the right to call to account for violations of legality, of party and Soviet democracy, and for lack of revolutionary morality, all officials without exception, not only of the party, including members of the Central Committee, but also, through mediation of the Workers' and Peasants' Inspection, the high officials of the state.

On January 23, through Krupskaya, Lenin sent for publication in *Pravda* an article[6] on the subject of his proposed reorganization of the central institutions. Fearing at once a traitorous blow from his disease and a no less traitorous response from the Secretariat, Lenin demanded that his article be printed in *Pravda* immediately; this implied a direct appeal to the party. Stalin refused Krupskaya this request on the ground of the necessity of discussing the question in the Political Bureau. Formally this meant merely a day's postponement. But the very procedure of referring it to the Political Bureau boded no good. At Lenin's direction Krupskaya turned to me for cooperation. I demanded an immediate meeting of the Political Bureau. Lenin's fears were completely confirmed: all the members and alternates present at the meeting, Stalin, Molotov, Kuibyshev, Rykov, Kalinin, and Bukharin, were not only against the reform proposed by Lenin, but also against printing his article. To console the sick man, whom any sharp emotional excitement threatened with disaster, Kuibyshev, the future head of the Central Control Commission, proposed that they print a special issue of *Pravda* containing Lenin's article, but consisting of only one copy. It was thus "fervently" that these people followed their teacher. I rejected with indignation the proposal to hoodwink Lenin, spoke essentially in favor of the reform proposed by him, and demanded the immediate publication of his article. I was supported by Kamenev who had come in an hour late. The attitude of the majority was at last broken down by the argument that Lenin in any case would put his article in circulation; it would be copied on typewriters and read with redoubled attention, and it would be thus all the more pointedly directed against the Political Bureau. The article appeared in *Pravda* the next morning, January 25. This episode also found its reflection in due season in official documents, upon the basis of which it is here described.

I consider it necessary in general to emphasize the fact that since I do not belong to the school of pure psychology, and since I am accustomed to trust firmly established facts rather than their emotional reflection in memory, the whole present exposition, with the exception of specially indicated episodes, is set forth by me on the basis of documents in my archives and with a careful verification of dates, testimony, and factual circumstances in general.

The disagreements between Lenin and Stalin

Organizational policy was not the only arena of Lenin's struggle against Stalin. The November plenum of the Central Committee (1922),[7] sitting without Lenin and without me, introduced unexpectedly a radical change in the system of foreign trade, undermining the very foundation of the state monopoly. In a conversation with Krassin, then people's commissar of foreign trade, I spoke of this resolution of the Central Committee approximately as follows: "They have not yet knocked the bottom out of the barrel, but they have bored several holes in it." Lenin heard of this. On December 13 he wrote me: "I earnestly urge you to take upon yourself at the coming plenum the defense of our common view as to the unconditional necessity of preserving and enforcing the monopoly. . . . The previous plenum took a decision in this matter wholly in conflict with monopoly of foreign trade."

Refusing any concessions upon this question, Lenin insisted that I appeal to the Central Committee and the congress. The blow was directed primarily against Stalin, responsible as general secretary for the presentation of questions at the plenums of the Central Committee. That time, however, the thing did not go to the point of open struggle. Sensing the danger, Stalin yielded without a struggle, and his friends with him. At the December plenum the November decision was revoked. "It seems we captured the position without firing a shot, by mere movements of maneuver," Lenin wrote me jokingly on December 21.

The disagreement in the sphere of national policy was

still sharper. In the autumn of 1922 we were preparing the transformation of the Soviet state into a federated union of national republics. Lenin considered it necessary to go as far as possible to meet the demands and claims of those nationalists who had long lived under oppression and were still far from recovering from its consequences. Stalin, on the other hand, who in his position as people's commissar for nationalities directed the preparatory work, was conducting in this sphere a policy of bureaucratic centralism. Lenin, convalescing in a village near Moscow, carried on a polemic with Stalin in letters addressed to the Political Bureau. In his first remarks on Stalin's project for the federated union, Lenin was extremely gentle and restrained. He was still hoping in those days—toward the end of September 1922—to adjust the question through the Political Bureau and without open conflict. Stalin's answers, on the other hand, contained a noticeable irritation. He thrust back at Lenin the reproach of "hurriedness," and with it an accusation of "national liberalism"—that is, indulgence to the nationalism of the outlanders. This correspondence, although extremely interesting politically, is still concealed from the party.

The bureaucratic national policy had already at that time provoked a keen opposition in Georgia, uniting the flower of Georgian Bolshevism against Stalin and his right-hand man, Ordzhonikidze. Through Krupskaya, Lenin got into private contact with the leaders of the Georgian opposition (Mdivani, Makharadze, etc.) against the faction of Stalin, Ordzhonikidze, and Dzerzhinsky. The struggle in the borderlands was too keen, and Stalin had bound himself too closely with definite groupings, to yield in silence as he had on the question of the monopoly of foreign trade. In the next few weeks Lenin became convinced that it would be necessary to appeal to the party.

At the end of December, he dictated a voluminous letter on the national question, which was to take the place of his speech at the party congress if illness prevented him from appearing.

Lenin employed against Stalin an accusation of administrative impulsiveness and spitefulness against an alleged nationalism. "Spitefulness in general," he wrote weightily, "plays the worst possible rôle in politics." The struggle against the just, even though at first exaggerated, demands of the nations formerly oppressed, Lenin qualified as a manifestation of Great Russian bureaucratism. He for the first time named his opponents by name: "It is, of course, necessary to hold Stalin and Dzerzhinsky responsible for all this out-and-out Great Russian nationalistic campaign." That the Great Russian, Lenin, accuses the Georgian, Dzhugashvili,[8] and the Pole, Dzerzhinsky, of Great Russian nationalism, may seem paradoxical; but the question here is not one of national feelings and partialities, but of two systems of politics whose differences reveal themselves in all spheres, the national question among them. In mercilessly condemning the methods of the Stalin faction, Rakovsky wrote some years later: "To the national question, as to all other questions, the bureaucracy makes its approach from the point of view of convenience of administration and regulation."[9] Nothing better could be said.

Stalin's verbal concessions did not quiet Lenin in the least, but on the contrary sharpened his suspicions. "Stalin will make a rotten compromise," Lenin warned me through his secretary "in order then to deceive." And that was just Stalin's course. He was ready to accept at the coming congress any theoretical formulation of the national policy provided it did not weaken his factional support in the center and in the borderlands. To be sure, Stalin had plenty of ground for fearing that Lenin saw through his plans completely. But on the other hand, the condition of the sick man was continually growing worse. Stalin coolly included this not unimportant factor in his calculations. The practical policy of the General Secretariat became the more decisive, the worse became Lenin's health. Stalin tried to isolate the dangerous supervisor from all information which might give him a weapon against the Secretariat and its allies. This policy of blockade naturally was directed against the people closest to Lenin. Krupskaya did what she could to protect the sick man from contact with the hostile machinations of the Secretariat. But Lenin knew how to guess a whole situation from accidental symptoms. He was clearly aware of the activities of Stalin, his motives and calculations. It is not difficult to imagine what reactions they provoked in his mind. We should remember that at that moment there already lay on Lenin's writing table, besides the testament insisting upon the removal of Stalin, also the documents on the national question which Lenin's secretaries Fotieva and Glyasser, sensitively reflecting the mood of their chief, were describing as "a bombshell against Stalin."

A half year of sharpening struggle

Lenin developed his idea of the rôle of the Central Control Commission as a protector of party law and unity in connection with the question of reorganizing the Workers' and Peasants' Inspection (Rabkrin), whose head for several preceding years had been Stalin. On March 4, 1923, *Pravda* published an article famous in the history of the party, "Better Fewer, but Better."[10] This work was written at several different times. Lenin did not like to, and could not, dictate. He had a hard time writing the article. On March 2 he finally listened to it with satisfaction: "At last it seems all right." This article included the reform of the guiding party institutions on a broad political perspective, both national and international. Upon this side of the question, however, we cannot pause here. Highly important for our theme, however, is the estimate which Lenin gave of the Workers' and Peasants' Inspection. Here are Lenin's words: "Let us speak frankly. The People's Commissariat of Rabkrin does not enjoy at the present moment a shadow of authority. Everybody knows that a worse organized institution than our Commissariat of Rabkrin does not exist, and that in the present circumstances you cannot expect a thing of that commissariat."

This extraordinarily biting allusion in print by the head of the government to one of the most important state institutions was a direct and unmitigated blow against Stalin as the organizer and head of this inspectorate. The reason for this should now be clear. The inspectorate was to serve chiefly as an antidote to bureaucratic distortions of the revolutionary dictatorship. This responsible function could be fulfilled successfully upon condition of complete loyalty in its leadership, but it was just this loyalty which Stalin lacked. He had converted the inspectorate like the party Secretariat into an implement of machine intrigues, of protection for "his men" and persecution of his opponents. In the article "Better Fewer, but Better" Lenin openly pointed out that his proposed reform of the inspectorate, at whose head Tsyurupa had not long ago been placed, must inevitably meet the resistance of "all our bureaucracy, both the Soviet and the party bureaucracy." In parenthesis Lenin adds significantly, "We have bureaucratism not only in the Soviet institutions but also in the party." This was a perfectly deliberate blow at Stalin as general secretary.

Thus it would be no exaggeration to say that the last half year of Lenin's political life, between his convalescence and his second illness, was filled with a sharpening struggle against Stalin. Let us recall once more the principal dates. In September 1922, Lenin opened fire against the national policy of Stalin. In the first part of December, he attacked Stalin on the question of the monopoly of foreign trade. On December 25, he wrote the first part of his testament. On December 30, he wrote his letter on the national question (the "bombshell"). On January 4, 1923, he added a postscript to his testament on the necessity of removing Stalin from his position as general secretary. On January 23, he drew up against Stalin a heavy battery: the project of a Control Commission. In an article on March 2, he dealt Stalin a double blow, both as organizer of the inspectorate and as general secretary. On March 5, he wrote me on the subject of his memorandum on the national question: "If you would agree to undertake its defense, I could be at rest." On that same day[11] he for the first time openly joined forces with the irreconcilable Georgian enemies of Stalin, informing them in a special note that he was backing their cause "with all my heart" and was preparing for them documents against Stalin, Ordzhonikidze, and Dzerzhinsky. "With all my heart"—this expression was not a frequent one with Lenin.

"This question [the national question] has worried him extremely," testifies his secretary, Fotieva, "and he was preparing to speak on it at the party congress."[12] But a month before the congress Lenin finally broke down, and without even having given instructions in regard to the article. A weight rolled from Stalin's shoulders. At the caucus of the Council of Elders at the Twelfth Congress he already made bold to speak, in the style characteristic of him, of Lenin's letter as the document of a sick man under the influence of "womenfolk." (That is, Krupskaya and the two secretaries.) Under pretext of the necessity of finding out the actual will of Lenin, it was decided to put the letter under lock and key. There it remains to this day.

The dramatic episodes enumerated above, vivid enough in themselves, do not in the remotest degree convey the fervor with which Lenin was living through the party events of the last months of his active life. In letters and articles he laid upon himself the usual very severe censorship. Lenin understood well enough from his first stroke the nature of his illness. After he returned to work in October 1922, the capillary vessels of his brain did not cease to remind him of themselves by a hardly noticeable, but ominous and more and more frequent nudge, obviously threatening a relapse. Lenin soberly estimated his own situation in spite of the quieting assurances of his physicians. At the beginning of March, when he was compelled again to withdraw from work, at least from meetings, interviews, and telephone conversations, he carried away into his sick room a number of troubling observations and dreads. The bureaucratic apparatus had become an independent factor in big politics with Stalin's secret factional staff in the Secretariat of the Central Committee. In the national sphere, where Lenin demanded special sensitiveness, the fangs of imperial centralism were revealing themselves more and more openly. The ideas and principles of the revolution were bending to the interests of combinations behind the scenes. The authority of the dictatorship was more and more often serving as a cover for the dictates of functionaries.

Lenin keenly sensed the approach of a political crisis and feared that the apparatus would strangle the party. The policies of Stalin became for Lenin in the last period of his life the incarnation of a rising monster of bureaucratism. The sick man must more than once have shuddered at the thought that he had not succeeded in carrying out that reform of the apparatus about which he had talked with me before his second illness. A terrible danger, it seemed to him, threatened the work of his whole life.

And Stalin? Having gone too far to retreat, spurred on by his own faction, fearing that concentrated attack whose threads all issued from the sickbed of his dread enemy, Stalin was already going headlong, was openly recruiting partisans by the distribution of party and Soviet positions, was terrorizing those who appealed to Lenin through Krupskaya, and was more and more persistently issuing rumors that Lenin was already not responsible for his actions. Such was the atmosphere from which rose Lenin's letter breaking with Stalin absolutely. No, it did not drop from a clear sky. It meant merely that the cup of endurance had run over. Not only chronologically, but politically and morally, it drew a last line under the attitude of Lenin to Stalin.

Is it not surprising that Ludwig, gratefully repeating the official story about the pupil faithful to his teacher "up to his very death," says not a word of this final letter or indeed of all the other circumstances which do not accord with the present Kremlin legends? Ludwig ought at least to know the fact of the letter, if only from my autobiography, with which he was once acquainted, for he gave it a favorable review. Maybe Ludwig had doubts of the authenticity of my testimony. But neither the existence of the letter nor its contents were ever disputed by anybody. Moreover, they are confirmed in stenographic minutes of the Central Committee. At the July plenum in 1926, Zinoviev said: "At the beginning of the year 1923, Vladimir Ilyich, in a personal letter to Comrade Stalin, broke off all comradely relations with him" (Stenographic Minutes of the Plenum, No. 4, page 32). And other speakers, among them M.I. Ulyanova, Lenin's sister, spoke of the letter as of a fact generally known in the circles of the Central Committee. In those days it could not even enter Stalin's head to oppose this testimony. Indeed, he has not ventured to do that so far as I know, in a direct form, even subsequently.[13]

It is true that the official historians have in recent years made literally gigantic efforts to wipe out of the memory of man this whole chapter of history. And so far as the Communist youth are concerned, these efforts have achieved certain results. But investigators exist, it would seem, exactly for the purpose of destroying legends and confirming the real facts in their rights. Or is this not true of psychologists?

The hypothesis of the 'duumvirate'

We have indicated above the signposts of the final struggle between Lenin and Stalin. At all these stages Lenin sought my support and found it. From the speeches, articles, and letters of Lenin you could without difficulty adduce dozens of testimonies to the fact that, after our temporary disagreement on the question of the trade unions,[14] throughout 1921 and 1922 and the beginning of 1923, Lenin did not lose one chance to emphasize in open forum his solidarity with me, to quote this or that statement from me, to support this or that step which I had taken. We must understand that his motives were not personal, but political. What may have alarmed him and grieved him in the last months, indeed, was my not-active-enough support of his fighting measures against Stalin. Yes, such is the paradox of the situation! Lenin, fearing in the future a split on the line of Stalin and Trotsky, demanded of me a more energetic struggle against Stalin. The contradiction here, however, is only superficial. It was in the interests of the stability of the party leadership in the future, that Lenin now wished to condemn Stalin sharply and disarm him. What restrained me was the fear that any sharp conflict in the ruling group at that time, when Lenin was struggling with death, might be understood by the party as a casting of lots for Lenin's mantle. I will not raise the question here as to whether my restraint in that case was right or not, nor the broader question as to whether it would have been possible at that time to ward off the advancing danger with organizational reforms and personal shiftings. But how far were all the actual positions of the actors from the picture which is given us by this popular German writer who so lightly picks the keys to all enigmas!

We heard from him that the testament "decided the fate of Trotsky"—that is, evidently served as a cause of Trotsky's losing power. According to another version of Ludwig, expounded alongside of this with not even an attempt to reconcile them, Lenin desired "a duumvirate of Trotsky and Stalin." This latter thought, also, doubtless suggested by Radek, gives excellent proof that even now, even in the close circle around Stalin, even in the tendentious manipulation of a foreign writer invited in for a conversation, nobody dared assert that Lenin saw his successor in Stalin. In order not to come into too crude conflict with the text of the testimony and a whole series of other documents, it is necessary to put forward ex post facto this idea of a duumvirate.

But how reconcile this story with Lenin's advice: remove the general secretary? That would have meant to deprive Stalin of all the weapons of his influence. You do not treat in this way the candidate for duumvir. No, and moreover this second hypothesis of Radek-Ludwig, although more cautious, finds no support in the text of the testament. The aim of the document was defined by its author—to guarantee the stability of the Central Committee. Lenin sought the road to this goal not in the artificial combination of a duumvirate, but in strengthening the collective control over the activity of the leaders. How in doing this he conceived the relative influence of individual members of the collective leadership—as to this the reader is free to draw his own conclusions on the basis of the above quotations from the testament. But he should not lose sight of the fact that the testament was not the last word of Lenin and that his attitude to Stalin became more severe the more closely he felt the denouement approaching.

Ludwig would not have made so capital a mistake in his appraisal of the meaning and spirit of the testament if he had interested himself a little bit in its further fate. Concealed by Stalin and his group from the party, the testament was reprinted and republished only by Oppositionists—of course, secretly. Hundreds of my friends and partisans were arrested and exiled for copying and distributing those two little pages. On November 7, 1927—the tenth anniversary of the October Revolution—the Moscow Oppositionists took part in the anniversary demonstration with a placard: "Fulfill the Testament of Lenin." Specially chosen troops of Stalinists broke into the line of march and snatched away the criminal placard. Two years later, at the moment of my banishment abroad, a story was even created of an insurrection in preparation by the "Trotskyists" on November 7, 1927. The summons to "fulfill the testament of Lenin" was interpreted by the Stalinist faction as a summons to insurrection! And even now the testament is forbidden publication by any section of the Communist International. The Left Opposition, on the contrary, is republishing the testament upon every appropriate occasion in all countries. Politically these facts exhaust the question.

Radek as a source of information

Still, where did that fantastic tale come from about how I leapt from my seat during the reading of the testament, or rather of the "six words" which are not in the testament, with the question: "What does it say there?" Of this I can only offer a hypothetical explanation. How correct it may be, let the reader judge.

Radek belongs to the tribe of professional wits and storytellers. By this I do not mean that he does not possess other qualities. Suffice it to say that at the Seventh Congress of the party on March 8, 1918, Lenin, who was in general very restrained in personal comments, considered it possible to say: "I return to Comrade Radek, and here I want to remark that he has accidentally succeeded in uttering a serious remark. . . ." And once again later on: "This time it did happen that we got a perfectly serious remark from Radek. . . ."[15]

People who speak seriously only by way of exception have an organic tendency to improve reality, for in its raw form reality is not always appropriate to their stories. My personal experience has taught me to adopt a very cautious attitude to Radek's testimonies. His custom is not to recount events, but to take them as the occasion for a witty discourse. Since every art, including the anecdotal, aspires toward a synthesis, Radek is inclined to unite together various facts or the brighter features of various episodes, even though they took place at different times and places. There is no malice in this. It is the manner of his calling.

And so it happened, apparently, this time. Radek, according to all the evidence, has combined a session of the Council of Elders at the Thirteenth Congress with a session of the plenum of the Central Committee of 1926, in spite of the fact that an interval of more than two years lay between the two. At that plenum also, secret manuscripts were read, among them the testament. This time Stalin did actually read them, and not Kamenev, who was then already sitting beside me in the Opposition benches. The reading was provoked by the fact that during those days copies of the testament, Lenin's letter on the national question, and other documents kept under lock and key were already circulating rather broadly in the party. The party apparatus was getting nervous and wanted to find out what it was that Lenin actually said. "The Opposition knows and we don't know," they were saying. After prolonged resistance Stalin found himself compelled to read the forbidden documents at a session of the Central Committee—thus automatically bringing them into the stenographic record, printed in secret notebooks for the heads of the party apparatus.

This time also, there were no exclamations during the reading of the testament, for the document was long ago too well known to the members of the Central Committee. But I did actually interrupt Stalin during the reading of the correspondence on the national question. The episode in itself is not so important, but maybe it will be of use to the psychologists for certain inferences.

Lenin was extremely economical in his literary means and methods. He carried on his business correspondence with close colleagues in telegraphic language. The form of address was always the last name of the addressee with the letter "T" (*Tovarishch:* comrade), and the signature was "Lenin." Complicated explanations were replaced by a double or triple underlining of separate words, extra exclamation points, etc. We all well knew the peculiarities of Lenin's manner, and therefore even a slight departure from his laconic custom attracted attention.

In sending his letter on the national question Lenin wrote me on March 5:

> Esteemed Comrade Trotsky:
>
> I earnestly ask you to undertake the defense of the Georgian affair at the Central Committee of the party. That affair is now under "prosecution" at the hands of Stalin and Dzerzhinsky and I cannot rely on their impartiality. Indeed, quite the contrary! If you would agree to undertake its defense, I could be at rest. If for some reason you do not agree, send me back all the papers. I will consider that a sign of your disagreement.
>
> With the very best comradely greetings,
> *Lenin*
> MARCH 5, 1923

Both the content and the tone of this slight note, dictated by Lenin during the last day of his political life, were no less painful to Stalin than the testament. A lack of "impartiality"—does not this imply, indeed, that same lack of loyalty? The last thing to be felt in this note is any confidence in Stalin—"indeed, quite the contrary"—the thing emphasized is confidence in me. A confirmation of the tacit union between Lenin and me against Stalin and his faction was at hand. Stalin controlled himself badly during the reading. When he arrived at the signature he hesitated: "With the very best comradely greetings"—that was too demonstrative from Lenin's pen. Stalin read: "With communist greetings." That sounded more dry and official. At that moment I did rise in my seat and ask: "What is written there?" Stalin was obliged, not without embarrassment, to read the authentic text of Lenin. Someone of his close friends shouted at me that I was quibbling over details although I had only sought to verify a text. That slight incident made an impression. There was talk about it among the heads of the party. Radek, who at that time was no longer a member of the Central Committee, learned of it at the plenum from others and perhaps from me. Five years later when he was already with Stalin and no longer with me, his flexible memory evidently helped him to compose this synthetic episode which stimulated Ludwig to so effective and so mistaken an inference.

Although Lenin, as we have seen, found no reason to declare in his testament that my non-Bolshevik past was "not accidental," still I am ready to adopt that formula on my own authority. In the spiritual world the law of causation is as inflexible as in the physical world. In that general sense my political orbit was, of course, "not accidental," but the fact that I became a Bolshevik was also not accidental. The question how seriously and permanently I came over to Bolshevism is not to be decided either by a bare chronological record or by the guesses of literary psychology. A theoretical and political analysis is necessary. This, of course, is too big a theme and lies wholly outside the frame of the present article. For our purpose it suffices that Lenin, in describing the conduct of Zinoviev and Kamenev in 1917 as "not accidental," was not making a philosophical reference to the laws of determinism, but a political warning for the future. It is exactly for this reason that Radek found it necessary, through Ludwig, to transfer this warning from Zinoviev and Kamenev to me.

The legend of 'Trotskyism'

Let us recall the chief signposts of this question. From 1917 to 1924, not a word was spoken of the contrast between Trotskyism and Leninism. In this period occurred the October Revolution, the civil war, the construction of the Soviet state, the creation of the Red Army, the working out of the party program, the establishment of the Communist International, the formation of its cadres, and the drawing up of its fundamental documents. After the withdrawal of Lenin from his work in the nucleus of the Central Committee, serious disagreements developed. In 1924 the specter of "Trotskyism"—after careful preparation behind the scenes—was brought forth on the stage. The entire inner struggle of the party was henceforth carried on within the frame of a contrast between Trotskyism and Leninism. In other words, the disagreements created by new circumstances and new tasks between me and the epigones were presented as a continuation of my old disagreements with Lenin. A vast literature was created upon this theme. The sharpshooters were always Zinoviev and Kamenev. In their character of old and very close colleagues of Lenin they stood at the head of "the Bolshevik Old Guard" against Trotskyism. But under the pressure of deep social processes this group itself fell apart. Zinoviev and Kamenev found themselves obliged to acknowledge that the so-called . . . "Trotskyists" had been right upon fundamental questions. New thousands of Old Bolshevists adhered to "Trotskyism."

At the July 1926 plenum, Zinoviev announced that his struggle against me had been the greatest mistake of his life—"*more dangerous* than the mistake of 1917."

Ordzhonikidze was not entirely wrong in calling to him from his seat: "Then why did you dupe the entire party?" (See the already quoted stenographic minutes.) To this weighty rejoinder Zinoviev officially found no answer. But he gave an unofficial explanation at a conference of the Opposition in October 1926. "You must understand," he said in my presence, to his closest friends, some Leningrad workers who honestly believed in the legend of Trotskyism, "you must understand that it was a struggle for power. The trick was to string together the old disagreements with new issues. For this purpose 'Trotskyism' was invented. . . ."

During their two-year stay in the Opposition, Zinoviev and Kamenev managed to expose completely the backstage mechanics of the preceding period when they with Stalin had created the legend of "Trotskyism" by conspiratorial methods. A year later, when it became finally clear that the Opposition would be compelled to swim long and stubbornly against the current, Zinoviev and Kamenev threw themselves on the mercy of the victor. As a first condition of their party rehabilitation it was demanded that they rehabilitate the legend of Trotskyism. They agreed. At that time I decided to reinforce their own previous declarations on this matter through a series of authoritative testimonials.[16] It was Radek, no other than Karl Radek, who gave the following written testimony:

> I was present at the conversation with Kamenev when L.B. [Kamenev] said he would openly declare at the Plenum of the Central Committee how they, that is, Kamenev and Zinoviev, together with Stalin, decided to utilize the old disagreements between L.D. [Trotsky] and Lenin so as to keep Comrade Trotsky from the leadership of the party after Lenin's death. Moreover, I

have heard repeated from the lips of Zinoviev and Kamenev the tale of how they had "invented" Trotskyism as a topical slogan.

K. Radek

DECEMBER 25, 1927

Similar written testimonies were given by Preobrazhensky, Pyatakov, Rakovsky, and Eltsin. Pyatakov, the present director of the State Bank, summed up Zinoviev's testimony in the following words: "'Trotskyism' had been invented in order to replace the real differences of opinion with fictitious differences, that is, to utilize past differences which had no bearing upon the present but which were resurrected artificially for the definite purpose mentioned above."

This is clear enough, is it not? And V. Eltsin, a representative of the younger generation, wrote: "None of the supporters of the 1925 group (the Zinovievists) who were present raised any objections to this. Everyone received this information of Zinoviev as a generally known fact."

The above-cited testimony of Radek was submitted by him on December 25, 1927. A few weeks later he was already in exile, and a few months later, on the meridian of Tomsk, he became convinced of the correctness of Stalin's position, a thing which had not been revealed to him earlier in Moscow. But from Radek also the powers demanded, as a condition sine qua non, an acknowledgment of the reality of this same legend of "Trotskyism." After Radek agreed to this, he had nothing left to do but repeat the old formulas of Zinoviev which the latter had himself exposed in 1926, only to return to them again in 1928. Radek has gone further. In a conversation with a credulous foreigner he has amended the testament of Lenin in order to find in it support for this epigonist legend of "Trotskyism."

From this short historic review, resting exclusively upon documentary data, many conclusions may be drawn. One is that a revolution is an austere process and does not spare its human vertebrae.

The course of subsequent events in the Kremlin and in the Soviet Union was determined not by a single document, even though it were the testament of Lenin, but by historical causes of a far deeper order. A political reaction after the enormous effort of the years of the insurrection and the civil war was inevitable. The concept of reaction must here be strictly distinguished from the concept of counter-revolution. Reaction does not necessarily imply a social overturn—that is, a transfer of power from one class to another. Even tsarism had its periods of progressive reform and its periods of reaction. The mood and orientation of the ruling class changes according to circumstances. This is true also of the working class. The pressure of the petty bourgeoisie upon the proletariat, tired from the tumult, entailed a revival of petty bourgeois tendencies in the proletariat itself and a first deep reaction on the crest of which the present bureaucratic apparatus headed by Stalin rose to power.

Those qualities which Lenin valued in Stalin—stubbornness of character and craftiness—remained, of course, even then. But they found a new field of action and a new point of application. Those features which in the past had represented a minus in Stalin's personality—narrowness of outlook, lack of creative imagination, empiricism—now gained an effective significance important in the highest degree. They permitted Stalin to become the semiconscious instrument of the Soviet bureaucracy, and they impelled the bureaucracy to see in Stalin its inspired leader. This ten-year struggle among the heads of the Bolshevik Party has indubitably proved that under the conditions of this new stage of the revolution, Stalin has been developing to the limit those very traits of his political character against which Lenin in the last period of his life waged irreconcilable war. But this question, standing even now at the focus of Soviet politics, would carry us far beyond the limits of our historic theme.

Many years have passed since the events we have related. If even ten years ago there were factors in action far more powerful than the counsel of Lenin, it would now be utterly naive to appeal to the testament as an effective political document. The international struggle between the two groups which have grown out of Bolshevism long ago outgrew the question of the fate of individuals. Lenin's letter, known under the name of his testament, has henceforward chiefly a historic interest. But history, we may venture to think, has also its rights, which moreover do not always conflict with the interests of politics. The most elementary of scientific demands—correctly to establish facts and to verify rumors by document—may at least be recommended alike to politician and historian. And this demand might well be extended even to the psychologist.

DECEMBER 31, 1932

Notes to
‘On the suppressed testament of Lenin’

1. According to the version published in Lenin’s *Collected Works,* vol. 36, pp. 593 ff., the first part of the testament was dictated on December 24–25, 1922, and taken down by M. Volodicheva. The addition to the testament on January 4, 1923, was taken down by another of Lenin’s secretaries, L. Fotieva. The document is also published in *Lenin’s Final Fight* (Pathfinder, 2010), pp. 221–44.

2. Lenin made this remark at a session of the Petersburg Committee of the Bolshevik Party on November 1 (14), 1917. (At this time Russia was still on the old-style Julian calendar, which was thirteen days behind the Gregorian calendar used in the West, hence the double date.) The minutes of this meeting were originally included in a collection of minutes of the Petrograd (Petersburg) Committee published in 1927, but they were expunged from the book at the last moment. The corrected galley proofs fell into the hands of the Opposition and Trotsky published them together with photostats of the originals in *Biulleten Oppozitsii* (Bulletin of the Opposition), the Russian-language organ he edited in exile (no. 7, November-December 1929, pp. 31–37). See pp. 145–163 of the present volume.

   Lenin’s speech does not appear in the *Collected Works.*

3. See “Greetings to Italian, French and German Communists,” *Collected Works,* vol. 30, pp. 55–56. Trotsky’s emphasis.

4. See “Speech in Memory of Y.M. Sverdlov,” *Collected Works,* vol. 29, pp. 89–94, for this and preceding citations. Trotsky’s emphasis.

5. This document has not been located.

6. The reference is to “How We Should Reorganize the Workers’ and Peasants’ Inspection,” contained in *Collected Works,* vol. 33, pp. 481–86 and *Lenin’s Final Fight,* pp. 273–80.

7. The plenum was actually held on October 6, 1922.

8. Dzhugashvili, Stalin's real name.
9. The source has not been located.
10. Reprinted in *Collected Works,* vol 33, pp. 487–502 and *Lenin's Final Fight,* pp. 283–301.
11. Actually, on the next day, March 6.
12. For the full text of Fotieva's statement in a letter dated March 16, 1923, see *Lenin's Final Fight,* pp. 356–58. According to Lewin, *Lenin's Last Struggle,* pp. 155–56, the Institute of Marxism-Leninism confirms the existence of this letter and states that Fotieva sent it to the Political Bureau on April 16, 1923.
13. This letter, dated March 5, 1923, was first published in the U.S.S.R. after Stalin's death. It is reprinted in *Collected Works,* vol. 45, p. 608 and *Lenin's Final Fight,* p. 304.
14. For Lenin's views on the Russian Communist Party's 1920–21 discussion on trade unions, see *Collected Works,* vol. 32. Trotsky's later assessment of it can be found in *My Life,* chapter 38 (Pathfinder, 1970), pp. 604–14.
15. See *Collected Works,* vol. 27, p. 110, where Lenin's remarks are directed against Ryazanov rather than Radek. The following note about this quotation appears in the findings of the Dewey Commission, which investigated the charges against Trotsky in the Moscow trials, published in 1938 in *Not Guilty* (Pathfinder, 1938, 1972, 2008), p. 257: "In checking this quotation we find that it appears as Trotsky gave it in Lenin's *Collected Works,* State Publishers, 1925 (Vol. XV, pp. 131–2). In the Third Russian edition of Lenin's *Collected Works,* published in 1935, the name of Riazanov has been substituted for that of Radek (Vol. XXII, p. 331). The editors neither explain the change nor even state that in earlier editions Radek's name figured in place of Riazanov's."
16. The full text of these testimonials, together with photostats of the Russian originals, can be found elsewhere in the present volume.

Index

REVOLUTIONARY LEADERS IN THEIR OWN WORDS

New Edition!

In Defense of Marxism

LEON TROTSKY

Trotsky sharply poses—and answers—what remains the decisive question for working people the world over: What is the class character and composition of the political leadership the working class must forge to prepare for coming revolutionary battles? As conflicts intensify among the world's dominant capitalist powers, the rulers are once again dragging humanity toward social catastrophes, fascist dictatorships, another Holocaust for the Jews, and a nuclear World War III. This is the world in which the lessons of Trotsky's *In Defense of Marxism* are needed more than ever. $17. An earlier edition is available in Spanish, French, Farsi.

The Struggle for a Proletarian Party

JAMES P. CANNON

"The workers of America have power enough to topple the structure of capitalism at home and to lift the whole world with them when they rise," Cannon asserts. At the start of World War II, a founder of the communist movement in the US and a leader of the Communist International in Lenin's time defends the program and party-building norms of Bolshevism. $20. Also in Spanish and Farsi.

Thomas Sankara Speaks

The Burkina Faso Revolution, 1983–87

Under Sankara's guidance, Burkina Faso's revolutionary government led peasants, workers, women, and youth to expand literacy; to sink wells, plant trees, erect housing; to combat women's oppression; to carry out land reform; to join others worldwide to free themselves from the imperialist yoke. $20. Also in French.

Is Socialist Revolution in the US Possible?

A Necessary Debate Among Working People

MARY-ALICE WATERS

Fighting for a society only working people can create, it is our own capacities we will discover. And we will answer the question posed here with a resounding "Yes." Revolution is possible but not inevitable. That depends on us. $7. Also in Spanish, French, Farsi.

Maurice Bishop Speaks

The Grenada Revolution and Its Overthrow, 1979–83

The triumph of the 1979 revolution in the Caribbean island of Grenada under the leadership of Maurice Bishop gave hope to millions throughout the Americas. Invaluable lessons from the workers and farmers government destroyed by a Stalinist-led counterrevolution in 1983. $20

Malcolm X Talks to Young People

"The young generation of whites, Blacks, browns, whatever else—you're living at a time of revolution," said Malcolm in 1964. "And I for one will join with anyone, I don't care what color you are, as long as you want to change this miserable condition that exists on this earth." Four talks and an interview in the last months of Malcolm's life. $12. Also in Spanish, French, Farsi, Greek, Arabic.

OTHER WRITINGS BY LEON TROTSKY

The Revolution Betrayed

What Is the Soviet Union and Where Is It Going?

In 1917 workers and peasants of Russia were the motor force of one of the deepest revolutions in history. Yet within ten years a political counterrevolution by a privileged social layer, whose chief spokesperson was Joseph Stalin, was being consolidated. The classic study of the Soviet workers state and its degeneration. $17. Also in Spanish, Farsi, Greek.

The Third International After Lenin

Leon Trotsky's 1928 defense of the Marxist course that had guided the Communist International in its early years. Writing in the heat of political battle, Trotsky addresses the key challenge facing working people today: building communist parties throughout the world capable of leading workers and farmers to take power. $20. Also in Farsi.

The History of the Russian Revolution

How, under Lenin's leadership, the Bolshevik Party led millions of workers and farmers to overthrow the state power of the landlords and capitalists in 1917 and bring to power a government that advanced their class interests at home and worldwide. Unabridged, 3 vols. in one. Written by one of the central leaders of that socialist revolution. $30. Also in French and Russian.

THE CUBAN REVOLUTION AND ITS IMPACT FROM AFRICA TO THE US

New!

Cuba and the Independence War in Guinea-Bissau and Cape Verde

The Fall of the Last Colonial Empire in Africa

VÍCTOR DREKE

In 1974–75 the people of two West African countries, Guinea-Bissau and Cape Verde, put an end to 500 years of Portuguese colonial exploitation. Led by a popular movement forged by Amílcar Cabral, their struggle triggered the collapse of Portugal's entire colonial empire and brought down the 40-year fascist dictatorship in Portugal itself. Víctor Dreke's firsthand account brings to life this decisive victory. $12. Also in Spanish and French.

October 1962

The 'Missile' Crisis as Seen from Cuba

TOMÁS DIEZ ACOSTA

In October 1962 Washington pushed the world to the edge of nuclear war. Here the full story of that historic moment is told from the perspective of the Cuban people, whose determination to defend their sovereignty and their socialist revolution blocked US plans for a devastating military assault. $17

Red Zone

Cuba and the Battle Against Ebola in West Africa

ENRIQUE UBIETA GÓMEZ

In 2014 West Africa was hit by the largest recorded Ebola epidemic. Answering a global call, Cuba's revolutionary socialist government provided what no other country even tried to—more than 200 volunteer doctors and nurses. "The heroic actions of Cuba's army of white coats occupies a place of honor in history," said Cuban leader Fidel Castro. $17. Also in Spanish and French.

FROM PATHFINDER

The Fight Against Jew-Hatred and Pogroms in the Imperialist Epoch

Stakes for the International Working Class

V.I. LENIN, LEON TROTSKY
FARRELL DOBBS, JAMES P. CANNON
JACK BARNES, DAVE PRINCE

Jew-hatred and pogroms—such as Hamas carried out on October 7, 2023—are part of the social convulsions and wars of the imperialist epoch. The authors explain why fighting Jew-hatred is decisive to the working class and oppressed nations of the world—and *what is to be done to end it*. $10. Also in Spanish, French, Greek.

The Low Point of Labor Resistance Is Behind Us

The Socialist Workers Party Looks Forward

JACK BARNES, MARY-ALICE WATERS, STEVE CLARK

The global order imposed by Washington is shattering. A long retreat by the working class and unions has come to an end. The bosses and their government are stepping up attacks on our wages, conditions, and constitutional rights. This book highlights opportunities for building a mass proletarian party able to lead the struggle to end capitalist rule, opening a socialist future for humanity. $10. Also in Spanish, French, Greek.

Panama: The Truth About the U.S. Invasion

CINDY JAQUITH, DON ROJAS, FIDEL CASTRO

Washington's probes to retake control of the Panama Canal and broader military operations in the Americas are good reason to recall the invasion of Panama in 1989, at the time the biggest US military action since Vietnam. A threat to the sovereignty of every nation in Latin America, these moves mark US imperialism's determination to crush the example set by Cuba's socialist revolution. Includes speech by Fidel Castro. $5

The Teamster Series

FARRELL DOBBS

Four books on the 1930s strikes, organizing drives, and political campaigns that transformed the Teamsters into a militant industrial union movement. Written by the organizer of these battles and leader of the Socialist Workers Party. A tool for workers seeking to use union power and advance the fight for a party of labor. $16 each, series $50. Also in Spanish. *Teamster Rebellion* is also available in French, Farsi, Greek.

Women in Cuba: The Making of a Revolution Within the Revolution

VILMA ESPÍN, ASELA DE LOS SANTOS
YOLANDA FERRER

The integration of women in the ranks and leadership of the Cuban Revolution was intertwined with the proletarian course led by Fidel Castro from the start. This is the story of that revolution and how it transformed the women and men who made it. $17. Also in Spanish, Farsi, Greek.

Malcolm X, Black Liberation and the Road to Workers Power

JACK BARNES

"The conquest of state power by a class-conscious vanguard of the working class is the mightiest weapon possible in the fight against Black oppression, the subjugation of women, Jew-hatred, and every form of human degradation inherited from class society." $20. Also in Spanish, French, Farsi, Greek, Arabic.

PATHFINDERPRESS.COM

COMMUNIST CONTINUITY AND PROGRAM

The Transitional Program for Socialist Revolution

LEON TROTSKY

The Socialist Workers Party program, drafted by Bolshevik leader Trotsky in 1938, still guides communists the world over. The party "uncompromisingly gives battle to all political groupings tied to the apron strings of the bourgeoisie. Its task—the abolition of capitalism's domination. Its aim—socialism. Its method—the proletarian revolution." $17. Also in Farsi.

Lenin's Final Fight

Speeches and Writings, 1922–23

V.I. LENIN

In 1922 and 1923, V.I. Lenin, central leader of the world's first socialist revolution, waged what was to be his last political battle—one that was lost after his death. At stake was whether that revolutionary government and the world communist movement it led would remain on the revolutionary proletarian course that brought workers and peasants to power in Russia in 1917. $17. Also in Spanish, Farsi, Greek.

Their Trotsky and Ours

JACK BARNES

To lead the working class in a successful revolution, a mass proletarian party is needed whose cadres, well beforehand, have absorbed a world communist program, are proletarian in life and work, derive deep satisfaction from doing politics, and have forged a leadership with an acute sense of what to do next. This book is about building such a party. $12. Also in Spanish, French, Farsi.

The Communist Manifesto

KARL MARX
AND FREDERICK ENGELS

Communism, say the founding leaders of the revolutionary workers movement, is not a set of ideas or preconceived "principles." It springs from a "movement going on under our very eyes." It is workers' line of march to power. $5. Also in Spanish, French, Farsi, Arabic.

Maoism vs. Bolshevism

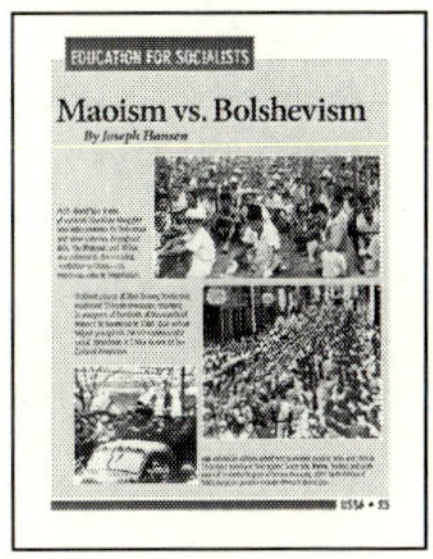

The 1965 Catastrophe in Indonesia
China's 'Cultural Revolution'
and the Disintegration of World Stalinism

JOSEPH HANSEN

Following the Chinese revolution of 1949, many workers and youth—inspired by that historic blow to imperialism—were diverted from a revolutionary course as they followed the Mao Zedong leadership. Joseph Hansen develops the communist alternative to Mao's Stalinist, class-collaborationist course, which in 1965 paved the way for a CIA-backed coup in Indonesia, and for which more than half a million workers, peasants, and youths paid with their lives. $6

Socialism: Utopian and Scientific

FREDERICK ENGELS

"To make men the masters of their own form of social organization—to make them free—is the mission of the modern proletariat," writes Engels. A classic guide to the operations of capitalism and struggles of the working class. $10. Also in Spanish and Farsi.

DEFENDING CONSTITUTIONAL FREEDOMS

Under the constitution "the power of censorship rests with the people over the government, not the government over the people."
—James Madison, *1794*

50 Years of Covert Operations in the US

Washington's Political Police and the American Working Class

LARRY SEIGLE, FARRELL DOBBS
STEVE CLARK

How class-conscious workers have defended constitutional freedoms and fought the capitalists' drive to build the "national security" state essential to maintaining their rule. $10. Also in Spanish and Farsi.

Socialism on Trial

Testimony at Minneapolis Sedition Trial

JAMES P. CANNON

The revolutionary program of the working class presented in federal court in 1941 on the eve of US entry into World War II. The frame-up charges of "seditious conspiracy" targeted leaders of the Socialist Workers Party. $15. Also in Spanish, French, Farsi.

FBI on Trial

The Victory in the Socialist Workers Party Suit Against Government Spying

MARGARET JAYKO

The record of a historic victory in the fight for political rights, including the 1986 federal court ruling against government spying and excerpts from trial testimony by SWP leaders Farrell Dobbs and Jack Barnes. $17

New International

A MAGAZINE OF MARXIST POLITICS AND THEORY

NEW INTERNATIONAL NO. 7

Opening Guns of World War III: Washington's Assault on Iraq

JACK BARNES

The murderous assault on Iraq in 1990–91 heralded increasingly sharp conflicts among imperialist powers, growing instability of capitalism, and more wars. Also includes:

1945: When US Troops Said 'No!'
by Mary-Alice Waters
Lessons from the Iran-Iraq War
by Samad Sharif

$14. Also in Spanish, French, Farsi.

NEW INTERNATIONAL NO. 11

U.S. Imperialism Has Lost the Cold War

JACK BARNES

The collapse of regimes across Eastern Europe and the USSR claiming to be communist did not mean workers and farmers there had been crushed. In today's sharpening class conflicts and wars, these toilers are joining working people the world over in the class struggle against capitalist exploitation. $14. Also in Spanish, French, Farsi, Greek.

NEW INTERNATIONAL NO. 12

Capitalism's Long Hot Winter Has Begun

JACK BARNES

Today's global capitalist crisis is but the opening stage of decades of economic, financial, and social convulsions and class battles. Class-conscious workers confront this historic turning point for imperialism with confidence, Jack Barnes writes, drawing satisfaction from being "in their face" as we chart a revolutionary course to take power. $14. Also in Spanish, French, Farsi, Greek, Arabic.

PATHFINDERPRESS.COM

EXPAND YOUR REVOLUTIONARY LIBRARY

Imperialism's March Toward Fascism and War

JACK BARNES

"There will be new Hitlers, new Mussolinis. That is inevitable. What is not inevitable is that they will triumph. The working-class vanguard will organize our class to fight back against the devastating toll we are made to pay for the capitalist crisis. The future of humanity will be decided in the contest between these contending class forces." In *New International* no. 10. $14. Also in Spanish, French, Farsi, Greek.

Are They Rich Because They're Smart?

Class, Privilege, and Learning Under Capitalism

JACK BARNES

Exposes growing class inequalities in the US and the self-serving rationalizations of well-paid professionals who think their "brilliance" equips them to "regulate" working people, who don't know what's in our own best interest. $10. Also in Spanish, French, Farsi, Greek, Arabic.

Cuba and Angola: The War for Freedom

HARRY VILLEGAS ("POMBO")

The story of Cuba's unparalleled contribution to the fight to free Africa from the scourge of apartheid. And how, in the doing, Cuba's socialist revolution was strengthened. $10. Also in Spanish, Farsi, Greek.

Cosmetics, Fashion, and the Exploitation of Women

MARY-ALICE WATERS
JOSEPH HANSEN, EVELYN REED

"Norms of beauty and fashion are inseparable from the class struggle." That's the title of the opening chapter of this new expanded edition of a lively 1950s debate in the *Militant*, a socialist newsweekly. How cosmetics and fashion monopolies rake in profits from social insecurities of women and adolescents. Why women's integration into the workforce and unions is a major advance in the fight for emancipation. A Marxist classic on the origins of women's oppression and the working-class road forward. $15. Also in Spanish, French, Farsi, Greek.

Imperialism, the Highest Stage of Capitalism

V.I. LENIN

"I trust that this pamphlet will help the reader to understand the fundamental economic question, that of the economic essence of imperialism," Lenin wrote in 1917. "For unless this is studied, it will be impossible to understand and appraise modern war and modern politics." $5. Also in Spanish, Farsi, Greek.

Pathfinder Press **accessible e-books** for the blind, those with low vision, or other challenges reading print books

For a list of current accessible titles, go to: pathfinderpress.com/collections/books-for-the-blind.

Visit bookshare.org for information on how to sign up.